My Mother's Son
– JEFF PEARCE –

Published by Jeff Pearce
Copyright © Jeff Pearce 2008

ISBN 978-0-9561235-0-3

Printed on FSC-friendly paper by
www.printondemand-worldwide.com

In loving memory of
Elsie
My Mother,
for having given me the greatest gift
a son could ever wish for.

★ ★ ★ ★ ★

It is also dedicated to
the three other women in my life,
Gina, Katie and Faye
for all their love, laughter and support over the years;
and
with particular thanks to
Gina
for having lived this story every day for the past year.

Acknowledgements

I am eternally grateful to Kit Knowles, my friend and part-time assistant who deciphered my hieroglyphics, dotted the 'I's and crossed my 'T's patiently over the past twelve months.

A special thank you to Lesley, for being on the other end of the phone whenever I needed her input on the family history; and for being my big sister.

A big thanks to my mate Danny Tallon, whose enthusiasm encouraged me to keep going and to finish my story.

And finally, Olwyn Dean, for proof reading my manuscript, and finding the title hidden in my book.

Contents

Prologue
1992

In the dark of an early winter morning a flashing red light on the dashboard caught my attention. Glancing down I realised it was the diesel gauge. The bastard was on empty. This was all I needed.

Pulling into the nearest petrol station, I jumped out and felt for my wallet. "Oh, shit!" In my haste to leave the house I had forgotten it. With not a penny in my pocket, nor for that matter in the world, and no time to spare, I proceeded to put £10 worth of diesel in the tank.

As I walked up to the window, I was patting my pockets, creating the impression that I was panicking and looking for something.

"Sorry," I apologised, "I seem to have come out without my wallet."

"Well, that wagon's not going anywhere mate," the cashier replied. This was not going to be easy.

"Don't be silly, it's only £10," I argued. "I'll call back later and drop it off then."

"Against the rules mate, can't let you do that."

Time was ticking on. "Look," undoing the strap on my Cartier wristwatch I handed it over. "Take this as security, with my name and address," I had really wound him up now, solving his problem for him.

He picked up my watch suspiciously, looking at it closely. "How do I know that this is worth ten quid?"

I sighed. "What difference does it make if it isn't?"

"A lot" he replied. Taking a pen and paper he made a careful note of my registration number and contact details. I was half expecting him to take my finger prints the way he was carrying on!

Climbing back in the cab I thought about his comments – 'Is it worth a tenner?' What a cheek! Gina had paid three and a half grand for it not that long ago. Still I had the juice and I was on my way!

Foot to the metal I anxiously headed towards Liverpool; back to where it had all begun. After fifteen years absence I was curious as to how I would be greeted by my former colleagues. Getting closer to my destination, the familiarity of it all strengthened, and as I pulled into the busy car park it almost seemed as if I had never been away.

The traders were busy, rushing around putting their stalls up with great speed and accuracy. Time was of the essence – the quicker it was erected the sooner they could empty their vans and set out the display of their goods in readiness for the days trading.

Weaving my way through the bustle I headed for the Market Inspectors office as I needed to see if there was a pitch available; I was desperately hoping that it would be someone I knew. My luck was changing; I was greeted by a familiar face.

"Hi Jeff! What are you doing here?" Ken had been the first Inspector I had ever met all those years ago.

"It's a long story," I said, "And I promise to tell it to you later. But right now I need a pitch."

"It's going to be hard," he said, "being so close to Christmas, but let's see what we can do. Picking up his clipboard he headed outside telling me to follow. As I walked alongside him I silently sent a word of thanks to my clever Mother for the words of wisdom she had given me; look after people as you move up the ladder of success, as you never know whom you might meet on the way down. If ever there was a true saying this was definitely one of them.

Ken turned to me. "Right Jeff, where are you parked?"

"There," I said, pointing to my wagon some twenty yards away.

"A frigging horse box!" he exclaimed, reading the words on the side out loud. "Jaguar Polo Team! What are you selling? Horse meat?"

"No, as I told you, it's a long story!"

"Polo horses in Toxteth? What's that all about?" Anyone else would have given up, but Ken was made of sterner stuff.

He instructed me to turn the wagon around, dropping the tailgate on to an empty space between two stalls, and to trade out of the back.

"Thanks Ken," I told him. "I owe you one!"

"It's alright Jeff," he replied, "More like I owe you one."

As I went about following his instructions and setting up my pitch, I couldn't help but notice that the horsebox and my arrival had caused a bit of a commotion. There were several other traders standing around watching me as I laid out my boxes on the ramps and the buzz of conversation was getting louder and louder.

One of them must have recognized me as I could hear him telling the others, "You know who that is don't you?"

"Who?" was the reply.

"That's Jeff Pearce that's who."

"Piss off you soft git, he's a millionaire. He wouldn't be here, not nowadays."

"I'm telling you it is." I heard my name being called out so stopped and looked up.

"Fucking hell!" There was a chorus of disbelieving voices. "What are you doing here Mr Big Time?"

"The same as you lads; trying to make a living."

They wouldn't give up. "Don't be daft, we have to be here, you don't."

I felt as if I had been hooked and they weren't letting go. Turning towards them, slightly irritated by their comments, I replied.

"Look lads, I assure you that if I didn't need to be here I certainly wouldn't, so back off and leave me alone!"

They took the hint and left, still not convinced about my real reasons for being there.

Once the boxes were out of the wagon and in position, I soon realised that the back had not been cleaned and there was horse shit all over the floor. I needed to get it sorted so that customers could come inside. Most of the women around here had never seen a horse box let alone walked up the ramp of one. They may need to come inside and try garments on so the shit had to go.

Having borrowed a brush and shovel, I literally shoved the shit into an empty box which I hid under the wagon. I then borrowed a can of air freshener to get rid of the smell of manure. When I opened the boxes I was pleasantly surprised to find that they were full of good quality jumpers which I had personally designed for Harrods some six months earlier.

It did not take me long to get back in to character. "Come on girls," I called out, "Hurry up and take a look - They're first class and going fast." My spiel continued, "Step up and have a look, a tenner a piece or two for fifteen. Don't be shy, come and buy! Jeff's my name, fashion's my game."

To draw a crowd is difficult, but to keep it is an art; you have to create a feeling of excitement and desire amongst the punters. Never sell to them, let them buy from you.

The banter amongst the people on the market went back and forth, Scouser humor at its best.

One lady called out another, "Go on Mary! You've always wanted a roll in the hay! Get in there you dirty mare!" Everyone burst out laughing.

My hands were soon full of ten pound notes in no time. My fellow traders looked on in awe at the speed in which I carried out my performance, tossing garments at customers as they called out the size and colour they wanted.

By the end of the day I was exhausted, but my bulging pockets full of money were clearly telling me that I had 'done the business'.

Not forgetting to call in at the office to pay my rent, I slipped Ken an extra tenner and thanked him for his help.

"No problem Jeff!" he answered, "Same again next week?"

"Yes please," I smiled.

As I set off on the long journey home, I felt good about myself for the first time in ages. I couldn't wait to tell Gina the good news and sang along to familiar songs playing on the radio all the way home not forgetting to stop off at the garage to redeem my watch.

When I walked into the kitchen Gina was sitting down with Katie and Faye helping them with their homework. She gave me her usual kiss hello, asking where I had been all this time.

Emptying my bulging pockets of the money on to the kitchen table in a big heap, I just said, "Gina, we're back!"

The four of us set about counting the money, the girls helping as well. There was £750 in front of us, enough I reckoned to get us back into business.

Lying in bed that night I couldn't stop thinking what a difference one day had made. In less than twenty-four hours my life had gone back fifteen years, yet I was more than happy to go back to the beginning in order to prove my worth.

Leaving school at the age of fourteen, a boy from the slums of Liverpool, I had worked harder than most people could ever imagine to achieve my ambitions.

Successfully hiding my flaws from the world as I built up an international fashion empire, I had led a double life; on one side the successful business entrepreneur and on the other an illiterate man who couldn't even write his own name. I created a fairytale lifestyle for my wife and two daughters, which in a cruel twist of fate had been taken away, literally overnight.

However, rather than accept that it had been circumstances beyond my control, I had blamed myself. In my guilt I felt like an impostor who had been found out and this was my punishment. Despair had kept me pinned to my bed night after night, unable to escape, almost driving me to the point of suicide.

Caught up in this nightmare I had silently called out for help. My cries had been answered when I heard my Mother's voice. "Stop crying and feeling sorry for yourself. You did it before, you can do it again." Her words had brought me back to reality, urging me out of bed and into my wagon that morning.

In another twist of fate I found myself back on the markets, almost at the point where I had once started so many years ago. Events had fallen into place in the most bizarre manner as the day went by, whilst being back amongst my customers had restored my self-esteem and given me a purpose in life to continue on my journey.

Chapter One
Any Old Rags

I was born to trade and my life trading started one day when I was four years old and sitting with my feet in the gutter whilst the other kids played. A horse and cart came down the street, and the man driving the cart was shouting out loud.

"Any old rags, any old bones, any old iron."

He pulled his horse to a stop. His cart was quite big and full of all kinds of things: old bikes, bits of metal, huge bundles of rags and boxes full of old bones left over from cooking. Most of the kids I was playing with were slightly older than me and seemed to know what to do. They all ran off to their own houses and within minutes were back with hands full of old clothes. These clothes were worn to the point of being almost threadbare, virtually beyond repair, rags in the truest sense of the word.

The children formed a line, passing their bundles up to the man on the cart. He in turn inspected each small bundle carefully before deciding whether or not they were worthy of a balloon tied to a piece of string. Most children received a balloon, but for those that were refused, it meant a quick trip back to their house before they once again emerged with a few more rags to add to the bundle. Only when he was satisfied would he hand over a balloon, and no one ever argued with him at his decision because he looked so stern and grumpy.

As he was nearing the end of his collection, I noticed Mum standing beside the cart talking to him. They seemed to be coming to some arrangement, as I then saw her getting up on the back of the cart, and begin rummaging through the bundles of rags heaped up there.

After a little while she got down, an assortment of jumpers and other clothes in her arms. Still negotiating, she opened her purse and took out a few coppers, passing them up to the rag and bone man.

Heading towards our front door, arms full, she called out to me, "Come on Jeff, we have work to do." I followed after her, leaving my friends and their balloons behind.

Once in the house we went through to the small kitchen at the back. Mum had two small metal buckets full of boiling water, which she carried out to the back yard emptying them into a larger tub - the Dolly Tub. Using a Dolly Peg she was able to create the same effect as a washing machine, cleaning the clothes as quickly as possible, and stopping any fleas or lice invading our house.

After about ten minutes, using a long pair of wooden tongs, my mother took the clothes out of the hot water and dropped them into another bucket full of cold water for rinsing. She would then pass me one end of each item of clothing to hold firm whilst she twisted the other end tighter and tighter, ringing out the excess water.

This stage of the washing completed, Mum then told me that the next job was mine. Mangling!

Mum would carefully feed the clothes through the rollers. I stood on a stool turning the handle, so that the rubber rollers squeezed the last remains of water out of the fabric; they were now ready to be hung out to dry on the line.

I was quite proud of myself and my ability to help with such an important job, and felt even better when Mum told me that all my hard work mangling would give me muscles like Tarzan. I may have got the muscles but I never got a balloon.

Finally, clothes clean and dry, Mum would then sit for hours and hours darning through the night before selling them on the market.

I also started going to the markets with Mum when I was four or at least that's when my earliest memories go back!

We would go to the market on Great Hommer Street, more commonly known as Paddy's Market, which was held only on Saturdays. It had got its nickname by way of the huge number of Irish immigrants that had settled in the area many years before. Paddy's Market was also close to Scotland Road, a very poor area of Liverpool, inhabited by tough, hardened families who lived in the terrible slums.

Most of the stallholders sold second hand items in those days. My mother would rent a small space for a few shillings. There were lots of ways of building up stock, and apart from the rag and bone man, another way was *'going on the knocker'*. This literally meant knocking on rich people's front doors and asking if they had any old clothes they didn't want. If you were very lucky you might even find things which you could also pawn.

There was one spring morning when I remember Mum knocking on the front door of a very large house overlooking Sefton Park. Normally the door would be opened by a member of the household staff, who would quite often chase us away, but on this occasion it was the lady of the house who appeared at the front door.

Mum politely said good morning, asking her if she had any old rags and clothes she wanted to get rid of.

I think that the lady was impressed by Mum's ladylike approach, and suggested that she wait on the step while she went to have a look. A few minutes later she returned, carrying a large bundle wrapped up in a sheet, passing it to Mum. The lady told Mum that she didn't want paying for them; in fact she was glad to get rid of the things, so Mum thanked her and walked down the steps.

The bundle was enormous, and Mum had quite a task carrying it to the bus stop, and keeping an eye on me – holding firmly on to her coat. We had to stop once or twice so that she could get her breath, but eventually we caught the bus, and were soon on our way back to Durden Street.

When we got home, Mum put the bundle on the table in the living room, carefully starting to undo the knots, all the time making sure that nothing fell to the floor.

"Look Jeff," Mum exclaimed, "Look at this! A fur coat!" Mum slipped the coat over her shoulders, and spun around the room as if she was dancing with Fred Astaire.

"Mum, you look fantastic," I laughed, being caught up in her excitement.

"Mink – Jeff, this is a real mink coat!" Her voice was brimming with joy. "Mink is worth a fortune, and this is a real mink coat!"

The next item Mum picked up was a man's overcoat, a camelhair crombie. Reverently running her hands over the lapels she looked at the label on the inside breast pocket.

"This is cashmere – real cashmere! I just don't believe it. Oh Jeff, this will fit your father, he will look so handsome in it!"

Mum was almost at a loss for words as she went through the rest of the bundle, looking through jumpers, dresses, skirts and lots of other beautiful things.

"Jeff," by now her voice was almost a whisper, "Can you believe our luck? All this wonderful stuff, we can make so much money from it, and it didn't cost us a single penny!"

She suddenly stopped what she was doing, looked at me, and gently put her hands on my shoulders. "God has been so good to us today. If you are a good person in life, then He will always look after you."

When my oldest sister Lesley later came home from school, Mum sent her to Browner's the Pawn shop with the mink coat. Within a little while she was back, almost tripping over herself in her haste and excitement to give Mum the profits from her visit. Holding out her hand, she passed Mum not one, but two ten pounds notes as if they were a king's ransom.

Mum held the money to her chest, before she turned and looked at the two of us standing there. "We're rich! We're rich! This is one of those days I was telling you about; this is a great day!" It was one of those rare moments when I saw Mum happy and laughing.

Mum would get ready for the markets the night before, showing me how to organise everything, sorting out the different categories of clothing, before neatly tying them into small bundles depending on the price. There were only two prices, one shilling or a tanner. Having finished this task, we would put these small bundles into two bigger bundles and tie each one up with a tarpaulin sheet which would keep the rain off.

This was very important as Mum's only form of transport to the market was a large old fashioned pram with big wheels making it easier to maneuver on and off the pavements with a heavy load. Mum and I would be up, dressed and washed in record time, leaving the house at 6 o'clock in the morning. Mum would push the pram along Tunnel Road, which to me seemed like a very long way, my little legs finding it impossible to keep up with her at times.

When we arrived she would hire a table for the day. Opening the tarpaulins she would put everything that was a shilling on the table, whilst everything that was a tanner would be laid neatly on top of the tarpaulin on the ground; once the stall was set up she would start with her spiel.

"Come on folks, everything a shilling on the table and a tanner on the floor," repeating this regularly throughout the day. Another one of Mum's popular spiels was, "Here Johnny, Johnny, lookee, Johnny, Johnny, here Johnny, Johnny."

'Johnny' was the name given to black sailors who predominantly worked in the engine rooms on most of the big cargo ships that visited Liverpool Docks. The market was very popular with the sailors whenever they were in port; they loved to buy umbrellas and hats - ladies hats and especially men's trilbies in any colour and condition, even if they had holes, as long as they were cheap. Mum told me that these hats would then be taken back to Africa where they would be given as gifts to their loved ones, protecting them from the heat of the sun.

I guess it would also have been seen as some sort of status symbol, perhaps the ultimate fashion statement, or proof that they had been to foreign countries all over the world.

Johnnies always moved around the market in a group of at least three or four. They would form a line, one behind the other, so close that the man behind was almost a part of the man in front, moving as one with a shuffling sort of dance-like step. What was amazing however was the number of hats on their heads, all shapes and sizes, colours and styles, stacked up ten high, towering above their heads and those of the crowds around them and tilting in different directions. Their arms would be similarly adorned with umbrellas, eight or nine on each arm, the handles neatly arranged like tribal bracelets.

Travelling in groups gave them a feeling of safety, the story being that the one in the middle always had the money.

I asked Mum why they were all called Johnnies. She told me that over the years when anybody had ever asked their name they would always say Johnny. In response the market traders would laugh amongst themselves, shouting out to one another that "they must all be called Johnny in their country," and so the nickname stuck.

After a couple of years I had become a regular trader with Mum. One particularly sunny morning the market was buzzing with the calls of the other traders getting their stalls ready for the day's business. The air was full of cries of 'Alright Gert? Tess, Dave, Alice?' 'The best of luck to you today, have a good'un, hope you take lots of money.' The atmosphere was great, humming with energy, everybody was in a lovely mood, and a lot of people were rummaging; all was right in the world of retail.

This particular day we had a small hand operated sewing machine to sell on the stall. Mum had gone to the toilet and had left me in charge when a lady came over and asked me about the machine.

"How much is this Son?" she asked, turning the wheel and checking the mechanical aspects. Mum had told me earlier how much she wanted to sell it for, but I couldn't remember what she had said. Not wanting to lose a sale, I quickly came up with a sum.

"Five pounds that, love" I answered, "Just five pounds." (I'd always heard Mum saying 'just' before stating any price).

Tousling my hair, the lady smiled, "You're very grown up for your age young man," and gave me the money, a big crisp five pound note, whilst the man who was with her picked up the machine, then they left. As soon as the money was in my hand I folded it up into a very small square, hiding it in the depths of my pocket to keep it safe.

Mum got back and immediately noticed that the machine was gone.

"Where's the sewing machine?" she asked, a note of worry in her voice.

"Sold and paid for' I replied.

"Did you get the three pounds I was asking for it?" she queried.

"No," I paused, "I got five.' Pulling the note out of my pocket I passed it over to her. Mum was lost for words; she pulled me into a big hug and squeezed me tightly.

"Well done, Jeff! You are now a real market trader and that's official! Go and get a big bag of sweets to celebrate," as she gave me a shilling.

After that I thought I was all grown up; seven years old, selling by myself, and five pounds worth in one go. I felt as if I could handle anything now, my confidence soared.

I was always on the lookout for 'business' opportunities.

One day, the house was quiet apart from the sounds of my Mother downstairs in the kitchen preparing tea for the family. I was on my own in the bedroom that I shared with my parents, wondering what to do as I was bored, when I decided to investigate the chest of drawers used by my Father.

Opening the bottom drawer I found some of his clothes, ties, socks, handkerchiefs and other things all neatly folded away but with nothing of any great interest. The second drawer was pretty much the same, so I moved on to the top. Pulling it open, the runners slightly sticking, I found an assortment of various things, tins, a jar of Brylcream, belts and braces. There was also a small wooden box, bright yellow in colour, with King Edwards Imperial Cigars emblazoned across the lid.

These were the cigars that my Father bought from the sailors and then sold on to the night club owners in town. Taking one out of the box, I stood in front of the mirror, looking at myself as I posed with the cigar between my lips, the image of an eight year old with red curly hair grinning back at me.

"My mates would love this," I thought to myself, and decided to take it in to school the following day to play a bit of a joke on them. Quickly closing the drawer, I searched the room for somewhere to hide the cigar, but could not find a suitable spot. Maybe I could hide it somewhere downstairs.

The floorboard creaked as I made my way out of the bedroom.

"Is that you Jeff?" I heard Mum call. "What are you doing?"

"Nothing Mum," I replied, coming down the stairs. My school blazer was draped over the banisters at the bottom of the stairs and I quickly hid the cigar in my pocket before going into the kitchen.

The next day, sitting behind my desk at school, I waited until our teacher had his back to the class, before pulling the cigar out of my pocket. Giving Raj, who was sitting next to me a quick nudge I showed him my surprise. His eyes were like saucers as he whispered to me, "Where did you get that?"

"It's one of my Dad's," I whispered back. I then stuck the cigar in my mouth and pretended to smoke it, catching the attention of the other boys sitting nearby.

Word spread like wildfire through the class, as one boy after another saw what I was doing, bursting into laughter at the sight of me sitting there like a miniature Winston Churchill puffing away. Before the teacher could catch me, the cigar disappeared back into the depths of my blazer, and I was the epitome of good behaviour and innocence.

Hisses of "show it me" and "let's see it again" were sent in my direction, but I just mouthed "later" gesturing with my finger towards the classroom door. It was quite clear that come playtime my mates were in for a treat.

The bell rang and I was one of the first out, followed by an impatient gang of lads. Heading for the block of toilets in the playground, I found myself surrounded by about ten of my mates, all eager for a look at my cigar. We had, being the inquisitive types, all experimented smoking a Woodbine at some stage but a cigar was different. This was big and fat and smelt of rich tobacco and was just so grown up. This is what real men smoked.

As I stood there, holding the cigar in my fingers allowing them to run their nose along it for a quick smell, and warning everyone to be careful as I did not want it damaged (I still had to return it to its box) some of the lads started asking me if I was going to light it, if any of them could have a smoke. I said no. This cigar was for look-see only.

"I'll pay yer for a puff," said one lad.

"Me too," said another, "A penny for a puff, see I have got the money here." He put his hand in his pocket and pulled out a coin. I couldn't believe it; looking around at the ten boys in the toilets with me, including the guy on *dixie* by the toilet entrance I started to think that for a penny a puff I could make nearly a shilling.

Feeling a little bit under pressure with the response that my cigar had caused, I felt that I needed time to work things out; my friends were rushing me. That night as I replaced the cigar in its box I looked at the contents; there were loads and loads of them, surely one wouldn't be missed, and it would mean that I could make lots of money and give it to Mum.

On the following day, although I had left the cigar safely at home, I was still being pestered for the chance of a puff from lots more boys this time. The amount of money that I could make was too good a chance to miss out on so I finally gave in and agreed to bring the cigar back at the end of the week; nervous in one way but excited in another - I was in business.

The day of 'the big smoke' dawned, and having managed to get some matches out of a box that Mum kept in the kitchen, I was well prepared. First Playtime came, and we all made our way to the toilets, one at a time, trying to avoid the attention of the teacher on playground duty. That in itself was fun, watching carefully for the right moment, and then making a dash for the toilet block. With a lad on *dixie*, we gathered around one of the cubicles and, having taken the cigar out of my pocket, I then removed a match, striking it against the wall.

Holding the flame to the end of the cigar, I puffed once or twice, lighting the tobacco as everyone watched in fascination. The end started to glow and a plume of smoke rose in the air; they all took a sniff at its pungent aroma. We had all seen adults with cigars, or one of our heroes in the movies, but we had never been this close to the real thing before.

Puffing a few more times to make sure that the cigar was well lit, I then held it out for the first lad to have a go, urging him to hurry up.

The cubicle was now filling up with smoke, the taste in my mouth was awful and my eyes were watering. As I watched carefully to ensure that everyone paid me their penny and that they all had equal amounts, the cigar was passed, literally down the row, until within minutes, there were ten lads all in the same boat, streaming eyes, coughing a little, and feeling far more grown up and a little bit queasy.

Everyone agreed that it was worth a penny, though I think that the 'naughtiness' of it all was more enjoyable than the actual cigar – the thought that any moment a teacher could walk in and catch us made the excitement even greater.

We had only smoked a small amount of the cigar, and as I saw this as being a great money-spinner, was very careful about stumping the lit end out on the floor, whilst my mates left the toilets one at a time.

I was a bit of a hero as far as the others were concerned, and naturally my reputation spread quickly throughout the school. Before long there were loads of boys queuing up for a puff on 'Red's Cigar'. The money was rolling in and I was able to give Mum quite a few shillings, telling her it was my winnings from a game of marbles.

However, as the cigar was coming to the end of its life, getting smaller and smaller so was my business venture. I was not going to chance another cigar as I felt it was only a matter of time before I got caught. It was all becoming too risky and there were now too many giveaways – the lingering smell of cigar smoke in the toilets alone was enough, not to mention the number of boys that were developing a cough!

Then one day we were right in the middle of our last smoking session when *dixie* sounded the alarm shouting:

"Quick, there is a teacher coming!"

Hastily, we all scrambled in the direction of the nearest urinal, unzipping our flies and pretending that we were all just innocently having a wee.

Unfortunately for poor Jonesy, he was left in the cubicle right in the middle of his 'puff' when *dixie* called the warning. He panicked, slamming the door shut and locking it just before the teacher burst into the toilets.

"We're done for!" I muttered to myself.

Mr O'Reilly stood blocking the entrance, searchingly looking at each and every boy standing at the urinals, before walking down the row of cubicle doors. He moved quietly, taking one step at a time, pausing outside each door and pushing on it with one finger, standing there watching as it swung back until it hit the tiled wall with a loud bang. He repeated this process with each door, one bang after another sounding like the heavy footsteps of an approaching executioner, ensuring that each cubicle was empty. Then he found the door that was locked.

We all stood there, a long row of boys facing the urinals, holding our willies and pretending to pee, acting as if nothing was wrong.

"Come on out," O'Reilly called, banging on the cubicle door. "I know that you are in there, and I know what you are up to."

"I'm on the toilet, Sir," Jonesy squeaked.

"No you are not. I know what you are doing, now open up!" O'Reilly replied.

Jonesy was stalling for time. "Honest Sir, I'm still sitting on the toilet, I'm not finished yet."

"Not finished?" O'Reilly bellowed. "By the time I am finished with you, you won't be able to sit on anything, let alone a toilet for quite some time! Now open up."

There was a few moments silence, broken only by the sound of a toilet being flushed. Those who could turned to see what was going on as the cubicle door opened and a thick cloud of heavy smoke billowed out. It was so dense we couldn't see a thing and for a moment it looked as if Jonesy had escaped. Sadly, he too emerged and O'Reilly who had now finished coughing and waving his hand about to clear the air, took hold of him by the ear.

Not letting go of Jonesy, O'Reilly peered into the cubicle looking for evidence and saw it, a small brown object floating in the toilet bowl. The cigar had refused to collaborate!

Jonesy was literally marched off by his ear to the Head Master's office, whilst everyone else got on with spreading the terrible news. Smoking a cigar at school could mean being expelled, and although I put on a brave face I knew that it wouldn't be long before Jonesy would crack under interrogation.

I was right, Jonesy squealed. Receiving my summons to go immediately to the Head Master's office, I was questioned closely as to where I had got the cigar from – the Head Master wanted to make sure that it hadn't been stolen from a shop. Once I admitted that it had been my father's I was sent home to fetch my Mother, and told to hurry back with her as quickly as I could.

I ran all the way home, my heart in my mouth, wondering all the time what she was going to do or say. I was in serious trouble and could not see anyway that she would be able to save me. I had certainly never done anything as bad as this before in my entire life. In fact, I was more scared of facing my mother, and her response, than I was of anything that the Head Master could do to me.

The journey from the house back to school was made in near silence, my mother's face grim, and her footsteps very determined. I sat outside the Head Master's Office for what seemed an eternity, until she finally emerged, the look on her face giving me a clear indication as to the extent of her anger.

We returned home, mother still not talking to me, but as soon as the door was closed, she literally went 'ballistic'. She told me off for stealing the cigar from the drawer, and for even looking in the drawers in the first place. She told me that I should have been expelled, and that she was so ashamed that she had been taken down to the school because I was in such bad trouble. She was furious that she almost had to plead on my behalf, promising that I would never misbehave again if I was allowed to stay at school.

I was sent to bed without any tea, which wasn't too bad. What was worse however was that she did not look at or speak to me for days, as if I didn't exist, and that hurt me most of all.

A good few days later, Mum was doing some ironing and I was sitting at the table drawing when she turned to me and asked, "How much did you charge for a go on that cigar?"

"A penny a puff, Mum" I replied.

"A penny a puff?" she almost sounded pleased. As she looked away, I could see the hint of a smile at the corners of her mouth.

Some forty odd years later I can just imagine the scene in the staff room during playtime. One of the teachers is standing by the window looking over the playground, and comments on the little puffs of smoke he can see from time to time.

Meanwhile, one of his colleagues, seated in a leather armchair, mentions the outbreak of coughing amongst many of the pupils.

The teacher at the window turns to look at him as the penny drops. "The little bleeders are smoking!"

★ ★ ★

Whereas Mum was good at trading, Dad taught me the art of selling, in particular the importance of a good spiel.

Christmas was only six weeks away and this year it was going to be different. Mum had come up with another one of her clever business ideas.

With a little financial assistance from Aunty Joyce and the help of her gentleman friend, Mac, Mum put her plan into action - Dad and Mac were going into business together, selling ladies stockings. On Saturdays the two of them would become street traders outside TJ Hughes on London Road right in the heart of Liverpool.

Mum organised everything - from where to buy the stock, to how it should be sold and for how much. She put an old suitcase on the kitchen table and carefully filled it with very small plastic bags containing ladies stockings.

That first Saturday morning, I sat on the stairs listening to all the discussions going on about what they were planning to do. It all sounded so exciting. As I sat there I built up enough courage to say, "Dad, can I come with you? Can I? Go on, can I?"

"It would be very good for him you know Les," said Mum, "A son should spend time with his Father, and he would be an asset to you. I have taught him lots on the markets."

Dad shook his head from side to side, a clear 'No' in any language, and then he stopped while he thought about what Mum had said. He smiled, "Yes, of course you can. Go get your coat on Jeff, and I might even buy you a pint on the way home."

Mum's response to this last comment was a clear, "Don't you even think about it!"

It was busy when we arrived, with barrow boys setting up their carts down the middle of the road selling everything imaginable, whilst on either side of the road were the big department stores. The barrow boys were 'legal' and had street trading licences which were normally passed down from generation to generation. Dad could not have got one of these street licences even if he could have afforded one as they were like gold dust. We, on the other hand were 'illegal' traders or fly pitchers. Should we have been caught by the police whilst trading, it would have meant instant arrest, confiscation of property and then an appearance in court a few weeks later where the fine could be anywhere between ten and twenty pounds. The stakes were high.

Dad and Mac discussed the best position and the getaway strategy should the *bizzies* show up. They agreed to set up just inside the corner entrance of TJ Hughes as there were no other fly pitchers on that spot (it was an unwritten law amongst fly pitchers that you did not take someone else's spot) so off we went. Mac stood across from us where he had a good view up and down the road, able to spot trouble in time. Dad in the meantime took up his place on what was now our pitch. Dressed in his camel crombie overcoat, with his signature starched collar and wearing a bright yellow tie tied in a large Windsor knot, he looked as if he owned the department store.

Dad had charm. Not only did he have the looks to go with the charm, but he had a way of talking to people that made them feel important, and listening to the words he uttered was like collecting pearls of wisdom. He could also twist people around his little finger.

So there we were on a cold winter's Saturday morning, with Pearce, Son & Associates ready to battle with both the elements and potential customers. It had started.

"Here we are ladies, here we are," Dad would call, the patter rolling off his tongue. "Nineteen denier stockings, two pair for half a crown.... All perfect just like me!" Women of all ages gathered around to have a look.

"Me old man's on nights," said one, "I wouldn't mind a bit of company if you know what I mean."

"I'll take four pair off yer, if you will put them on for me handsome," called out a very large lady at the top of her voice.

Everyone laughed at this, which got the day well and truly off to a fine start.

Before we started, I had been told how important my job was. I had to kneel down on the ground in the doorway, next to the open suitcase and pass the stockings up to my Dad as and when he needed them. Above all, however, I was to do what I was told. With Dad selling, Mac would be keeping dixie and as soon as he saw a policeman in the distance he would give Dad a warning nod. Dad would then let me know so that I could close the suitcase and stroll into the store calmly and casually, drawing as little attention to myself as possible. I was then to make my way to the side entrance where Dad would meet me and we would go and have a pot of tea with Mac in the café across the road until the coast was clear and the bizzies gone. Then we would take up position again and continue trading as if nothing had happened.

When Dad was in position, ready to start his spiel, he would put his hands in the two big pockets on the front of his crombie overcoat, shaking a handful of half crowns up and down making them jingle. That way he would get the attention of the passers-by, the ladies turning their heads to see where the noise was coming from. Then he would start all over again.

"Come on girls, nineteen denier stockings, two pairs for half a crown," he would call out, announcing our return to business.

Every Saturday night, when we had finished at about five o'clock, we would head into the café where Dad would order a large pot of tea and he and Mac would talk to the other traders. Emptying out his pockets one at a time laying all the coins on the table so that I could stack them in order, one on top of the other Dad would then split the money with Mac, passing any left-over small change to me saying "Well son, there's your wages".

This Saturday night tradition would then continue with Dad stopping off at the pub on the way home for a couple of pints, whilst I waited outside with the obligatory bottle of lemonade and a packet of crisps.

Mum was very pleased with the way that the stockings were selling, and the fact that Dad was beginning to give her some decent money. However she felt that as Christmas was getting closer it was time for a change, for something more festive, so she decided we would sell sheets of coloured wrapping paper.

Setting off for the wholesalers on the bus, Mum would get as much paper as she could fit in to two large shopping bags. When she got home, we would all help sorting out the different coloured sheets and then we would make them up into packs of twelve, one of each colour. She would then carefully put them in the suitcase in neat parcels, just like she had done with the stockings, and leave the suitcase by the front door before going to bed.

Come Saturday, and positioned on our pitch, Dad would start the day's business this time with calls of, "Come on girls, come and get your Christmas paper, twelve sheets for shilling girls, just a shilling for twelve."

Again it would not be long before the ladies would start gathering around, and I would be passing out parcels to him as fast as I could. There was no doubt about it, Dad could sell. He would use his charm and good looks, and I would notice the effect that this had on the women who would gather around and how they would look at him. I am sure that if I had understood half the things they said to him, I would have been shocked, but luckily I was too young. I would mention these things to Mum later once we were home, but she would just laugh and say, "They can look at him all they want as long as they keep on buying."

A few days to go before Christmas and everything was going well. We were eating good food; we had warm clothes, enough money for coal, and even the occasional treat. We felt very proud of ourselves – The Pearce's were coming up in the world again.

One Saturday morning, mid-trading I suddenly got a nod and a kick from Dad. There was a policeman headed straight our way. I panicked, forgetting all my instructions about remaining calm, and having snapped the case closed lifted it over my head and legged it straight into the store. All that would have been visible to the shoppers inside TJ Hughes was a large suitcase on top of a pair of skinny, little legs running straight at them.

A path quickly opened up, as if I was Moses parting the Red Sea. My dash for freedom suddenly ended as I collided with a large protruding stomach belonging to a man with grey trousers and dirty boots (they were all I could see). The suitcase bounced back off his stomach flying through the air behind me; I looked up and saw the angry red face of a store detective staring down at me menacingly. He quickly grabbed me by the arm with one hand, picked up the suitcase with the other, and marched me towards the stairs leading to the manager's office.

He was a big man in a scruffy uniform with a flat hat, dragging a small frightened kid up a stairwell. I kept pulling hard trying to escape his clutches, but the more I tried the redder his face would become and the tighter his grip. He hauled me inside the office closing the door closed behind us, and then banged the suitcase down on the floor at my feet. He turned to the manager sitting behind the desk.

"Here he is sir, one of the culprits who sell right outside our shop." Lifting the suitcase on to the desk, he started to open it up as if I had just robbed the Bank of England and he was going to find hundreds of pound notes inside. The manager looked first at the large suitcase, then at me, then at the store detective.

"Surely the case must be empty," he said, looking me up and down, realising that I was clearly small enough to fit inside the case myself.

Whilst I was being detained, Dad had gone around the corner to meet me at the side door so that we could go for our usual cup of tea. After a reasonable amount of time had passed, and I still had not shown up, he realised that something must have gone wrong so went into the store to look for me.

He asked everyone standing about if they had seen a small boy with a large suitcase. "Yes," one man called out, "The store detective grabbed him and took him up those stairs."

By this time, I was now being asked who my accomplices were. Right in the middle of this interrogation the door was suddenly thrown open with so much force that it nearly flew off its hinges and Dad appeared. He seemed to look like a cross between Hop-Along-Cassidy and Flash Gordon as he burst into the room; a man with a mission.

"That's my son," he yelled, lifting me up with one hand. "And that's my suitcase" he added picking the case up off the desk. "I will thank you to leave them both alone!"

The store detective leaped forward as if to stop him, but Dad just swung the suitcase in his direction, making him retreat behind the Managers desk, out of the reach of Dad's wrath.

The Manager started shouting back, "We don't want you outside our shop selling. NOT ever… you got that?

Turning his back on the two men blustering from behind the safety of their desk, Dad merely tipped his head back towards them as he replied, "I'll make a note and you know what I'll do with it then…. don't you?"

Nobody ever bothered us again; that corner entrance to TJ Hughes became Dad's pitch and he sold his wares and chatted-up ladies from that spot for many years to come. We were moderately successful in selling our stock, and hugely successful in avoiding the bizzies.

Chapter Two
The Boss

I f only The Boss could have been more of a father; but he wasn't. There were times when he seemed to live in a completely different world from the rest of us. Apart from when we were working together he wasn't really around. In fact, I rarely saw him whilst I was growing up, and if I did it was mostly when I came home from school at 4 o'clock when I would find him at the kitchen sink shaving.

Seeing me standing there, he would put his hand in his pocket and jingling the coins before taking out a coin or two.

"Son, go and get me pack of twenty Rothman's King size cigarettes and a packet of Seven O'clock razor blades."

It always had to be Rothman's as my father would smoke nothing else; as far as he was concerned, Woodbines and Senior Service were common, and he was too good for them.

Setting off to run my errand, I would hear Mum chiding me to "Be quick Jeff be quick; don't keep your Dad waiting."

My Father's afternoon preparations were a ritual with Mum waiting on him hand and foot as he readied himself for work. She treated him as if he was a Hollywood movie star, making sure that his shirts and collars were freshly laundered at the Chinese Laundry on a regular basis. He had to have a clean shirt every day, with particular emphasis on the starched collar and cuffs, in which he always wore a tie and a pair of gleaming cufflinks.

His preparations did not end with a shave and a clean shirt. He would blacken his moustache with a cosmetic pencil, and apply vast amounts of brillcream using his fingers to carefully position the waves in his thick black hair, frequently checking his reflection in the mirror, his vanity needing constant reassurance of his good looks; it was an attention to detail bordering on the excessive.

Mum would have polished his shoes earlier and before putting them on he would turn them over to check that she had even polished the arch on the sole! She was also responsible for ensuring that the shoulders of his jacket were given one last brush down before he left the house. Mum was very much his 'gentleman's valet.'

Despite his failings as a provider, Mum adored him and dreamed that one day soon he would change becoming the perfect husband and a good father to his children.

The reality however was different. My father lived a lie, pretending to the world that he was an affluent man; if his appearance was anything to go by he certainly looked like a man of wealth and stature. Once away from his house and his family we all ceased to exist. If anyone approached him for a bob or two he would oblige even if it was his last pound. The fact that he was never repaid never bothered him, nor did he ever ask for the money back.

For many years my father hardly contributed a single penny towards the household costs, spending the money he earned either on getting drunk or looking after his friends.

Mum hated his so called friends referring to them as his cronies; they would feed his make-believe world and his ego with compliments and flattery. Nicknaming him 'The Boss' these cronies flattered him into believing that he not only looked but behaved like a wealthy businessman, and being the weak person he was he was easily caught up in their lies. He refused to grow up, turning his back on the true responsibility of his family and wife in favour of so many insignificant people.

He shared a black city cab with one of his best friends, Nobbie, who lived a couple of streets away. Nobbie worked the permanent day shift whilst my father did the nights. Working out of the clubs, in the seedier side of town, he would chauffeur the prostitutes and their 'clients' to and from the nearby ships that were in port at the time. This ferrying backwards and forwards would go on throughout the night, and was apparently a very lucrative business for the girls as well as my father, as he would earn at least five pounds for a return trip.

Besides seeing him in the afternoons when I came home the only other time I occasionally saw him was in the morning as I left for school. He no longer looked well groomed and tidy; instead he was almost frightening with bloodshot eyes, his hair in an untidy mess and his tie skewiff - slouched in the chair stinking of booze and tobacco. We wouldn't bother talking to him as he couldn't string a sentence together he was so drunk. Sometimes he would go on a bender for days at a time; how he managed to avoid any fatal accidents, I will never know.

Until I started working with Dad, I only ever went out with him twice, and only because my Mother forced him in to it. She would point out that he never took his children out anywhere telling him that 'a boy should spend time with his father'. She wanted him to take me out boating on the lake in the park, knowing I would really enjoy it.

One day, obviously after mother had another go at him, he came up to me. "Come on Son, I am taking you out for the day. How about we go to Greenbank Park and get a boat out for an hour or two? You can row me around the lake!"

At this time I was only 6 years old, the thought of going out with Dad all by myself filled me with so much happiness I felt I would burst. Mum got me dressed in my best Sunday clothes, and we set off for the bus stop. Greenbank Park was about six stops down Smithdown Road; once we got on the big green double-decker bus, I sat with Dad upstairs so that he could have a smoke. I felt immensely proud and grown up sitting there next to him. The journey passed quickly, and it seemed only like a few minutes before Dad was telling me that our stop was the next one.

I was so excited with the thought of rowing the boat around the lake that I jumped up quickly as the bus pulled up at the stop, and clattered down the curved stairs to the platform below. We got off, just outside a large pub called the Brook House. I could see Dad looking at the pub, with a smile on his face, and was not too surprised when he turned to me.

"Come on son," he said, "I am just going to have a quick pint before we go to the park."

Leaving me at the door to the pub he told me to wait outside making me promise that I wouldn't move. I think about twenty minutes must have gone by before he came out, "Great," I thought to myself, "Great we are going to the park now." Instead he handed me a small bottle of lemonade and a packet of crisps and then went back inside with hardly a word.

All I could do was wait for him to come back out again. This time hours passed, and not wanting to dirty my best Sunday clothes, I stood by the door, rather than sitting down on the pavement or the filthy steps leading inside the public house. It was quite hot, and I was getting bored and tired just standing there. There was nothing for me to do and nobody to talk to, so I tried to amuse myself by watching the buses going up and down the road, and watching the men coming in and out of the pub. The worst of it was that every time the door opened I could see Dad leaning on the bar talking to other men, laughing and joking, enjoying himself, whilst I was outside, I was on my own.

As the afternoon wore on the pub started to empty, and I could hear the man behind the bar shouting for last orders, and time to drink up. Did this mean that Dad would be coming out, and that we could go to the Park? Finally, he emerged, one of the last to leave.

"Come on," he said, "Let's go to the Park and take a look at these boats." He smelt of beer and cigarettes. We made our way to the park and then across to the lake. As we got closer I could sense that something was wrong, there were no boats on the water. By the time we got to the boat-hire hut, I could see that it was closed, and all the boats were chained up along the little wooden jetty. My heart sank. Dad spoke to the man in charge, trying to persuade him to let us take a boat out for a short while. I could hear the man telling him that they had closed at 4 o'clock, and it was now 4.30. There was no chance.

As we turned to head back, Dad apologised, trying to take hold of my hand. I didn't want him to touch me. He continued to say he was sorry all the way back to the bus stop. It didn't matter what he said to me though, I just simply hated him that day.

When we arrived home Mum could tell from the miserable look on my face and the smell of booze on his breath that it had all gone very wrong. She started to get angry, asking him what had happened. Dad, knowing that he was in the wrong, started to shout back, and before long they were yelling at each other. It was frightening for us kids, and we all ran upstairs out of the way of the noise.

Almost a year later, Dad took me out again; this was a proper day out as we were going to Southport, a coastal resort famous for the amusement arcades and funfair and a popular destination for families during the holidays and weekends.

I had heard from my mates who had been there before, that it was a great place to go. There were traditional seaside attractions and the fairground was massive, with every possible ride you could ever imagine. There were sweets galore, and lots of other nice things to eat, as well as stalls where you could win prizes, if you were lucky or a good shot. I was so looking forward to it, sharing the fun of the rides with Dad and enjoying all sorts of goodies like toffee apples and candy floss.

We had to make an early start and being a child full of excitement I woke up even earlier than normal. We started off on the bus, which took us to a railway station, where we then caught a train to Southport. I cannot remember much of the two hour journey, anticipation made the time fly.

As we got off the train at Southport Station, I could feel the holiday atmosphere in the air. There were crowds of people, Mums and Dads with their children hurriedly making their way towards the sea and the fairground carrying baskets and bags full of goodies for the day, or laden down with buckets and spades for the beach, whilst there were others simply holding hands as they walked along. Everyone looked so happy, filled with the thought of the day ahead.

As we made our way out of the station, I could see the big wheel of the fairground in the distance, slowly going around with the carriages full of people laughing and waving. That would be me soon, I thought to myself, holding Dad's hand firmly with mine. I was terrified of losing him in all the crowds around us.

When we arrived, we went straight to the fairground and Dad put me on a couple of the small rides, telling me that we could have a go on the bigger ones later. He bought us each an ice-cream, and I was really beginning to enjoy myself, looking around as we walked along, planning which I would go on next.

While we were walking along Dad bumped into some man whom he seemed to know. This man was there with his three sons who were slightly older than me, and like us, were there for a day out together, just the four of them. We joined up into a group and continued to walk along, Dad talking to his friend, whilst I was left trailing along behind with the three older boys who ignored me. I felt so much smaller and younger than them so just kept quiet, thinking about the adventures to come.

After a few minutes we stopped, Dad put his hand in his pocket and pulled out a half crown. "Take this Son," he said handing me the coin. "I am going in there for a pint with my friend. You run along with these lads and have fun. Just be good and don't get lost. But don't worry about me, I will only be here," he finished, pointing towards a red-brick pub.

As Dad and his friend walked inside, I turned around to the other boys, but they had disappeared. I just caught sight of them running into the fairground, and reckoned that they must have been so excited at the thought of spending the money that their dad had given them, that they forgot to wait for me. Anyway, I didn't want to be with them, I wanted to be with my Dad, just the two of us going on all those promised rides together. I stood there not knowing what to do, A seven year old, rooted to the ground, too frightened to move from that spot, terrified at the thought of getting lost in the crowds of holiday makers.

There must have been hundreds of people all walking and moving around me, most of them bigger and faster, and I was scared at being swept up and carried away. What if I got lost? What if I couldn't find the pub again? I couldn't even see the name of the pub, and even if I had been able to I couldn't have read it. Even worse, what if Dad came out of the pub and couldn't find me? Or would he forget that he had even brought me with him, and go home without me, leaving me stranded in this strange place all on my own? I didn't think that I could find my way to the train station on my own, and I certainly wouldn't know which train to catch or where to get off.

Waves of panic were beginning to engulf me, and I knew from past experience that the best thing to do was to get as close to the pub door which I had seen Dad go in, and to stay there until he finally came out.

Once again I found myself just standing and watching the world go by, unable to join in like all the other kids with their parents around me. My half crown was burning a hole in my pocket, and I kept having to touch it to make sure that I hadn't lost it, but wanting to keep it hidden in case some bigger lad tried to nick it off me. I so wanted to buy something for myself, but I couldn't see any shops close by for me to go and get something (while still keeping an eye on the pub door) so all I could do was look at the other kids wistfully, walking past me wearing funny hats, eating sticks of rock or big lollipops, and enjoying themselves as kids should on a special day out.

Time passed slowly as I stood there. It was hot and I was thirsty. I also needed to wee and not wanting to wet my pants, plucked up courage to nip around the back of the pub as fast I could, and relieve myself behind some old boxes. I had to hurry though as I was terrified in case Dad came out and found me gone.

The three other lads eventually came back, full of stories of the rides they had been on which they were happy to share with me. I wasn't interested; I just wanted to get back to the safety of my home and my Mum. It was getting late, I was hot, tired and hungry, and feeling totally miserable.

When he finally staggered out, it was easy to see that Dad had been drinking heavily. He had to hold on to me for support as we walked along, and had to ask for directions to the station as he had forgotten where it was. After we got on the train, he fell asleep; unaware of the small boy next to him, his drunken snores were an embarrassment to me, making me wish that he was not my Dad.

Mum never let him take me out for the day ever again.

I kept the half crown hidden for a couple of weeks and eventually one day when I knew Mum needed some extra pennies to buy food I gave it to her, telling her it was from my day out with Dad.

Mum tried to protect her children as best she could from the antics of my father, but she was not always successful and sadly we always found out. My older brother and sisters had a greater awareness of what was going on and formed their own opinions accordingly. However, from my point of view as the youngest child at the time, my understanding was based on what I saw and how it made me feel.

There is, however, one particular memory which we all share, and which we are all agreed upon.

It was a cold, dark wintery evening, Mum was in the kitchen keeping Dad's evening meal warm (I think he had been absent for a day or two) and the four of us were clustered around our new 14 inch television; the lights were off and you could have heard a pin drop. The television was a new addition to our house, and had pride of place in the front parlour. This was Mum's favourite room, where she kept all her most valuable possessions; visitors were entertained, and where Christmas was celebrated.

I clearly remember we were watching a circus. There was a group of acrobats forming a human tower, leaping on to each other's shoulders. As the last man was about to be thrown into the air, the door to the parlour opened and we heard a drunken grunt. Without thinking, and as one voice, the four of us all chorused a loud 'shush'.

As the final acrobat flew through the air on the point of taking his place at the top of the 'tower' we all suddenly realised who was standing behind us.

"Tell me to shush will you? I'll show you who the fucking boss is in this house."

My father lurched over to the tv, picked it up, staggered over to the bay window at the front of the room, and hurled it with all his might through the glass onto the street outside. The noise was horrendous, as metal broke through glass, glass rained down on the cobbles outside, and he continued to roar out in anger.

We did not stay put for long, leaping to our feet and making a bolt for the safety of upstairs. The fact that the four of us managed to fit through the door all at once just proves how desperate we were to escape.

As we pounded upstairs, our feet making a loud noise on the brown lino that covered the floor, Mum came out of the kitchen, attracted by the shouting. Wiping her hands on her apron she was asking, "What is going on? Will someone tell me what is going on?"

I guess she must have gone into the front parlour and seen the devastation to the window. I could hear my father still ranting, but perhaps the realization of what he had done might have started to dawn on him, as his voice quieted down, his anger turning to self-justification for his outburst of rage.

What I do know is what I saw a little while later when I managed to pluck up the courage to pull back the curtains from the window above my bed. Although there was no sight of my father, the neighbours were out in force, peering from behind their net curtains, or being even bolder and standing on their front steps watching and gossiping to one another about the spectacle before them.

My Mum was out on the street, a vulnerable figure of a woman, down on her hands and knees picking up the pieces of the wreckage. As the streetlamp shone down on her face I could see the light glinting on the tears streaming down her cheeks. It was symbolic of our life as a family; for all the good that Mum managed to achieve my father would destroy in one drunken moment.

He did a great many unpleasant things as far as my mother was concerned, but in hindsight I believe that this was one of the lowest moments of their married life. The complete and utter humiliation that he subjected her to has remained with me as clearly as the image of her tears as she knelt in the street outside.

★ ★ ★

My Mother was a woman of incredible spirit and courage, and like women all over the world would stoop to almost anything in order to protect and provide for her children.

Like so many other small kids living in the Liverpool slums, we were cold, worn clothes providing little or no warmth. When times were hard, we would huddle around the fire in the living room, where literally anything would be thrown on to burn; I can even remember Mum throwing worn out old shoes and boots into the embers to keep the fire going. Great Britain was still experiencing the tail end of World War II rationing, and jobs were very hard to find.

Although Mum worked hard, and had a good reputation locally, cleaning jobs were not always available. In the winter months, the Saturday markets would often be almost empty thanks to freezing cold weather.

They were really difficult times, and even as a small child I could often feel the sense of pure desperation and worry that seemed to permanently enshroud my mother, especially when it came to money. Without money she couldn't feed us.

One bitter February morning I found Mum sitting at the small table in the living room, taking her coppers out of her purse and laying them on the table as she counted them. She seemed to be lost in thought, as if weighing up something very carefully. I must have made a noise as I approached her, as she suddenly looked up at me before getting to her feet.

Taking me by the hand, she led me to where our coats were hanging. She put on her old black coat, and dressed me up as best she could in my winter coat and a handmade woolen hat pulled right down to cover my ears. "We are going to the Co-Op," she said, knotting a floral head scarf under her chin, before opening the back door and stepping out in to the jigga.

The jigga was about two minutes walk from the Co-Op; in its day, the Co-Op was regarded as a very modern way of shopping, larger than the normal corner shop which people were used to.

When we arrived at the shop entrance, she took both my hands in hers and looked me straight in my eyes saying, "Jeff, listen to me. I want you to stay right here. Do you understand? Don't you dare move; I promise I won't be long," all the time fastening my coat and wiping my runny nose with her handkerchief.

I didn't think to say anything other than "Yes, Mum", but I couldn't understand why she wouldn't let me go in with her this time. I stood by the door looking at the busy traffic going up and down Smithdown Road and all the people rushing around. As the wind whistled about the doorway I started to feel cold, wanting my Mum, and wishing she would hurry up. I seemed to be standing there forever as customers went in and out. Each time the door opened, I tried to look through the gap but I couldn't see in as I was too small and the door never stayed open long enough.

I wasn't used to being on my own, and became very upset crying with confusion whilst I couldn't stop shivering with cold. Suddenly this lady kneeled down in front of me, concern in her voice.

"What's up love?" she asked.

"It's me Mum. I want me Mum."

"Where is she?"

"She's in there," I replied pointing to the shop door behind me. Standing up, she took me by the hand and led me inside the store. It was warm in there so I started to feel a bit better.

The woman stopped in the middle of the store with me by her side. "Who does this child belong to?" she demanded in a loud voice. She repeated herself, "Who does this child belong to? Does he belong to anyone in here?"

Everyone looked around, and before long one of the sales assistants said, "He must belong to the woman in the office with the policeman and the manager". The next moment one of the staff took my hand and led me into the office.

As the door opened, I caught sight of my Mum, sitting on a chair crying. Still crying myself I ran to her, reaching out for her. She put her arms around me, and picked me up placing me on her lap covering my face with kisses.

"There, there son," she said, her voice beginning to soothe me. "I'm sorry, I'm so sorry. Everything will be alright now we're together".

There was a policeman standing next to my Mum's chair. He looked at me sitting on Mum's lap, and couldn't stop himself asking "Have you no pride? Theft is a very grave crime, even if it is only a loaf of bread."

He continued, "Stealing is serious. If I had my way I would be taking you down the station right now! You're very lucky the manager has decided not to prosecute. He says he knows you, and you come here shopping quite a lot. He says you have never stolen from here before, so he's letting you go."

They walked us to the door speaking loudly so that everyone could hear the policeman saying, "Don't let me catch you stealing ever again!" The manager added, "You should be ashamed of yourself. Don't you ever show your face in here again."

Mum quickly turned out the door and almost immediately into the jigga heading for home, grasping my hand, willing me to keep up with her. As soon as we were through the door, she quickly shut it behind us, before leaning back, closing her eyes and sighing with relief at being in the safety of her own home. Then she groaned as if with despair as the shame of it hit her.

"Has it come to this?" she cried out. "Having to steal a loaf of bread to feed my children?"

"What have I done?" she moaned. "What in heaven have I done? The neighbours....." her voice trailed off as the reality sank in. My Mum knew that within ten minutes of our leaving the shop everybody from streets around would know what had happened. They would have something new to gossip about now, and for once it wasn't my Dad.

My poor little Mum. She must have felt so miserable, knowing this time she had brought shame to the house, and it was almost too much for her to bear. She broke down, weeping for the longest time, and I stood there with my arms wrapped around her knees, trying to comfort her.

I didn't understand much of it then but it has stayed with me all my life, like a bad dream coming back to haunt me from time to time. I have often thought how desperate my mother must have been that day to have to taken those drastic measures. As I grew older I could never understand why my father didn't share the burden of bringing up a family, just like the other fathers did instead of leaving it all up to Mum.

★ ★ ★

There was another occasion which also still bothers me, when I recall standing quietly in the kitchen watching my Mother going through the now familiar routine of counting her money. It was such a familiar sight watching her separate coins from the meager pile; she would put the shillings to one side for the electricity and gas meters, whilst any other coins would be used for food for the rest of the week. Her pain and frustration at the lack of money yet again was obvious even to a child as young as me.

As I watched, I could hear her going through her shopping list as she counted out enough change for a loaf of bread and some paraffin. Seeing me in the doorway a gentle smile came over her face as she beckoned me forward. I leant against her knee as her arm came around me and she stroked my ginger-topped head. Her voice was soft and with no hint of her usual briskness. 'Jeff, son, we are going to Mr. Cohen's, for some paraffin and soap.'

Mr Cohen's chandler's shop was across from our street, on the corner of Smithdown Road. We needed paraffin for the small black stove, which was placed in each of the bedrooms, to warm them on winter nights. Whoever went to bed first according to age would have the chill taken off their room for half an hour before bedtime. Mum would then carefully move the heater on to the next room. Once we were all in bed, she would leave the heater on the landing next to the potty throughout the night.

She was still stroking my hair as she said, 'We are going to play a little game. You're going to be a good boy for your mum. While I'm talking to Mr. Cohen, I'm going to leave my bag on the floor next to the soap and I want you to be very clever and put a bar of soap in my bag. Remember only one bar of soap.'

So I said, 'Yes, Mum.' I took this very seriously and thought it sounded like a great game. Off we went across the road and into Mr. Cohen's Chandlers. He was a Fagin-like old man who wore a dark brown apron and stood behind a tall counter. I never saw his face clearly, but I do remember the fingerless gloves on his hands revealing his blackened fingernails.

The floor was covered in sawdust and I kicked at it a couple of times with my foot a fun thing to do for us little boys, which probably irritated the hell out of Mr Cohen as it sent dust flying everywhere. There was a strange mixture of powerful smells whenever we went in there, made up of carbolic soap and paraffin, white spirit and turps and a faint hint of ammonia. Tins of paint were stacked up on dusty shelves and there were lots of other things crammed into every nook and cranny of the shop. There was just about enough floor space for me to stand beside Mum, as even the floor was covered with boxes and bags full of things for sale. Mum stood in front of the counter with me wedged between her and the dusty pile of soap on the floor. She placed the bag down on the floor next to me and started to talk to Mr Cohen. As she leant over the counter she asked him for some paraffin, passing him the gallon tin can to fill.

I was in my own world with bars of soap to play with. I picked up the first bar and ran my hands over its waxy surface. Mr Cohen must have turned away, as my dream was interrupted by Mum nudging me with her foot and nodding towards the soap with her head. I was already cradling a bar and I smiled up at her, causing her to smile back at me. I placed the soap in the bag. I thought I was quite good. Then without looking at Mum, I got another bar and another bar, and I kept loading them up until I had put eight bars in the bag. It was like playing with building bricks and I loved it.

Mum bent over to pick up the shopping bag and immediately noticed the heavy weight. Her hands were now full, so nudging me out of the shop with her knees and telling me to move as quickly as possible, we made a hasty exit. Out on the street, and needing to cross the busy road, she ordered me to grab hold of her coat. We crossed the road and made our way straight down the jigga into our house.

Unlocking the back door she silently dragged me in, anger written all over her face, before closing it, so that the neighbours couldn't overhear us. She then got very cross and told me exactly what she thought of my behavior. Putting me over her knee she gave me a really good spanking all the time repeating, "One bar of soap, I said one bar of soap! Don't you ever, ever do that again! We only needed one bar. You're a naughty boy! You took so many when we just needed one bar."

Normally, evening times would be special as Mum would stand me up in the porcelain Belfast Sink in our tiny kitchen to give me a wash. In order to do this she would have to heat a pan of water on the gas cooker as there was only a cold water tap above the sink. Once washed, she would stand me in front of the fire in the living room and dry me off with a big towel. It used to be a lovely time as she got me ready for bed. There'd be stories and then she'd sing me to sleep, one of her favourite songs being Doris Day's, Que Sera Sera. Not surprisingly it still remains one of my favourites to this day.

That night she put me to bed very early. I clearly recall that it felt so strange to be going to bed while it was still light outside. There was no story, no song, just a quiet anger about her. She did not heat my room either and I lay curled up under the blankets feeling utterly miserable trying to warm up as best I could, when I heard her leave the house.

The next morning she told me she had taken the seven bars of soap back to Mr. Cohen's. I wondered if he had told her off, but some time later she told me that she had hidden them among the brushes and other household items, on display in the big baskets and dustbins along the pavement outside the shop. It was only then that I was able to feel relieved and glad because Mr. Cohen was not likely to come after me.

My Mother never ever encouraged any of her children to steal, and would have condemned such behaviour from any of us; however her need to keep us clean at that moment in time was far greater than the morals of the crime we committed. As for me, I learned a very valuable lesson that day; necessity is one thing, whilst greed is another.

Chapter Three
Number 36

I was born with a silver spoon in my mouth. Not because I was born into an aristocratic family, unfortunately, but because my birth coincided with the Coronation of our new Queen.

In 1953, any child born within a week of the Queen's Coronation received a commemorative silver spoon to celebrate the official crowning of Queen Elizabeth II. The Coronation was to be held on Tuesday, 2nd June 1953, and I was born on Saturday 30th May, entitling me to this beautiful gift; a gift I still treasure 55 years later.

I was born James Jeffrey Pearce to my proud parents Elsie May and Leslie Norman. Three days after I was born, Mum and I were allowed to home. I could not have chosen a better day. My timing was perfect! Tuesday, 2nd June, the day the whole country was celebrating the Queens Coronation.

This was a time of rejoicing. The Second World War had ended eight years earlier, and England had been going through a long period of rebuilding and recovery. Rationing had only just finished, and a feeling of wellbeing had begun to pervade the nation. Thousands of street parties were being held up and down the country, streamers and bunting hung from street lamps, tables of every size and description set out in long rows down the centers of the street covered with plates of sandwiches, small cakes and other simple offerings.

The whole nation seemed to have joined together in one enormous party, the streets filled with laughter and celebration as neighbours sat down on chairs outside their front doors, whilst children in party hats tucked into the food laid out in front of them, or raced up and down calling out to one another.

My Father picked us up from the hospital in his black cab and no sooner had we pulled up outside our red front door than my brother and sisters ran over to Mum to say hello and to see me for the first time. As she stepped out of the taxi Mum was swamped by my siblings and their friends, all standing on tip toe and craning their necks to get a better look at me.

I was introduced to my sister Lesley first. She was a pretty blonde eight year old and the eldest child. Next in line was my brother Barry, a cheeky six year old with a tousled mop of dark curls. Standing right behind was Sheila, a solemn two year old with bright auburn hair and lots of freckles who had been the baby of the family before my arrival.

They gathered around me to have a closer look, all the time asking my Mum, "Where is it Mum? Where is it?"

Mum was puzzled. "Where's what?" she asked.

"The present off the Queen", they chorused in reply. "The spoon!"

Mum laughed, taking the precious silver spoon out of her hand bag and passing it to Lesley. "Don't let it out of your sight," she warned.

Grasping the spoon carefully in her hands, Lesley ran off a little way down the street. Hot on her heels was a cluster of children of all ages, calling out excitedly.

"Please Lesley, let's have a look."

"Slow down Lesley, I want to see it! Stop!"

Coming to a standstill, she was soon lost amongst the other children, all of whom were begging for a look at the treasure in her hands. As she carefully opened her hand, revealing the silver spoon lying on her palm a gasp of awe could be heard, before silence descended over the small crowd.

"Look" said Lesley, pointing to the hallmarks on the back of the spoon. "That's real silver that is. It was made for the Queen, and she took it out of one of her kitchen drawers to give to us, as a special present for our new baby!"

As the children's minds were filled with images of the Queen in her palace choosing a spoon for a new baby, Mum quietly sat down with me on her lap to enjoy the celebrations for the rest of the day.

★ ★ ★

I loved our house and all my memories of growing up there. We had two and a half rooms upstairs (the smallest being too small to call a proper room), and two and a half rooms downstairs. Somehow Mum managed to fit us all in. Even with four children to look after and all the extra jobs my mum had, she still managed to keep the house clean and tidy.

Being house proud was something that all the women had in common, and presenting the right outward appearance took up a great deal of their time. The women who had brass on their front doors would start their morning's polishing until a spotless gold-mirror-effect was achieved. Then they would turn their attention to the windowsill, applying another healthy dose of elbow grease to achieve near-perfection. The final chore, and the most important, was the front step leading into the house.

The state of your front step said a lot about you and the way in which you kept your house, and many a reputation could be ruined by a dirty entrance. On their knees, bums in air, the women would set to work. Armed with a bucket of hot water, a scrubbing brush, some Vim, and a piece of sandstone or a small white block called a 'Donkey Stone', (depending on preference) they would scrub and clean until their muscles ached and the step would pass close inspection.

Having finished their cleaning, these good ladies would sit back on their heels to admire their handiwork, the perspiration shining on their foreheads, knees aching from the hardness of the ground, every muscle in their bodies hurting from the strenuous activity. Cleaning your front step was a real workout, a far cry from the lycra and hi-tech paraphernalia to be found in the fitness centers so popular with today's women.

The morning's activity provided the perfect opportunity for gossip, either when they had finished their chores, or during the cleaning. Steps and nets were the main topic, leading the way into far juicier subjects. The sight of two women standing together, their arms crossed creating a platform for their matronly chests to rest upon, shaking their heads, and muttering to one another, was a familiar one.

"Have you seen the state of her step? It's rotten?" said one.

"Step? Never mind the step, have you seen her nets? God I feel ashamed for her!" her companion would retort.

"It makes you think what the rest of the house is like!"

"No bloody wonder, she is always out gallivanting, that one." And with these profound words, some poor unsuspecting housewife's reputation was ruined – there and then.

★ ★ ★

There was one thing however that cleanliness was no match for.

Every night Mum would tuck us into bed, and wish us a "Good night, sleep tight, hope the bed bugs don't bite," before leaving us to go to sleep. An hour or two after we had gone to bed, she always popped her head into our bedrooms to check on us and see if we were fast asleep. Sometimes we weren't, as we tossed and turned where we lay tormented by a terrible itching. Mum would respond immediately, getting us out of bed so that she could check our bodies for bite marks. These marks would let her know what type of insect to look for and where to find them - like gathering military intelligence for an attack on the enemy.

Mum would silently and quickly pull back the blankets, revealing three or four bugs running in different directions away from the light. Like a trained mercenary, Mum would strike out, grabbing a bug and killing it between her thumb nails, our blood squirting out from the strength of her attack. With split second precision, she moved from the first to the second, and then to the third, our tormentors meeting their fate bodies being squished firmly, none of them managing to escape.

Satisfied that all had been killed, mum would roll up the blankets and sheets taking them outside to the backyard and giving them all a good shake, just in case one or two bugs had managed to evade her.

Bedding aired, Mum would return to the bedroom with a tin of bug powder, firstly taking the mattress off the bed and checking it carefully both sides before shaking the powder all over the metal frame. Using the powder she would then make a circle on the floor at the base of the four bed legs, which would stop the bugs climbing up to the mattress and attacking us all over again.

Although it was brilliant watching Mum killing the enemy, most of the time we were too caught up in standing and scratching, trying to find some relief from the bites we had received, and dreading the moment when we had to return to bed. Mum always assured us that the bed bugs would not come back, but we knew the truce would not last long, and they would inevitably return. Funnily enough, although it was something never talked about, it was a well known fact that all the houses in the street suffered from the same problems, no matter how gleaming the brass on the front door or spotless the nets and front step were!

Once a year, the Corporation would send a special truck to our street (and all the other streets nearby) to fumigate the houses. The residents would have to wait outside on the pavement whilst the trucks sprayed some sort of chemical smoke into each house – the idea being that all the bugs and insects which had taken up residence over the preceding year would be killed, and we humans would actually have the houses to ourselves for a while. The houses stank afterwards, making us all cough, the spray didn't really work judging from the speed in which the bugs returned, and we would all be itching again in a matter of days. It was just a small part of life.

★ ★ ★

Living in our house was at times an adventure in itself. During the night a potty would be placed on the upstairs landing for anyone who needed to have a wee. Anything larger meant a trip to the outside toilet.

I could handle the potty by myself, however, if I needed to go outside, the job of taking me would fall to Lesley, as I was too small to go on my own especially in the dark winter when the cold would chill you to your bones.

The first thing I had to do was wake up Lesley, and this in itself could take some time. I would get out of bed, quietly calling her name, and go into her room shaking her shoulder, or tugging her hair, to get some response. Occasionally I had to jump on her before she would wake up.

Getting out of bed, Lesley would take me downstairs to the kitchen where she would wrap herself up in Dad's old RAF coat. Then placing me on her hip, holding on to me with one arm, the other free to hold a lit candle we would go out into the icy night air to the lav at bottom of the yard. This consisted of a brick shed with a hole in the ground which was very basic; literally a wooden box with a round hole cut in the top. The box was placed directly above another hole in the ground which led to the sewers. As for toilet paper, Mum would cut up sheets of newspaper into smaller squares which would be hung to one side on a piece of string.

As Lesley traipsed across the yard, I would cling on grimly, my arms wrapped around her neck, not letting go until she had plonked me down on the cold wooden seat, leaving the candle next to me to stop me being scared.

Sitting there, my eyes would be firmly fixed on the ground making sure the big slugs that lived in the toilet came nowhere near me. (On some occasions when the slugs got really bad, Mum had a magical way of making them disappear by sprinkling them with large amounts of salt!)

Whilst I was doing my business, poor Lesley would be out in the cold, her teeth chattering, hopping around trying to keep warm, and constantly telling me to hurry up.

My mission completed and the paper work done, we couldn't wait to get back indoors. Putting my arms around her neck and my legs around her waist, she would wrap me inside Dad's coat; we would bolt for the house and the warmth of our beds as quickly as possible. By the time I got back to bed I too would be shivering from the cold. Tucking the blankets snuggly around me, Lesley would finally place Dad's RAF coat on top of me leaving me to get back to sleep.

* * *

Our street was a fantastic place for playing all types of games in, though football was the boy's favourite and was also the most challenging. The street seemed to be lined with glass on either side due to the never ending row of bay windows, one immediately after another, whose glass often fell victim to a flying football.

I managed to easily achieve this on a couple of occasions, pretending that I was playing for England in the World Cup which was all we spoke about at the time; I was Alan Ball, and about to take a very important corner kick. My mates would be lined up by a makeshift goal mouth waiting patiently; I would take a long run up to the ball, kicking as hard as I could, watching the ball leave the ground at great speed. Smash! The sound of breaking glass falling on to the pavement would be the signal for all the kids would run like mad into their own houses, whilst I stood there frozen to the spot, waiting for the trouble to begin.

Within seconds the woman of the house appeared, shouting, "Who the hell did that?"

By this time I was the only child left in the whole street. Spotting me standing there she would continued, "It was you, you little bastard!"

Neighbours heads would be appearing out of doors, or peering through their net curtains to witness the commotion.

Shutting her front door firmly behind her, and straightening the headscarf she wrapped around her head, she advanced in my direction. A determined look on her face clearly indicated that there was no chance of escape for me at all!

Tight lipped, she grabbed me by the ear dragging me towards our house. Banging on our front door, she shouted, "Your son has smashed my windows! What are you going to do about it?" as she stood there with me cowering by her side.

Mum would open the door, listening to what the neighbour had to say, before calming the situation down by offering to pay for the damage and finding somebody to fix it as soon as possible.

Once she got me inside the house, however, she would go mad at me. "How am I going to find the money to pay for that?" she would shout, "Why is it always you?" She would then slap my bottom very hard before sending me to bed with no tea (evening meal). My Mum was right. No matter how hard I tried to be a good boy, I was the one who caused the most problems, as if I was accident prone, and I am sure that there were many occasions, where once having gotten me out of the way, Mum would then sit down to try and figure out how she was ever going to find the money to repair the damage I had caused.

Durden Street was one of a series of narrow streets nestled between Smithdown Road and Earl Road both being main roads leading in and out of the city, and teeming with traffic and activity.

There was every type of shop that you could possibly imagine, and both roads had more than their fair share of pubs; in fact it would be true to say that there was a public house on every other street corner.

Pubs were popular with the male population, who would call in on their way home from work, staying until their money had run out before they staggered home. The pubs did well, as the majority of wages earned were spent there, the shillings never making it back to the families who needed to be fed. But it was the way of life, and a lucrative one for breweries and landlords alike, with somewhere in the region of two thousand pubs dotted around Liverpool.

On our street you would often find around thirty kids playing outside, boys and girls together, ages ranging from about three to ten years old. Once you got past ten, you were too big to play with the little 'uns, and moved on to other forms of entertainment elsewhere.

We all had nicknames, Scousers are famous for them, and mine soon became Red, due to the colour of my hair. Shouts of 'Come on Red, pass the ball' would be heard up and down our street whilst we kids were playing.

The girls would spend hours skipping, an old rope as long as the street was wide, being looped whilst they chanted skipping songs, calling in their very best friend to join them as they leapt over the rope passing under their feet. Sometimes the boys would be allowed to join in as well, but it was very much a girl's game. The girls were also very good at throwing two tennis balls against a wall, juggling them in different ways and singing songs relevant to that particular game. Hula hooping was very popular at this time, and again it was the girls who showed their skills.

Boys and girls alike would play hopscotch, rounders, tick (tag), kick-the-can, catch-the-girl-kiss-the girl, and jacks; large groups of us gathered together, enjoying each others company.

The boys had their own games, and the most popular was marbles also known as 'ollies'using very small glass or metal balls, and would be played in the gutters running along the side of the pavements.

On a hot summer's day, we would collect used ice-lolly sticks off the pavements and streets nearby. Each boy would try to collect at least fifteen sticks, before sitting alongside each other on the side-walk, our feet in the gutter, occupied with weaving the sticks in and out of each other as if making baskets. After a little while we would end up with a flat six inch square of interwoven sticks, which would then need to be joined or kept in place.

The hot summer sun would melt the black tar in between the granite cobbles that covered most of the streets in our area heating it to a point where it would bubble up. Using a spare stick, we would burst the bubble, spreading the tar like glue across the joints of our woven stick-squares, before putting them in the shade for an hour to harden. Once the tar had hardened these squares would be transformed into flying-saucers which we could throw to one another in the same way people do today with Frisbees. If we had a heavy downpour of rain we would use them as rafts or boats racing them down the gutters on the deluge of water that would pour away.

A lot of the older boys made their own steering carts out of bits of old wood and pram wheels they had found. The driver would sit at the front steering the cart with a small piece of rope attached to the front wheels. A second boy would be tasked with pushing the cart from behind as hard as he could, running along until the cart built up speed and was going too fast for him to keep up. He would then leap on the back of the cart, holding on to the driver's shoulders as they rattled along at great speed, until eventually the cart slowed down, at which point the boys would swap duties and start all over again.

Conkers was a popular game in September through to November, and could only be played at this time of year, as that was the time when the conkers would fall from the horse chestnut trees. When I was growing up there were no patches of grass, or trees growing in our streets only row upon row of terraced houses, so we would make our way to Sefton Park, the nearest public park which was about an hours walk away.

Mum encouraged us all, as well as the other kids in our street, to visit the park on school holidays and sunny Sundays so that we could play and get as much fresh air as possible. She would make us jam or banana butties with a large bottle of tap water to quench our thirst. As I was the youngest I had to wait until last before I could have a swig out of the bottle and by this time there would be lots of bits of bread floating around in the water. It didn't bother us that much after all we were family and friends.

Once the word was out on the street that conkers were falling, nearly every young boy and his mates were off to the park. It was only when our pockets were bulging with lovely light brown conkers, and we could carry no more, that we would leave.

We learnt all our games from our older brothers and sisters, games which had been passed down from generation to generation. They were activities that encouraged us to use our imagination and to be resourceful and we spent many happy hours from sun-up until called in for bed, playing happily together in our street.

Chapter Four
My Mother's Son

F rom a very early age I had a special closeness with Mum
and being the youngest I accompanied her everywhere
like her shadow, whilst my three older siblings were at school.

Money was always scarce in our house; Mum had to find
lots of different jobs in order to keep food on the table and
shoes on our feet. One of her many jobs was cleaning local
pubs in the morning, which was a fairly reliable source of
income. She was good at her job, fast and efficient, and would
quite easily get through three pubs before opening time at
11.00.

Immediately, setting off once my brother and sisters had
left for school, she would strap me into a little wooden seat
perched above the rear wheel of her bicycle. Pulling away
from the pavement, the first heave of the pedal was always the
trickiest bit, before moving out into the traffic. I would wrap
my arms around her waist, and lean into her, my face pressed
against her familiar black coat, taking refuge in the warm
shelter which she created, protecting me from whatever the
weather decided to throw at us.

I held on tight, the wheels bumping over the granite cobble sets of the road, and the bicycle chain squeaking a familiar tune.

Once we arrived at the pub, Mum would place me on the floor in a corner of the room, out of the way of broom and mop,

She always gave me bottle tops to keep me occupied whilst she was cleaning. I soon learnt not to put them in my mouth, because of the tinny taste and sharp edges. I would stack them on top of each other like building bricks and then knock them down with a clatter. Even now when I walk into a pub and the smell of stale ale hits me, I am taken back to my early childhood and the hours spent sitting on the floor playing with bottle tops.

As soon as she had finished, Mum would collect her few shillings, scoop me up and we would be off to the next job.

★ ★ ★

I started attending Lawrence Road Infant School when I was five. I was not looking forward to being separated from my mother, as we were so close and had not been parted from each other before. I dreaded the twenty-five minute walk there every morning holding tightly on to her hand knowing that once the large metal gates were in sight I would soon have to say good bye.

Mum knew I was unhappy, so having dropped me off at 8.30 in the morning she would then return at 10.00 during play time and talk to me through the railings. When dinner time came, I would rush out into the playground, anxiously looking to see if she was in her usual spot by the railings. She was always there and would pass me a sandwich.

I always knew it was time for her to leave when she wet the corner of her handkerchief with the tip of her tongue before wiping around my mouth. After a kiss through the railings she would walk away, stopping to turn back to wave. It took a few weeks, but I eventually did settle into school which meant that Mum was once again free to go about her daily activities.

There were about twenty boys and girls in a class and I am sure that none of us found it easy at the beginning, particularly learning to read and write. It should have got easier with time, but sadly it didn't, no matter how hard I tried - I found anything to do with letters too difficult. As a popular young child with an inquisitive mind this was especially hard as I wanted to learn, and I could see that my class mates were doing better than me. I also sensed the teachers were unhappy with my progress, that they thought I wasn't trying hard enough, whilst Mum did her best to help me whatever way she could.

At first, thinking I had bad eyesight, she asked my teachers to let me sit at the front of the class so I could see the blackboard more easily. Then she arranged for me to have my eyes tested, and I was fitted with glasses.

I hated them! They were too big for my face, had heavy dark frames and made my ears stick out. I don't think that they helped at all, but Mum insisted that I have them, convinced that the problem lay with my eyes and to persuade me to wear them she told me that they would help to make me very clever.

All this however was to no avail. With or without glasses the words just got mixed up, so Mum would sit with me for hours in the evening teaching me simple spellings like cat, hat, mat, dog and frog, until I knew them by heart. Half an hour later we would go through the words again and I just couldn't remember them at all. I had forgotten such easy words in less than thirty minutes; it was as if all our hard work had never happened.

One of the most important words which I just couldn't spell was my first name James; when I came to write it down the five different letters all became jumbled up, no matter what. One day, Mum must've had enough as she decided there and then that I was going to be called Jeff. This was not an official change, but it was a highly effective one, and I have enjoyed being Jeff ever since.

One afternoon Lesley came to pick me up from school, which was a little bit unusual as Mum was always there to meet me at the school gates. As we got nearer our house, I ran ahead, bursting through the kitchen door, full of happiness at being home.

I found Mum sitting in an armchair by the fire in the living room; she was rocking backwards and forwards holding a large, white handkerchief to her mouth.

Going over to her side, I leant forward so I could see her face better. "What's wrong Mum," I asked. "Are you feeling sick?"

All she did was shake her head from side to side, as if to say no.

I was beginning to feel a bit worried, this wasn't like Mum. I could feel a note of panic welling up in my voice, and tears starting to form at the back of my eyes. "Please Mum, please tell me what's wrong?"

Looking at me properly for the first time, she slowly lowered the handkerchief from her mouth and I caught a glimpse of blood on the white cotton and on her hands.

I jumped to my feet, my voice almost hysterical, "Who's done it Mum?" I cried, "What's happened?"

Moving back to her side, I looked at her mouth in horror; where once she'd had beautiful teeth, all that remained were red gums. Her teeth had disappeared.

She was trying to talk to me and sounded like a different person, muffled and old. It wasn't the Mum I knew - I didn't want this person for my Mum.

"I hate you!" I shouted, "I don't love you anymore. Who's done it? Who's done it?" I ran out of the room, slamming the door behind me as I headed upstairs for the safety of my bed.

Throwing myself across the covers, I sobbed my heart out. I was frightened and confused. What had happened to my Mum?

She'd had lovely teeth, with a gap in the middle just like mine. Mum had always said that we were lucky as the gap meant wealth and one day we would be wealthy.

Once Lesley came in Mum must have sent her upstairs to calm me down. She sat on my bed, gently stroking my head, and soothing my loud sobs, until they subsided to hiccups and sniffles.

"What's wrong, Jeff?" she asked.

My face buried in my pillow I uttered a muffled 'go away, leave me alone'.

Lesley did not give up so easily however and coaxed me into sitting up, snuggling me closer as she sat me on her lap. "Come on Jeff, you can tell me what's wrong."

"I don't love Mum no more, something is wrong with her and she hasn't got any teeth no more, and she can't even speak to me properly!" It all rushed out in one long sentence.

Lesley explained that Mum had lost all her teeth because of some nasty germs in her gums. She told me that the germs had attacked the teeth and made it painful for Mum and it was the dentist who had taken them all out. She also told me that the dentist was going to be nice and make Mum some beautiful new teeth for her mouth.

(Years later Mum told me that my outburst about not loving her that day had actually been more painful than the loss of her teeth.)

I am sure there was a well worn path from our house to the top of Smithdown Road. There were three sets of foot prints that frequently headed that way – one set belonging to my father as he went to the Boundary Pub, and the other two belonging to Mum and one of her children, going towards the doctor's surgery – ironically situated directly opposite the pub.

Dr Dover had a soft spot for my mother, and knew that she had a lot to deal with not only in terms of her children's and her own health, but also at home. Mum had bad duodenal ulcers throughout her life, and had even been rushed to hospital because of internal hemorrhaging on one occasion.

Quite often Dr Dover would overlook the shilling fee that it used to cost in those days for an appointment, and would give Mum prescriptions for free, doing whatever he could to help her. He was a nice man, very reassuring in his manner, and had a genuine interest in his patients. Working in a poor area of a large city meant that he must have seen such a variety of injuries and illnesses, but he always managed to maintain a level of patience and kindness that made him feel more of a friend than a daunting professional.

Lesley had suffered from Pinks Disease as a small child, the most common cause of which was the use of teething powders containing mercury and could be fatal.

Barry had purpura, a blood disorder, which also caused a great deal of problems and at one point he spent six months in hospital.

From the age of four, I was prone to bronchitis every winter, coughing up huge amounts of phlegm every night, and suffering problems with my breathing. Mum used to dread the onset of winter as she never knew what triggered this bronchitis, wondering whether it was the pollution in the air, or the cold and dampness of the bedroom or if I suffered from a weak chest.

I also worried her with my constant 'rocking'. Every night once she had tucked me in bed and given me a kiss, I would lie there, rocking my head from side to side on my pillow. I would be wide awake unable to sleep, and my mind would be racing from adventure to adventure. Mum would come and check on me and find me in this almost trance like state, and she would despair. Sitting on the bed next to me, she would gently shake me back to reality, then soothing my head with her hand she would talk quietly to me, softly telling me to go to sleep.

This rocking baffled her – I showed no signs of any mental handicap, and she wondered if it had anything to do with my learning difficulties, however Dr Dover calmed her fears telling her that it was most probably my way of dealing with an excess of energy at night in a way, exhausting myself so that I could then sleep soundly. I can clearly recall him describing me as a fine figure of a boy, which made me feel very grown up.

Sefton General Hospital was another frequently visited establishment. Mum was very competent with first aid for minor injuries, but some of the 'war wounds' that I would return with were too much for even her medical skills.

My bessie-mate was Ian Watt, who lived in the same street, a few doors away. We always played together, quite often on one of the bomb sites a few streets down. We would play at being soldiers, making dug-outs for ourselves and using stones and broken pieces of brick as ammunition, which we would hurl through the air with accompanying cries of "whoosh" and "kaboom" as if they were hand grenades and other such weapons.

Our war games were (not surprisingly) based on the recently ended war, the British fighting the Germans, or inspired by the movies we had seen at the Bug House. Unlike the real battlefield, however, we boys would take it in turns – pulling the pins out with our teeth, before hurling the 'grenade' through the air. Common sense told us that until the weapon had landed, we were to stay put, hidden down in our fox holes, heads covered by our arms or old pieces of wood that were lying around.

I had finished my throw, and was crouching down, waiting for Ian's missile to come my way. I seemed to be waiting for ever, and so, being the impatient type, and wondering if everything was ok his end, I stood up, raising my head above the safety of ground level. I can only surmise that his weapon was a miniature doodle bug, as there was no sound as the rock flew through the air, and like a doodle bug a lot of sound as it made contact with my forehead. Right smack in the middle!

It was a direct hit for Ian, as I keeled over backwards, landing on a pile of rubble behind me. Blood streaming down my face, I staggered to my feet, wiping the blood out of my eyes and smearing it all over my face and my ears. Ian took one look of me and scarpered into the distance, knowing full well that he was in for some big trouble, his young life seemingly coming to an end in his mind as visions of police cells and prison flooded his imagination.

Howling loudly I ran home, calling out for Mum all the way. Mum must have heard the racket, because as I came down the jigga and entered the back yard, she appeared at the kitchen door. She started to ask what was wrong, but then stopped dead in her tracks as the full impact of the sight before her sank in - her small son, dirty, bedraggled, and covered in blood. I had my hands clamped to my head, afraid of letting go in case my brains fell out, and the noise I was making left no doubt as to the fear and pain I was feeling.

"What?...." she almost seemed at a loss for words. "Come here? What have you done? Who did this?" Reaching out for me she drew me closer to her, leading me inside the house so that she could see what damage had been done.

Safe now that I was with Mum, my howling turned to loud sobs as I went into the house with her, making it clear who was to blame. "Ian Watt did it Mum," I said in between loud sniffs and whimpers of pain, "Ian Watt threw the bomb Mum."

One look at my head and Mum knew that she would have to take me to hospital, a bus trip to Sefton General – some four stops away! I am not sure what was going through her mind as I sat on her lap on the bus, but I imagine she was planning her revenge on Ian Watt, and couldn't wait to get her hands on him! Six stitches later, and a bandage wrapped around the top of my head like a turban, and I was given permission to go straight home. Mum had other plans however, and as we got off the bus, I was marched straight to the Watt house.

Standing outside the house, Mum banged loudly on the front door, and within a few minutes it was opened by Mrs Watt. Mum wasted no time on pleasantries.

"Look what your son had done to mine!" she exclaimed angrily, thrusting me in front of her. "I have had to take him down the hospital, three holes in his head to stitch up. Your son did this. Six stitches he got!" She was almost incoherent with rage.

Ian's Mother was not too happy either. "Ian, get yourself down here now!" she shouted in the direction of the back kitchen. "Ian, come here at once!"

Ian's head appeared cautiously around the edge of the door as he slowly made his way towards his Mum. Looking at me, standing there, like a half wrapped mummy, his face reflected the terror he was feeling. For all he knew he had nearly killed me, and it was a miracle that the doctors had been able to save my life!

As he got within reach, his mother grabbed him by the sleeve, and pulled him closer. "Did you do that?" she demanded, pointing to me standing out the front. "You stupid little bugger," she shouted, cuffing him around the head. "What were you thinking of, throwing stones at him?"

My mother, seemingly satisfied that Ian's 'crime' was now public knowledge, gave strict instructions that Ian was to keep away from me and our house, and that I was never to play with him again. I was kept in for the rest of the day, and made to rest.

The next day, as I went out to play, Mum told me again to keep away from Ian Watt. As soon as I was out of sight of the house however, I couldn't wait to find Ian, and to tell him all about my adventures at the hospital. As with all children within minutes we were best mates again!

The jigga was a popular place for us kids to play in. It was long and narrow, with back-yard doors leading off it every eight feet or so on both sides. Ian and I had been playing outside one late afternoon, when Mum had called me in for tea.

As we climbed down from our perches on top of the walls, Ian spied an empty glass milk bottle on the ground, and being a typical boy decided that it obviously needed breaking! I agreed with him, but suggested that he let me get back to mine before he threw it, so that neither of us would get in trouble for the crime.

"Don't throw it yet," I said to him. "Give me a chance to get back to mine before you do."

"Ok", he replied, picking up the bottle.

We were standing outside his backyard door, some forty feet from mine, so I set off at a run towards ours when I heard a loud crash as the bottle landed just behind me. Ian had thrown it too soon. Before I had the chance to move further away, I felt a sharp pain in the back of my leg, and looking down saw a large piece of glass, about six inches long sticking out, with a steady flow of blood disappearing down into my sock.

I hobbled the remainder of the way through our yard and into the kitchen; Mum was standing at the cooker preparing everyone's tea. You can imagine the look on her face, when I showed her the back of my leg.

"Mum, look at what Ian has done!" I said pointing with my finger.

"I'll swing for that little bastard one day," was her only response. She cleaned me up as best she could, removing the glass and wrapping my leg in an old piece of clean cloth.

Lesley was at home that evening, and she took me to the hospital on the bus, sitting with me whilst I had four stitches in my leg, before bringing me back, which meant that for once, Mum didn't have to drop everything to take me herself.

As for Ian Watt, although I still carry the scars that he gave me, I remember the fun we had growing up in Liverpool together, and how we were bessie-mates for many, many years.

Chapter Five
As Bright as a Button

Mum was very inventive and had all kinds of weird and wonderful ways of making money, most of which involved us kids.

One of our jobs was selling firewood in the winter months. Within a one mile radius of where we lived there were many bomb sites, areas where buildings had once stood and which had been flattened by the Luftwaffe. Almost every other street had a bomb site, and apart from being a great place for kids to play, they were also an excellent source of wood and other building rubble.

Having woken us up in the morning Mum would tell us that we had a job to do that day. Putting Lesley and Barry in charge, the four of us would set off taking Barry's steering cart to transport our findings. Going to the bomb-sites and around all the neighbouring jiggas, we would load up our cart until it was full of pieces of wood before returning home, where it would then be unpacked. We did this all day until we had a large stack of wood piled up, and were too tired and dirty to carry on!

The following day, Mum would oversee a small production line in the back yard. She and Barry would chop the wood into smaller pieces using the sharp axes she kept for this purpose, before Sheila and I placed the wood into a small clamp, tying them into little bundles with a thin piece of wire. Bundles assembled, we would give them to Lesley who would carefully stack the cart getting as many bundles on as possible. Cart loaded, the three of us set off (leaving Barry and Mum behind) knocking on doors and selling the bundles for tuppence each.

There was one simple rule that we had to adhere to – we were allowed to sell our bundles anywhere we wanted, except on our street; Mum did not want the neighbours knowing our business.

Another winter money maker for the four of us was snow shifting, especially if it had snowed heavily during the night. Mum would get us up early the following morning, wrapping us up in our winter coats with warm hats perched on our heads, gloves protecting our hands and Wellies on our feet.

Armed with shovels and stiff brushes we would set off, heading in the direction of the shops first. Barry would go into the shops, politely asking the store keeper if they wanted the snow shifted from their shop fronts, trying to present a professional impression as if he had a team of qualified snow shifters waiting outside!

As the storekeepers were inevitably too busy with readying their stores for the day, they nearly always said yes. Lesley and Barry gave Sheila and me instructions like Sergeants organizing their troops. Once we had shoveled all the snow into the gutter and brushed the sidewalk clean, Barry would finish off with a sprinkle of salt all over the pavement.

We had no set price for snow shifting, relying on the good will of the storekeeper, and the good job we had done to reap our reward. This must have worked well, as I can remember that in addition to the few coppers we would be given, we often received little extras such as an apple each from the fruit-monger, or a small bag of sweets from the tobacconist.

At midday Mum would come and look for us, calling us home for our dinner, a nice bowl of hot soup sometimes served with a chunk of bread on the side. Mum would dry our clothes by the fire while we were having our soup, then we would head back out to do some more snow shifting.

In the afternoon, we would focus our attention on the older neighbours, particularly elderly women who lived on their own and were unable to shift the snow themselves.

Whilst we were being industrious, we could see all the other kids playing with each other in the snow. I am sure that there was a nickname for us, relating to the fact that we quite often spent our time working instead of playing, but it didn't bother us. We were happy being together laughing and joking and best of all we were helping Mum. At the end of the day we would give her all the money we had made, and she in turn would always reward us with pennies to go and buy ourselves some sweets.

In the summer months, the four of us would go jam jar collecting. Barry would put two big wooden crates on his steering cart, tying them up with rope to keep them from falling off. Setting out, we would get to the first street, before splitting up and knocking on every door asking for any old jam jars and newspaper which they did not want.

If we were asked what we needed them for, we would reply, "For school Missus, for washing our paint brushes in". It always worked, as people liked helping children who were doing something for their school, so they would often come out arms laden with as many empty jam jars and newspapers as they could find.

As soon as the crates were full we would go back home. We would unload, and then head back out again, leaving Mum to wash out all the old jars, and put the newspaper into neat piles in the shed. When there were no more jam jars to collect, we would take them, now clean, down to the rag and bone yard, off Smithdown Road where the man would pay us one penny for four jars. On a good day we would collect around sixty jars and make half a crown.

When times were particularly hard, Mum would tell us to get the pile of newspapers from the shed and take them to the local fish and chip shop. Our nearest 'chippy' was run by a Chinese Man, Mr Foo, who I think, knowing what was really going on would give four large bags of piping hot chips, sprinkled generously with salt and vinegar in exchange for our old papers. Those hot chips were the best chips in the whole wide world – particularly when you were a small starving child.

Mum was a very good cleaner, and could often find work in the large houses on Mather Avenue, a smarter part of Liverpool, only a couple of miles away from where we lived. Cleaning, ironing, making up fires, she would turn her hand to anything except cooking – whether it was because she was not a kosher cook, or because she was not the world's best cook I am not sure.

She did a lot of work for the Jewish community whose families had settled close to the local Synagogue on Mather Avenue. There was one particular lady she cleaned for, who, to ensure Mum did a thorough job, would hide half-pennies underneath the ornaments. In doing this, the lady would be able to see if Mum had been thorough in her dusting, and also if she could be trusted not to steal anything lying around.

Mum wised to this from the start. As soon as she got into the house, she would quickly go from room to room picking everything up, collecting the coins, and then stacking them on a grand mantle piece in the main room so that they were clearly visible to the lady of the house when she returned. Whether or not Mum actually returned and dusted underneath all the items was debatable, however she showed a high degree of honesty which was appreciated by her employer.

Her employer would show her appreciation in a variety of different ways. Sometimes it was a few extra pennies, other times a small bundle of firewood. The best parcels contained exotic homemade breads, smelling of cinnamon and other warm spices, dotted with dried fruits and sweet to the taste. There would sometimes be flavoured meat dishes, cooked in such a way that the meat would melt in our mouths, or delicious chicken broth with noodles to warm our souls. Such charity, whatever inspired it, never bothered us children. We would wait eagerly for such a banquet, and relish it with a gratitude I can remember to this day.

Mum had the ability to make a feast out of nothing. Sitting in the warmth of the living room, the smell of the Scouse bubbling away on the cooker wafting through, she would conjure up a feast for us. Other times it may only have been a jam buttie, or a mug of Oxo with a chunk of bread to help it down, but it all tasted great. My favourite was 'pobs', chunks of bread floating in a bowl of hot milk, with a sprinkling of sugar on top.

Mum's greatest gift was that you always loved being home with her as the house always seemed warmer when she was there. Although everything was always left to her, bringing up the kid's, taking care of the house and finding the money to do so, she still managed to give us more love than a lot of other children got from both their parents.

We learned from Mum that if we wanted something in life, we needed to work, to earn money. Nothing came for free. As I grew up, I inherited jobs from my older siblings – it was almost like a family tradition passing a job down from one to the other like hand-me-downs.

My first solo job was running errands for Mrs Gilbert who lived at the bottom of our street at Number 8. Every afternoon once school was finished, I would rush home and quickly change out of my uniform into old clothes. I had to be quick as Mrs Gilbert expected me to be at her house by no later that 4.45; any later and I would be too late for the shops as they all closed at 5.30 and I would not be able to get her shopping done in good time.

Mrs Gilbert was massive. We reckoned that she must have weighed about 25 stone and she found it very difficult to move around. As a result she never left her house. So that she didn't have to get up she always left her front door slightly ajar for me, and having arrived at her house, I would take a deep breath before opening the door and going in.

That deep breath was so important – and the longer that I could hold on to it the better it was for me. Dashing down the hallway and into the living room, I would take the money and the shopping list off the top of a dresser where she had left it, before speeding towards the front door and fresh air. Once outside and gasping for breath, I would enjoy a couple of lungfuls before heading on my way.

Mrs Gilbert's house stank. She had cats. So many cats that nobody, including Mrs Gilbert, knew exactly how many there were, and those cats lived in the house hardly ever going outside.

When I first started my job working for Mrs Gilbert, I could not read the shopping list that she would leave out, having to head back home so that Mum or one of my sisters could translate it. After a while however I got used to her handwriting, and as the lists were nearly always the same would be able to head for the shops as quickly as possible.

I would get the groceries that she needed, going to the Co-Op or the bakery or wherever. Everyday, however, without fail, I would have to go to the pet store, and whilst the owner was weighing and slicing my slab of cat food for me, I would stand gazing at the mice and the goldfish and talking to the parrots in their cages.

I did this job for about three years, as had Lesley and Barry and Sheila – Mrs Gilbert got at least twelve years good service out of The Pearces! I was paid once a week, two shillings and six pence, and worked Monday to Friday. I would give my Mum the money and in return would receive some pennies, which I would then go and spend on sweets. What I didn't realise at the time though, was that by ensuring we were all gainfully employed, Mum was not only instilling us with a good work ethic, but more importantly keeping us all out of trouble!

★ ★ ★

When the money ran out we ran out to Grandma Turner's. Mum would send us to her Mother's to ask her for a loan; this was another job that had been passed down from one child to the other over many years.

Grandma Turner was our last surviving grandparent, the only one whom I had ever known. She had always been a successful business woman in her own way, and had a reputation as a money-lender in the neighbourhood. She knew that our visits were predominantly 'business related' as well.

Going through her front door, which was inevitably left ajar, I would call out to her as I ran down the hallway towards the living room.

"Hi Grandma!" I would puff, "Mum has sent me to borrow half a crown."

She would nearly always be sitting in front of her fire in a large armchair when I arrived, her skirts up around her knees stirring the coals with a long poker.

Instead of grandmotherly hugs and treats she would listen to my request, pulling a disapproving face and 'tut-tutting' several times as if to add some verbal emphasis. Slowly raising herself out of the chair she would continue to tut and sigh before starting the most extraordinary ritual.

Once on her feet, she would lift up her long black skirt, revealing several grubby petticoats underneath almost reaching down to her ankles. I would stand there watching her as one by one she would slowly raise each petticoat holding them with one hand, using her free hand to peel back the next layer.

Finally she would have got to the right layer. She wore old flat black shoes, out of which protruded a saggy pair of socks, faded to an ancient grey and wrinkled around her ankles. Her legs, blotched with chilblains from the heat of the fire came to an abrupt halt as they disappeared into a long pair of bloomers.

Digging into a small 'pinny' with pockets that she wore on top of her bloomers, she would pull out a tiny book, letting the 'curtains' of petticoats drop to the floor.

This little book had an equally short length of pencil attached to it, tied on by a piece of string. Putting the tip of the pencil into her mouth, she would lick the lead first, before turning to the 'Elsie' page where she would make another entry.

"Tell your Mother that she needs to come and see me," she would instruct, "she hasn't paid me for a long time. Are you listening to me?

"Yes Grandma," I would reply. "I am listening."

"This borrowing has got to stop. She has to pay me back the money and all the interest she owes me or she can't borrow any more until she does. Do you understand?"

"Yes, Grandma," I would say again, feeling uncomfortable and just wishing that she would give me the money so that I could get back home to Mum.

She would stop writing for a moment looking directly at me, "Are you listening to me. She has to pay me back."

Book-keeping done, the whole process of raising the petticoats would start all over again, until the pinny was found and she could return the book to its safe place. She would then pull out a small purse extracting the money and giving it to me, placing it firmly in the palm of my hand and closing my fingers over the coin. "Take care of this now," she would warn, "don't go losing it because I won't be giving your mother another one."

Clutching the money tightly in my hand, and Grandma's message firmly imprinted in my brain, I would run off as fast I could. I always felt so guilty, as if I was the one borrowing the money – not running the errand. Talk about shooting the messenger!

* * *

When Barry was fifteen, Mum found him a full-time job in Browners, the pawnbrokers on Smithdown Road. It was an imposing double-fronted corner shop, specialising in men's clothing and household goods (most of which had been pawned at some time or other, and never redeemed).

If you came in to pawn something, Tom Brown, the owner of the shop would carefully inspect each item before setting a pledge-value and a time limit in which to repay the money and interest accumulated.

If you accepted the offer, Tom would give you the cash and a pledge ticket, which would clearly tell you how much you would have to pay, and the date when the pledge expired. If you were unable to make the payment in time you lost your item, and it ended up in the shop selling for a lot more. Both Barry and Lesley had been regular visitors on Mum's behalf, slipping in through the side door so that the neighbours could not see what was going on.

Barry joined Browners with high hopes and expectations. He had visions of standing behind a glass counter in a smart suit, a tailor's tape measure draped around his neck, selling suits, shirts and ties to gentleman.

Instead he was banished to the loft where he spent the first year scurrying around like an attic rat. He operated the dumb waiter, a simple contraption which raised and lowered a small box-like cupboard from floor to floor controlled by a mechanism of ropes and pulleys.

Everything at Browners worked efficiently. When a customer came in to redeem a pledge he would give his ticket to Tom Brown. Mr Brown would then walk over to a small cupboard set in a wall and opening the doors would place the ticket in a metal box on the dumb waiter, close the doors and then press the bell.

Barry, some four floors up, would hear the bell ringing and would have to pull the dumbwaiter up hauling on the rope mechanism. Extracting the ticket he would search for the correct item, sorting through thousands of things stacked up on shelves and in boxes, piled on the floor, or neatly arranged on hundreds of hangers suspended on rails along one wall.

There was hardly any space to spare, with items crammed into every small nook and cranny. The clothes would be so tightly pressed together on the rails that if Barry was not careful taking one item out could mean that several more would follow.

It was a demanding job at the best of times, never mind for a young lad. Barry had to know where everything went, and where everything was to be found. He would have to carry all shapes and sizes and weights of items to and from the dumbwaiter, sometimes manhandling small rugs or clocks across the room, and then squeezing them into the small compartment before carefully lowering them to the shop floor. And this all had to be done in record time; Barry never stopped scurrying.

★ ★ ★

I inherited a new job when I was nine, taking over from Barry when he started at Browners. It was a little bit of a challenge as I was fairly small in stature and not really old enough to be working as a 'security guard'. My new job was at the Wash House on Lodge Lane, part of a large community facility which had been in operation for almost a hundred years. The facility consisted of the swimming and public baths and the Wash House.

The swimming baths were very popular with the children, especially if you were able to swim four lengths without stopping; if you managed to do this, you got a free yearly pass. Mum encouraged us all to go to the baths and so Lesley and Barry taught Sheila and me how to swim. I am sure that Lesley was a much kinder teacher with Sheila than Barry was with me; he just pushed me in one day at the deep end, when I was about five, and watched as I floundered to the edge telling me to get on with it. And get on with it I did; it was not long before I was swimming and as confidently as the others.

The public baths were for anyone and everyone who wanted a hot bath. For one shilling, you could soak in a large tub full of steaming hot water, a real luxury when you think that there was no running hot water in the houses in that area. If you wanted a bath at home you would have to boil kettle after kettle until you had enough hot water to fill a large metal hipbath, inevitably placed in the kitchen. Every house had one, hanging on a nail in the backyard, but because bathing at home took so much effort, one bath would often be shared by the whole family, and it was not a regular occurrence.

Friday nights at the public baths was a hive of activity. Girls that worked in shops and factories, men that worked on the building sites and the docks – everyone would congregate there between 5 and 7pm in the evening.

Although the bathing areas were segregated into men and women, the before-and-after-bath was a great time to meet and have a chat. Many a marriage may have started at the baths – and many a friendship was definitely made.

The wash house was the forerunner to the public laundry, a place where women could take their laundry to do their weekly wash. As most of the women had large families to look after, with some members of the family doing very dirty jobs, the laundry could quite often be an all-day task. These women literally came from miles around, large bundles of washing tied up in a sheet and perched on top of a push pram. A push-pram was in a way their best friend, their only means of transporting bulky items everywhere, not to mention clusters of small children. In other words prams were the same as the small runabouts of today.

At seven o'clock on a Saturday morning I would be there, come rain or shine, ready for a days work. Saturday morning was the busiest day of the week for the Wash House and my job was to look after the prams whilst their owners disappeared inside to do their laundry.

At 7.15 in the morning the doors would open, twenty women going in at a time. At 8.15 another twenty would be allowed in, and so it went until midday.

Inside the wash-house all was constant activity. The first hour would be spent doing a hot wash; each woman would have her own three-sided cubicle, with a sink a large dolly-tub, and unlimited hot water. Sleeves rolled up, aprons on, they would be up to their elbows in hot suds, using *Aunt Sally* a chalky red liquid detergent to clean their washing.

They had an hour to do their washing, before they had to move to the wringers – where the items would be passed through large mangles and all the water squeezed out. In the meantime the next group of women would be allowed in.

Mangling done (and this would take an hour)the washing was then hung out to dry, in an incredibly hot room, heated by all the hot water pipes that ran through from the boilers to the Wash House and the public baths. Whilst everything was drying, the women would escape from their chores and the heat and the steam of the drying room to the fresh air, indulging in a cigarette or two, a sandwich, and a good exchange of local news and gossip.

I would be on the outside, standing by the door, keeping guard over the long row of prams left along Grierson Street by their owners. The prams were a popular target for gangs of young lads who were always on the lookout for wheels and other bits and pieces that could be used in making steering carts.

Barry had shown me how to tie the prams together, attaching a long rope around a cast iron railing at one end with plenty of knots, and then threading it through the front two wheels until they were all linked together, before tying the other end of the rope to a different railing. This was the best way of keeping the prams together, and stopping the lads from running off with them. There was no way I could have chased after one vanishing pram, never mind two or three at the same time, particularly if they had all been vanishing in different directions.

Saturday mornings were the busiest at the wash-house and therefore busy for me. Knowing that the prams would be congregated outside on the street, the lads would turn up in groups, some groups as many as six, like hyenas prowling for pickings, laughing and taunting.

They would circle, bombarding me with rude comments and pushing me about from side to side. I had to keep my distance, so that they could not grab a hold of me. If I fell into their trap, I would be finished, and the prams would be nicked. So constantly on the move, I would dodge their lunges, moving quickly from side to side, all the time getting closer to the steps leading up to the main entrance.

If it all got too much I would dart inside, calling out for help.

"Quick missus, quick they are robbing your prams" I would yell. "Help, missus, I need some help."

Like a stampeding herd of Wildebeest the women closest to the entrance charged towards the door. As they emerged out into the daylight, sleeves rolled up above their elbows, they would be shouting at the lads outside.

"Get your effin' hands off those prams you little bastards."

It was an awesome sight. Red faces, sweat dripping off their chins, hair tucked up under white mob caps, they were not women to be argued with. I stood there feeling invincible, a pint size general with an army behind him, watching my antagonists disappearing like rats down the sewers.

Commotion over, the women would return to their washing, occasionally coming out for a cigarette or to mind the prams while they sent me off for some more *Aunt Sally*.

Armed with a handful of coins, an empty jar or bottle or two I would head down Grierson Street, to a small nondescript house halfway down on the left hand-side. An old woman would answer the door and take my bottles, filling them up with the detergent from a large metal barrel resting on a table in her front room. Once the bottles were full I would hand over the pennies and head back to the Wash House, errand complete.

I looked after those prams until I was twelve and made good money week after week; three pence a pram every Saturday morning. In addition to the pram money, I would run around the wash house after all the women had left, checking for empty glass bottles or jars and loading them into an old crate. Having scoured every possible nook and cranny, I would take my findings to the old lady who sold the *Aunt Sally* in exchange for a few extra pennies.

My long rope rolled up tidily and slung over my shoulder, pockets jingling with all the money I had made, I would return home extremely content with the morning's takings.

Chapter Six
The Perfect Couple

The electricity went off on a regular basis because the meter was empty, and Mum's purse was just as bare. Picking up the baby, she would head off on the hunt for my father. As this had been happening for as long as Mum could remember, at least since the War, there had nearly always been a baby who couldn't be left on its own in the house. She also took a degree of comfort from the presence of her child, whether it was for moral support, or perhaps because she hoped that seeing one of his children would shame my father into putting his hand into his pocket.

Going from pub to pub, Mum would stand in the doorway, baby in her arms, peering through the crowd of men and cigarette smoke searching for a glimpse of her husband. If she was lucky to spot him, she would gesture frantically trying to catch his attention. More often than not this would fail, as either he was too busy enjoying himself with his mates, or too drunk to notice what was going on.

Mum would have to venture into the pub, carefully making her way through the press of bodies until she reached his side. Tapping him quietly she would try to gain his attention without causing too much of a stir. My father's response would vary depending on how much he had drunk. Sometimes he would give her a shilling for the meter and some extra for food, other times he would insist she went home, annoyed by her interruption.

Occasionally, he was harder to track down.

If Mum couldn't find him, she would look for his taxi, sometimes he would be there waiting for a fare, other times it would be empty and she might spend a few minutes sitting inside in case he showed up. Whichever way it worked out, Mum never went hunting for Dad on her own.

Lesley clearly remembers she was with Mum one time as they searched the city centre for his taxi. She recalls that they found the cab parked in a dark side street, so dark they could not see if there was anyone inside the car. Mum tried the door handle and found the cab locked. She and Lesley were about to walk away when the door opened, and Dad's angry voice rang out across the cobbles.

"What are you doing here? Are you bloody spying on me? Following me around or something?" he demanded.

As Mum explained that she had no money for the meter, she and Lesley moved closer to the taxi. Through the gap left by the open door, they could clearly see Ruby Brown in a clear state of undress in the back of the cab next to Dad.

My Mother was stunned – Ruby Brown was her best friend; as young girls they had been almost inseparable, going dancing together, and sharing all their girlhood secrets. This friendship had continued through the War, and into the early days of her marriage, when Ruby had joined them for a drink in the pub on numerous occasions. Mum always included her in their outings to the pub, as she felt sorry for Ruby being on her own, her husband away at sea for long stretches of time.

Mustering as much dignity as possible, she took Lesley by the hand and turned away – a woman betrayed.

I often wondered how Mum's life had changed so much, from the day when she walked down the aisle as a beautiful young bride towards a future of happiness and love, to the harsh reality of her life as it turned out.

Elsie was 19 years old and working in her mothers shop when she first saw my Father. Her mother, Mary Louise Turner was the proud owner of not one, but two sweet and tobacco shops on Lodge Lane. Her father, George Turner was employed full time as a sheet metal worker for the Gas Board and in his free time helped out in the family business.

Mr and Mrs. Turner had 11 children - 7 girls and 4 boys, and Elsie was the sixth eldest child. When she was 11 years old she became very ill with pneumonia and ended up spending a large part of her childhood in a special home in Southport for very sick children. It must have been quite a difficult time for her, because whilst she was convalescing she was kept indoors and told to rest. Although this meant that she could not enjoy the normal playful activities of healthier children, Elsie turned her mind to reading and writing, building upon a natural inquisitiveness and intelligence to the point that when she left, she had furthered her education by several years and was miles ahead of many of her healthier contemporaries. Her Mother soon realised how gifted Elsie was and quickly put her to work in the shop, knowing that it would not be long before she had mastered the necessary skills.

Leslie Norman Pearce was born and grew up in the same area as Elsie. He lived at number 52 Wendle Street just off Smithdown Road, in a small two-up-two-down terrace house with his mother, Emily Jane Pearce and his father, James Henry Pearce, who was a taxi driver.

The Pearce's had six children. There were two older boys, both of whom were away at sea, then three girls, and finally Les, as he was called, who was the youngest by about seven years. His early childhood was unsettled as his father left home to set up with another woman and raised a second family. When Les was barely eight, tragically his Mother died of thrombosis, and Les and the youngest of his three sisters, Joyce were put into an orphanage. Les and Joyce hated life in the orphanage, with Joyce vowing to remove them both once she was sixteen and legally able to do so.

On her sixteenth birthday Joyce left taking Les who was now nine years old with her, and went back to the family home. The three sisters then raised Les, spoiling him outrageously to make up for the loss of his parents at such an early age, fussing over and protecting him as if he was a little prince.

Liverpool was one of the most important seaports in the world. History shows at the beginning of the 20th Century, somewhere in the region of 25% of Liverpool's male population were involved in something maritime, either working on the docks or actually away at sea on one of the many merchant ships that frequented the Port.

Unlike his older brothers however, Leslie's first job was working for the Liverpool Corporation Road Department maintaining the roads, and his work often took him along Lodge Lane, in the vicinity of one of the shops where Elsie worked.

In 1938, he was only 16 when he set eyes on Elsie for the first time. Going in to the shop for a packet of cigarettes one day he saw her, a pretty young girl, petite in stature, with a fabulous smile and warm personality, and the most beautiful head of auburn hair that framed her face like a halo.

Once he had seen her that day, he couldn't stop himself from going back, finding excuses to go into the shop to see if she was serving. Sometimes, if the shop was busy he would peer in through the window trying to catch a glimpse of her. He was smitten. Eventually he found the courage to say a few words to her, and a couple of days later he asked her out for a date. Elsie said yes. They made an attractive couple. Les was very tall with dark hair and bore an uncanny resemblance to Clarke Gable; in fact he had been told so many times he was the actor's double that it was no surprise that he modeled himself upon the American movie star.

Elsie's sisters thought he was very handsome, giggling whenever he came into the shop. They were more than a little disappointed when he asked Elsie out for a date, clearly showing who he was interested in. 'Else and Les' as they became known, started to see a lot of each other and spent most of their time together dancing at Reece's Tea Rooms.

Both were good dancers, but Elsie shone on the floor. She had a natural rhythm and love of music, and had always been a favourite with the various bands who used to play around town; her sisters would tease her about one particular band leader, Joe Loss, who had a terrible crush on her, and would always ask her out on a date – Elsie always smiled and said no, as she had already fallen in love with Les.

Not long after her 20th birthday, Elsie found herself pregnant, and as was the unspoken rule in those days, when a young man got a girl in trouble, he did the right thing and married her. There was a degree of resistance to this idea from his sisters, as they felt that Les, who was only 17, was not much more than a child himself.

On the 23rd August 1939, they were married at St Bede's Parish Church in Hartington Road. It was a fairly respectable wedding with all the family gathered from both sides to join in the celebrations; everyone would have made a determined effort to ensure they had a good day, even if they did not necessarily agree with the marriage. Within a matter of weeks of the wedding Great Britain had declared war on Germany.

After a long and difficult birth, their first baby, Pamela, was born in February 1940. Unfortunately, Pamela was not strong enough to survive the trauma of the delivery, and died a few hours later. The young couple was devastated to have lost their first child so soon, and grief overwhelmed them. Elsie must have felt a terrible loss as she held her small child, knowing that she would never see her baby smile, or be able to inhale the warm scent so particular to small babies the world over. Les was at a loss, too young and inexperienced to know how to comfort his wife, let alone deal with the grief that he felt.

Within weeks of Pamela's death, in April 1940 the Phony War came to an end, and troops were mobilized overnight. Les had already joined up, and found himself posted to RAF Brize Norton in Oxfordshire, where he served as a member of the Catering Corps, leaving his wife on her own.

Liverpool suffered greatly at the hands of the Germans during the War, coming only second to London in terms of devastation and casualties caused during the bombing raids.

With its huge docklands stretching from the north to the south of the city, this western coast port was the main link between Britain and the USA and saw food, fuel, raw materials, weapons and troops enter in and out of the country, therefore making it a prime target for the Luftwaffe air raids.

In 1941, for seven consecutive nights, from the first to the seventh of May (now referred to as the May Blitz), 681 German planes dropped 870 tonnes of high explosives with over 112,000 incendiary devices on the area, killing in excess of 1,700 people and making around 76,000 people homeless. The May Blitz was the heaviest, most concentrated period of bombing experienced by the city, throughout the duration of the War.

For anyone living in Liverpool during this time, it would have been terrifying as everything familiar was flattened, loved ones and homes lost, the simplest aspects of everyday life disrupted. Despite all this, the people of Liverpool were brought together their sense of unity and comradeship overcoming the hardships and loss.

With her husband posted to the south of England, Elsie, like so many other women with husbands and loved ones away got on with her life. She continued working in the family shop until it was destroyed during a raid, and then found work at Freemans, a small department store on Wavertree Road, looking after the hosiery counter.

Even the safety of the small house that she and Les rented on Galloway Street would have come under threat, for although it remained unscathed during the air raids, the house was located close to major gas works, a prime target for German bombers.

Les, in the meantime, was enjoying life in the RAF. He was fortunate in that he was not posted overseas, and was able to get home leave on a regular basis. The outcome of this was that Elsie suffered a further two miscarriages between 1941 and 1943, when she then joined the WRNS (Women's Royal Naval Service).

Life in the WRNS was disciplined but fun, with a sense of camaraderie amongst them that extended beyond the confines of duty. She was based at the Royal Liver Building, working in the communications centre located deep in the basements. The Royal Liver Building was also the home of the wireless station for Liverpool which was situated on the top of the building.

(Mum once told me a story of how she was taken to the top, and through a door opening on to a small platform, providing a magnificent viewpoint of the coast, and the host of warships on the River Mersey. The best thing about this story, however, was that as she turned to go back into the building, she realised the door was actually the number '6' on the clock face! To this day, whenever I am in Liverpool, I always make a point of looking up at the clock, and visualise Mum standing there in her WRNS uniform.)

Towards the end of 1944, finding herself pregnant again, Elsie was discharged from the WRNS, and Lesley, her first surviving child was born in the front parlour of Grandma Turner's house in July 1945. Her joy was immense, as for the first time in six long years she was finally able to hold a beautiful healthy baby in her arms.

Later that year Les was sent over to Germany as part of the Occupying Forces. His role had changed somewhat by then, and he was now serving as a batman to a Colonel in the RAF. The role of batman suited him well, as he enjoyed the duties of 'gentleman's valet' and all the perks that went with the job.

One of the greatest benefits was an almost unregulated access to the 'stores' where all the unit's supplies were kept. Les was required to ensure that the Colonel was well looked after by whatever means possible. If there was a shortage of fresh 'luxuries', Les would requisition packets of cigarettes, and head off into the local villages, where a black market operation was beginning to develop. In exchange for the packets of smokes, Les would be able to obtain whatever fresh produce was available, such as eggs, smoked meats, the occasional bottle of schnapps or even German Marks. The Americans were also a good source of supplies, and bartering would take place amongst the various Allied Occupying forces, with exchanges of coffee for whisky taking place for example.

Les built up a reputation for being able to supply almost anything, his smooth talking and convincing manner opening doors wherever he went. He found that there were financial gains to be made, as well as greater 'freedoms' which he took advantage of. On one occasion, in the absence of his colonel, Les dressed himself up in the senior officers uniform, and ventured out on the town, enjoying the attention of women drawn to his good looks and pips on his shoulders.

Les became an accomplished womaniser, encouraging and reveling in female attention wherever he went, and without doubt indulged in more than the occasional dalliance. However he did not completely forget his wife, sending her

German marks rolled into a tight bundle, hidden in the middle of a tin of coffee, whenever he could. Marks were of no use in England, however, the American troops heading out to Germany would readily exchange them for dollars, which had a much higher street value in England.

Les returned briefly to England in November 1946, bringing a few little luxuries as presents for his wife and family. When he returned to Germany, he left Elsie pregnant once again; Barry was born the following year, in August 1947.

Les had been demobbed by this time and was actually at home when Barry was born. As one pregnancy followed another, Elsie soon realised that getting too close to Les meant more babies as she fell pregnant again within a year of Barry's birth.

Ian was born in 1949, sadly dying nine days later from hydrocephalus, commonly known as water on the brain. This was the second time that they had to bury a small child, and Elsie once again found herself being the stronger of the two in their time of grief.

Continuing the two year pattern, Elsie gave birth to Sheila in June 1951, and I was born some two years later in May 1953.

Chapter Seven
Sun, Sea and Scrap

Dad's continual drinking and irresponsible behaviour was a source of constant worry and distress to Mum. The uncertainty of the future plagued her, and she knew that for as long as my father carried on working night shifts driving a taxi the problem would persist.

In order for any improvement, something had to change, and so Mum started to formulate a business idea. In post War Britain there was a high demand for scrap metal, and there was plenty of it to hand with all the bomb sites, demolition and reconstruction going on. It was a relatively straight forward business, requiring a wagon, a driver, and some 'sales skills'. Dad was more than capable of both the driving and the negotiating. All that remained was a wagon.

She started by borrowing some money from her sisters, enough to put a deposit down on a second hand wagon suitable for the scrap metal business with a long flat-bed and drop down sides.

One day Dad pulled up outside our house with a navy blue Bedford wagon, with a covered cab at the front. Inside the cab were two seats and in between the seats was a metal cover concealing the engine. Dad put an old blanket over it and that is where Barry, Lesley and I used to sit. Dad would drive the wagon and the passenger seat belonged to Jack, Dad's friend, who had a lot of experience and contacts in the scrap business and just like Dad could talk his way in and out of everything. As Mum would say 'they both had the gift of the gab.'

Mum even had a telephone installed (the only one in our street) and some smart white business cards printed. It was a substantial card, printed with bold black print.

L. N. Pearce & Sons,
Scrap Metal Merchants

Our address and telephone number were also on the card, and Mum was so proud of how professional it all looked. We were now officially in business.

Setting off at the beginning of the day, Les and Jack would drive around the streets of Liverpool, literally looking for scraps of metal left abandoned. It could be anything, an old bicycle, an old pram, or debris on bomb sites; literally anything that they could get their hands on.

Meanwhile, Mum was also branching into the haulage business, contacting small companies and arranging contracts whereby Dad would collect and deliver all kinds of items. One particular job, which was exciting for us kids, was a contract he had with a rope manufacturer. He would go to the factory on the outskirts of Liverpool to collect large coils of rope, which once loaded on to the wagon would then be delivered to customers in the city.

Whilst Jack and Dad were loading the wagon, we were having the time of our life. The factory was huge, about the size of a football field, with long swathes of rope hanging down from the beams across the roof to the floor below. The walls and the floors were hidden under small mountains of coiled ropes, of all sizes and heights – everywhere you looked there were ropes, and ropes and ropes.

Grabbing hold of one end of a rope which was hanging down, we would swing from one mountain to the other, traversing the length of the factory, covering distances of up 20 meters in one go – it was childhood heaven as we imagined ourselves to be Tarzan moving through the jungle, or even Swiss Family Robinson descending from our house at the top of the trees.

Some adventures were not so much fun however, and Barry certainly had one of them.

One day the wagon was in a scrap merchant's yard in the Old Swan area. The load had been weighed, and the deal agreed, and all that remained was for the wagon to be unloaded. The quickest way to do this was with a large magnet, attached to a tall crane. The magnet would be moved from wagon to wagon, attracting the metal and swinging it over to a large heap, where it would then be dropped. It was a fast process, and required a high degree of skill and precision on the part of the crane operator.

Barry was sitting on the tailgate, watching the crane come to collect the metal from the back of our wagon. We had a good collection this time, loads of metal girders of varying lengths and widths. As the magnet made contact with the metal it caused some of the lower pieces to shift and a small mouse darted out. Barry, forgetting everything else, lunged forward to grab it draping himself over a long beam, which unbeknownst to him was a part of the first grab.

Suddenly he found himself in the air, being moved at some speed towards a mighty metal mountain. He wrapped his arms tightly around the metal girder, and started to scream for help, yelling at the top of his voice as he swung through the air.

With all the noise of the machinery no one could hear Barry's cries for help and the crane operator in his cab was totally oblivious to his distress. Fortunately for Barry, my Father came out of the office at that moment and hearing something happened to glance up towards the crane.

Immediately realising the imminent danger that Barry was facing, Dad was spurred into action racing over towards the operator, waving and shouting, flapping his arms and jumping in the air, doing everything that he could to get the operator's attention. If the operator pressed the release button, Barry would be sent hurtling to a horrible death, impaled on a mountain of broken metal and crushed by girders falling from above.

As the operator was about to press the button he noticed a 'madman' tearing towards him out of the corner of his eye, and wondering what was going on, immediately stopped what he was doing.

He got out of his cab and walked over to my Father to find out what all the commotion was about. Pointing to the pile of metal suspended on the end of the magnet, the operator saw a young boy hanging some sixty feet in the air, and holding on for dear life. Within minutes my brother was safely returned to the ground, shaking and white with terror.

The ordeal was not over however, as the operator proceeded to give both Barry and my Dad one hell of a telling off. From that moment on, whenever we visited the scrap yard, neither Barry nor I were allowed out the cab.

Dad also earned decent money selling wooden blocks. These small oak blocks had originally been used as paving on many of the streets and roads around the city, but were being replaced with granite sets as they became slippery and dangerous when wet.

The blocks were stored in huge piles in a large yard near the city centre, and Dad had won a contract to remove and dispose of them. Soaked in tar (from when they had originally been laid) Dad soon discovered that they burnt very well, trying a few on the fire at home. Although they were a bit smokey, most of it disappeared up the chimney; however they burnt for ages, and would make great firewood to sell!

Every morning, having loaded up the wagon with at least a thousand blocks, we would head for an area where the streets were close to each other. Barry and Jack would go knocking on doors calling out their sales spiel as they went:

> 'We have served the Duke of York,
> The King of Cork and all the Royal Family,
> Get your burning blocks now,
> Ten for a shilling - your burning blocks.'

In the meantime, Dad would be driving the wagon slowly along the middle of the street, beeping his horn to get peoples attention.

Our blocks of wood soon proved to be very popular as a means of heating a house as they were cheaper than coal.

On the back of the wagon, I would be stacking the blocks into piles of ten, ready for Barry and Jack to collect, keeping little piles ready for them to handover to the housewives coming out with their money. It would take us all day to empty one wagon load. We didn't stop until every last one was sold. It was dirty work, and we were as black as tar ourselves by the time we were finished.

Listening to Dad and Jack talking, we soon learnt that it was worth all the hard work. On a good day we could make as much as five to seven pounds profit, which considering the average weekly wage was four to five pounds made it very good money.

Come the end of the day, Dad would announce that he would have to 'take his medicine'. Essentially this meant his driving to the nearest pub where he would enjoy pint after pint. Barry and I would remain outside, looking after the wagon, with a bottle of lemonade and a packet of crisps to keep us going. 'Taking his medicine' quite often lasted up to three hours, and did not always happen in the best parts of the city.

At times the two of us found ourselves fighting for our lives or so it seemed, against gangs of lads who would be out on the mooch. In some dark and dingy city backstreet, Barry and I would find ourselves guarding whatever was left on the wagon, whilst Dad made merry elsewhere. It was not just a few blocks of wood that we were protecting either – we could sometimes have piles of scrap metal, or the next day's haulage load, that Dad had decided to pick up ahead of schedule. Whatever it was, it made for excellent pickings for these gangs of professional hoodlums.

Armed with long sticks, supposedly to intimidate them with, we must have made a sight. Two relatively small boys, guarding a wagon full of goodies as if it were the Crown Jewels. Sometimes we were lucky, and there may only be three or four – we could handle a small group like this. However if there were more, we were definitely outnumbered, as we battled against one half whilst the other half helped themselves. We couldn't even go for help, as Dad was not to be disturbed once he got into a pub. We hated every minute of those lonely nights; it didn't matter so much that these hoods were stealing Dad's drinking money, but that it was just as much Mum's money as well.

Despite all this, financially things started to improve and Mum started to take us on more days out; one of her favourites was going on the ferry boat across the Mersey to New Brighton.

The swimming baths in New Brighton was one of my favourite places as they had a huge open-air pool with a fifty-foot diving board, reaching high up into the sky. Lesley and Barry were brave enough to leap off the top, whilst Sheila and I would only jump off the board a quarter of the way up.

On one very rare occasion Dad joined us on a day out at the baths and announced that he was going to dive off the top board. We all watched nervously as he climbed the many steps one by one, to the platform at the top. Standing at the end of the diving board, he waved to us, a seemingly small figure in the distance, a hero about to take flight. He certainly seemed like a hero to me as no-one ever dived off the top board at all.

The swimming baths were busy that day, and a hush fell over the crowd, as thousands of pairs of eyes turned their attention towards the man high above the water. All that could be heard was the drone of an insect in the heat of the summer sun.

Perfectly balanced at the end of the board, his arms outstretched, his toes gripping to the edge, he looked ready for flight. As I watched him push off and fly through the air, I was so proud – that was my Dad diving off the top.

Seconds later he landed on the water, the watching crowd gasping in sympathy, groaning as they acknowledged his pain. My Dad had done the most perfect belly flop from fifty feet in the air and when he landed nearly all the water came out of the pool soaking everyone who was sunbathing!

Eventually a small head broke the surface of the water, and made its way to the steps at the side of the pool. Slowly he emerged, sheepishly pulling himself up the ladder. As he turned to walk towards us everyone could see his bright red chest and belly, and the tops of his legs, crimson from the impact with the water. The eyes of the crowd still followed him, stiffly walking towards us, there was no doubt my Dad was in pain.

As he sat down beside us, Mum looked at his chest and grinned. "You daft bugger," she said. "I thought you said you could dive." We all burst out laughing, including Dad.

In the summer months Dad and Jack liked going over to North Wales, where they would visit farms on the scout for disused farm equipment. Doing a deal with the farmer, they would load up the wagon and return to Liverpool, taking their collection to the scrap metal yard. It was another profitable venture.

Mum now decided that as Dad was spending so much time in Wales the family was also going to Wales, but for us it would be our first family holiday.

For our first summer Mum organised a small caravan in Gronant, near Prestatyn for two weeks. In comparison to the city streets of Liverpool it was the most amazing experience, with wide open spaces and green fields to run in, sand dunes to climb on and beaches that seemed to go on for miles. We swam in the sea, and built kingdoms from sand, out in the sun and the fresh air all day.

One afternoon, the four of us were out exploring the fields around the campsite. We were walking in single file along the top of an old Welsh dry-stone wall, arms spread out on either side like tightrope walkers in a circus as we carefully negotiated our way along. Barry and Lesley were in the front, followed by Sheila, whilst I lagged behind, bringing up the rear. Afraid that they were going to go too fast and would leave me behind I started to quicken my pace, trying to catch up with them all.

A loud scream suddenly broke the stillness of the summer afternoon. Barry and Lesley stopped dead in their tracks and turned back to see what was going on. Much to their dismay they could only see Sheila standing directly behind them, whilst there was no sight of me anywhere.

Turning around to retrace their steps, Barry suddenly noticed that the tops of the nettles growing on one side of the wall seemed to be moving a lot, and muffled yelping was coming from the depths of the deep overgrowth.

"I think he is in there!" Sheila said, pointing at the nettles. "What are we going to do?"

"I am not getting in to pull him out," said Barry, "No way on earth!"

Eventually, and after much coaxing from Barry and Lesley, I slowly made my way to the wall crying out with every step as the nettles continued their relentless stinging. Taking my hands Barry pulled me to the safety of the top of the stones. I was a big red lump, covered in so many hives that they seemed to be all joined into one – my body totally unprotected apart from the area covered by my swimming trunks. The pain was horrible. It felt like my body was on fire and as the tears ran down my face the saltiness of them cruelly made the rashes on my cheeks sting even more. It was pure torture.

My mother, needless to say, was horrified when she saw me. She immediately sent my siblings off to look for as many dock leaves as they could find, crushing them in her hands before she rubbed them gently over my skin. After a couple of hours, when the initial sting had subsided, she finally smothered me in calamine lotion so I ended up spending the next few days looking like a little pink shrimp.

Mum relished watching her children playing together and having a good time. She never stopped smiling all the time we were there and decided that without fail we would come back the following year. Before we left, she arranged the holiday in advance, negotiating six weeks rental on a small wooden hut across the road from the campsite where we had stayed.

The second summer was the best holiday we ever had. We fell in love with our little wooden hut from the moment we opened the door and walked in. It was very basic with a main room containing two sets of wooden bunks on facing walls, and a table and four chairs. In one corner of the room, there was a small table with a Baby Belling cooker sitting on top, with shelves arranged above it, and a sink attached to the wall beside it. That was the kitchen. There was another small room with a double bed, ideal for Mum (and Dad when he came to stay). Toilet facilities were available at the campsite across the road.

Most of our summer was spent playing and having fun, but we did occasionally resort to ways and means of earning money – some ideas more imaginative than others.

Next to the long sandy beach was a shop that sold buckets and spades, ice creams, sweets and lemonade. At the end of a hot summer's day we would walk along the beach collecting empty lemonade bottles before taking them back to the shop.

The lady who ran the shop would give us half a penny for each bottle and we would then buy sweets. It didn't take Barry and Lesley very long to realise that the empty bottles were stacked in crates around the back. On a quiet day, if we had not collected as many empty bottles as was needed to buy enough sweets, Barry and Lesley would sneak around the back then remove some of the empties from the crates so as to make up the numbers.

Sadly one day, it all went wrong. We had collected our bottles, been paid our money, and had bought our sweets. Lesley divided them out, and had started to walk up the hill back to our 'hut' with Barry on one side of her and Sheila on the other, all happily chewing away.

I remained behind, standing outside this wonderful place, where like magic Lesley and Barry produced sweeties from nowhere. As I put most of my sweets in my pocket (and some in my mouth), I noticed some full bottles of lemonade by the door. Thinking that everything in this magic place was free, and that Barry and Lesley would love a full bottle of lemonade each, I picked two up, one in each hand, and set off at a steady pace behind them.

Just as they got to the top of the hill, Lesley heard somebody shouting. Looking back down the hill, they could see me, half way up the hill, struggling to keep hold of two full bottles of lemonade, with an irate shop owner chasing after me, waving her fist in the air and shouting, "Stop thief. Put them down you little thief."

In a flash, Barry was racing down the hill towards me. Reaching my side, he grabbed the two bottles from my hands, placed them carefully on the ground, picked me up and half threw me over his shoulder before turning and running up the hill as fast as he could. Once out of sight of the lady, and a safe distance away, he dumped me on the pavement.

"What were you doing?" they all shouted at the same time.

"I don't know," I replied, "I just wanted to give you some lemonade."

"You just wanted to give us some lemonade?" Lesley scolded. "You are supposed to buy it, not steal it you idiot!"

They made me cross my heart and hope to die as I promised not to tell Mum, as well as swearing that I would never do something like that ever again. Apparently I had now spoiled everything as we couldn't go back there anymore in case we were reported to the police.

The day I decided to help myself to a biscuit, was the day I excelled myself in causing problems for my mother. We were playing outside our little wooden hut, when I started to feel hungry. The biscuits were kept on the shelf above the cooker.

Going inside I pulled a chair over to the cooker, and stood on it and trying to reach the jar. It was no good – I was still too short. So I put one foot on to the corner of the little table which the cooker was resting on to give myself a little extra height. I was still not tall enough – but almost there, so I leaned forward, putting all my weight on the front of the table and stretching as high as I could towards the jar of biscuits, my fingers brushing against the coolness of the glass. I was almost there, just an inch more.

Suddenly the table gave way, my weight causing it to topple forwards. Thrown from my precarious position, I landed face down on the floor, a pan of boiling water (which I had not noticed, being so focused on reaching the jar of biscuits) flying in my direction as the cooker slid off the table top. Within seconds of my hitting the floor, the pan and its contents had landed on top of me. All I can remember was the excruciating pain across my back as I screamed out in terror.

Once again I was only wearing my swimming trunks and my back was quickly covered in blisters the size of Mum's hands. Instructing Lesley to look after the others, she picked me up and carried me as carefully as she could for the two mile walk to the nearest bus stop. She couldn't cover me with anything as my back was too badly burnt, and every movement was sheer agony making me scream out in pain.

The bus seemed to take forever to arrive, and even longer to travel the ten miles to the nearest hospital in Rhyl. It must have been a horrible journey for Mum as well: the other passengers on the bus would have been looking at the two of us, my blistered back exposed for all to see, possibly passing judgment on her abilities as a parent; she had a small child, who was badly injured sitting on her lap, sobbing piteously in her arms and she was unable to take away the pain. Throughout this time she would have been silently wishing the driver to hurry up.

The bus driver, realising the gravity of the situation, dropped Mum right outside the hospital before returning to his normal route. Mum rushed in, calling out for immediate help, and within a few minutes we were taken away by some nurses who began the process of attending to my injuries.

We remained at the hospital for the next two days. I was too distraught to let Mum out of my sight, and she was reluctant to leave me on my own. After several phone calls Mum was able to finally speak to the lady who owned the campsite, and asked her to tell Lesley that she would be staying at the hospital with me overnight.

Apparently my burns were quite serious, and for the first twenty-four hours the doctors closely monitored my progress in case I needed to have skin-grafts. After two days and on the basis that Mum followed the strict instructions given to her to keep me out of the sun and the sea, we were allowed home.

My brother and sisters were so nice to me when I got home, the sympathy and 'looking after' lasting for a good couple of days before they got bored with it all, reverting to normal – playing and fighting as children do.

My Mother however, virtually kept me under lock and key, not letting me out of her sight, and certainly not letting me out in to the sun to play with the others. I must have nagged her constantly as my back was healing and I was feeling no pain whatsoever. After a week, she finally relented giving me permission to go to the beach with the others.

I was only allowed to go as long as I promised not to take off my top, and not to go into the water, Lesley being instructed to make sure that I stuck to my promise.

Lesley took her responsibility seriously, watching over me like a hawk, constantly telling me to be careful. I was not allowed to take of my hat or my top, and she got quite cross when I went too near the waters edge. After a considerable while, she must have dropped her guard a little, as I remember she went for a short walk with Barry, who was looking for driftwood whilst she searched for shells.

Sheila and I stayed where we were, running around after each other, and jumping in and out of the shallow pools created by the tide going out, in amongst the small sandbars. We were having so much fun, splashing and messing about. Suddenly I tripped, landing on my back in less than a foot of water; it didn't hurt so I got up and carried on playing.

I don't even think that I realised that my top was wet until Lesley came back. Taking one look at me, the happy sister of a few moments ago disappeared, to be replaced by a furious one.

"How come your t-shirt is wet?" she demanded, grabbing my arm, almost shaking me.

"I don't know," I said, "we've just been playing."

"You stupid little boy!" she hissed at me. "Give me your t-shirt as I need to make sure that it is dry before Mum sees it."

I took off my top and passed it to her, and then turned to head back to my games with Sheila. Lesley let out a piercing shriek.

"What have you done to your back?" she exclaimed. "Oh my god, what have you done? Your blisters are back, they are full of water again."

"You've got jelly fish all over your back!" said Barry who had been standing to one side, watching this all going on. "Jelly man – Mum will kill you! Jelly man!"

"I only fell in a little bit of water," I protested trying to peer over my shoulder to see what they were talking about, "I haven't been in the sea, I promise."

"He is telling the truth," said Sheila, who had now come to stand by my side. "He hasn't been swimming or anything, we were just playing around down there, where there is hardly any water," she added, pointing to the puddles and the sandbars where we had been earlier.

Muttering that "Mum was going to kill her" we all packed up and Lesley took me back to the hut, with Barry and Sheila trailing behind. This time Mum was silent when she saw what I had done, as she quietly gathered her things together, putting them all in her hand bag.

I think that she must have taken Lesley to one side, and had a few sharp words with her, as Lesley looked totally miserable when Mum and I left, setting off on the long journey to the hospital again.

This time the trip was different; I was feeling no pain and was able to cover my back. We travelled in virtual silence, Mum staring out of the window and no doubt wondering what she had done to deserve such a child. As for me, I sat there and studied the other passengers, unaware of the shame that was yet to come, at least as far as Mum was concerned.

There was no desperate rush when we got to the hospital, although the nurses, having taken one look at my back, were pretty quick to take me away to be checked by a doctor. Mum followed behind putting on a brave face and knowing full well that her skills as a mother were about to be called into question.

After a thorough examination, and realising the water was most probably from the sea, the 'balloons' on my back were burst, and I was wrapped in bandages. I felt no pain, and sat there quietly while the nurse and doctor went about their tasks. Before letting us go, the doctor gave my mother a real dressing down.

In clipped tones, he reminded her of the instructions he had given, demanded to know how she could have ignored them, asked her what sort of woman she was, and advised her that he really did not want to see her again! Mum suffered more that day than I did, but it was not until I was much older, did I really understand the extent of humiliation and shame that I had innocently caused her that time.

The holiday eventually came to an end. We all had the most fabulous six weeks; even Mum enjoyed herself despite my burns and the trouble I had caused. Sadly we never holidayed again as a family – our six weeks of sunshine was the second and the last holiday we ever had together.

Once back in Durden Street, life carried on as normal, a million miles away from the sea and sand and the simple happiness of our little hut by the beach.

Our scrap wagon business was continuing to do well although Dad was having a few problems with parking the wagon at the end of the day. He would normally park it outside the house in the evening, but the police would knock on the door and ask him to move it.

Apparently it was too wide for our narrow street. Dad decided to park it on a piece of waste ground next to Bernard's Bike shop on Smithdown Road literally a minute away from our house.

One morning dad, Barry and I were walking towards the wagon to go to work. As we got closer Dad noticed that there was something wrong, and on closer inspection we found that the tyres were flat. Luckily they were not slashed, just flat, six pancakes wrapped around the wheels, including the spare which was bolted underneath.

Pity for Dad was not something that Barry and I ever felt, but that day we felt sorry for him. His face was so full of sadness and concern; not only did he have to get the wagon back on the road, but how much time and money would it take and how many days work would he lose, would have been his other major concerns.

All that aggravation caused by a bunch of kids, thinking that letting air out of tyres was a good laugh! Little did they know that Dad ended up losing two days work as a result, which no one in our family found funny.

Not long afterwards, Dad slipped a disc in his back whilst lifting a piece of steel on to the wagon. He had to be taken to hospital as he was in too much pain and could not move. He ended up spending two months in traction before he was allowed home, and even then he was denied a decent nights rest as he had to sleep on a wooden board.

With Dad not being able to work, Mum tried to keep the business going by employing a driver to work alongside Jack. Unfortunately, after a couple of months it didn't work and she could no longer keep up the payments on the wagon, so it was repossessed by the finance company.

The scrap business, whilst it lasted, had been good to us, enabling the family to have two fantastic summer holidays; we had also experienced the normality of family-life for the first time, where money or the lack of it was not the overriding concern.

Having learnt from the scrap wagon business, Mum started to think of new ideas whilst Dad returned to the taxis.

Old habits die hard, and the ritual of getting ready for a night in his cab was reinstated. Only this time there was a new layer to be added. My Dad now needed a corset, as prescribed by the doctors to provide support for his back – he couldn't leave the house without it. Dad selected this garment with care, choosing a corset as 'worn by the stars'. Occasionally we would catch a glimpse of him putting it on, standing upright with the corset wrapped around his torso. As he held it in place Mum would be behind him, pulling the laces as tightly as she could, whilst Dad emitted little squeaks of protest and grunts of disgust as he was firmly tied in place. Mum all the while would be smiling broadly from the safety of behind his back.

Chapter Eight
Tears and Torment

I remember the day I started at Junior School, aged seven. Mum didn't want me to follow Barry to Earl Road School, just at the bottom of our street as she felt that the boys there were too rough. I am sure she thought they would pick on me, especially as I couldn't even write my own name, so she chose Sefton Park Secondary Modern Juniors for Boys.

I was very nervous. Mum had taken me to school, and as we stood outside the entrance she bent down, straightened my tie and told me that I looked good in my new uniform. Aged seven, I was still in short trousers and would not graduate to 'longs' until I was eleven and about to move into the Seniors.

It was a big school with about one hundred boys to every year split into three bands; Band A was for the 'Bright Sparks', Band B for the 'Average Joes' and Band C for those more commonly referred to as 'The Thickies'.

Although I was a confident young lad in so many ways, I was always apprehensive about school. My first day was made even more traumatic as we all had to sit for some exams, the results of which would determine which band we would be put in to.

Exams were pure torture. I would find myself staring at a piece of paper, my eyes darting all over the page as I tried to pick out words that were familiar to me. The tick of the clock would be sounding loudly as I endeavoured to make sense of it all, knowing that the minutes were not in my favour. As my tension and panic increased the words would almost seem to vanish from the page, and I would find myself glancing at the boys on either side – as if for reassurance that I was not alone.

By copying their actions and flicking through pages, or resting my head on my hand while I appeared to study the question before me, I created an image of being in control, whilst in reality I felt I was drowning. If only there had been a calming voice or a helping hand to lead me through, to take the edge off my tension – then things may have been different. As it was, I was alone in my misery feeling like the only stupid person in the whole world.

The excitement of a new school and new friends to meet was overshadowed by the horror of those first two days and I cried myself to sleep both nights. Only Mum knew what I was going through.

I was placed in Band C, with thirty-three other boys of mixed race and background and we were a bunch of misfits, almost regarded as no-hopers. Some of the boys came from one parent families and had grown up without a father and no discipline in their lives at all. Others were sons of first and second generation immigrants, some arrived so recently that they spoke hardly any English. Then there were others like me, who were hindered by a learning difficulty, but rather than being singled out for assistance we were put to one side, not worth the time or trouble, left to make our own way.

The teachers dreaded coming into our classroom and this came across very clearly in the way they taught us all. Rather than imparting knowledge they spent most of their time trying to enforce discipline, using detentions as a way of establishing a certain degree of calm and control.

I actually found myself to be quite popular in my class. Although I was small I had confidence and was able to think on my feet. I showed no fear of my peers (only teachers) and would not allow myself to be bullied.

Although there were boys from different backgrounds, there was nobody who wore a turban in our school. One morning, just after we had gone through the register, there was a knock on the door and a new boy entered. He told the teacher he was Ranjitt Singh and then waited politely by the door.

There was a sudden outburst of rude comments from across the classroom.

"Wotsa marra with yer noggin, lar?" one of the lads cried out, "Have yer been playing tick with an 'atchet?" Everyone burst out laughing.

"That's some bandage you've got there Sabu," another sniped, "Don't pick it or it'll never get better."

The sniping went on and on; by this time the whole of the class was in uproar, laughing so much that they were falling off their seats, some even had tears rolling down their cheeks with the mirth of it all.

I suddenly noticed Ranjitt standing by the door. He too was crying, but these were tears of a different kind. His were tears of shame, shame caused by the taunts of a group of ignorant seven year olds who knew no better. I felt sorry for him and sat there silently watching him in sympathy.

The following Monday morning on the way to school, I saw Ranjitt walking along by himself looking miserable. I walked up to him, and smiled.

"Hi," I said. He didn't respond. "Hi," I said again nudging him with my elbow. He continued to walk, head down, still not looking at me.

"How do you say your name again?" I asked him.

"Ranjitt Singh," was the mumbled response.

"What kind of name is that?" I asked, "I'll never remember that! What about Ran? Is that alright?"

He just looked at me as if I was talking a different language and continued walking even faster.

Catching up with him I said, "Slow down, we've plenty of time, we don't have to be in for another ten minutes." I told him what I had been doing over the weekend and how I helped my mum at the market; once I started I couldn't stop.

He must have caught me taking a breath because he asked, "Do you like working at the market?" We then carried on along the road, chatting away and starting to feel more at ease with each other.

To my surprise, just as we neared the school, Ranjitt said something that stopped me in my tracks.

"Do you want to go ahead by yourself now? I won't blame you, and I know the rest of your friends won't like you being with me."

I looked at him as if he was talking nonsense. "No. We are mates now, aren't we? Unless you don't want to walk in with me?" I replied.

Ran didn't answer so we just walked in together.

He was right, my other mates didn't like it.

"Warra yer doin talking to 'im?" One of the lads shouted over.

I looked straight at him and shouted back, "I'll talk to anybody, even the likes of you." At that moment the bell went and every kid did the hundred-yard dash to get in before the bell stopped. During playtime we walked about in the yard together. After a little while a couple of my pals came over to ask if I wanted to kick a ball around with them.

"Ok," I agreed. "Come on Ran" I said to him. "Let's go take up position."

"Why dus he 'ave to play?" someone snarled.

"He doesn't have to if he don't want to," I snarled back, "But if he wants to... he can, all right." This was not a question, it was a statement and a silence fell over our small group as time seemed to stop for a few moments.

All of a sudden one of the boys kicked the ball towards me and suddenly we were off. From that day on Ran was one of the gang.

I started to enjoy my time at Sefton Park Juniors, if only because of all the school activities. I joined the football team, the swimming team, and everything else that was going on, including the school chess club.

However, lessons that contained any form of reading or writing were still a problem and not getting any easier. Some teachers did try to help but quickly gave up, unable to understand how it was that somebody who could talk so well and appear so bright would read and write so poorly.

On some occasions one or two of the teachers would get angry with me, calling me lazy, and saying that I showed no interest in the lessons. They would stand me in the corner of the classroom, facing the wall with a tall, pointed dunce's hat on my head. I was to stand there for the remainder of the lesson, and rather than reprimand or encourage me to do better, this just humiliated me and made me feel worse.

One teacher in particular really had it in for me, and said if I didn't try harder I would be sent to a special school where backward children went. I knew what she meant as I had seen the groups of handicapped children in the morning, lined up waiting for their special bus to collect them; the thought of this frightened the life out of me.

Ignorance about dyslexia in the 1960's was still prevalent in many schools, with research into the 'disorder' barely filtering down to the educational system. Dyslexia was still believed to be a form of mental illness in some quarters, whilst others believed it to be an excuse for laziness.

It wasn't until the middle sixties that it became known as it is today; a difficulty resulting from a reduced ability to associate visual symbols with verbal sounds. Up until that point it was referred to as 'word blindness' and the study of dyslexia was primarily the domain of medical specialists.

It was also something of a taboo in schools in England. Whether this was because so little was known about it, how to identify the disorder and how to 'treat' it, or whether it was because teachers did not have the regular training that they have today, I am not sure. I am certain, however, that although dyslexia is a lifelong condition, with the right help it can be overcome and dyslexics can learn to adapt to the limitations imposed upon them.

However, in my case, and the cases of thousands of other children, help was not available. Whether as a result of sheer ignorance, or from a lack of time, knowledge or inclination, I was led to believe by my teachers that I was suffering from a mental illness. They destroyed my self-confidence, humiliated me on a regular basis and it took many years for the scars to heal. Not surprisingly, an element of bitterness still remains with me today.

I certainly wasn't Mr Goodie-Two-Shoes when I was young and quickly developed entrepreneurial skills which I would employ during our hours out in the playground. The playground was the perfect 'black market' where quickly conducted business deals would take place whilst a teacher's back was turned. Money would exchange hands very quickly, as we sold Woodbine *loosies*, lost bets on a game of conkers, or paid the purchase price of a bag of ollies.

Ollies were good business for me. I played the game well, and used to walk around with my pockets full of small glass balls, clinking together as I moved. To buy a bag of ollies from the sweet shop would cost tuppence whereas I cannily charged half price for a bag, ensuring a good turnover. The ironic thing was that many a boy who lost his ollies to me during a game, would end up buying them back from me the following day.

Chapter Nine
Penny For The Guy

When I turned eight, I finally felt as if I was starting to grow up. The nice thing was that my aunties felt the same way too, always telling my Mum that I was old for my age.

Mum was constantly tired and it worried me. She was becoming more irritable, snapping at everybody, and shouting at me for the slightest misdemeanor. It just wasn't like her and I asked Sheila if she had noticed it too. Was Mum sick?

I'd lie in bed at night listening to Mum and Dad shouting at each other down stairs. This had been going on for some weeks when one afternoon I found out what the problem was. I was coming downstairs when I overheard Lesley and Sheila talking in their bedroom; Lesley was telling Sheila that Mum was pregnant.

Hurtling down the rest of the stairs, I ran into the kitchen straight over to Mum. "Is it true Mum?" I asked, "Are you going to have another baby?"

She stopped what she was doing and bent down to give me a big hug. "Yes, Jeff, it's true." We stayed there for a few minutes our arms around each other. "The baby is due in November."

I didn't know what to say and just enjoyed being held close to her.

Taking my silence for concern, Mum continued, "Just think, you will have a little brother or sister to play with this Christmas. Santa is coming early."

All the shouting that I had overheard over the past few weeks was Mum reading Dad the riot act which must have paid off. Dad was around a lot more and although he still smelt of alcohol in the mornings, he was nowhere near as drunk as before. What's more this improved behaviour seemed to last for several months, so there was a much happier atmosphere at home.

Lesley was now sixteen and had left school. She had started her first full-time job as a trainee assistant in a chemist on Whitechapel in the city centre so she was bringing home wages and even Dad was contributing a lot more.

It was now October, and our new baby was due very soon. We were all busy getting ready for Bonfire Night. There was a flurry of activity as all the local kids would be out collecting old timber and anything else that would burn for their bonfire. Streets would form 'gangs' working together, to ensure that their 'bommi' was the biggest and the best in the area.

Our gang would go on the prowl, quite a few streets away to steal backyard doors; but whilst we were out robbing elsewhere, another gang would be equally busy nicking our doors. We would even keep guard over our piles of wood to ensure that no-one stole pieces away in the middle of the night. There was a competition to see which gang had the biggest bonfire, and although there was no prize as such, there was a huge degree of status attached.

In order to buy fireworks, children everywhere would go around asking for a 'penny for the guy'.

A 'guy' is a giant rag doll, made out old clothes and newspapers. Tying string around the bottoms of the trouser legs, and the cuffs of the shirts, we would then stuff them with scrunched up newspaper making the body. The head and face would either be made from a balloon or an old brown paper bag, also stuffed with paper, upon which we would draw a face.

Joining the body together we would place our guy into a pram or a steering cart, if necessary tying him in place, before finally putting an old hat on his head. The more realistic looking the guy, the more money we would collect.

At 5.30 in the evening we would set off, heading for the bus stop, where we would stand chanting out, "A penny for the guy," to all the passengers as they got off the bus, "A penny for the guy please, Miss."

With the guy by our side and a hat in our outstretched hand, we would continue our spiel until the home-time rush was over. From the bus stop we would move to a pub – trying to find one where there were no other kids pitched outside.

Collecting pennies outside a pub was a much trickier business as it was important to avoid the drunks, moving out of their way as they staggered along – sometimes they would ignore us, other times they could be quite nasty. Most of the people coming out of the pub however were in a good mood, and would be happy to give us a penny or two, dropping the coins into our hat.

We would give all our money to Mum to save for our fireworks and in return she would make sure that the fireworks were divided out equally amongst us.

Recently Lesley told me a funny story. She and Barry were supposed to be looking after Sheila and me while Mum was out, as I was only about three or four at the time. It was very close to bonfire night and they needed a Guy Fawkes, so rather than make one they decided to use me instead, making a cardboard mask with two holes cut out for my eye and an elastic band at the back to hold it in position. Putting the mask over my face, sticking a hat on my head and a pair of gloves on my hands – I was ready, the job was done.

Apparently, everything was going well until they decided to pitch up outside the Boundary Pub. Quite a few people had come out and had given them some pennies for their 'little guy'. Then two men emerged, and Barry who was not paying any attention, asked for a 'penny for the guy, please mister'.

At that moment he looked up and realised that the Mister he was talking to was none other than Dad. Dad was not at all happy, he was furious, chasing us all the way home where he then gave us a real telling off. As far as he was concerned, what we had been doing was no better than begging, the Pearce Family were above that sort of behaviour.

Perhaps if he hadn't spent so much of his life nursing a pint in a pub, and had paid attention to what was happening in the real world, i.e. that which went on outside the pub doors, he would have known that asking for a 'penny for the guy' was actually a tradition and had nothing to do with begging at all.

It was the day before bonfire night and I was out collecting wood with all my mates for the massive bonfire we always had every year in Harvey Street which was next to ours.

I suddenly heard Barry shouting for me, telling me to 'come in the house now'. I was enjoying myself but I knew from the tone of his voice he meant *now*; I also knew that when I irritated him he would give me a sly dig when Mum wasn't looking. Dead arms and dead legs were his favourite form of punishment – sometimes given to me for no other reason than I was his younger brother.

When I asked him why he did this he explained to me in great detail - it was an older brothers' privilege to pick on their little brothers, if only to keep them in line. For years his pet nickname for me was 'Fat Man' which I hated as I was not fat. I think that the six year age difference was the cause as we never got on as children.

Hearing him calling I ran home as quickly as I could. When I got in the house, Lesley told us to sit down around the table in the living room.

"Mum has been rushed to hospital," she said, "She is going to be alright, but you all have to be good for me as I am in charge of you lot while Mum is away."

To our dismay Lesley wanted to keep us in on Bonfire Night, one of the best nights of the year. What a disaster. After all the collecting of wood for the bonfire, the saving of pennies for fireworks, and all the excitement and planning that we had gone through – this was total disappointment. As far as we were concerned life could not get much worse than this.

"Oh please Les," we begged, "please let us go out. We promise to be good, pleeeeeease Lesley." Looking at our crestfallen faces, she relented.

"Tell you what," she promised, "I will talk to Mum when I go and see her at the hospital this afternoon. And then depending on what she says you might be able to go out. But you have to be good. OK?"

We couldn't wait for Lesley to get back and were so happy when she told us that Sheila and I could go to the bonfire as long as we promised to stay together and to be home by 9 o'clock at the latest.

Sheila and I had a fantastic time. We joined all our friends at our bommi, gathering together on Harvey Street at 6.30 that evening. You had to be there on time, watching the flames as they licked their way up the wood towards the guy who was tied to the top. By the time the guy started to burn the bonfires were taller than the houses, the flames reaching up to the sky, the sparks shooting out in all directions crackling and spitting.

The black night sky was a perfect backdrop for the colours of the fireworks going off, the smoke from the bonfires mixing with the smoke from the fireworks as they fizzed their way skywards.

On the ground watching this all going on, we were warmed by the heat given off from the bommi, our faces glowing pink in the reflection of the flames, the smell of smoke all around us. There were always nice things to eat as well, toffee apples, treacle toffee and pieces of cinder toffee being the most popular. Mum normally would have made these for us, but with her being in hospital we were happy to share with our friends whatever they had to offer.

Keeping our promise to Lesley, Sheila and I were at home by nine, happy, tired and smelling of wood smoke and fell straight to sleep once our heads hit our pillows.

In the early hours of the following morning, November 6th 1961, Mum gave birth to a perfect little baby girl, June Karen Pearce. When she came home a few days later, bringing our little sister with her, Mum told us that it was the sound of the fireworks that had woken little June up, which is why she was born when she was!

To make room for the new arrival Mum moved all the beds around, putting bunk beds in Barry's tiny room. She decided that as Barry and I constantly fought it would be best if Lesley shared a room with him, but this arrangement only lasted for one night.

Both Barry and Lesley were in bed, Barry on the bottom bunk and Lesley on the top. Lesley was trying to get to sleep and Barry was trying to keep her awake by lying on his back with the soles of his feet pushed up against the base of her mattress.

This way he could not only kick her through the thin mattress that divided them both, but also push her up into the air, sort of bumping her around as he did it. He then got it into his brain to undo the metal clips above his head which held the top bunk bed to the bottom one, this now allowed him to 'raise' her up in the air, again with his feet, like some weight lifter in a gym.

Unfortunately, Barry's plan backfired, most probably because he wasn't strong enough! Before he had a chance to move out of the way, the whole of the top bunk with Lesley as well, landed on Barry at an angle. He couldn't breath as the metal frame of the base had fallen across his throat, and his arms were pinned by his sides under the weight of everything else. He was trapped.

Lesley found herself crashing down on to the bed below, and hearing no noise from Barry other than a strangulated gasping, realised that something was very wrong, climbing off the bed as quickly as she could.

Summoning up his last bit of strength, Barry gave an almighty shove, managing to lift the mattress and the base high enough to push it off his throat. Gasping for air, he just lay there, totally without a smart comment for once in his life.

Mum reorganized the sleeping arrangements the next day, putting me in with Barry, and Lesley and Sheila together. She was very firm with Barry, telling him in no uncertain terms, that he had to behave, and Barry still being in shock at how narrow an escape he'd had, took it on board. As Mum told us all, with a new baby to care for, all she wanted was a little peace and quiet and a good night's sleep, if that was possible, please!

Mum was confined to the house after having baby June, and was still weak from the birth. Considering that she was forty-two at the time, her slight build and the fact that she weighed only seven and a half stone, the successful arrival of my baby sister was a real tribute to what a remarkably strong and resilient woman she really was.

Chapter Ten
On the Never-Never

Despite the difficulties of winter, Mum always made Christmas the most magical time of year. In the run up to Christmas Lesley and Mum would distemper the house, going from room to room freshening the walls with a lick of paint.

Once the walls were dry, we would then decorate the living room and front parlour with paper chains that we had made.

We would have at least a six foot Christmas tree and Sheila and I would be tasked with decorating it. Once the tree was complete, Mum would then hang little chocolate figures of Father Christmas covered in brightly coloured tin foil on to the branches.

"Now I have counted them," she would say as she looped the little pieces of string over the pine needles, "and I know how many there are, so don't you lot go eating them before Christmas day. I will be watching!"

The Father Christmases never lasted long, but no-one ever owned up to eating them. No doubt Mum, seeing them disappearing so quickly from the tree, had helped herself to one or two before they all vanished – whatever the reason she never made an issue about their disappearance.

We would be sent to bed quite early on Christmas Eve – too excited to sleep, whilst Mum enjoyed a little peace and quiet downstairs without her boisterous children underfoot. Sitting at the table in the living room, she would spend hours carefully wrapping oranges, apples and nuts in remnants of wallpaper and other scraps of brightly coloured paper that she had saved.

Once wrapped, these little items would be put into each of our sacks, together with one big present that we had previously asked Father Christmas for. Mum would know exactly what to get as well, because she would have taken us to visit Father Christmas in his Grotto at Blacklers Department Store in the city centre, and would have overheard our conversation with him whilst we sat on his knee.

One year I asked Father Christmas for a violin. I had been inspired by the musicians whom I had seen on tv, and could just see myself playing with the same skill, producing beautiful music for the whole family to enjoy. Father Christmas obliged, and having unwrapped the highly polished instrument, I stood in the front parlour, violin tucked under my chin, feet firmly planted slightly apart, bow in my hand.

I touched the bow to the strings, drawing it across them backwards and forwards. A loud screech pierced my ear drums, making me stop. This wasn't right. Not one to be daunted, I raised my bow and started all over again. The violin still screamed in protest at my inexperience.

"Shut up Fat Man," Barry ordered. "Mum, tell him to stop. What did you get him that for? He is going to drive us mad with that noise!"

Mum came into the front parlour to see what was going on. "Oh Barry, leave him alone. Let him have a play and enjoy his present. You won't be saying that when he's playing for the Philharmonic Orchestra. "

"There's more chance of him flying to the moon, than his learning to play that thing! He sounds like he is killing a cat!" Barry responded, totally unconvinced by my musical potential.

After an hour of trying, I put my violin down and went to find Mum, disappointment written all over my face.

"Mum, they are no good those violins, they don't work properly."

The violin disappeared sometime that afternoon, as I think that Barry hid it away. It was no great loss; I never bothered to find out what had happened to it. My musical career came to an end, and Mum recouped her investment, taking it back to the shop where she had found it for a full refund in return.

On Christmas morning we would wake up early, scrambling for the sack of goodies that lay waiting for us at the foot of our bed. I would take my sack into Sheila and Lesley's room, waking Sheila up so that we could share the fun of opening our presents together.

No matter what our circumstances were, we never missed having a spectacular Christmas dinner. If we didn't have a turkey Mum would ensure that we had a fat chicken, with lots of vegetables, roast potatoes, stuffing and gravy.

The table in the living room would be decorated with pieces of holly and ivy in the middle, and Christmas crackers placed in front of each chair. Turning to the person next to us, we would pull a cracker putting on the hats, laughing at the jokes, and playing with the little toys that would be hiding inside.

Sitting in front of an almost overflowing plate, the wonderful smells wafting up, we would tuck in to what was definitely the best meal of the year. We could have a choice of either cream soda or dandelion and burdock to drink, and if we had room – we could have second helpings. After the turkey was over it was time for pudding, a traditional plum pudding served with hot custard. There would always be a couple of shiny sixpences hidden in its plummy depths, and whoever found a coin would be allowed to keep it. Finding a sixpence was as nice as eating the pudding itself.

So stuffed that another mouthful was almost impossible to swallow, Mum would urge us to finish off, all the time keeping an eye on the clock. At five minutes to three we would be herded into the front parlour where we would sit down in front of the television to await the Queen's Speech, Mum's favourite programme.

Sitting in the middle of the sofa, with her children at her feet and on either side, she would be like a queen in her own little kingdom, as we all sat in silence listening to the Her Majesty's Address to the Nation. Households up and down the country would all be doing the same thing and the streets would be eerily empty; the Queens Speech was not to be missed at any cost.

★ ★ ★

The aftermath of Christmas brought debt for many, and Mum was no exception. In our area this was a way of life; a custom almost like Christmas trees and chocolate Santas.

For people like us, with no savings or extra money to spend, there would only be one option available, and that would be to apply for credit from certain companies who would specialize in 'helping'. The Provident was one of the best known, to the point that the nickname of 'Provi Cheque' was coined and well known throughout Merseyside. In the weeks before Christmas a representative or salesman from the Provi would be out knocking on doors asking if you needed any help over Christmas. The answer was always 'yes'.

A sum would be agreed, anywhere between £20 - £40 and then the interest calculated (which was always high), the two figures added together, and finally the weekly repayments worked out. Within a week the salesman would come by again, bringing you your Provi Cheque. This was a special visit, because in a way he was giving you Christmas, that cheque was the difference between Christmas feast and Christmas famine. The cheque could be used in quite a few department stores such as Colliers on London Road or Freemans on Wavertree Road. What a difference it made, so easy to come by, though so hard to pay back.

Mum would spend the majority of her cheque on a new school uniform for each of us, and most importantly a new pair of shoes. She would also make sure that we all had one good present each – mostly because we had dropped unsubtle hints for weeks and weeks beforehand.

Another form of credit available came from a most obliging Jewish gentleman called Harry Shaperio. Harry did not offer cheques but instead would call at the door laden with items that any housewife could not live without. Warm blankets in the middle of a cold winter, a beautiful table cloth just as the final touches were being put to Christmas decorations, whatever it was it had to be bought.

"You can have them, Mrs Pearce," he would say, "for ten shillings, and you can pay me only a shilling a week until you are clear." It was a good deal, and the items would be purchased.

Within two weeks he would be back with something else that was really needed, and again within minutes another deal would be done. And so it went on, almost like a form of rolling credit, never paying off what was owed, for many, many years.

He would call every Friday without fail to collect his money. Sometimes, Mum didn't have a shilling for him, so she would tell me, "When Harry Shaperio comes don't open the door. Just tell him that 'me mum's not in' do you understand." Rolling my eyes with exasperation, I would tell her I understood.

The knock came at the door and I'd go to it. "Me Mum says to tell you she is not in," I stated in what I thought was a grown up voice.

After a few moments silence the letterbox flap was raised, and Harry Shaperio's eyes peered at me. Then he moved his head so that his mouth was framed by the letter box and very slowly and loudly said, "Go back and tell your Mother she is in and I want my shilling."

"Ok." I said. I returned to the kitchen, "Mum, he said you are in and he wants his shilling."

"Tell him that I am not in and I haven't got it this week," she replied, speaking quietly so as not to be heard.

I walked back down the hallway to the front door. Bending over I called out, "Me Mum said that she is not in, and she hasn't got it this week."

The flap opened again. "Fine. You tell your mother I want my two shillings next week or else!"

I returned to the kitchen relaying Mr Shaperio's message to Mum. "Alright," she replied. "Tell him that I'll give him his bloody shillings next week. I promise."

As I walked down the hall, I repeated Mums message under my breath several times so that I didn't forget it. Leaning towards the letterbox flap this time, I waited for it to open. I didn't need to wait for long as if by magic it lifted and I found myself looking him straight in the eye.

"Me Mum says you'll get your shillings next week. Oh and she bloody promises."

He looked at me for a moment, before dropping the flap, then I'd hear the sound of his footsteps as he walked away, no doubt going to the next house to go through it all over again!

There was also the Co-Op man who would call once a week for a penny payment towards funeral insurance, and the 'Pools Man' who would come to collect the weekly coupon for the Littlewoods Football Pools. Mum used to say winning it would get us out of this mess one day. Friday afternoon and early evening would see the streets a buzz of activity as all the different collectors would be out knocking trying to collect what was owing. Some of the shops also offered credit and our favourite was Mary's.

Mary was a middle aged woman who ran a small corner shop on Smithdown Road; she lived in the flat above running the business on her own and stayed open quite late in the evening. There were shelves around the edge of the room, reaching up to the ceiling and an 'L' shaped counter, from behind which Mary served her customers. The shelves were stacked with dry provisions such as tea and sugar and tinned goods whilst she also sold milk and butter and bread.

Best of all were the rows of jars full of sweets which were prominently displayed so that children of all ages and heights could see them. Glass jars full of such a variety of colours and flavours; lemon sherbets, Drumsticks and Refreshers, wine gums and everton mints – everything a kid could wish for. Some sweets would be sold by the weight, tuppence a quarter, and Mary would carefully weigh them out on a small set of scales before pouring them into a little white paper bag, twisting the top of the bag closed. More often than not though, I would go into the shop asking Mary for a penny mix, a small selection of sweets of my choice whilst Sheila would choose sherbet Dib Dabs and a packet of Love Hearts.

We also ran to Mary's for groceries for Mum, who would send us off to pick whatever she needed with the instruction that we were to ask Mary to put it in the book. Getting to the shop we would repeat Mum's request, and Mary would pull out her 'tally' book from underneath the counter and make an entry in it, recording whatever it was that we required.

On quite a few occasions I would ask Mary for something and she would refuse, telling me to go back and tell Mum that we couldn't have anything else until our 'account' had been settled. Inevitably we had to steer clear of Mary's for a while until Mum had enough money to pay the bill.

Going to Mary's meant going past Barnard's Bike shop and I would always stop and look through the window at the shiny stainless steel wheels and handle bars, and all the different coloured bikes. I would be lost in another world, dreaming of winning a race on such a lovely machine, my hands cupped around either side of my face as I pressed up close to the glass.

Such was my absorption that Mum would often come out looking for me, telling me to get 'a hurry on' down to Mary's because she needed whatever it was that I was supposed to be fetching. Rushing off I would complete my errand, and if I could I would stop on the way back for just one more, quick peek.

I never realised it, but Mum was aware of my longing for a bike and one day she took me to the shop. It was the morning of my eleventh birthday when Mum said, "Come on Jeff, you are coming with me. I have got a special treat for the birthday boy."

Following her out of the house, I found myself on the step leading into Barnard's. "Go on Jeff, pick the one that you want."

It was a dream come true, and I looked at her not sure if I was hearing correctly. Patting me on the shoulder she repeated, "Go on Jeff, before I change my mind!"

I did not hesitate. I knew exactly which one I wanted, a red ten gear Raleigh racing bike with every possible extra. It even came with a padlock and chain.

Mum must have already spoken to Mr Barnard to organise the finances over a three year period. The bike cost thirty-two pounds which was an absolute fortune for anyone in those days, let alone for a family constantly trying to make ends meet.

My dreamlike state continued – I could not believe how lucky I was, most probably the luckiest and proudest boy in the whole of Liverpool. I loved that bike so much that I almost did not want to ride it.

My mates were all admiring of my new bike begging me for a ride on it, and hours later when Mum wasn't looking I would give them a quick go, carefully inspecting it after each ride to make sure that it was still in perfect condition.

Once Mum was happy that I could ride my bicycle safely I would be able to go a bit further afield and if I was very good I could take it to school. So I practiced and practiced, moving from the relative safety of Durden Street to the challenges of Smithdown Road.

When Mum felt I was ready to cycle to school, I had to take good care of it, promising to chain it up properly in the bike shed every day.

There were quite a few other boys who had bikes but these lads were older, so I was definitely the envy of everyone else. Everyday I would pedal down Smithdown Road building up a great speed, overtaking buses full of friends going to school who would see me flying past on my speed machine. The journey home was never quite so speedy or glorious, as I would be lagging behind the bus, pedaling hard the whole way up the hill encouraged by the shouts of 'faster Red, come on faster!' from my friends through the windows.

I'd had my bike for four weeks when our football team was scheduled to play an away-match at Otters Pool, about four miles from school. Opting to go on my bike, a friend of mine, Alan Joel, and I decided to cycle together. We left school just after four in the afternoon thinking we would make it in plenty of time for the 5 o'clock kick off. We managed to get a bit lost on the way and it took longer to get to the playing ground than we had planned, arriving at just after five! The game had already started and as we pedaled up the path towards the changing rooms our games teacher spotted us.

Running in our direction he shouted out to us to get a move on, "Come on you boys, get in there and get changed quick as you can. We need you on the field now – we are losing. Now hurry up!"

Putting our bikes down alongside the others, Alan and I grabbed our sports bags and headed into the changing rooms emerging on the field a few minutes later. The adrenalin was pumping as we raced over to join our team mates, losing ourselves in the challenge of the game. We won, four goals to three and were all feeling so pleased with ourselves as we headed back to the dressing room, patting each other on the back and telling each other how brilliant we had been.

Glancing over towards the pile of bikes, to admire my lovely red racer from afar, my stomach suddenly lurched with horror. I couldn't see it anywhere. I broke into a run, heading as fast as I could to where I had left it, but it wasn't there. Had one of the other boys hidden it for a laugh?

My mind was a jumble of panicked thoughts – had someone borrowed it during the game or moved it somewhere else for a prank. Alan's bike was still where he had left it, and I noticed that he hadn't chained it up. "Oh shit," I thought to myself, "Did I lock mine?"

I ran around the changing room block looking everywhere to see if it had been hidden, but still could not find it. Otters Pool was a large complex of four football fields, and I could not see anyone amongst the crowds of boys who had been involved in other matches with anything that remotely looked like my bike.

My heart sank as I slowly made my way back into the changing room, starting to feel sick with worry. Repeatedly going over the moments after we arrived at the grounds in my mind, I tried to remember what I had done. The more I thought about it, the worse I began to feel as the horrible reality started to dawn on me. Bending over to pick up my sports bag from amongst the jumble of other bags on the floor, the weight of the bag told me that my nightmare was real. There in the bottom of the bag was the padlock and chain.

I went in search of my teacher, expecting that he would be able to perform some miracle. I found him, talking to a group of other teachers, and hardly waiting for him to finish his sentence, I interrupted.

"Sir," I blurted out, "Sir, please Sir, my bike has been nicked!"

He turned quickly towards me, "What did you say? What has happened? Slow down Pearce and tell me again."

I repeated my story, telling him where I had looked, and asking him for his help.

He turned towards the other teachers who had all been listening, and they all agreed to have a quick look around. I didn't really pay much attention to what they were saying, remaining where I stood, drowning in despair. After a while they all came back, but it was clear from the looks on their faces that they'd had no success.

"I'm sorry Pearce," my teacher said, "There's nothing much else that we can do. No sign of your bike and no one has seen anything suspicious. I suggest that you go to the Police Station and report it."

Locked in my own small world of misery the journey back on the school bus was awful as I ran through the scene ahead of me, breaking the news to Mum.

"Mum" I said to myself quietly. "What am I going to tell Mum?" I wanted to cry with the shame of it all, but not a tear came. Thirty-two pounds for a bike and it was gone. I had well and truly let her down.

Even my team mates seemed to understand what I was going through, and although there was pleasure at our success in the match it was now rather subdued.

Finding Mum in the kitchen I quietly and nervously started to tell her what had happened. Without letting me finish my sorry tale Mum had taken me down to the Police Station in Lawrence Road, and I was standing in front of a Policeman telling him what had happened.

With encouragement to speak up from Mum I told my story. As I neared the end Mum took over, trying to impress upon him the urgency of the situation.

"It's a new red racing bike the only one in the area," she explained. "It's brand new. You must be able to find it."

The Sergeant was sitting at a large desk with a black notebook in front of him, listening carefully to what she had to say, and making notes.

Mum continued, "You must go and find it now; it's only four weeks old and it cost thirty-two pounds. It must be easy to find around here, no-one would have one like it."

The sergeant paused in his note taking and looked up at her. "Mrs Pearce, I am sorry, but it is most probably a different colour by now."

Looking at me, he continued, "Young man, you could call in every other day to see if anyone has found it, but other than that there is not much else we can do."

As Mum and I walked home we were almost silent; I desperately wanted to say something to make it better, and a simple "I am sorry" was not nearly enough to make up for the hurt that I had caused her, so instead I just said nothing, my head down focusing on my feet. Looking at my feet made me realise that I would now have to walk or take a bus, and the days of freedom and fun cycling everywhere were now a thing of the past.

Apart from asking me 'why is it always you?' Mum never got cross or punished me for having been so careless. I went to the Police Station every couple of days to ask if there was news, and all my friends kept look out as well, but it was never seen nor heard of again.

In the meantime, Mum continued to make her monthly payments until after three years the debt was cleared – thirty two pounds of bicycle for somebody else to enjoy.

Chapter Eleven
Blazing Glory

After a four year stint at the Junior School it was time to move on. My fellow inmates from Band C and I travelled the lengthy distance of about 50 metres to Sefton Park Seniors which was just next door.

It was a move that none of us were looking forward to. Our reputation as a class of disruptive no-hopers had preceded us, and we all knew that our teachers would certainly not be giving us a warm welcome. From my own point of view I was dreading it. If I could have left school when I was eleven I would have, but I knew that if I wanted to succeed in any kind of job I would have to be able to read and write. There was no avoiding it, I had another four years to do before I could escape from these educational institutions!

My only saving grace was that I was not going to be alone this time. My mates and I were doing this together; we had shared our lives for four years in the Juniors and knew each others strengths and weaknesses; we were now about to complete the next stage of our growing up and this final stage of our schooling felt a lot less daunting because we had each other to rely on. What's more, for the first time we could all now wear long trousers, something which certainly set us apart from the little 'uns, and made us feel more like 'men'.

Mr Beesley was my favourite teacher; he was an inspiration to many hundreds of pupils who came his way. He knew how to get the best out of us all, finding a strength in each individual child, making them all feel as if they had something worthwhile to contribute; as far as school was concerned, Mr Beesley made the difference.

He was a small man with a youthful appearance, who had to wear a moustache to differentiate himself from the pupils. He drove a little yellow car, a three-wheeled Regal Reliant, and he used to take students to matches and sporting events in it. With three boys crammed in the back, the boot and any spare space stuffed with our sports kit and equipment, and another boy sitting next to him in the front we would literally chug along to our destination.

It was amazing how much we could fit in to that small car, and they were great little cars too. However, they were vulnerable to wind and the slightest gust would catch under the front of the car, raising the front wheel off the road and the bonnet up in the air. All that could be seen from the windscreen was the sky.

Whenever this happened, Mr Beesley would call out to us, "Lean forward boys! Lean forward!" So we would all lean forward, Mr Beesley over the steering wheel and we passengers in our seats, and the front wheel would bump down making contact with the road again. It must have been quite a sight to watch, particularly in autumn when the wind would blow quite strongly, a little car literally bouncing up and down as it drove along full of school boys bobbing about inside it.

Mr Beesley organised all types of different sporting activities, with many of the activities offering extra privileges and benefits (i.e. leaving classes/school early, or returning to class late because of extended training). As a result he had many keen sportsmen, me being one of them, signing up for anything that we could get involved in.

★ ★ ★

I loved swimming. We were fortunate to have a small pool in the school basement and the swim team could use it every dinner time for training; although it was tiny, it made all the difference, building up our technique and speed. This practice began to pay off once we started swimming against other schools in the area and after a while began winning more and more races.

Mr Beesley felt that I was a very promising swimmer encouraging me and spending lots of time on extra training; he even organised a trial for me with the Liverpool School Boys Swimming Team.

One evening, after school, he took me to Anfield School for the trials; they had a large swimming pool where all the training programmes were held.

After having taken part in five different races both he and I felt confident that I had done well, and therefore we were both pleased when I was offered a place in the Liverpool Junior Swimming Team.

My hopes of swimming glory and fame were short-lived however when I learnt that training was held every Saturday and Sunday morning; I couldn't go as it conflicted with my job at the Wash House. Mr Beesley did his best to plead my case with the Senior Coach, but to no avail. If I was not available for training on both mornings I couldn't be part of the team.

Although I was disappointed, it didn't take me too long to get over it. I had my job at the Wash House to do, I could still keep on swimming and racing for the school.

Occasionally Mum and my little sister June would come along to watch and support me in my races. Mum was always proud of me no matter how well I did, but she loved it when I won; we would walk home laughing and talking about the competition all the way, with me narrating every second of my race and June tagging along listening with a smile on her face to her big brother's achievements.

One day at school, Paul Cole started to tease me when I was out in the playground. He had a reputation for being a bit of a hard case, which translated into being a good fighter. Surrounded by his mates, he called out names of 'Mummy's boy' at me.

"Who is a mummy's boy then?" he taunted. "I saw yer last night, walking home with your Mummy!"

His friends were all laughing and teasing me, shouting out 'little boy' and 'Mummy's pet', as well as other unpleasant comments about my mother. I could take his skitting me, but bringing my mother into it was not allowed.

I saw red. I was boiling inside with rage and without stopping to think, ran straight at him, hitting him in his stomach, knocking him to the ground. Landing on top of him, I continued to hit out, and within seconds we were rolling around on top of each.

The bell rang. Our friends pulled us apart, and as we got to our feet, he shouted, "I'll have you out at four o'clock, Pearce."

The school grapevine worked fast; within a couple of hours the whole school knew - the message being passed from boy to boy that 'Cole and Pearce were having a fight at four o'clock.'

I did not want to fight Cole at all but there was no way out. He had laid down the challenge and unless I wanted to be looked upon as a coward by all my friends and literally everyone in the school, I would have to face up to fighting him later that day.

Our crowds of supporters started to build. There was a split in the school, the boys who supported Cole, and those that supported me. Both sides wanted blood. Those with allegiance to Cole supported him because he was ranked as sixth 'cock' of the school, i.e. the sixth best fighter. As for me, I was an unknown, untried, small amateur in the second year; I was a 'nobody'.

As four o'clock drew nearer my supporters started to give me more and more advice, all done in an effort to be helpful. Anyone would have thought that they were professional trainers working in some boxing club for all the wisdom they spouted, yet I could not remember any of them having been involved in a fight themselves. My mind was being filled with nonsense, my stomach was churning with nerves, and there was nothing I could do except put up a brave front.

The clock ticked onwards, the school bell announced the end of the day, and almost as if one massive body, hundreds of boys swarmed through the school doors, across the playground and out of the gates to the 'field of honour', a wide alleyway nearby. Any teachers watching must have realised that there was something afoot, but as soon as we were out of sight, we were out of mind, and were allowed to continue on our way.

I was swept along, surrounded by my group of supporters, pressed in on all sides by helpful advisors. Cole and his crowd were ahead of us, with lads turning back to continue the taunting.

When we got to the alleyway a circle started to form, one half made up of Cole's followers, the other half mine. Hands were pulling off my blazer and more advice was being given as I stood there facing my opponent.

"Cole is going to kill Pearce," someone shouted.

"Cole is history," came back from my side, "He is a piece of piss."

"Pearce is going to knock shit out of him!" called out another from somewhere behind me.

"Pearce is f★ ★ ★and so it went on.

While the two crowds enjoyed hurling abuse at each other, I stood there, almost paralysed to the spot, staring at Cole who was punching the air with his fists looking like a professional featherweight.

I wanted to turn and run. I wanted to say to them all, "I am sorry lads, I have to go and do Mrs Gilbert's shopping," but by this stage there was obviously no chance of that working.

If they had wanted blood before, they really wanted it now; they did not care whose it was. There was no way that I was going to take the risk of disappointing them!

To a chorus of 'oooh, oooh, oooh' and 'fight, fight, fight', cat calls and cheers, I found myself being pushed into the middle of the circle face to face with Cole. He was in front of me, a matter of inches away. I knew he was only two years older, and he was slightly bigger in build, but it was his reputation that was scary. I had been in a couple of small scraps but nothing like this. This was my first title fight, with a whole future lying ahead of me in this new sporting venture.

The adrenaline was rushing through my body, and I found myself feeling exactly the same as I had when I had been on the back of Dad's wagon, or standing in front of the Wash House guarding the prams.

Barry's words rang through my head, as clearly as if he was standing next to me. "Attack, Jeff," I could hear him say, "Attack is the best form of defence."

I just steamed in, hitting him as many times as I could in the face, the ribs, the chest, anywhere I could land a punch. As my knuckles made contact with his nose, pressing it flat against his face, I felt the warm stickiness of his blood starting to trickle down to his chin. The sight of blood spurred me on and I continued to lash out until suddenly he fell to the ground, curling up in a ball to protect himself with his arms around his head.

"Kick him! Kick him!" the spectators were urging me on. "Kick him hard Pearce!"

"No more! No more!" Cole was crying out, wanting me to stop.

I did, and the fight was over. Out of breath I stood there, looking down at Cole where he lay on the ground. I couldn't quite believe it – it really was all over. I was unscathed without even one punch having hit me while Cole lay in a small huddle at my feet. My supporters crowded around me, raising my hands into the air, as if I was a professional boxer who had just been called the winner in some world title fight.

As stated by the rules of school warfare, I automatically took over his position in the school pecking order as sixth cock, meaning I was now the sixth best fighter in the school. Although I liked the title I did not want to have to fight every other day to maintain my position, preferring to keep my head down. As it was I got into enough trouble both in and out of school and wasn't planning on looking for any more!

★ ★ ★

One morning I was enjoying a game of football with the lads in the playground. I was running down the wing with the ball, when I was intercepted by someone from the other team. I tried to push my way past him but he blocked me, and we ended up pushing and shoving each other for a few seconds, before he ran away from me dribbling the ball.

As he ran off I looked down at my hand – how could he be getting away from me if I still had hold of his sleeve. I looked at him again, he was still moving, and then I realised that although he was wearing his school blazer one of the sleeves was now white. It was his white shirt and I had part of his blazer in my possession.

Holding the sleeve up, I waved it about in the air, showing my trophy off to the other players. Everyone stopped what they were doing, falling about with laughter.

"It's alright Red," one of the lads called out, "no need to worry about him – he's 'armless!" This just made us laugh even more.

Once we all stopped laughing I went over to him and apologised, giving him his sleeve back. He looked horrified.

"Thanks a lot Pearce," he said, "Me Mum's going to bloody kill me for this!" Putting his hand into the sleeve, he pulled it back up his arm, trying to make it look as if it was still attached to the rest of his blazer. "I am bloody in for it," he added, "Bloody dead, that's what I am!"

Game over, we headed back into class and got on with our lessons; I gave it no further thought.

The next morning, while we were all gathered in assembly, my name was called out and I was told to report to the Headmaster's Office immediately. Puzzled as to what I had done wrong this time, I made my way upstairs to the office and knocked on the door. I was told to enter, and as I did my questions were answered.

A group of three people stood around the Mr Wolley's desk, solemn expressions on their faces. The blazer was lying flat across the desk with the sleeve placed neatly alongside it.

Mr Woolley, the boy and his mother were all staring at the jacket as if it was the body of a loved one laid out to rest.

"Did you do this Pearce?" the Headmaster demanded.

"Well, yes Sir," I replied hesitantly. "It was an accident Sir, we were just playing."

"What do you have to say for yourself, Pearce?" my interrogator continued. "Do you feel any remorse?"

"Well, y-yes Sir," I stumbled, "I am sorry Sir, but it was just an accident. It happened while we were playing football."

The boy's Mother took over, her shrill tones slicing through the heavy atmosphere in the room. "You are a wicked boy, you have ruined this blazer!"

I stood there dumfounded; my silence taken as an admission of guilt.

"I want a new blazer", she continued to screech. "This one is ruined."

"Go outside Pearce" the stern tones of Mr Woolley cutting through the mothers complaints. "I will deal with you shortly."

After a little while, I was told to go home returning immediately with my Mother. Mum was surprised to see me, and asked me what was wrong. I explained that she needed to come back with me to school, telling her the full story.

Mum sat talking with the Headmaster in his office while I stood outside the door. I could hear everything that was being said. Mum was being told to buy a brand new blazer to replace the damaged one.

I could hear the indignation in Mum's voice as she responded to Mr Woolley's statement. She told him, in no uncertain terms, that the blazer which had been damaged was a hand-me-down, at least five years old, and anyone with any common sense could see that the other woman was trying to pull a fast one.

"It's worth repairing," Mum continued, "But not replacing. I have got five kids of my own to look after, never mind buying her a new one. Who does she think she is?"

Mr Woolley agreed to let Mum have a go at repairing it. He warned her however, that if she did not do a good job of it and it was clear to see that it had been mended, he would have to insist that Mum replaced the blazer.

I was sent back to class whilst Mum went home. I can't really remember the rest of the day as my mind was taken up with the guilt of having caused Mum even more work, worries, and possible financial burden on top of it all!

When I got home later that afternoon she had already started work on it. Pausing in her sewing she said, "Jeff, you have done it again! You are a walking disaster!"

"Mum, I am sorry, I really am sorry. It was an accident, we were just playing," I replied, "I didn't do it on purpose."

She stayed up most of the night, invisibly mending the blazer until it was impossible to tell that the sleeve had ever come off.

Next morning she gave the blazer to me, "Say a prayer on your way to school that your headmaster likes my needle work," was all she said. She had done a superb job, not only mending but cleaning and ironing the garment and making it look better than it had in a long, long time!

Thankfully, the blazer passed Mr Woolley's inspection and we didn't have to buy a new one; from that day on I was very careful when playing football.

★ ★ ★

I was now well into my second year of the Senior's when a new boy enrolled. Steve was a good foot taller than me, being as big as some of the fourth year boys.

I had lots of friends at school, but for some reason was drawn to Steve, and he and I became good friends. It was odd really as we were so different. For example, I was passionate about sport, whilst he wasn't. I made friends easily, he didn't. I walked on the sunny side of the street, he preferred the shadows.

Steve was shy, almost to the point of being introverted. He hardly ever spoke to new people as he had a slight stammer, preferring to spend time with people with whom he felt comfortable. As I got to know him better I discovered, little by little, that he'd had it rough as a child.

He had only been at school for a couple of weeks when John Thomson (Tommo) started to shove him around. Tommo had a quick temper, picking on anyone who was smaller or weaker than him. He would head to the front of the queue at dinner time, pushing his way past anyone who was waiting to be served. If you had something he liked, he would take it off you, and if you tried to stop him he would punch you for your efforts. He was a bully and to go with it a good fighter, frightened of no-one, which had earned him the title first cock of the school. He enjoyed his position in the school pecking order, and took pleasure in bullying everyone else.

One afternoon Tommo came up to Steve and started having another go at him, calling him names, and mimicking his stammer, egged on by his mates around him. Steve's face was starting to redden, and he was shaking.

I tried to intervene. "Leave him alone Tommo, he's alright, he's one of the lads."

Having told me to 'shut-it Pearce', Tommo continued to push Steve. "Do you fancy a go? Do you fancy taking me on? Do ya? Do ya?" shoving and punching him in the arm.

There was a flash of movement, as Steve head-butted him in the face; Tommo went down like a sack of spuds to the ground, blood pouring out of his nose.

I suddenly noticed that everyone on the playground was standing still, watching what was going on, waiting to see if Tommo was going to get up. He didn't and as he lay there a buzz of voices started to spread, one boy telling the other about what they had seen. The cock of the school was down, and it was Steve 'who did it'.

His mates rapidly disappeared with fright in case they were next, so it was left to us to pick Tommo up off the tarmac and cover for Steve as a teacher came over to see what was going on.

"He fell over Sir" we said, "It was an accident. He tripped."

Knowing that he would get nothing further out of us, the teacher took Tommo to the school nurse, and as we later found out he'd had to go to hospital as he had a broken nose.

Steve automatically became the cock of the school. It wasn't just the fact that he stood up to the older bully, but it was the speed in which he had taken him out. Steve was the youngest cock of the school ever, achieving that position at the tender age of 12.

He relished his new position in the school, often fighting to hold on to his title in larger 'matches' at four o'clock, and definitely enjoying smaller brawls during the day. He remained number one until the day he left.

Ironically enough, Steve wasn't a bully. Having been on the receiving end of bullying for much of his childhood, he knew exactly what it felt like, and therefore never subjected anyone else to it.

★ ★ ★

Our school definitely believed in corporal punishment; misbehaviour was unacceptable and dealt with immediately.

Mr Woolley was a frail figure of a man, with thinning white hair, who looked ghostly and much older than his years. We all thought that he must have been at least eighty years old if not more, but anyone older than thirty looks ancient to a young boy.

He was a disciplinarian and strongly believed that if any boy stepped out of line in any way, they should be properly punished. His favourite saying was 'You need knocking into shape boy', and he would certainly 'knock'.

If we were caught misbehaving in class, for example talking or throwing paper pellets at each other, we were either dealt with on the spot or sent to see Mr Woolley.

Once outside the Headmaster's Office, we had to knock on the door and wait for a response. Sometimes a few minutes would go by, so we would knock again and remain outside until a voice called out, "Come in boy."

It was a sizeable office, with windows overlooking the playground. In the middle of the room was an oversized desk at which he sat, and behind him in the left hand corner stood an ornate coat stand. As you approached across the highly polished parquet floor he would continue writing, head down looking at his papers.

"Why are you here boy?"

"I have been sent by Mr Roberts, Sir," I would say.

He would slowly raise his head, his eyes focusing on me over the top of his glasses, which were balanced on the end of his nose. "Ah Pearce," he stated, knowing my name well as I was such a regular visitor, "And why has Mr Roberts sent you?"

"For misbehaving Sir."

"What type of misbehaving, Pearce?" he would ask.

"Talking Sir," I would reply. (No matter what the real crime, we would always plead the lesser offence which was talking, therefore receiving the lightest sentence.)

"You are here to learn boy, not to talk in class. I'll teach you not to talk in class, hold your hand out."

Getting up out of his chair he walked over to the coat stand in the corner and contemplated the bamboo canes which were arranged in the rack at the bottom, in amongst a black umbrella or two.

He'd glance at me, as if sizing me up as though it bore a direct relevance on his selection of cane, before making his choice. He pulled a thin strip of bamboo out of the umbrella rack and flexed it, bending it backwards and forwards and slashing it through the air a few times like a swordsman with a rapier as he walked over to where I stood.

Standing in front of his desk with my arm held out at a right angle to my body, palm upturned, I would watch as he positioned himself in front of me, resting the cane lightly on the palm of my hand, lining it up.

He would slowly raise his hand right back so that the cane was almost completely over his shoulder, before bringing it down with great speed on to my waiting hand. There would be a searing feeling as the bamboo made contact with my skin, the pain shooting up my arm and registering with my brain, making me want to check that my fingers were still attached.

I endured this a couple of times before I started to realise that it was actually a matter of the punishment not fitting the crime; such lashings were out of proportion with the misdemeanours committed by small boys.

I talked about it with my friends and found out that Mr Woolley was actually supposed to be as blind as a bat; there was a way to be punished without feeling a thing.

Timing was everything. As the cane sliced down through the air, and at exactly the precise moment of contact, I would snatch my hand back towards my mouth, protesting with pain, blowing on the palm and acting as if the bamboo had really hit me.

Once Mr Woolley had finished with the first hand, he would instruct me to hold out the other, and the process would begin all over again. After the required number of lashes, Mr Woolley would finish off with a short lecture, whilst I would stand there shaking both my hands in the air, and blowing on the palms 'trying' to alleviate the pain.

Back in the classroom, I continued with my Oscar winning performance for the benefit of the teacher who had sent me in the first place; a subdued entrance, head hanging as if in shame, gently blowing on my painful hands and looking very sorry for myself.

Once the teacher was satisfied that I had been suitably chastised, I would return to my desk, quickly sending a glance out to my mates that I was ok, and if I could, giving them all a quick thumbs up – Woolley had missed again!

Woolley must have got wise to this as he suddenly changed tactic. Prepared for a caning on our hands we were all thrown by his order to 'bend over' so that we could be caned on the backside. Not to be defeated however, we came up with our own strategy, placing an exercise book down the seat of our trousers before going in to his office.

Woolley must have been deaf as well as blind – bamboo hitting a notebook is a very different sound to bamboo hitting a soft bottom, and yet he never seemed to notice!

Mr Sutcliffe was our Geography teacher, a large overweight man, whose personality seemed as unpleasant as his appearance. He must have weighed at least 20 stone and was very pale, with slightly bulging eyes and thinning hair which he wore in a comb over. His hands were very podgy and always felt cold and damp, a bit like the skin on a toad. His favourite implement of torture was a metal ruler, which he would wrap across the back of your hand, making sure to get the knuckles if possible.

He would patrol up and down the aisles between the rows of desks, hitting the palm of his hand with his ruler, on the lookout for someone he could chastise on the flimsiest of reasons. If he thought that you were talking, not looking at the right page in your book, or even not sitting correctly (to name a few crimes) he would grab hold of your arm at the wrist, holding it in front of him with one hand whilst he lashed down on your knuckles with the ruler held in the other. And then he would do it again and again and again until he was satisfied that he had hurt you enough. This normally meant that the knuckles had started to swell, or at the very least the skin was broken and he could see blood.

When he was not patrolling the classroom, or sitting at his desk, he would stand in front of the blackboard drawing a map, or writing country names for us to learn.

Even though his back was turned to the class he was still aware of every sound and movement we made. If there was anything that seemed out of place, he would suddenly turn, hurling the blackboard duster in the direction of the noise, with the same speed and accuracy that a toad strikes out at an insect with its tongue.

The wooden duster sped through the air like a missile launched from a rocket and anyone in the firing line would duck, whilst the rest of us would watch in fascinated horror. As the duster hit either a desk, or a wall, there would be a sharp noise, instilling fear in all the boys in the room. In hindsight it was fortunate that the duster never made contact with someone's head, as the hard wooden edges would have caused a grave injury; as it was there were enough bruises received as it bounced off a shoulder or arm before landing on the floor.

Sutcliffe enjoyed being cruel.

Mr Cooper, the Deputy Headmaster was the most feared. He was over six foot tall, a giant of a man with the strength to match his size. He would give you two of the best on the palm of each hand, his cane never missing its target, and the strength and speed behind each lash made it exceedingly painful.

Every boy in the school was terrified of Mr Cooper, except one, my mate Steve.

One day, Mr Cooper was taking our class when Steve arrived ten minutes late. Quietly opening the door, he tried to sneak in and get to his desk without Mr Cooper noticing, but he was not in luck.

Just as he sat down, Mr Cooper called out, "Stand up Chan. Why are you late? And what is that you are wearing?"

Steve had come into school wearing the latest fashion, a dark navy denim bib and brace which he had bleached in the bath at home. It was certainly not the school uniform and he was asking for trouble.

"Come here boy; at once." Mr Cooper instructed.

Steve got out of his seat and walked over to where Mr Cooper was standing.

"Why haven't you got your school uniform on?" the teacher demanded.

Steve looked up at him. "I can't afford one Sir," he said, before turning around to look at the rest of us, throwing us all a quick, furtive smile.

"Nonsense, boy. What do you mean you can't afford a school uniform?" By now Mr Cooper was leaning over Steve where he stood, shouting at him as if he was trying to subdue Steve into nothingness on the classroom floor.

"I live with my grandmother Sir," said Steve, "And she hasn't got any money to buy me a uniform."

Mr Cooper was not interested in what Steve had to say. "Rubbish! That is just a pack of lies. You go home at once and DO NOT DARE to come back to this school until you are wearing the correct school uniform."

Mr Cooper was getting very annoyed as Steve was not cowering in front of him; instead he remained still, holding his ground. We all sat there spellbound as the drama continued to unfold.

Something must have snapped inside Mr Cooper, as he started to shout even louder. "I told you to get out now!" he bellowed, starting to push at Steve as if to propel him towards the door.

Steve did not move an inch. Pulling himself up to his full height, he looked at the Deputy Head and said very quietly, "Don't you dare push me again. Get your hands off me now."

Cooper did not listen; instead he pushed Steve even harder, this time with both hands on the chest and continued shouting at him. "Get out of here at once!"

As we all watched, Steve leant back, as if giving way to the pressure being exerted by the teacher. Suddenly the tables were turned as he catapulted forward, his forehead making contact with Mr Coopers face. It was without a doubt, the most spectacular "scouser kiss" that we had ever seen.

For a split second the Deputy Head remained upright, before his legs buckled underneath him and he fell to the floor; he was out for the count. There was not one single boy who did not gasp out loud before a horrified silence descended over the classroom. What Steve had done was unthinkable, nobody fought back with a teacher, let alone knocked them out. Not a word was said as we all sat there.

It was Steve who broke the silence. "You can stick your fucking school up your fucking arse, Cooper" he said, looking down at the prostrate body of the teacher at his feet.

Thirty-three pairs of eyes watched him as he walked towards the door. "Come on Jeff," he called over to me, "Let's go and leave this fucking shit heap of a school now."

Thirty-two pairs of eyes turned in my direction, waiting for my reply. I sat firm in my seat, and looked at my mate, weighing up my options. "No way mate," I finally said. "I am sorry Steve, but I have only got six months left, and I intended to stick it to the end."

Steve never returned to school.

Chapter Twelve
Silver Blades

O ccasionally in life you may find yourself being in the right place at the right time.

Growing up in the sixties was an exciting time for any teenager, let alone for those lucky enough to be in Liverpool. Barry and Lesley were two of these lucky teenagers.

A new sound was emerging which was called the Mersey Beat, with the Beatles leading the way. They had one hit after the other, and Beatlemania started to spread further south before taking the world by storm.

Fashion changed dramatically, and in many cases overnight. Heavily influenced by their pop idols teenagers would dress as replicas. Beatle hair cuts were massively popular with young men, as were the round collared suits with narrow bottom trousers and pointed Cuban heeled boots. Barry was so meticulous in his attention to detail that he was sometimes mistaken for one of the Beatles (something which he loved!).

For the first time teenagers were developing an identity of their own. They found their voice, expressing it in the way they dressed, the music they listened to and how they danced.

What was more, having found their voice, they were making themselves heard, and were standing up for what they believed in. It was the start of a revolution.

Barry was very much part of this revolution. He spent a great deal of his time at the Cavern Club, listening to the music and dancing. Barry was a good dancer, and was asked if he would like to appear on a television programme that was being filmed about the Beatles the following week. Of course he accepted!

Barry asked his boss, Tom Browner if he could have the afternoon off, but was told in no uncertain terms that would not be possible. When Barry explained the reason why, it made no difference whatsoever, to the point that Mr Browner warned him that if he didn't show up for work then he wouldn't have a job to come back to.

So he decided it was worth the risk, and took the day off. On the 17th October 1962 he spent the afternoon and early evening at the Cavern Club, dancing to the Beatles as the played live for a Granada Television Programme entitled 'People and Places'. Mum, Lesley, Sheila and I watched it on tv, singing along to the popular hits such as 'Some Other Guy' and 'Love Me Do'.

It was a little bit of television history for all of us. For the Beatles it was their first television performance, whilst for the Pearce's it was the first time anyone in our family had appeared on television. We all caught a glimpse of Barry doing the Cavern Stomp, right by the stage, in such close proximity to the 'Fab Four'.

The fact that he had appeared on tv made Barry, in my eyes, almost as famous as the Beatles himself, and as most of the kids in our street had also seen the programme, he became a local legend for a little while.

Unfortunately, Mr Browner was not so impressed, and when Barry reported for work the following day, he was told that he no longer had a job. His unemployment lasted for four weeks before Mr Browner offered him his old job back.

Although I was too young to really be involved, I loved watching Barry getting ready to go out. Sitting on my bunk, I would be impressed by his Beatle hair cut, and black pointy-toed, Cuban-heeled boots. I particularly loved the boots, and managed to persuade Mum to buy me a pair for Christmas that year as my main present.

They had two inch heels, and I felt so cool as I swaggered down to see Ian and my other friends on Christmas day. Well, I thought I swaggered, but in reality I staggered, and wobbled from side to side and fell off them every few steps of the way, but after a short while I got the knack of it. Nine year old boys are not really designed to wear two inch Cuban heels! Once I had my Beatle Boots I became a slave to fashion.

Lesley was now seventeen, and very attractive. On Friday evenings I would be waiting for her at the bus stop, as Fridays were pay day, and she would always buy Sheila and me a bag of sweets each on her way home.

As the six o'clock bus slowed down, Lesley would be standing on the platform at the back of the bus waiting for it to stop. Stepping down on to the pavement, she would pause for a minute, allowing her admirers to do what they did best – admire her!

Lesley was tall and slim, with long blonde hair that fell in soft curls down her back, and a lovely smile. Dressed in a mini skirt with long legs that disappeared into knee high boots she was the latest thing in fashion. Lesley used her walk. She had an almost feline sensuality in the way she swung her hips, head held high, and arm draped casually across my shoulder.

There was something about Lesley and her impact on men. If she walked past a guy in the street, he would inevitably stop and look back at her for a second glance. If she was on the bus, blokes would sit in awe, casting surreptitious glances in her direction, trying to catch her attention.

Rising to get off the bus, she would afford them a clear view of her sheer gorgeousness, so that by the time she had stepped off the bus, the small windows used for ventilation would have been opened, and wolf whistles and shouts of "What are you doing tonight beautiful?" could be heard.

She also seemed to have a constant stream of admirers who would come knocking on our front door in the hopes of being able to ask her out on a date. Most were unsuccessful as Mum would answer the door, sending them packing in no time, however, if Lesley got there first then there was a faint glimmer of hope for the young suitor.

She was very astute and knew what most of the lads were after, so she created a safety mechanism in her little brother.

After accepting the invitation, she would tell her new date that she had to look after me, and that if he wanted to take her out, I would have to come too. They nearly always agreed, and we would go to either the cinema or to the local fairground.

Trips to the cinema were the most amusing. I can remember going to see Cliff Richard in 'Summer Holiday', and sitting next to Lesley on one side, whilst her date was on the other. The lights had dimmed, I had my bag of sweets, and was starting to enjoy the film, when I felt something brushing across the top of my head. Batting whatever it was away with my hand, I settled back in to my seat, eyes on the screen. A few minutes later I felt it again, something moving lightly across the top of my head.

"Stop it," I called out in a loud voice.

There was a flurry of movement and a giggle from Lesley before I realised what was going on. Her poor date had been trying to slowly put his arm around her shoulder without Lesley noticing, and my outburst had stopped him dead in his tracks. No doubt he had another go, but would have taken care to avoid my head.

When we went to the fair I was not in the least bit bothered if I was left to my own devices for ten minutes or so while the young man tried to sneak a quick kiss with Lesley; I was having too much fun and going on as many rides as I could. Being Lesley's chaperone was great for me but I am not too sure that her admirers felt the same way, I was the perfect pain in the arse.

★ ★ ★

Good fortune also smiled upon Sheila and me, as we too found ourselves in the right place at the right time.

Dad's oldest sister Aunty Doris worked in the Silver Blades Ice Rink in Kensington about three to four miles from our house; one afternoon she came by with two free tickets for the rink which she gave to Sheila and me. The following Sunday the two of us caught a bus to Kensington, and using the tickets we had been given entered a whole new world, which we both fell in love with. After our first visit, and seeing how much fun we had, Aunty Doris tried to get us tickets as often as possible.

The first impression that hit us was the smell of sweaty feet as we lined up to hire our skates. Shoes in one hand, we would slowly shuffle along to the counter, where we exchanged them for boots. The closer you got, the stronger the smell. The whole hire shop smelt of hundreds if not thousands of sweaty feet.

Boots on, we made our way out to the ice. Both hands gripping the barrier tightly, as if holding on for dear life, we cautiously put one foot and then the other on to the icy surface. As soon as the metal blades made contact with the ice our feet shot off in different directions taking our legs with them. Having only just got them back under control they would disappear again, either going sideways to the left and the right or shooting out to the back or the front, making us tumble to the ice in an untidy bruised heap.

After a while we progressed to holding on with one hand, but this was a little trickier and we started to fall more frequently. The longer we skated, the more we laughed, until we found ourselves laughing the whole time. The funniest thing was when we both fell over at the same time, lying flat on the ice legs in the air, and paralysed with giggles. Although we would try to help each other up, it would just make matters worse, and the only way to get up on our feet was to crawl back to the barrier, so we could start all over again.

Skating was fun – we laughed a lot as we improved, and soon learnt to love the freedom of movement as we glided around and around the rink.

Little did I know when I started skating, that the Silver Blades Ice Rink would in fact become, my saving grace.

The poorer areas of Liverpool, like any big city, were also the rougher areas, and crime flourished from an early age. It was almost an accepted part of growing up, as smaller boys were encouraged to follow in the footsteps of the older lads, starting with petty theft before graduating to more serious crimes.

The lads I knocked around with were no exception to this rule. Unlocked cars and the backs of lorries were our first training grounds, on the lookout for anything worth nicking. The next step in this criminal education was instruction in the art of breaking in to small shops, which if completed successfully meant promotion to the more profitable targets – people's houses.

Although I explored the 'criminal underworld' on a couple of occasions, I never did feel comfortable and used to suffer from a permanent sick feeling at the bottom of my stomach whenever we were up to no good. I liked my friends and wanted to be accepted as part of the gang, but this was not the way it was going to happen, this was not the life for me.

My growing passion for skating meant that I spent less and less time hanging around on street corners, part of a gang of lads just looking for something to do.

Instead I found myself on the ice, surrounded by all sorts of people, some like Sheila and me, and others who stood apart from us all because of the way they were dressed, and the way that they skated. The girls would wear little skirts or skating tutu's, their legs encased in opaque tights, whilst the boys wore slim fitting trousers and smart waistcoats.

During the interval we would go and see Aunty Doris who worked in the refreshment kiosk, who would always give us a bottle of Coca Cola and a packet of Toffee Poppets. She knew that we didn't have any money, and loved to treat us in whatever way she could, getting great pleasure just from seeing us having a wonderful time.

Both Sheila and I slowly started to make new friends at the ice rink, which made going there even more fun. I teamed up with a boy called Bernie Snag who lived not too far away from me. Bernie and I had history in common, both suffering from an absent father. He lived with his Mother (whom he adored), his brother Terry, and sister Cathleen in a run down four-storey tenement block, ironically called Paddington Gardens. Like me, Bernie was on the verge of falling in with the wrong crowd until he came ice-skating one day, and found something that he would much rather do with his time.

The Silver Blades Ice Rink was the only one in Liverpool and was a very popular meeting place. Bernie and I would meet up on Sunday afternoons and Wednesday nights to begin with so that we could skate together. I was still very busy with all my jobs, running errands for Mrs Gilbert every afternoon after school, and working Saturday mornings at the Wash House.

Sheila got on very well with one of our cousins Beverly, who was about the same age as her, and they started skating together whilst Bernie and I were keeping each other company. It was a nice foursome, as the girls could do what they wanted, whilst Bernie and I would be more adventurous, testing our new found skills, and practising skating faster and faster, whilst still all keeping and eye on each other.

Arriving early, Bernie and I used to watch the 'posh' kids having their lessons, listening to what the teacher had to say, and paying close attention to what was going on. As soon as the lessons were over, and the ice cleared for the next session, Bernie and I would put on our skates and head down to the rink, practicing what we had seen and heard, until we became as good as the others.

It was the skates, however which separated those with more money from those with less. Good skaters and those who could afford them wore their own boots, black if you were a boy and white if you were a girl. Bernie and I wore rental boots, which were black with a white stripe on them, making them very identifiable as hire boots. They were so horrible to look at that no one would have ever wanted to steal them.

As you came into the ice rink there was small shop in the lobby which sold new boots, but they were way too expensive for us to buy. There was a notice board however, where second hand boots were advertised for sale. As the four of us longed to own our own boots, we all saved up for a while, and a few months later we soon realised our dream.

Sitting on the benches, putting *our* boots on and doing up the laces we felt so proud – we were the bee's knee's. And what an improvement to our skating. Bernie and I with black boots on our feet suddenly became Kings of the Ice, swishing and slicing, flying forwards and back, and spinning around. Not only were the boots actually better for skating in, but psychologically we were now in a different category altogether – we were seen as serious skaters.

We had also made friends with a boy called John, one of the 'posh' kids who had lessons, he would help us some of the time, passing on what he had learned in his private lessons that morning so Bernie and I found ourselves getting better and better; we could skate backwards as fast as we could skate forwards, altering direction as we moved in a straight line, skating in figure eights the loops getting smaller and smaller all the time.

We skated to music played by a man in a smart white jacket and red bow-tie sitting at the organ. Half way through a session, he would solemnly announce that it was time for all the skaters to clear the ice, as the next fifteen minutes were for the more advance skaters only. Suddenly the ice rink would clear, and instead of one hundred and fifty skaters crowding its surface there would be twenty or so left. Bernie, John and I loved this time, as we had the chance to strut our stuff, practising all the moves we had learnt, and even attracting the attention of some of the girls sitting on the benches around the rink.

The Silver Blades had the most peculiar opening hours. This was due to the fact that ice can only survive for so many hours before it needs to be resurfaced and refrozen. At weekends, and during school holidays, they had three daily sessions, from 9.30 – 12.30, 2.00 – 5.00 and 7.30-10.30pm, whilst during the week they were only open in the evenings from 7.30 – 10.30.

If we wanted to enjoy all three sessions on a Sunday, we had to pay three times. This wasn't a problem for John, who had a monthly pass paid for by his parents, but for Bernie and me it was a different matter; there was no way we could afford it, so we devised a plan.

There was a balcony on the first floor which ran the whole way around the rink, hardly used by spectators, in fact almost no one ever went up there. Whilst Bernie and I had been exploring one afternoon, we had found a door at the back of the balcony, through which were steps leading to an old changing room. This room was used by the speed skating team, when they came for their practices on Tuesday and Thursday night and no one else. We decided to hide in there between sessions; hopefully no-one would think of looking for two stowaways, and we would remain undiscovered.

The first Sunday Bernie and I put our plan into action, we were like nervous wrecks. As 12.30 approached I told Sheila that I was going to Bernie's house and would see her later. I couldn't tell her what I was really up to as she would never have allowed me to do anything like that, particularly with Aunty Doris working at the rink – it would have been too embarrassing for all the family if we were caught. As quickly and as quietly as possible we made our way upstairs, reaching the shelter of the changing room where we then sat down to wait.

The room had benches lining the walls on three sides, with pegs above the benches. In the middle of the room was a row of metal lockers, and we decided that if we heard footsteps on the stairs we could climb inside the lockers and remain hidden until the coast was clear.

We were so nervous of being found out that we dared not make a noise, hardly breathing let alone whispering in case anyone overheard us. The time seemed to drag so slowly, and every creak or sound we heard became a warning of imminent disaster, we were about to be discovered.

Finally, one and a half hours later, we heard the organ music starting up, and knew that we had almost succeeded. Now all we had to do was to get back down on to the ice without being detected. We opened the locker room door as quietly as possible, and tiptoed down the stairs, pausing if a stair creaked. Then, opening the door on to the balcony, we peered through the narrow gap to make sure that the coast was clear.

Fortunately, there was no sign of the dreaded Mr Kay, who was the Manager of the rink, a man who seemed to have eyes in the back of his head, never missing a trick. Keeping low, we made a dash for the stairs, skates clutched to our chest so that they wouldn't bump against anything and make a noise.

The relief of success made our enjoyment of being back on the ice even greater; John came over to congratulate us on our adventure, and as we laughed and skated around, Bernie and I felt like we had reached our destination in one piece, two stowaways who had crossed the Seven Seas.

We managed to pull this off, for at least the next eight or nine Sundays, each time spending the whole day and night at the rink, and only paying once. Then something happened which changed it all.

A man named Hughie ran the ice-gang, and Bernie and I had been pestering him for months, begging him to give us a job in his gang. One afternoon, we had emerged from our hiding spot and were about to head out on to the ice for the beginning of the seven thirty session, when a hand landed on my shoulder. Startled I turned to find Hughie standing behind me with a solemn expression on his face. I immediately thought that Bernie and I had been found out and were about to be punished. As the weight of Hughie's hand bore down on my shoulder, I started to imagine all the different types of punishment that awaited me. Was it to be public humiliation in front of everyone (including Aunty Doris)? A lashing at the hands of Mr Kay while being watched by my friends and family? Or something even worse – being banned for life from the ice rink, never to be able to skate ever again?

I was finished; it was all over for Bernie and me.

Before I could say anything, Hughie spoke.

"Lads, I need to talk to you in my office." Bernie and I looked at each other, fear written all over our face. Letting go of my shoulder Hughie started to walk in front of us, with Bernie and me behind. Our legs were shaking so badly we could hardly keep up, and we were frantically signaling to one another about what fate awaited us. Bernie was doing a wonderful impersonation of a hang mans noose – yes, we were dead men!

Getting to his office, Hughie sat down at his desk before he continued.

"You know those jobs which you two have been mithering me about, well they are now available. What do you think? Do you still want them?"

I was so overwhelmed with relief I nearly wet my pants. Hughie was waiting for our answer, so seeing that I had lost my voice, Bernie jumped in for us both.

"Dead right we do," he almost shouted. I just stood there next to him, nodding as if my head was on a spring, a big grin on my face.

So we became part of the ice-gang, working for Hughie, and in return we got a small wage, but most importantly free permanent passes which allowed us to come in and out of the rink whenever we wanted. Our dreams had become true.

I was totally hooked on skating, and gave up my job at the Wash House to be able to better concentrate on my new job at the rink, and my passion for the sport. Bernie and I literally lived there during every free moment; in the eight weeks of the summer holidays we never missed a day, and if we could, we would have slept there every night. It was the best time of our lives. For the first time we both felt really important doing proper jobs, and we also felt as if we belonged to something bigger than the small worlds we had grown up in.

Starting on the brushes, we work hard for the first year, becoming experienced scrapers. This was a job normally done by older boys, who could skate well, but there we were, twelve years old and equally as good. We were good skaters by now and ready for the next challenge in our lives.

As with everything in the sixties, times were changing, and Mr Kay announced that he was going to build a discotheque on the balcony. He had cottoned on to the popularity of the music scene elsewhere and decided to capitalise on the unused space to attract teenagers who were not just interested in skating but also wanted to dance. So the organist left, and was replaced by a DJ who played the latest records.

At about this time Bernie and I discovered our hormones. Suddenly girls were mysterious, they smelt nice, they moved differently, and we noticed that they had a beauty about them which hadn't been apparent to us before. The girls we saw and knew where also changing, developing into young women, and these physical changes fascinated us. Girls were no longer just sisters or friends, they were objects of desire.

One day I was on the ice with Bernie when a girl skated over and told me that her friend fancied me. She pointed towards another girl who was on the other side of the rink, sort of looking in our direction. Seeing me looking over towards her, she gave me a little smile of encouragement, before spinning off in the opposite direction.

I had never been told that a girl fancied me before, and this was a new and exciting situation to be in.

Over the next two weeks my life changed again. Every time I was at the rink I was constantly on the lookout for her, sometimes so busily looking around me that I would bump into other skaters. If I did catch a glimpse of her, I would do a complicated skating routine to impress her.

I washed my hair every day. Mum noticed my sudden interest in my appearance and commented that if I washed it any more it would all fall out. I was helping myself to Barry's Old Spice, which I would liberally splash all over my face, and leave the house smelling like a tart's boudoir, generating some peculiar looks from the men on the bus as I travelled to the ice rink. I reeked!

Clothes became important, with Mum trying to keep up with my laundry demands for my favourite jeans and shirts, and even my boots got more polishing than usual! It was all part and parcel of creating the right impression.

I was a young teenager with a crush, and I don't even think I really realised what was going on. A girl had sent her friend over to me to tell me that she fancied me, and I was behaving in a totally strange manner. I couldn't even think straight.

She became the focal point of my thoughts, both day and night, which was odd as I had not spoken to her, and did not even know her name. The power of the word 'fancy' was quite overwhelming and my whole life was changing because of it. And then one day, my new, fragile world shattered.

I was on the rink with Bernie, doing my stuff for the benefit of the new interest in my life, when her friend glided over to me. Swishing to a stop next to me, she said in a very matter of fact tone, "My friend doesn't fancy you any more. She fancies your mate!" before skating off, leaving me devastated.

I looked at Bernie, confused. How could she change her mind, what had I done wrong? She had never spoken to me, let alone kissed me, how could she know what I was like? How could she do this to me? One minute make me feel special, a lad a girl fancied out of the hundreds of other lads on the rink, and then ...... nothing. I was even more confused than before, and worse than that experiencing female rejection for the first time.

Looking at Bernie, I gave him my opinion. "Now it's your bloody turn. Good luck mate, you will need it."

The new discotheque had now opened, and it was called the Bee Hive. As we were not sixteen, Bernie and I had to content ourselves with sitting on the balcony watching the boys and girls dancing with each other through the glass that made up two sides of the dance floor.

We could see them performing intricate steps, swaying their bodies in time to the music, arms making complicated patterns in the air, whilst their feet kept beat on the dance floor. The music was new as well, as it came from further afield than Liverpool. Interspersed with songs from our favourites were new tunes performed by groups such as The Four Tops, and the Stylistics, The Temptations and Diana Ross; Tamla Motown had arrived in Liverpool.

Clothing and styles were becoming more diversified too, with the boys wearing their hair in shorter styles, looking like Perry Como. Suits became sharper, and more tailored, and were made out of shiny sharkskin or two-tone mohair, whilst shirts had button down collars and were made by designers like Ben Sherman. Como shoes were also in fashion, with the favourite colour being the deep red of ox-blood. The girls were the female mirror image, with short skirted suits also made from mohair. A more feminine Ben Sherman shirt would be tucked into their waistbands and their feet would be tucked into lace up brogues. Their hair was stylish and sharp, cut short at the back with longer pieces arranged on either side of their face, echoing their jaw-lines.

These boys and girls we saw dancing at the Bee Hive were the mods and modettes of the sixties; whilst the youth of Great Britain set a new craze, Bernie and I found our new look.

★ ★ ★

Not long after my first 'failed' romance, I noticed a very pretty young girl called Kimberley, known to everyone as Kim. She not only was the about the same age as me, but also the same height, which made it (in my opinion) a perfect match. She had lovely shoulder length golden blonde hair which she wore in a pony tail, and big blue eyes.

Whenever I spotted her on the ice with her friends, I would start to skate closer to her, casually getting nearer and nearer until I was able to suddenly appear surprised at seeing her there. After I had done this a couple of times, I plucked up courage to not only start skating alongside her, but also to talk to her. And our conversations were fascinating.

"Hi," I would say, as we started to skate around the rink together.

"Hi," she would respond, smiling at me. Silence would then fall for a few moments.

"How are you?" I would ask as we started on our second lap.

"Fine," she would reply, "And you?"

"Good," as we corned into the third lap, and a few more minutes silence.

"Not too busy today." I would say, starting up the conversation again."

"No, it's good," she would reply.

On our fourth lap, she noticed some of her friends standing talking. "Must go. Bye" With a dazzling smile and a wave she was off.

"See you soon," I would call after her retreating back, my heart pounding with happiness. I had waited all week for this moment, and now I had another week to go before I could speak to her again. Enough time to practice my lines.

And that's how I fell in love.

Teenage hormones kicked into overdrive causing havoc with my emotions. Although the feelings were similar to my first encounter with a member of the opposite sex, everything was different this time. For a start I was doing the chasing, and started to feel like any other young man when he finds an attractive girl to pursue.

Having decided that I really fancied her, I made a momentous decision; Kim was going to be my first real girlfriend, and I was going to ask her out on a date.

Such a major undertaking required a great deal of planning, and I discussed my strategy with Bernie endlessly, what was the best way to make it all happen. In the end I decided on a very simple plan.

Kim caught the same bus home as I did, getting off a couple of stops before I did. After a great deal of input on

Bernie's part, and endless speculation on mine, I decided to keep it as simple as possible. I would ask her if I could escort her home after we had both been skating.

I was so nervous, and like all young boys, scared of rejection, so it took me several weeks to pluck up the courage and finally ask her. From the way I was behaving, anyone would have thought that I was about to propose to her, offering her a life long commitment, not just a simple bus ride home which she made every day in any case!

We had been circling the ice for a good few minutes and she was on her own, her friends having gone for refreshments, which made it so much easier, as I would have not have an audience if she said 'no', and therefore no-one to laugh at my shame. Taking a deep breath, I launched into my proposal, trying to sound as casual as possible, hoping that she wouldn't notice the tremor in my voice, and praying that my voice wouldn't turn into a high pitched squeak.

"Can I take you home after skating tonight?" I asked.

"Yes." She smiled at me as if she had known for some weeks that I was going to ask her this, and she had rehearsed her answer.

Was it really that simple? I let out my breath with a huge sigh of relief, which I am sure was heard the whole way around the rink. I was amazed. She had said yes!

I suddenly had to tell Bernie, and mumbling some excuse, skated away as fast as I could, looking for my friend everywhere so that I could share my good news with him. It was official, I was about to have my first date!

So much planning had gone into my first date that I knew exactly what I had to do. We were going to get off the bus together at her stop and then I was going to walk her to her front door. When we were there, after a few minutes of casual conversation, I was going to lean forward and give her a kiss goodnight, creating the impression that this was something I had done lots of times before. Kim was going to be so impressed that she would want to go out with me again.

That evening once the ice rink had closed, we left the building walking towards the bus stop, side by side. Kim linked her arm through mine as if it was the most natural thing in the world. I felt like an adult – this whole dating thing was so grown up; we were like a young couple of twenty year olds, not youngsters of thirteen.

My confidence started to wane however as we stood waiting for the bus to arrive, a wait which seemed to go on for ever and ever. There were quite a few men and women waiting as well, and most of them seemed to have been to the pub judging from the raucous laughter and slightly rowdy behaviour. I realised that as far as the other people there were concerned we were just two kids, and it might look a bit silly if I continued to play the courting couple with her. I didn't want to let myself open for teasing, not on such an important evening! At that moment I also wished that she would let go of my arm.

As the minutes ticked by, I found myself becoming quieter and quieter, even losing my ability to talk to Kim, so the two of us just stood there awkwardly, an uncomfortable silence between us. The sight of the headlights coming along the road was most welcoming; once we were on the bus it would all be ok and I could carry on as planned.

Slowing to a halt at the stop, the conductor called out 'Upstairs only,' to the waiting passengers indicating that downstairs was full. We climbed the circular staircase, me leading the way with Kim following closely behind. As soon as I was able to see, I started scanning the crowded level, looking for two seats together.

I could not have picked a worse evening for a first date. The top deck was almost completely full with lots of men and women who had all been out to the pubs around town. The conversation was loud, the air was thick with cigarette smoke, and I was having a problem finding somewhere to sit. I certainly did not want to be separated from Kim if possible, as this was not part of my plan.

Suddenly I saw two seats together at the very back of the bus, and taking Kim's hand literally dragged her towards them before anyone else saw them and tried to push past. We sat down together and I felt as if the pressure was momentarily off. I gave a little sigh of relief to myself before I continued my role of leading man.

A moment or two went by and then Kim leant over and whispered in my ear.

"I have lost my shoe," she said.

"What?" I couldn't believe what I had heard.

Again she leant into me and whispered, "I have lost my shoe, and I think it is downstairs."

I looked down in disbelief at her feet and saw that she wasn't joking. Sure enough there was one foot in a shoe, and the other without. I looked up at her and frowned.

Sheepishly looking at me in the eyes she continued, "Please can you go and get it for me?"

This was too much, and I must have looked pretty annoyed as I looked back at her. I was beginning to feel really rather hot and bothered, sweating almost at the thought of walking past all those drunken men and women and before having to go down those stairs looking for a shoe! It was just so embarrassing.

Years of experience of drunken behaviour of adults had told me that adults could be very unpredictable after a pint too many. I had seen my father fly off the handle often enough, his rages in some cases caused by the most trivial thing! The last thing I needed was for one of the passengers to let rip at me as I searched the bus for a missing shoe. Then another thought entered my mind, they could all start to take the micky if they found out what I was looking for

With these thoughts going through my mind, I got up and started to walk back the way we came, holding on to the back of the seat rails to help keep my balance as the bus rattled and swayed along the road, and keeping my eyes pinned to the floor trying to catch a glimpse of a shoe in amongst all the ankles and trousers legs, and shoes and feet that seemed to fill up the smallest spaces. What a stupid girl she was losing her stupid shoe.

Having walked slowly down the aisle and then even more slowly down the stairs, I kept on looking. Reaching the platform at the bottom of the stairs, I could hear everyone laughing very loudly.

The conductor was standing on the platform at the back of the bus, his back turned towards me facing his audience of passengers. My arrival behind him prompted another, louder outburst of laughter, and I could feel my face burning up with embarrassment.

Sensing my presence, the conductor turned around to where I was standing. With a small bow he held out his hand revealing Kim's shoe. I stood there not knowing what to do or say. Should I snatch the shoe and run back upstairs, or just jump off the bus leaving Kim to find her shoe herself.

"Are you looking for Cinderella's shoe, Prince Charming?"

The laughter from downstairs got even louder. "Yes," I gulped, trying not to snatch the shoe out of his hand. "Thanks," I mumbled taking it from him before heading for the safety of the top deck. But it was not to end there.

The conductor followed behind me, and as I made my way to the back of the bus where Kim was waiting for me, I could hear him broadcasting to all the upstairs passengers what had happened. I could feel everyone looking at my retreating back, as he referred to me as Prince Charming who had come to find Cinderella's slipper.

All of a sudden, Kim and I were as popular as the happy couple from the fairytale with everyone wanting to say something to us, or make a comment on our version of the 'romance'.

I didn't need this sort of attention, this was not part of my script, and I had never dreamt that something so embarrassing could ever happen to us! No, what I needed was a quiet corner in which I could curl up and die! My first date, and I was the centre of ridicule and amusement, not envy as to my good fortune. It was too much for a teenage boy embarking on romance.

As the bus pulled up at Kim's stop, I let her get off, staying firmly in my seat, all my hopes of a tender kiss good night a thing of the past. I think that she tried to say good bye to me, but I sat in stony silence, head turned towards the glass and my face still a burning shade of crimson. I could see her reflection in the glass, and watched her as she made her way off the bus.

I never asked Kimberley out again, and in fact cannot really remember ever talking to her again either. Bernie and everybody else who knew me thought it was hilarious and laughed for weeks after.

As for me, I think that in some way it scarred me for life, as I can still clearly remember every embarrassing moment of it as if it had only happened yesterday!

Chapter Thirteen
Mum Shocks Us All

At the start of 1967 Lesley had left home and gone to live in London. Within a few weeks of her arriving there, she met a young science teacher called Roy Smith and married him shortly afterwards. (Despite predictions of doom and gloom and the marriage not lasting, they were happily married until the time of Roy's death in 2008.) Barry was 19 and doing very well as an assistant sales manager in a television shop on Allerton Road called Johnson Brothers. He had also passed his driving test and was now the proud owner of a grey mini-van.

When Sheila was fifteen and ready to leave school Mum helped her find a job as a sales assistant in Sayers Confectioners, working in their Lodge Lane Shop.

I liked Sheila working at the bakery. She would bring back all sorts of goodies which hadn't sold during the day, and rather than throw them away she would ask her manager if she could take them home instead.

She knew all of our favourites; mine was jam donuts, particularly the challenge of eating a whole donut without licking the sugar off my lips.

Sheila and I were still pretty close, although now she was working and I was still at school she was a little more grown up. In many ways we were as alike as two peas in a pod, both of a similar height, and both with red hair (which she hated! as do most children who have red hair and freckles whilst they are young). The reality was that her hair was as lovely as Mum's; long thick curly, auburn locks, which I often found useful for grabbing hold of whenever we argued!

I was 13 years old, whilst my lovely baby sister June was now five and growing up very quickly. We got on well she and I; she was a typical cheeky little madam with me, but as far as I was concerned she was special. I was the older brother who would often put her on my shoulders and take her for sweets. If she had been good for Mum, and if I had the extra pennies, as a treat I would often buy her an ice-cream cornet whenever the ice cream van came down our street.

Dad was Dad. We didn't see him much; during the week he still worked nights driving taxis, spending the days sleeping off the effects of too much drink the night before.

As for my darling Mum, she started to look a lot older than 47. The constant despairing of my father's behaviour and the continual worry about money were beginning to take their toll on her.

As we went about our daily lives, little did we know of the dramatic change that was about to take place.

★ ★ ★

We were all sitting around the table having our tea (Dad was off in his taxi) when Mum broke the news to us.

"I've got something to tell you all," she said. We carried on eating looking up to see what she was about to say. "We're moving."

"What?" Barry was the first to speak, his fork still suspended in the air in front of his mouth. "What do you mean we're moving?"

"We are going. We are leaving this house, moving to something bigger and better, away from this place." There was a note of excitement in her voice as she spoke.

"What about my job?" demanded Sheila, "Where are we moving to?"

"When are we going? The sooner the better, as far as I am concerned, away from this dump!" Barry interrupted before Mum could answer Sheila's question.

"I am not changing school now!" I piped up. "I haven't got long to go! And what about my job at the ice rink – I can't leave that!"

June must have only picked up on the mention of a new house, and added her own little bit to ours. "Do we have a new house Mum? Are we going to a new house?"

Holding her hand up for silence, Mum said "If you just all be quiet for a minute, I'll tell you exactly what's happening."

"In two weeks time we are moving to a lovely modern Corporation House in West Derby. I went there today to see it and it is perfect for us. There is so much more space and even a garden."

"But, Mum what about my new job and Jeff's school?" Sheila asked.

"Don't worry love," Mum said looking at Sheila, "They have a Sayers not far away and you can ask for a transfer. As for Jeff, he can carry on at the same school and continue to work at the ice rink; he'll just have to get up a bit earlier to catch his buses."

Barry personally was not too bothered, as he had his own transport and could get to and from work without any problems. But he did raise a good point.

"Dad will go ballistic!" Barry stated. "He won't move all the way out there, it's miles away!"

Barry was spot on. Dad was going to suffer the most – as he would have to travel the furthest to his favourite pubs.

However, judging from Mum's reply that had been her intention all along.

"That is my worry Son, not yours." She believed that in moving us all further away, and extracting Dad from the clutches of his drinking partners at the Boundary Pub, he might end up drinking less.

It was a plan that she had masterminded some years earlier, when she had put our name down on a Corporation Housing list and had not told a soul; it had been such a long time ago I think that she had almost completely given up on it. However, one day she had received notification that a house was available, and after a long trip that involved three buses and several hours she went to see a house 'in the country'. Her prayers had been answered and her mind was made up. This time, as far as she was concerned, there was no going back: we were moving.

Needless to say, Dad wasn't happy at all and came up with all sorts of reasons and excuses for why we shouldn't have to move. He literally tried every trick in the book even adding a few of his own, but Mum stood fast. She wasn't having any of it; we were moving whether he liked it or not and she was determined that her children would have a new life, away from the slums where we had lived for so many years.

Although we didn't have a lot to pack, they were all in Mum's eyes, treasured possessions, and she insisted that everything was carefully wrapped up in newspaper, before being packed away in old tea chests which I had collected.

Dad got involved by borrowing a van off somebody he knew.

The day of the move finally dawned, and we were all up bright and early, getting stuck in to the job of loading the van with all our belongings.

Job finally completed, it was time for me to say goodbye to everyone whom I had known for so many years, and who had become such a part of my daily life. Setting off at a run, I went to say goodbye first of all to Mrs Gilbert. She thanked me for looking after her and her cats for all those years, gave me a half crown and wished me luck.

Then there was Mary from the sweet shop.

I walked in to the shop calling out, "See you Mary, we are going now. I just came to say goodbye."

"One minute Jeff, wait" she said, coming out from behind the counter, with a bag in her hands. "These are for you for the journey."

Ruffling my hair, with one hand she gave me the bag of sweets. "I am going to miss you Jeff and your big cheeky smile."

I was definitely going to miss Mary as she had become my friend.

My mates were all hanging around by the van, not sure what to do with themselves. Ian Watt was looking particularly uncomfortable, staring down at the pavement, and not saying much. After all we had been bezzie mates ever since we were allowed to play out in the street, and now I was leaving.

As I shook their hands good bye endeavouring to be as grown up as I could, I still had a lump in my throat as I said my farewells fighting with my emotions and trying not to let any tears show in my eyes.

I promised them all that I would come back and see them soon, a part of me knew that I never would. I was moving to a whole new life, and even though it was only a few miles away, I could have been travelling to the other side of the world for all the difference it made. Sadly, I never saw any of them ever again.

Finally we all set off in convoy, Barry leading the way in his van, with June sitting on Mum's lap, whilst Sheila and I followed behind with Dad in the borrowed van.

It must have taken us an hour or so to get there. As we moved further from Durden Street and closer to Princess Drive, the scenery started to dramatically change. Instead of the grey of old buildings there were more and more trees and open expanses of greenery and grass. It was almost like being out in the country, and reminded us of our trips to Wales.

West Derby was on the outskirts of the city and had been predominantly farm land before World War II. After the war however, and as a result of the devastation that Liverpool had suffered at the hands of the Luftwaffe during the bombing raids, Liverpool Corporation had acquired and built housing estates in these areas to accommodate families that had been made homeless. The estates also catered for the overspill of people who lived in derelict houses in the inner city which were due to be pulled down as they were deemed to be worse than slum dwellings.

As we pulled up outside our new house we could see several things. Firstly, it was a corner house, and had its own front and side garden.

It also looked much newer and larger than our old house in Durden Street having been built in the late fifties.

I was the first out of the van, running over to a little white wooden gate, tucked in the middle of two five foot high privet hedges. I had only ever seen front gardens and white wooden gates on television or in the movies and here I was opening our own.

I walked down the path towards the front door, which was painted a bright red, - ironically the same colour as our old front door.

Mum was immediately behind me, and my excitement was hard to contain as she searched for the keys in her handbag, and almost fumbled with her own anticipation as she put the key in the lock.

She finally managed to open the door, and we walked into our new home, into a square hallway. On the right hand side was a staircase leading upstairs, whilst on the left hand side and straight ahead of us were two doors, both closed, and inviting exploration. I decided to open the door on the left first of all, and it led me into a large room with a front window looking out on to the garden. There was a contraption fixed to the wall.

I shouted to Mum "Look it has got a funny thing on the wall. What is it?"

She looked and gave me the biggest smile. "That is our new gas fire, Jeff, just think no more making coal fires."

I pointed to some other square metal objects which were attached to other walls in the room. "What are they Mum?" I asked.

"Radiators," she said. "There are radiators in every room in the house and they give out lots of heat."

"Even the toilet?" I countered.

"Yes even in the toilet," Mum replied, adding "Just wait until you see that room."

I followed Mum out of the front room back into the hallway, and she opened the other door. As we both walked in I could see it was a lovely long kitchen with fitted cupboards and a stainless steel sink with running hot and cold water. I turned the tap on with the letter 'H' and fair enough, within a few minutes piping hot water came rushing out.

"Does this mean you don't have to boil any more kettles for hot water, Mum?" I was teasing her. She just laughed in response.

Above the kitchen sink there was a large window looking out on to another garden. Mum, seeing what I was looking at told me that it was our back garden, in such a way as if she had always had one.

Upstairs were three decent sized bedrooms. The front one was to be for Barry and myself. For the first time ever, we could split our bunk beds and have proper single beds on the floor; no more of Barry's antics waking me up in the middle of the night. There was another similar sized room for Sheila and June next door, and finally a quieter one at the back of the house for Mum and Dad.

I loved the new house, and every room in it, however, my favourite one, without a doubt had to be the room referred to as the bathroom. We had never had one of these before. This bathroom was amazing with a long white bath that you could stretch out in and get properly warm without any bits of your body getting cold, and with instant hot and cold water. There was also a sink just for washing your hands and face, and cleaning your teeth, and best of all a white porcelain toilet with a spotless white plastic seat. This was unashamed luxury.

As if one indoor toilet was not enough, there was another toilet downstairs, just as you came in through the kitchen door. So as to reflect our improved status in life, and perhaps in tribute to the joy of having indoor toilets, Mum never ever used old newspaper torn into squares ever again. Instead we used soft tissue paper on rolls.

The feeling of gratitude and love for my mother was overwhelming, and I understood why it had been so important for her to move us here. There was no need for words; as I wrapped my arms around her in a big hug, I knew she understood, and we stood there for a few moments, enjoying each others company and our new surroundings. After a quick kiss on the cheek, it was down to the business of unpacking and getting settled in.

It did not take the Pearce family too long to settle in. We all loved it here, the new house and all the creature comforts it had to offer. Mum organised our furniture and bits and pieces and within a matter of days it felt well and truly like our home. Dad loved the house, but he hated the location, mumbling to himself that we were no better off.

Not long after we moved in, Sheila got her transfer to the Dovecote branch of Sayers, less than a fifteen minute walk away. Little June started at the local school, conveniently located just around the corner and seemed to be very happy there. I had to get used to the buses, as it took me about an hour and twenty minutes to get to school, and the same to get back home. Although it took a big chunk out of the day, it was worth it, just to see how happy Mum was in the new house; she even arranged a free school bus pass for me. As for getting to and from the ice rink, that wasn't too bad as it only took an hour either way.

No, nothing could spoil the joy of living on Princess Drive, and even though my days seemed to be longer, I would never have dreamt of complaining to Mum.

Mum found herself in that house, and discovered the joys of gardening. If the weather was nice, you could be sure that she would be outside, digging over the soil, weeding the flower beds and tending to her roses; she was well and truly a different woman. Mum had, for the first time in her life, a few of her dreams come true.

Dad, however, once again managed to add a sour taste to it all. Mum's plan of moving him as far away as possible from bad influences seemed to backfire. He still kept on meeting up with his cronies, staying out and drinking, carrying on as if he had no other care in the world, and certainly no family or home to come back to. Sometimes he would come home very late, sometimes in the early hours of the morning, and sometimes simply not at all. As I soon found out, Mum would stay awake through the night, worrying herself sick about him and whether he had got himself into some awful sort of trouble such as fight or a crash. Other times, I imagine she wished that he hadn't bothered to come home at all, as he was such a disgrace, an embarrassment, staggering off the bus which stopped across from our house.

On these occasions, he was so drunk that he had to be helped in as he could not stand up, let alone walk on his own. My poor mother. I now recall that she seemed to spend half her evenings looking out of the front window every time she heard a bus to see if he was on it. I can only suppose that the alcohol made him totally unaware of how much he was managing to spoil my mother's hard won happiness.

Princess Drive was a reasonably busy dual carriage way that ran down the middle of a very large housing estate. If you turned right out of our house and carried on for about two and half miles you ended up in West Derby, which was regarded as a posh area.

However if you turned left out of our house, a mile down the road would bring you to Page Moss in Huyton an area of Liverpool with a notoriously bad reputation as being one of the hardest and roughest council estates in Liverpool, if not the UK. When building the Huyton Estate, the Liverpool Corporation had 'relocated' the hardened criminal community from the city centre, and moved them further out into the countryside.

The Eagle and Child Pub in Page Moss, only five minutes away, and the Bow and Arrow Pub which was almost directly opposite our house were notorious and known to be two of the most dangerous and violent pubs in Liverpool at that time. Such was their reputation that even the police were scared to go in either pub for fear of being caught up in a violent brawl.

Mum had certainly succeeded in keeping Dad out of the 'locals', as both places would have been too hazardous for a distinguished gentleman such as my Father.

Oh Mum, God love her! All she had ever wanted was to bring her children up in a safe environment, so she had moved us far away from big city squalor and crime to the benefits of a more rural setting. What a pity - she had miscalculated by only a mile in the wrong direction; we were now living deep in the heart of criminal country.

On the day we moved in, I was looking out of Mum's bedroom window, when I noticed a boy about the same age as me playing football in the garden next door. I opened the window to get a closer look, and caught his attention.

"Do you fancy a game?" he shouted.

"Sounds good," I replied.

Closing the window in Mum's room, I went outside, and within a few minutes we were passing the ball to one another. His name was Ronnie O'Toole and he lived next door with his mother and two older brothers. That first game was the beginning of a friendship that lasted many years.

Chapter Fourteen
Wots-A-Gofer-Do?

O nce we moved to our new home I found that time seemed to fly past. All of a sudden I was fourteen going on fifteen and was due to leave school in a matter of months so we were all sent individually to see the visiting careers officer to discuss our plans for the future.

We had to queue up alphabetically in the corridor, outside a classroom which was being used for the interviews. Most of the other boys were nervous as they waited their turn – asking each other for ideas as to what they should say, seeking inspiration for possible career plans. I wasn't nervous, I was confident. I had always worked, in fact I was born to work and had learned so much from my Mother and family ever since I could walk. I just wanted to get started in proper work. I was quiet in comparison to the other lads, going through everything in my mind and rehearsing what it was I wanted to say.

Finally it was my turn as my name was called. I entered the classroom and saw a rather tubby man dressed in a brown suit sitting at one of the desks. As I got closer I noticed that his hair was rather greasy, as was his tie, which was tied in a school boy knot instead of a mans' Windsor, like Dad always wore.

I sat down, and he looked at me with tired disinterested eyes. "Well, Mr Pearce, what job would you like to do when you leave school?"

This was the moment I had been waiting for, the first chance I'd had to turn my dreams into reality. Taking a deep breath I started on my plans for the future.

"Well, sir, I want to have my own business. Maybe start off on the markets like I did with my Mum, selling all kinds of things and when I have enough money, get my own shop. I want to be like Mr Hughes, Sir, when I am older, and have my own big store like his."

I paused for breath to see what reaction I was getting, if there were any signs of encouragement or inspiration, but I was met with a blank stare. Perhaps he didn't know who I was talking about.

"Mr Hughes, Sir," I repeated, "The one who owns TJ Hughes in London Road. Sir, you must know it, it's one of the biggest in Liverpool."

There was still no response from the man opposite me, so I sat there for a moment not sure what to say.

He then picked up a couple of pieces of paper from various piles which he had stacked in front of him, passing them to me. "Here you are young man, some things for you to look at and have a think about."

"Next," he shouted loudly, as I hesitantly got to my feet and slowly walked across the classroom floor. Glancing down at the leaflets he had given me, I couldn't make out any of the words written on them, but I could see pictures of soldiers and sailors. What was this all about? I wasn't interested in being a soldier or going to sea. That man hadn't even listened to a word I had said, and I left the room feeling very let down and disillusioned.

Mum knew that I had been looking forward to meeting the careers officer that day and when I told her what had happened she cheered me up.

"Don't worry Jeff, I am already looking for something special for you. Leave it to me, I know what I am doing."

Not long after that Mum gave me the good news – she had found me a proper job and had arranged a meeting with the Head Master.

As we both sat in his office, Mum explained that she had found a much sought after job for me working as an apprentice TV engineer, and that the position was available to start immediately.

She knew that I was meant to leave school at the start of the summer holidays with all the other boys, however, as she explained, with my poor academic abilities I would not stand a chance getting a job, never mind one as good as this against the competition of all the other school leavers.

She was therefore asking the Head Master for his assistance in obtaining permission for me to leave school before the official end of term date, so that I may start work as soon as possible.

The Head Master said that he would see what he could do, and about a week later Mum was called back for another meeting. Once again we found ourselves in his office, and he explained that having spoken to the relevant authorities, and after much deliberation, permission had been granted for me to leave school early.

On my last day at school I said goodbye to all my classmates and other friends that I had made over many years. They were all obviously envious of my early departure, and called me a 'lucky b★★★★★d'!

My form teacher Mrs Jones, was less congratulatory, saying that it had been a waste of time trying to teach me and no good would come from my Mother's efforts. She went on to imply that I would never amount to anything due to the fact that I did not want to learn. In her professional opinion I was a no hoper, a total waste of time.

As I walked across the school playground on that last afternoon, heading for the school gates and a new life, I was feeling very scared. The thought of my new employer discovering that I could not read or write made the safety of the school ground even more appealing, despite the harsh comments of teachers like Mrs Jones. I was fourteen years old, just a boy entering an adult's world.

Mum soon vanquished all the misgivings that had been bothering me as I had walked home that afternoon. She told me that televisions were the thing of the future, and that there would always be work when it came to their repair and installation. They were already part of people's everyday lives and Mum could see that the television was only going to go from strength to strength – as an engineer I would always be able to earn a living.

She was so enthusiastic that I couldn't help but feel excited at the prospect of my new job – the way Mum described it made it sound very grown up. I must admit the thought of repairing televisions all day did appeal to me as well!

★ ★ ★

The company I was joining was the same company where Barry worked, Johnson Brothers, which was a privately owned television and radio business, with six shops in and around the Merseyside area. They sold TVs and other electronic appliances and Barry was employed as an apprentice sales manager in one of their stores.

My job, however, was in their service department in Rose Lane, just off Allerton Road. My first Monday morning in the summer of 1968 was memorable. I arrived on the dot of nine, trying to look as grown up as possible as I carried my 'butty' box (containing some sandwiches Mum had made the night before), under my arm.

Walking towards the main entrance my first impression was of how busy it was. There were lots of vans coming and going in and out of the yard; there must have been as many as twenty, all painted white with big blue lettering on the side stating Johnson Brothers TV and Radios. As I walked through all the hustle and bustle towards the door marked Reception, I started to feel very nervous.

Entering the building I found myself in the reception area. On one side was a small square window, framing the head and shoulders of a lady busy doing something.

I walked over to the window and found myself having to stand on my toes so that I could see her. She kept on looking down at her typewriter. I didn't want to jump up and down to get her attention, so instead I cleared my throat and waited. It worked as she stopped typing and looked at me.

"Can I help you?" she asked.

"I am here to fix televisions," I blurted out.

Her eyebrows shot up as she looked at the pair of anxious eyes above a nose resting on the window sill in front of her.

"I am sorry?" she said. "What was that again?"

"I am here for the job," I answered.

"What job?"

"The television engineer job," I elaborated.

Pushing her chair back she stood up, leaning forward to get a better look at me. I found myself confronted by an overpowering cleavage as her body now filled up the window frame.

"Well, young man," she said, "You'd best take a seat hadn't you."

Picking up the microphone for the tannoy system, I heard her voice loud and clear and full of laughter as she put a call out.

"Frank, would Frank Johnson please come to reception."

There was a minute's pause before she repeated her call. "Frank to reception. The world's smallest tv engineer is waiting for you."

Sitting there in reception, my face red with embarrassment, I didn't know what to think. I wondered what she was laughing about; I was here for the job, what had I said wrong?

A short while later a door opened, and a man appeared walking towards me with a smile on his face.

"Hello there, I am Frank Johnson. What is your name young man."

Getting to my feet quickly I replied, "Jeff Pearce, Sir."

"Oh! Right, you're the new apprentice. Come on follow me," he said, walking off at a brisk pace.

I had to work hard to keep up with him, my shorter legs doing at least two strides for every one of his longer ones, as we made our way through a maze of hallways and doors.

As we sped along, he told me that he was one of the Johnson Brothers who owned the company and was in charge of the service department. He was my 'Big Boss'.

Finally we came to a door that led into a large room full of work benches arranged around the walls. These work benches were quite high, and the surfaces were covered with lots of televisions and radios all making different crackling sounds. In front of the benches there were tall stools, spaced about six feet apart, upon which sat the repair engineers, most of whom were women, all peering into the backs of the electronics and doing things.

There must have been about twelve women in total, and only two men, and they were all busy repairing the faults, many of them using soldering irons which smoked each time they made contact with some part of the television or radio. Everyone had their backs turned to us, and they were all so preoccupied with what they were doing that no-one notice us coming in. Mr Johnson called for attention, asking everyone to stop what they were doing so that he could introduce me to them.

"This is Jeff Pearce, and he is the new apprentice I was telling you about. I would like you to show him the ropes, and to help him settle in here."

I stood there shyly, feeling nervous and unsure of what to do. Sensing my apprehension Mr Johnson said to me, "It's alright Jeff. No need to worry, they'll look after you," before leaving the room.

It was as if his words had fallen on deaf ears; everyone had carried on with their work whilst he had been speaking, and continued to do so once he'd left. I remained in the middle of the room waiting for someone to notice that I was there and to tell me what to do, but nothing happened. After about ten minutes I plucked up enough courage to put my butty box down on the corner of one of the benches and to walk over to one of the women who had the kindest looking face. Making that choice was hard enough as they were all sitting on their stools, and were much higher than me, and most had their heads deep in the innards of a television or radio.

"Is there anything I can do to help you?" I asked in my politest voice.

"Bloody hell," she said, almost jumping off her seat, startled by the sudden interruption. "Who the hell are you?"

"I am Jeff," I answered, "the new apprentice."

"Oh you are here" was her reply. Turning to face the centre of the room, she called out loudly to her colleagues, "Our gofer's arrived!"

"Gofer?" This was a new expression to me, and meant nothing at all.

Seeing the look of puzzlement on my face, she smiled, "Go for this, go for that. Gofer. You know what I mean don't you?"

"I am sorry," I replied, "I don't."

"You go for messages, and run errands around the place," she said, making it much clearer to me what a gofer was.

I felt better now that I understood, but I still couldn't see what this had to do with repairing tv's.

"Where do I sit," I asked her looking around the room at all the benches.

She burst out laughing. "Not here love, come on follow me. I'll show you where you are going to be working," she added, getting off her stool and heading for another doorway.

She took me into a smaller room with two large oblong tables down the centre, and lots of chairs arranged around them. There was a sink and a cooker to one side, with cupboards on the walls above. A large clock, with oversized hands was ticking away above the door.

"We call this our canteen. It's not much of one is it?" she said looking at me.

"Now pay attention whilst I tell you what you have to do every day."

As I listened to her carefully she continued. "By ten o'clock every morning you have to make sure that you have made two large pots of tea, and you make them by putting four large teaspoons of tea into each pot before adding the boiling water. Remember boiling water, nothing else will do."

"You also have to make sure that all the teacups and saucers are clean and dry and laid out on the two tables, and this all has to be ready for ten o'clock, understand."

I nodded my head to let her know that I understood.

"Once our ten o'clock break is over you have to clean up any mess, washing all the cups and saucers, and wiping down the tables, ready for our dinner break at 12.30."

Her instructions continued. "At 11.30 you have to come next door and ask all of us what we want from the chippy for our dinner."

"Where's the chippy," I asked.

"On Rose Lane, about ten minutes away," she told me. "When you get back from the chippy, you have to put everything in the oven to keep it warm, and then make two more pots of tea and get the tables ready like before, for our break. We finish our dinner at 1.30 and you then have to clean up, making sure that it is all neat and tidy for tomorrow, when you will do the same all over again. So Jeff, you had better get cracking as we will all be in at ten and no one likes to be kept waiting."

Just before she left the room, she stopped and looked back at me, "And once you have finished clearing up after dinner, you have to get ready for the three o'clock tea-break then you must come and sweep up the workshop floor before you finish at 5.30. Understood?"

My head spun with all the instructions that I had been given, but I started to get to work as quickly as possible, rushing around the room like a headless chicken in my desire to have everything done by ten o'clock. I had just put the teapots down on the table when they all came through, each person heading to a seat around the table which apparently was their own special place. As they drank their tea, they teased me, either about my curly ginger hair, or the new nickname that they had decided to give me, 'The Ginger Gofer'. I didn't mind it at all as I enjoyed their sense of humour which made me feel part of the group.

At eleven thirty, and having devised a way of overcoming my lack of spelling, I went into the workshop with a pencil and a piece of paper, ready to take their dinner orders. Using _fc_ for fish and chips, _'skpc'_ for steak and kidney pie and chips and so on, I was able to write down the orders using my codes before setting off for the chippy on Rose Lane.

At the end of the week I received my first wage packet, which contained three pounds. I had also received tips from the men and women I worked with, and that amounted to almost a pound. I was so proud being able to give Mum all that money. In those days it was the tradition in Liverpool to give all of your first wage packet to your mother; but from then on you paid the agreed board and lodging, keeping the balance for yourself. I just gave Mum my wage packet, and in return she would give me ten shillings back to cover the cost of my bus fare. I never had to buy lunch as Mum always made my sandwiches, and I kept my tips for myself.

It took me a couple of weeks to get it all down to a fine art, and I soon found myself being able to spend more and more time in the workshop, running errands to the stores department to pick up transistors or large glass valves and tubes, all parts needed to replace the broken components in the tv's and radios which were being repaired.

It didn't quite live up to the expectations that I'd had when I left school and ventured forth into the big wide world. Making tea and being a gofer for a group of women was not my idea of a career, and after about three months I started to feel disappointed with my career choice. When I found out that I had to start going to an engineering college one day a week in the near future I started to panic; once again my fears of being found out reared their ugly heads. I began to look at other opportunities, my attention being drawn to the vans in the yard outside, constantly coming and going. Surely that would be more interesting and better for me.

I really liked the aerial rigging vans, with their big aluminium ladders strapped to the roofs which rattled loudly as they drove into the yard. The drivers seemed to be tall men, with big muscles who all had leather tool belts strapped around their waists full of hammers and spanners and other interesting looking tools. To a young boy they reminded me of cowboys with their gun belts slung low around their hips.

Each aerial rigging team consisted of two men; the main aerial rigger who would be in charge and also drive the van, and an aerial lad (or apprentice, who also acted as a gofer!). Aerial lads were normally quite big, aged between 16 and 18 and they had to be quite strong as they were expected to handle the three sixteen foot long sections of the aluminium ladder.

I found myself watching them every morning as they came to collect their list of jobs for the day and to stock up from the store with rolls and rolls of cables and lots of shiny aerials. It looked so exciting as the aerial lads loaded the vans first thing in the morning before setting off. They would go to houses all over Liverpool, climbing the roofs and attaching the aerials to chimney stacks. Sometimes they would return at dinner time, lots of vans all lined up whilst the teams sat in the sun eating their fish and chips and laughing with each other.

I felt so insignificant walking past with the women's dinner orders, so having laid everything out in the canteen I would go and stand outside in a spot where I couldn't be seen but from where I could listen to them and hear their stories. I so wanted to be like them, to grow up big and strong, and do something important; I envied the fact that the van lads didn't have to spend their days making tea, and putting up with a group of women taking the mickey out of them all the time.

I could not stop thinking about being an aerial lad, working in the outdoors all day, climbing up and down roofs, and wearing a tool belt around my waist. It was just such a manly job, and seemed such an adventure to me.

One sunny lunchtime, when all the aerial vans were in the yard and the teams having their usual good time, Mr Frank Johnson just happened to walk past me. Suddenly I found myself calling his name.

"Mr Johnson," I said, "I would really like to be an aerial rigger, just like them."

Mr Johnson stopped, and turned towards me with his usual smile. "Jeff, I really don't think that you want to be like them, out in all kinds of weather good or bad. A tv engineer is a far better job."

"Mr Johnson," I replied, "I really want to be an aerial rigger, and I don't want to be an engineer at all."

"I am sorry son, but you are too small," was his reply.

"No Sir," I was adamant, "No I am not too small at all."

"Come with me then," he said, as he set off in the direction of the riggers. I followed at his side until we had covered the short distance to where everyone was sitting. He stopped and put his hand on my shoulder.

"This young boy wants to be an aerial rigger. What do you think?"

They all burst out laughing. "There's nothing to him Frank," said one tall man with dark hair. "There's more fat on a sausage!"

"He needs to grow a bit more," said another, "Put a bit more meat on him otherwise he will be blown off the top of a roof on a windy day."

"See what I mean," said Mr Johnson, once again looking at me, "I think that it would be best if you forget this crazy idea."

Crestfallen I turned away, heading back to the canteen, Mr Johnson walking beside me.

"Wait a minute." There was a shout from the group behind us. Mr Johnson and I both stopped and turned around to see who had called out.

"George, what's up?" asked Mr Johnson, directing his question towards a tall, young man who was approaching the two of us.

"I am looking for a van lad, Frank," George replied, "and I have got an idea. This lad could be ok if he can prove it." Then turning to me, he asked me what my name was.

"Jeff Pearce," I said, my sudden bravado of a few minutes before suddenly disappearing. What did this man have in mind?

"Come on lads," said George, turning back to the group sitting around, "Lets see what the little fella is made of," giving them all a big wink and bringing them in on the joke.

Indicating that I should follow him, we walked over to his van, Mr Johnson and all the other riggers and lads in our wake.

Taking the three sections of the ladder down off the top of his van and balancing them on my shoulder, he told me that if I could walk over to the gates and back without dropping them, then I could have the job as his new van lad.

The gate was about fifty yards away from his van, so I had to safely cover one hundred yards in total. With my audience watching and laughing at me I headed off towards the gate. The further I walked the more difficult it became; the ladders were not heavy to carry, but they were difficult to balance, one minute tilting forwards and the next titling back in a non-stop rocking motion.

I reached the gates and slowly turned, walking back towards the van. By now I was beginning to feel quite a lot of pain in my shoulder and arms, and my knees were beginning to feel quite weak as if they would buckle out from under me any minute. The heat of the midday sun and the sheer exertion of completing my task was making sweat pour down my face and into my eyes.

As I got closer to the waiting crowd I realised that they were all cheering for me, urging me on to complete the task as I focused on the ever closing distance. About ten yards away from where they all stood I couldn't go on any further. Dropping to the ground, the ladders landing with a loud metallic crash beside me, I knelt there, my whole body aching with pain. The encouraging cheers had subsided and all I could hear now were words of defeat as they shared their "I told you so's" and comments as to how I was not big or strong enough.

George Williams came over to where I rested, picking his ladders up as if they were as light as feathers before putting them back on the top of his van. I just stayed where I was feeling so small and dejected, and miserable at the thought of another year making tea and running for fish and chips, my dreams in tatters around me.

"Hey kid," I heard George call out. "You have got a lot of guts you know. You weren't frightened to give it a go. I have got a mind to take you on as my lad."

His words were music to my ears as I raised my head, hope starting to dawn again in me. "Please mister, please," I looked at him imploringly, "Please give me the job."

"Hey Frank," George continued, "I fancy this kid and I am going to take him on."

The other drivers couldn't believe their ears and told him that he was making a big mistake – I was too small, not strong enough and too young. Had the sun got to him? Was he mad? George was told that I would never make a good riggers lad in a month of Sunday's.

George's only response was to tell them to wait and see. "In six months time," he said, "I reckon he will be the best lad on the yard!"

Mr Johnson, who had been quietly standing watching the whole proceedings, took me to one side. "Are you sure that this is what you want to do?"

"Yes definitely. It is what I want to do. I don't want to work in there any more." I was breathless with excitement and from my exertions of carrying the ladders, so I nodded my head frantically to emphasise my point. "Please Mr Johnson, it is just what I want to do."

"Alright," he said, once again smiling at me. "You can start on Monday as George's new lad. And tell your mother that it was nothing to do with me!"

"I will," I promised, bursting with happiness.

In truth Mum was a little disappointed at first, though once she realised how keen I was about my new job she accepted the change and seemed quite happy for me.

Chapter Fifteen
Up the Ladder

George Williams, my new boss, was the youngest rigger on the yard being only twenty, very tall with muscular arms, and was literally 'built like a brick shit house'. He had blonde hair which was styled in a fashionably long bob, and he also sported a Mexican-type moustache, which he believed made his youthful appearance seem older.

George had started out as an aerial lad himself, working his way up through the ranks and learning as he went along. He had started out in the days of the old 'H' and 'X' aerials, enormous metal contraptions which had been very difficult to install, and once he had passed his driving test was given a van of his own and promoted to the position of rigger. This promotion had only happened a few weeks before I joined his crew.

My first morning with George started well as the two of us loaded up the van with all the equipment required for the days work. Van loaded I climbed onto the front seat next to him as we set off for the day. I felt really grown up.

George tossed me the daily job slips, a bundle of pieces of paper held together with a large bulldog clip. Looking at the slips in dismay I realised that they were covered in writing, a jumble of words that I couldn't read.

"Where's our first job," George asked.

I looked over at him. "I don't know where these places are," I said stalling for time.

The next thing I knew a small book had landed on my lap.

"Look them up in there," George shouted, "and be quick about it as we don't have all day to get the jobs done."

I looked down and saw the letters A-Z on the cover, and the word Liverpool. "But I have never used one of these before."

I thought he was going to cuff me he looked so annoyed.

"Are you a fucking idiot?" he demanded. "What's your problem? Find the bloody streets – use the fucking maps!"

I realised that George did not have the patience of a saint, and that he was getting really annoyed. I glanced down at the job slips on my lap and couldn't even read the street name. If I couldn't read that how was I going to find it in the book? I started to feel cold and shaky, with that familiar sick feeling in the pit of my stomach.

George's driving was becoming erratic and I heard him swearing under his breath. Suddenly the van veered to one side of the road, mounting the curb and screeching to a halt as he yanked up the handbrake.

"What's your problem" he shouted. "Can't you bloody read? Are you stupid?"

My heart was in my mouth as I sat next to him – my secret was about to be discovered, it was the end of my new job. This was my worst nightmare.

"I just don't know how to do it, that's all" I said, hoping that this would put him off track.

George lunged in my direction, and grabbed the job slips and A-Z out of my hand. "Do you need me to show you what to do? Fucking hell, this is bloody stupid."

"It's as easy as this. Look, first the address, Paddington Street," he said pointing to the first line of writing on the job slip.

"Look in the index for Pad – P-A-D" he instructed, opening the back of the book and running his finger down all the words beginning with 'P' until he found the one he was looking for. "Look, see, there it is," he pointed it out to me.

"See what it says next to it, 2D, p67. That is the map reference and the page number of the map," he carried on. Turning the pages of the book he showed me how to find page 67, and then use the map references to find 2D. "Look, there it is there."

"What you need to do now is tell me how to get there, keeping an eye out for the correct house number."

I struggled through that day and sensed that George was beginning to regret his decision. However, I was not returning to the role of glorified tea-boy, and was going to get the better of this current challenge.

At the end of my first day, I slipped the A-Z into my butty box without George noticing, smuggling it home with me to study.

Mum was waiting for me when I got home dying to hear the news all about my first day in my new job.

"How did it go Jeff?" she asked, almost as soon as I had come through the front door.

Hanging my coat up I told her. "It was horrible, Mum. My new boss got angry with me, shouting and screaming and getting really cross. I think that he'll want to get rid of me now."

"Why Jeff, what did you do wrong?"

"I didn't do anything wrong, Mum, it was what I couldn't do."

Taking my butty box, she said, "Come on lets go and have a brew," before heading into the kitchen.

I sat down on a chair at the kitchen table, slumped forward with my head buried in my arms. Mum opened my buttie box and found the A-Z. "What's this?" she asked.

I raised my head a little and saw the book in her hand. "That's what wrong with my job," my voice was totally flat with despair. "Mum, why can't I read like everyone else?"

Mum put a cup of tea down in front of me. "I wish I knew Son. What I can't understand is that you are so clever in so many other ways, it just doesn't make sense."

"Everyday I have to sort out the job slips and give George directions on how to get there using this book. And I have to be fast about it, as he gets annoyed really quickly," I explained.

"Jeff, life is full of obstacles, or hurdles, and everyone comes across them from time to time. If you want to achieve things in life you have to learn how to overcome them, whether it be by tackling them head on, or sometimes going around them if there is no other way." She took a sip of her tea. "What we need to do is work out a way that we can overcome this particular obstacle together," she said, gesturing to the book in front of her.

We sat there drinking our tea for a few minutes in companionable silence, my gaze never leaving her face. I loved watching Mum when she was 'busy' thinking, as her face took on a very crafty look.

"I've got it!" she stated. "I know how we are going to get the better of this little book!"

I sat up straighter in my seat, despair and dejection completely vanquished. When Mum came up with a plan it was always a winner and I couldn't wait to hear what she had to say.

"Every night I am going to write down street names taken from the back of this book," she explained. "And every night, Jeff, you are going to find those streets as quickly as you can on the maps."

It was a simple plan, but a good one, and for the next week she and I spent hours and hours working together around the kitchen table, until it got to the point where I was literally beating the clock, reading the names and finding the locations on the maps in a matter of seconds. Not only was I speedy but I started to enjoy it. That little book was no longer a demon to me but a friend, and having mastered the art of giving directions from one address to another, I would then plan the whole days' journey telling George where to go.

George was very impressed at how quick I was in getting us from one job to another, telling all the other drivers that I knew Liverpool like the back of my hand!

The next hurdle to master was the ladders which took a little bit longer. It was not so much a matter of strength but one of balance. When carried horizontally across my shoulder it was fairly straight forward to adjust to the slight see-sawing motion that they made – but I still managed to keep up a good speed.

However, sometimes it was not possible to carry the ladders horizontally, so there was no option other than a vertical up-lift. I must have presented the most terrifying sight to pedestrians walking by. A little lad, well short of five foot, hurrying along with sixteen feet of metal balanced against his shoulder reaching up into the sky.

As I darted along, weaving to avoid obstacles on the ground, the ladders swayed like palm trees from side to side bending in a strong tropical storm. Pedestrians dived for cover, scrambling in their haste to get out of my way. It might have looked dangerous, but I was in control of those unwieldy pieces of aluminium.

Ladders and maps were just some of the things that I learned. The biggest change however was that this was a proper job, I was now part of the adult world, and soon learnt to toughen up a lot.

George was more than happy with my work and how quickly I picked things up, though you wouldn't have known it from the way he treated me. We would be in the van driving along, and suddenly I would feel his clenched fist crashing into my shoulder, or just above my knee. The initial pain was unbelievable, and would be replaced by a dull throbbing that would last for the next half hour.

If I ever asked him to stop it, he would tell me to stop moaning and being such a wimp. Apparently it had happened to him and a lot worse too; as far as he was concerned all lads should get a thumping every now and then, it toughened us up!

One day, about six months after I had started working with him, George and I were on our way to a job. I was making up a lashing kit, which fitted around the chimney stacks, in readiness for the next job; it was my custom to use the time spent travelling in the van to get everything ready, making the installation process quicker once we arrived at our destination.

I had almost finished making the lashing kit, and all that remained was the metal bracket which I was holding in my hands, when suddenly, and totally out of the blue, I felt George's fist coming into contact with my leg. It was the hardest blow I had received to date, and without thinking, I hit back.

Unfortunately for George, I was not empty handed as the metal bracket made contact with his forehead, cutting the skin above his eyebrow, making him yell out in pain.

I looked over to see what I had done and saw a thick river of blood gushing down the side of his face blinding his sight. George let go of the steering wheel and clasped his head in this hands as he moaned and swore with pain.

"I am going to kill you, you bastard," he groaned, rocking back and forth in agony. "Just wait until I get my hands on you, you little bastard. Don't think that you can escape. You're dead!"

I cowered in my corner as far away from him as possible, pressed up against the door, desperately trying to work out how I was going to get away from the van and from George. Luck was on my side.

The van was now totally out of control as it careered across the road mounting the kerb and ending up on the grass strip that ran down the middle of Queens Drive. George must have put his foot down on the brake as the van lurched forward, grinding to a standstill.

I opened the door and threw myself out, half landing on my knees, scrambling to my feet and running away as fast as my legs would go, desperately trying to increase the distance between myself and the van. All I wanted to do was to get as far away as possible; George wanted to kill me, so I did not slow down until I was well and truly out of sight.

It took me two hours to walk home. As I sat in the kitchen talking to Mum, I told her about all the previous occasions when George had hit out at me.

"I've had enough, Mum" I said to her, "I am packing it in. Chances are that I will be sacked anyway for nearly killing him!"

"You did the right thing Jeff, standing up for yourself like that." Mum replied. "I'll have a word with George or Mr Johnson in the morning and we will get to the bottom of it all."

George normally picked me up at 8.30 sharp every morning for work, but as far as I was concerned I was not going back. "No Mum, he won't come by tomorrow morning, and anyway, even if he did I am not going to work with him ever again. And that's final."

Mum said nothing further on the matter, realising that I was really upset by it all.

The following morning, 8.30 sharp, I heard George beeping the horn in his van as he usually did. Climbing out from under my bed covers, I opened the curtains a fraction, peering out into the street below.

I could see my Mother walking with great purpose towards the van where George waited. She was talking to him angrily, wagging her finger to emphasise her point, and from what I could see, continued to tell him off. This went on for a few minutes until she eventually returned to the house, whilst George drove away.

She had hardly closed the door before I was down the stairs demanding to know what had happened.

"Well, it's quite simple. I told him that if he ever laid a finger on you ever again, I would swing for him."

I looked at Mum standing in front of me, and an image of this petite woman taking on an overgrown man sprang to mind, it was positively David and Goliath, but I knew that my mother would be the winner whatever.

"What did he look like Mum" was my next question, wanting to hear all the gory details.

"A bit sorry for himself," Mum replied. "I told him that you weren't coming back today, and that you will only come back to work if he promises never to do it again!"

I couldn't believe my ears. Mum had got George to agree to never hit me again, not to press charges, and to treat me a bit better. Mum was amazing.

"But what did his head look like?" I asked her again.

"He had a big plaster above his eye, and it looked a bit red and puffy. He said that it was very sore."

"What's going to happen now Mum?"

"Well, I told him that you didn't want to come back, but suggested that he pass by tomorrow to see if you had changed your mind. So he will be here tomorrow morning, and you can go back to work. He did promise not to hit you anymore."

It was a little bit uncomfortable the next morning when George picked me up, as we were not sure what to say to each other. Once the day's jobs got underway we soon started talking and before long it was almost as if nothing had ever happened.

Our relationship had altered subtly however; George showed me a greater degree of respect, and he certainly never hit me ever again. As time passed, we became good friends and enjoyed each others company working well as a team. He took great pleasure in telling the other riggers that I was brilliant at my job, and it was quietly recognized on the yard that I was definitely the best aerial lad.

"I never even have to get out of the van," he would boast. "Jeff is so quick and so good at what he does, that I can sit there with my brew and enjoy the papers, only stopping to get the job signed off or to go to the next job." I was a valuable asset.

"They were fools not to recognize that the best things come in small packages."

My mother's predictions with regard the growth and popularity of television were, as usual, accurate. Everyone wanted a television with an aerial, but not everyone was able to pay the full price. Spotting a gap in the market, George and I stocked up on the necessary equipment from a small local manufacturer in Aintree.

Loading the gear into our van, alongside the equipment from Johnsons, we would set off on the day's official jobs. George and I were quick at installations, turning them around in less than fifteen minutes, which gave us more than enough time to do 'foreigners'.

A 'foreigner' is a way of referring to jobs on the side, and all tradesmen all over the country 'do foreigners'.

The process of generating business was simple. We would arrive in our van to do a Johnson installation, and no sooner had we unloaded the ladders we would be approached by a neighbour or two wanting to know how much it cost.

"Our company charges ten pounds Missus," we would say, waiting for the moment when their face would fall at the price.

"But now that we are here we can put one up for you, right now for a fiver. Five pounds cash." Nearly eighty percent of all customers agreed to the offer, and we ended up doing loads of foreigners in a day.

We were busy. We were completing between fifty to sixty installations a week for Johnson Brothers, which made Mr Johnson very happy as we were beating our target. He knew we all did foreigners, but as long as we hit out targets he would turn a blind eye.

We were visiting our own manufacturer at least twice if not three times a week stocking up with materials for our own jobs, and yet we could not keep up with the demand.

And most importantly, we were also making three times our salaries on foreigners alone, George splitting the profit equally between us both, something I really appreciated.

George was the only rigger who did this, as most of the others gave their lads a small percentage of the profits. His reason however was quite simple; I was worth my weight in gold, doing all the roof work, bringing the new business in, and essentially ensuring that we finished in record time.

George and I were so good at what we did, that we would have finished all our work by midday, heading off to a café in Kensington to meet up with all the other riggers.

The café was like our guildhall, as men would gather around the tables, discussing the days jobs, exchanging information on technical details and generally putting the world of television to right. It was also the perfect hunting ground for two small operatives Jimmy MacCabe and Billy Johnston.

Billy and Jimmy both ran their own little businesses, and worked in friendly competition with one another. They would come in at lunchtime looking for good experienced lads to work with them for the afternoon.

An aerial lad could expect to earn £4 a week working for a company like Johnson Brothers. Working in the afternoon, for someone like Billy or Jimmy, could earn them an extra £1 a day, thus allowing them to double their earnings by the end of the week. I had worked with both of them on numerous occasions.

Billy and Jimmy would bid against each other for my services for the afternoon. George told me not to sell myself short, encouraging me to charge £3 for an afternoon's work. As he put it – I was making the money for them, they could afford the extra pound or two.

So I would sit in the café, listening to the two of them debating as to who was going to hire me for the afternoon. As long as I got three pounds I didn't mind as they were both good men to work for.

It was becoming ridiculous – I was making so much money. There I was, a sixteen year old lad making as much money each week as someone in a recognized profession.

Chapter Sixteen
Girls, Girls, Girls!

That extra money made such a difference to both Mum and me. I loved the job I was doing, but I loved being able to spoil her. Not only was she no longer worried about paying bills and debt collectors knocking at the door but she was able to indulge herself as a woman.

She was the happiest I had ever seen her. I ensured that she had her hair done once a month, and would take her shopping for a new dress, encouraging her to splash out on something pretty and frivolous. She also had an extra £10 'pocket money' a week to do whatever she wanted to do or go wherever she wanted to go. (In typical Mother fashion, all she would do was save it up, spending it on little treats for her children. It seemed silly at the time, but in hindsight it made her happy and that was all that mattered.)

Mum had always had an interest in 'the horses' and now she was in a position where she could have a little flutter if there was a horse which took her fancy. I used to see her sitting in the kitchen in the morning, going through the form on the days racing, a Woodbine in one hand, and a pencil in the other, as she marked off the horses which sounded like good runners. She had a knack with it too – almost as if she had 'the sight' and her shilling-each-way bets would nearly always pay off.

A new Bingo Hall had opened a mile away from the house, and Mum, after a little encouragement would go for a night out, sometimes on her own, and sometimes with Sheila. Again she had a lucky streak, and would often come home with her winnings, enjoying her luck as much as she had the night out.

When she'd had a win, she would tell me that one day she would hit the jackpot, and that she'd take us all away to somewhere really nice to live.

I started to drag Ronnie, my new best friend and next-door neighbour, to the ice-rink with me at the weekends, where we would meet up with Bernie Snagg. He didn't skate, in fact his sense of balance was so bad that he spent most of the time holding on to the edge moving slowly around. But he liked the girls and found the disco a great attraction. Now that we were sixteen, we were allowed in to the Bee Hive

Girls, girls, girls! Three sixteen year old lads with one thing on their mind, and that was girls. We would skate for an hour or so and then head up to the disco standing in a small huddle at the edge of the room. Bernie and I would be keen to get on to the dance floor, but the only way that we could do that was by finding a girl to dance with. In those days you never danced without a girl.

Hormones raging at the proximity of all this female beauty, we would prowl the perimeter, looking for a reasonably attractive pair of girls who were not dancing with anyone else. Suddenly the prey would be spotted, a hasty allocation made as to who would dance with who, and then a concerted dash to get to the side of the chosen female.

The competition to get to the prettiest girl first was fierce. This is when the testosterone kicked in, as if driven by some primitive urge we would charge to the side of our chosen partner, arriving rather out of breath and no doubt looking a little flushed.

Hearts pounding there would be a moment of agony as we waited for a response to our arrival. Would they ignore us both continuing to dance with one another? Or even worse would they take one look at the two red faced lads standing awkwardly near by, before grabbing their handbags and rapidly moving away, leaving us looking like two complete and utter idiots as we danced with fresh air, abandoned before we had even been rescued.

The worst part over, rejection avoided, a quick transformation would then take place as we started to dance, our bodies moving in time to the music, standing alongside one another as we went through the steps, each one of us in synchronisation with the other.

Bernie and I enjoyed dancing and were confident movers, whilst poor Ronnie found that it was as difficult for him as skating. It was not a question of two left feet, more a lack of balance and when he tried to dance it looked as if he was permanently on the point of falling over. So I gave him lessons in the privacy of his bedroom and after a little while he was as accomplished a mover as the two of us.

It was all part of growing up, about meeting girls in the comparative safety of the Bee Hive and maybe exchanging a few words with them over the noise of the music being played. If it went well, there were lots of other places to go to – down on to the rink for some skating (if you weren't sure how pretty she was) or to a quiet corner in some part of the building (if she was a cracker) for a quick kiss.

Learning about kissing was a whole new minefield in itself. We all thought of ourselves as being cool and tried to appear as if we knew what we were doing. The reality was very different however!

We were as much beginners as the girls we met and no doubt they were experiencing the same awkwardness as we experimented with kissing and cuddling. Having smooched a couple of times the desire to discover more led to the fumbling attempts of further exploration, youthful passion and excitement encouraging us to be bolder and bolder.

I had been in a quiet corner with a pretty girl one evening and couldn't wait to find my two friends to share the excitement of my big moment. Scanning the building I spotted them on one of the benches down near the ice and headed over as fast as I could.

Throwing myself down next to Bernie, I blurted out, "I've done it!"

They looked at me blankly. "Done what?" Ronnie asked.

"I felt her tits!" I replied, my voice quite loud with pride at my achievement.

"Keep it down!" Bernie hissed. "What was it like?"

"A bit awkward really," I said.

"What do you mean awkward?" Ronnie asked.

"There I was having a good kiss, getting a grip of her, with my hands all over her back and her waist and stuff, when I realised that her blouse was untucked so I thought that it would be a good chance to get my hands up it, see how far she would let me go!"

"Well did she let you?" it was Bernie this time demanding the details.

"Well, sort of. I couldn't tell, it all happened so fast."

"Were they massive?" Bernie interrupted again.

"Well, let me finish…. I put my hand up her back and brought it around to the front and all I could feel was like spongy material"

"What? Are you saying her tits felt like spongy material, didn't they feel like big boobs or something?" Bernie was disappointed.

"Do you think that they were falsies?" Ronnie asked.

"Well, I didn't get the chance to find out, did I? She pushed me away."

"So what happened next," Ronnie asked, "Did you try again?"

"No it all went wrong after that. We were both really uncomfortable and didn't know what to do or say. She just pushed me away and went back to her friends. I feel like shit now."

"What do you mean?" this time it was Bernie. "Why do you feel like shit? I bet you she loved it, they all do!" Bernie and Ronnie were both pissing themselves laughing by now.

"I don't think it's as simple as that," I told him, "You should have seen the look on her face as she took off! How embarrassing! I hate to think what she's telling her friends! I won't be able to look at her in the face or dance with her again!" Putting my head in my hands I groaned at the complete embarrassment of it all.

"You'll be right mate, it's a breeze!" said Ronnie giving me a nudge.

"Well, I look forward to hearing your adventures," I replied, "Let's see how you get on and maybe it will be my turn to laugh next time!"

In order to even attract the attention of our female prey we had to look the part; Bernie, Ronnie and I were all mods. This required a considerable investment on our part in the way we presented ourselves, not just in terms of the clothes we wore, the way we walked and the music we talked about, but most significantly our hair.

To be a real mod I had to get rid of my curls, which was an appealing thought as I felt that losing my curls would make me look older.

One Saturday morning, Ronnie, Bernie and I went to Pee Wee's in Kingsley Road, Toxteth. Pee Wee was well known for his skill with a cut throat razor, and was regarded as being the only place to go for a real mod hair cut. Ringo Starr (although not a mod) was also known for preferring Pee Wee's barbering skills which made it even cooler.

We found Pee Wee's and went in. It was full so we had to wait by the door until a space came up on the bench that formed an 'L' shape around two sides of the room, waiting to be called. Lucky for Ronnie and I, Bernie was called first.

As he sat down in the barber's chair he looked very small and afraid, asking Pee Wee for a 'skiffle cut with a shaven part' so quietly that he could hardly be heard.

Pee Wee got to work. Picking up an electric trimmer with one hand, and placing the other hand on Bernie's head to tilt it about (and hold it steady) he started to run the trimmer from Bernie's forehead to the back of his neck in one long swiping movement. Ronnie and I sat there in horrified silence as we watched long chunks of hair falling away, landing on Bernie's shoulder before sliding down to the floor where they lay in a large dark hairy pile. Within a matter of four or five swipes Bernie was as good as bald, his scalp looking very strange, white skin made to look grey because of the dark stubble which was all that remained of his hair.

Then it got scary. Pee Wee discarded his trimmer in favour of a lethal looking cut-throat. As he sharpened it on the leather strap hanging down from the back of the chair, we could see Bernie's face reflected in the mirror, his eyes having gone from horror at his new bald image to sheer terror as he watched Pee Wee sharpening the blade.

Once again Bernie's head was held still in the vice like clamp of one of Pee Wee's hands, whilst the other slowly and carefully scraped a parting line down the left hand side of his skull with the accuracy and precision of a surgeon. The parting started from above the temple to just behind his ear; it looked like a parting, but it didn't feel like a parting. Bernie's eyes had welled up with tears, whether from fright or pain we did not know, but were soon to discover!

Ronnie and I glanced at each other – did we really want to go through with it? I could see my sudden urge to get up and walk out mirrored in Ronnie's eyes. If either of us had had the courage to stand up and make a move for the door, the other would have followed, we would have been gone, leaving Bernie to fend for himself.

But we couldn't, we were pals and we were committed. Anyway, mods were supposed to be 'tough' and we were signing up to the whole mod movement. Together we faced the barber's blade and together we emerged an hour later, transformed.

Coming out into the daylight of Kingsley Road the full impact of what we had done suddenly hit us. Looking at each other we all realised that we hated our new hair. None of us liked it, but none of us had the courage to say so. Instead nervous laughter broke out as a show of bravado was adopted, there was no going back and I think that we all secretly hoped that our hair would grow back rapidly. Even our faces were transformed and the reflection in shop windows as we passed by showed three youths who looked more like released POW's than three young men who were supposedly the height of fashion.

As I got closer to home a feeling of dread came over me. Grabbing Ronnie by the arm I towed him up the path to the front door. "You are coming in with me mate," I stated, "I need you there for support."

Mum was in the kitchen when I walked in. She took one glance at me before slamming the cup she held in her hand down on the counter, tea sloshing over the side.

"Jeff, what have you done?" she exclaimed. "Ronnie, you too? You look like a couple of convicts."

Not daring to break into her tirade, I stood there feeling even worse than I had when I'd left Pee Wee's.

"What have you done?" She demanded again. "Where are all your lovely curls?"

Ronnie got there first. "On the floor in Pee Wee's" he told her. I just gave him a quick kick on the ankle.

"It's all the fashion Mum," I tried to explain. "You can't be a mod without a hair cut like this!"

"I don't care about what the mods do. You look awful, it just doesn't suit you. In fact, you look like someone who has just been released from prison this morning – now you look like a hard knock!" and with that Mum made her thoughts on my hair cut quite clear.

The boys and I realised that the difference between a good hair cut and bad hair cut is a week; either because the hair grows a little, or perhaps because you just get used to it. The week theory did not apply to Mum – she never stopped hating it.

★ ★ ★

Top of the Pops, at seven o'clock Thursday evenings, was essential viewing for every teenager in Great Britain. Ronnie and I were no different as we sat there carefully watching the latest fashions being worn by our favourite bands and listening to the hits in the charts. The Who and The Small Faces were amongst our favourites, but paled into insignificance when it came to Debbie Harry (Blondie).

I was in love with her, as were Ronnie and Bernie, and every other hot blooded adolescent male in the country. She was gorgeous, sexy and the girl of our dreams. She was hot!

After watching Top of the Pops on Thursdays, most Saturdays were then spent in Liverpool, scouring shops like the Army & Navy Stores and the odd boutique looking for clothes that would fit the image and style we wanted to portray. We all became customers of Peter Pells on London Road where we were fitted for our tailor made suits; there was nothing off-the-peg about being a mod, we paid as much attention to our suiting as a gentleman frequenting Saville Row in London. We were passionate followers of fashion.

We felt the part and looked the part, immaculately turned out in tailored suits, shirts and ties. As with any other teenage movement, the loss of identity to the culture made us feel invincible, as, in our numbers, we were the voice of the future, we had the answers and the world was ready to listen.

Looking good on the dance floor and knowing all the latest moves helped increase pulling power. A couple of dances with the same girl could lead to a walk to the bus stop at the end of the evening. It was then a matter of plucking up the courage to try for a kiss and, if success was achieved, the next step was asking her out for a date.

Having waited until the last minute to ask with her bus coming into sight, and with heart pounding, the words "Do you fancy going out on a date?" would come tumbling out. The drama of the moment increased as she would wait until she was on the step of the bus before turning and saying yes.

The bus would then start to pull away, so I ran alongside, shouting out the arrangements, hoping that she could hear me.

"Meet you outside Dickie Lewis, Wednesday, seven o'clock Ok?"

"Ok," she would call back, waving and smiling in my direction.

With a sigh of relief that the worst bit was over, I would enjoy going home, pleased with my success at having arranged a date. I never understood why I (like all my friends) left something so important to the last minute, perhaps it was self preservation, that there was no need to remove ourselves from the scene covered in embarrassment if she said no – the bus would do that for us.

Dickie Lewis is an institution in Liverpool, a naked bronze of a man standing some ten feet tall at the front of a ship looking out to sea. Officially named 'Liverpool Resurgent', he was unofficially renamed Dickie Lewis by the people of Liverpool for two good reasons. His first name is in reference to the exposure of his private parts for the world to see and the second is in reference to his location, outside the front entrance of Lewis' Department Store.

During the week, the area around the base of the statue was a mass of anxious young men and women all waiting to meet their dates. Rather than standing still, everyone milled around, trying to find a spot where they could be seen, without being too conspicuous by standing too far away from the crowd, anxious looks on all their faces. They were all thinking the same thing – what does he look like? Will she turn up? What was his name? Is today the right day? Oh please let her be pretty! I hope his breath doesn't smell!

After a few successful dates with a girl I had met, I would then invite them home to meet my family. It didn't matter how nice I thought they were they never were good enough for Mum. She would wait until the next day to pass judgment, telling me that she was 'too tarty looking' or there was 'something not quite right, she is not the girl for you'. My natural response was to tell Mum that the girl had only been a date, not my intended wife to be! It made no difference though, Mum continued to take an interest in both my and Barry's girl-friends and none of them ever made the grade.

One thing that Mum did do however was to cleverly prevent disasters from happening. Barry and I were in our bedroom one evening and I was getting ready to go out when I opened one of my drawers.

"Barry," I said, "your things are in my drawer."

"What things?" he asked.

"Them things there," I said pointing into the drawer.

"Oh, the johnnies," he said casually. "No, they are not mine, they are yours."

"No they are not," I replied indignantly. "I don't have any of them."

"Yes, they are," Barry said. "Now that you are starting to court Mum will make sure that you've always got them."

"What do you mean?" I was confused.

"Mum will keep them stocked up for you and make sure that you have got a regular supply!"

"What? Mum knows about them? You mean she actually goes and buys them?" I was horrified at the thought of Mum knowing anything about condoms, let alone my sex-life! This was hard to believe.

"She certainly won't want you getting a girl pregnant will she? You know what she is like!" Barry retorted.

I never mentioned it to Mum, and I never saw her doing it, but there was always a regular supply in my bottom drawer!

Just as my life was getting really exciting and I was enjoying going out during the week and having lots of fun with my friends, the bus drivers in Liverpool went on strike. The whole city came to a standstill. As the strike continued, week after week, month after month, people rallied together finding alternative means of transport. For me personally, the strike was disastrous. I was no longer able to get into town in the evenings nor at weekends to meet up with my friends and go on dates. Worst of all was that getting to and from the ice-rink was now virtually impossible. I tried walking in once or twice but it took a good two hours each way, so in the end I simply stopped going.

Chapter Seventeen
Size Eights

George and I continued to work well together both for Johnsons and for ourselves. We had some hair-raising moments when the elements such as strong winds and lightning nearly killed us whilst we were putting up aerials. We were left stranded on the roof, clinging on for dear life whilst our ladders were blown to the ground and a passer by called the fire brigade to come and rescue us. The other riggers found this funny much to our embarrassment, but not as funny as another 'adventure' we had.

We were working on an installation in a maisonette in Kirkby. I was on the roof passing a cable down through the roof slates to George who was in the loft space. Suddenly there was a loud shout of pain and an agonized call for help. It sounded serious. I called out to George to see what was wrong, but got no response so I made my way as quickly as possible into the building, racing to the top floor.

A red faced, angry tenant was standing outside his front door, effing and blinding. "Are you with him?"

"With who?" I asked.

"Come here and I'll show you," he replied, indicating that I follow him into his flat.

"That fat bastard there," he said, pointing to a large pair of size ten workman's boots attached to a pair of solid legs, sticking through two holes in the ceiling directly above the television set in his lounge. One leg through each hole.

"What was keeping the rest of him from falling through", I wondered as I hastily made my way up into the attic.

"Are you alright George," I called out, "I'm on the way. Just hang on!"

"I ain't bloody going anywhere," was his reply.

Switching on my torch I found George straddled across a solid wooden joist, tears pouring down his cheeks and a rather strangulated sound coming from his mouth.

"My bollocks," he groaned, "My fucking bollocks are history! The family line stops here!"

I looked over to where he was stranded. "Come on George, stop messing about."

"Mess about? I'll bloody mess you about in a minute. Get over here and get me out!"

After much effort I eventually managed to pull George out of his holes. In the process he made them much larger as he kicked his way out, until there were two quite sizeable apertures above the lounge below.

Peering up at us were Mrs and Mrs Seriously-Pissed-Off, both of them giving us a very clear indication of what they thought about the whole thing.

"You had better come and fix this mess, you fat bastard!" shouted the husband, whilst the wife told us that there was no way we were going to get away with it.

Carefully climbing down the ladder, George first with me following behind, we made our way into their flat.

Seeing the amount of damage that George had done, and knowing that he was not the best person to be handling the situation, I quickly started to apologise, assuring them that

Johnson's would cover the cost of repairs. George stood beside me, mutely nodding his head in agreement.

"Why doesn't he say something," asked the woman.

"Yeah, you clumsy git, what have you got to say for yourself?" demanded her husband. George remained silent, so I intervened.

"He's not up to saying much at the moment," I replied on his behalf.

"Why, cat got your tongue?" asked the man.

George then spoke up. "No," he croaked, "The joist got my bloody bollocks!"

★ ★ ★

When I was sixteen I developed a new obsession, the need to learn how to drive; I wasn't legally old enough, but I didn't want to have to wait another year. After much nagging, George finally relented, teaching me in our van on the quieter back roads of Liverpool and on Ainsdale Beach, where I could happily and safely drive up and down for hours without getting in trouble with the police.

Dad also had a car, a blue Ford Cortina. It was actually Barry's, but he had decided to leave Liverpool and was going to work his way around Europe. Mum had a real battle convincing Barry to let Dad take over the payments on the car, and although Barry hated the idea he finally relented, and agreed to do it only because it mattered so much to Mum.

After a lot of persuasion from Mum, Dad agreed to give me the occasional lesson on a new housing estate, Cantril Farm, which was being built, just behind where we lived. The reality was that it was a housing estate without the houses; the infrastructure was in place, a complete network of streets and roads, which made it the perfect spot for a learner driver as there was no other sign of life.

For the first time, Dad took an interest in me and what I was doing, and he seemed to be very happy giving me driving lessons, in fact it was the beginning of new relationship for the two of us. He was a very good teacher, and it was not long before I was both confident and competent behind the wheel. In return for driving lessons, it was agreed that I would give Dad's car a full valet every Sunday morning, checking the oil and water, and making sure that it was spotless both inside and out. My involvement with cars made me feel that I had climbed another rung up the ladder of adult life.

Early one sunny Sunday morning, I was out cleaning my Father's Cortina, the radio blaring loudly as I worked away, when Ronnie, my best mate from next door came over asking if I fancied going to Southport for the day.

"Sorry mate," I replied. "I have to finish cleaning the car. Perhaps we can go later?"

"Come on, let's go now. It will be too late," he clearly was not enthused at the idea of waiting.

"You know I've gotta finish it, Dad'll go mad if I don't."

"Why don't we take this?" Ronnie said jokingly, patting the bonnet. "It'll be good for picking up the birds; it'll be a real pose!"

"Forget it. I haven't got a driver's licence," I replied. "I'm not old enough to be driving for one, and for two, Dad would kill me if he found out."

Ronnie laughed. "He won't know. He is fast asleep and by the time he wakes up we'll be back!"

The seed had been planted. What an exciting idea! Before I knew it, we were both dressed to the nines in our best gear, in the car and on our way to Southport. The windows rolled down, the latest sounds playing loudly, we felt so cool as we cruised along – two young men on the look out for some pretty girls.

We were enjoying ourselves and were only a couple of miles from our destination when the car in front of me slowed to a halt. After a few minutes of not going anywhere I asked Ronnie if he could see what the problem was.

"Can't see a thing," he said, "But hang on a moment, and I'll get out to have a look."

After a few seconds, he was back in the car. "Oh shit, it's a copper up ahead."

My face went white. "What?"

"There is a copper up ahead stopping the traffic."

"What, searching them?" I was getting worried.

"I don't know what he is doing," Ronnie replied. "Directing the traffic maybe?"

I looked around me. We were on a narrow country lane, with a car behind me and one in front. I wanted to get out of there as fast as I could, but there was not a lot of room and I was nowhere near confident enough to do a three point turn. I was stuck, and the only way to go was forward, past the policeman.

Ronnie sat nervously fidgeting beside me which was making matters worse. I was becoming more and more anxious. It would be just my luck if the policeman noticed that there was a very small person driving a very large car. I looked ridiculous; I was bound to get pulled over. I would lose my licence before I had even got it! And the thought of my having to tell my Father that the police had taken his car away was almost too much to think about.

"Ronnie, what am I going to do?"

"Look bigger!" he said.

I tried straightening up and puffing out my chest. The more I tried to sit up, the more my foot kept slipping off the brake.

"This isn't working, Ronnie," I said. "Bloody do something, otherwise we are dead."

Ronnie noticed that there was a checked blanket on the back seat. He hastily folded it into a small cushion like pillow, which he then shoved under my backside.

"That's a bit better," I said, "but still not enough. I need something else." By this stage there were a dozen cars between me and the policeman. All of a sudden, he indicated that our queue was to move forward.

"Ronnie, for God's sake quickly do something, we're moving."

Ronnie was searching around the car for something else for me to sit on. I was staring out of the windscreen my eyes glued to the policeman ahead.

Whipping off his jumper he shoved it under the blanket. "Is that any better?" he asked.

"A bit," I replied, "But I need something else."

"There's nothing! There's nothing!" he cried, "What do you want to do, sit on me?"

Ronnie had a flash of inspiration; he suddenly reached down into the footwell and pulled off his shoes adding them to the bottom of the pile.

I sat there gripping the wheel as I drove forward. As my luck would have it the policemen suddenly held up his hand and I had to stop right in front of him. I was so close I could almost see the colour of his eyes.

"Jeff, keep cool," I heard Ronnie hissing at me. "Look old, look grown up!"

"How the fuck are you supposed to do that?" I hissed back. I was sitting there sweat pouring down my face, my hands frozen to the wheel, hardly able to move. My legs were beginning to shake as I had them extended to their full length, my toes stretching as far as they could only just making contact with the brake pedal, desperately holding it down, thinking that if my foot slipped off the brake the car would roll forward and the policeman would end up spread-eagled across the bonnet.

The seconds ticked by slowly, it felt like forever. Ronnie had lowered the sun visor in front of me in order to help hide my face, but it was no comfort or protection at all.

Suddenly the policeman turned, beckoning me to move forward. I panicked again. What happened if I stalled the car?

Would he come over to see what was wrong? Trying desperately to remember everything I had learned I put the car into gear, eased off on the clutch and gave it some throttle. The Cortina moved forward, slowly and smoothly, as we drove safely by.

Once we were out of sight I pulled into a lay-by on the side of the road. I opened my door, almost falling off the top of my improvised perch as I got out of the car, the items tumbling to the ground around me. I felt sick and leant on the bonnet of the car gulping down huge breaths of fresh air, trying to calm my nerves.

Looking up, I saw Ronnie laughing at me through the windscreen.

"Pass me my shoes, mate" he called out.

His request broke the tension of the moment. As I picked them off the ground where they had fallen, I looked at the shiny brown leather realising that his size eights had well and truly saved the day.

I continued my driving lessons with Dad and George, right up until the day of my seventeenth birthday, when I could officially apply for my driving test. Finally, the big day of my test dawned and I passed with flying colours.

★　★　★

Now that I had passed my driving test, I couldn't wait to ask Frank Johnson for my own van and (even possibly) my own apprentice.

I went to see him in his office, knocking on the door and waiting to be called in. Feeling very confident and grown up, I decided to use his first name as all the other drivers did.

"Hey Frank," I said, "I have passed my driving test. Is there any chance of my own van and my own lad now?"

He almost choked with astonishment. "What was that again?"

"I've passed my test," I repeated. "I have got a full driver's licence."

"You can't be serious," was the reply.

"Why not?" I demanded.

"You're only ...... er? How old are you?"

"I am seventeen Frank," I told him proudly.

"No Jeff, I am sorry, you are far too young. You need to come back when you are at least twenty, if not twenty-one. Just carry on doing the good job that you are doing in the meantime."

He could see that I was disappointed with his response, and as I was leaving his office called out to me, "Well done, however, on passing your test Jeff. Whatever will you do next?"

George told me that he wasn't surprised that I had passed my test, but also said that I was expecting too much to have wanted my own van at my age. "No-one gets a van before they are twenty-one," he said. "I was exceptionally lucky getting my van at twenty." I appreciated his words, but they were small comfort to me.

As far as I was concerned what was the point of passing my driving test if I was not allowed to drive? There was no way that I could wait another four years; I was ambitious and had plans.

I carried on as normal for a couple of weeks until I could bear it no longer. One evening when I was sitting with Mum in the kitchen, having finished my tea, I decided to tell her about my plans.

"Mum, I want to start my own business."

"Doing what?" she asked.

"Aerials of course," I replied.

"Jeff, going into business is not as easy as that. You haven't even got a van, or ladders or anything." Mum was clearly shocked by my announcement.

"Jeff, you have got a good job," she continued, "You are earning good money, in fact more money than anyone twice your age. You don't want to risk everything, it might not work. How do you plan on getting your jobs – have you even thought this through?"

I had. "Mum, I have worked it all out. Listen to me. First I buy a van and some second hand ladders with my savings. Then I place an advert in the Liverpool Echo, advertising aerial installations, and giving this telephone number. Mum you can answer the phone and be my secretary booking the jobs. It will work! I know it will." I stopped for a moment to see what her reaction would be.

"Oh, Jeff," she was shaking her head. "This is a big risk you know. You have to slow down, you are far too young to be in business. Nobody will take you seriously, you are only just seventeen."

I hated being told that I was too young. "What do you mean they wouldn't take me seriously, I am one of the best aerial riggers out there, you know I am!"

Mum wasn't convinced. "Just slow down and think about it for a few days before you decide to do anything rash."

I had heard that there was a motor auction every Wednesday night in Tuebrook so Ronnie and I went along. There was a nice old dark blue Ford Anglia van with a roof rack already in place that looked ideal. I was nervous as I had never been to an auction before and wasn't sure what to do, so I watched the other people bidding. By the time the van came under the hammer I knew what to do. I wanted Ronnie to bid because he was a lot taller than me and therefore would be seen more clearly by the auctioneer; he was too shy and refused point blank.

Luckily I found an old crate to stand on, which now put me level with the rest of the crowd. The bidding started, and after a few tense minutes and sixty pounds later, the van was mine.

I joined a queue to pay for my van. When it was my turn, the lady behind the counter informed me that all items in the auction were 'sold as seen', and that they would not accept any comeback whatsoever. I wasn't bothered. Having paid my cash and collected the keys, I walked over to admire my purchase. Ronnie and I were so excited opening doors, looking under the bonnet and checking the tyres, that we were literally all over it like a rash.

As we drove away from the auction, Ronnie christened her Blue Betty. Her engine sounded good, and she was driving very nicely. As soon as I built up speed and put her into fourth gear, Blue Betty revealed her true personality. She refused to stay in fourth, spitting the gear stick back into neutral with a little clanking noise as soon as she could; this irritating habit meant that I had to keep the gear stick in fourth holding it firmly in place with one hand, whilst using the other to steer.

It was a whole new driving experience and probably a bad buy, but I was not going to own up to anybody for fear of being told 'you rushed into it; you should never buy cars from auctions'. Blue Betty was mine and I loved her, I now had the freedom to go wherever I wanted. She was my business partner and I was proud of her even if it did mean driving with one hand.

Once I had finished work that evening, I drove to Billy Johnson's house and bought a good set of second-hand aluminium ladders from him for fifteen pounds; they were pretty old but would still do the job. Billy was very generous and gave me a box of old tools which he knew would come in handy. Once I had tied the ladders onto the roof rack I felt so proud, standing back and admiring my van. It all looked so professional, I was now ready to go into business.

The following morning I went to see Frank Johnson and thanked him for all that he had done for me. I told him how much I had enjoyed working for him, but I was now going to work for myself and I was giving him a weeks notice.

"I have got to hand it to you, Jeff, when you make your mind up to do something nothing can stop you. Good luck, I wish you the very best."

The following Friday, at the end of my last days work with George, there was a certain feeling of sadness. We had built up a strong bond of friendship and although I knew that this would never disappear, I would miss his company and camaraderie.

As I left Johnson Brothers, I told all the riggers and their lads that they were not getting rid of me that easily.

"I'll be seeing you in the caff on Monday!" I called out, leaving the yard for the last time.

Mum placed a small notice in the *Liverpool Echo* advertising new aerial installations for five pounds, whilst Barry (who had now returned from his trip around Europe and was back working for Johnsons as the Manager of one of their shops) promised to pass as much work as he could. I also got my very first business cards printed which made me feel official.

I went to see the guy in Aintree that George and I used to buy our aerials from as I needed to stock up on all my spare parts. Because Tony knew me quite well by now he was happy to give me a little bit of credit, which helped me on my way. He, like everyone else, was very surprised that someone as young as me was going out on his own but at the same time was very supportive.

At the beginning business was slow, with very little response to my advert in the newspaper. Not being the type to sit around waiting for the phone to ring, I took to the streets in my van, driving around looking for any aerials that had fallen down and looked as if they could possibly be dangerous. I would knock at the door, hand over a business card, and inform the customer that their aerial was lying dangerously on the roof.

Most of the customers had no idea that their aerials were in such a bad state of repair. It wasn't that difficult to strike a deal, either agreeing to repair the old aerial or replace it with a new one; more often than not they opted for the new one. I always offered to take away the old aerials for free and the customer was always pleased with this suggestion.

Old aluminium aerials were nearly worth their weight in gold and having collected a reasonable amount I would take them to the nearest scrap yard turning them into cash which came in very useful during the quieter times.

After a couple of days of on-the-spot repairs, I called into the cafe to see if either Billy Johnson or Jimmy McCabe had some extra jobs which they wanted to pass on, splitting the profit between us with me taking the smaller share. It was not quite how I had imagined it all to be, but it was better than nothing, and it was up to me to make it work.

As the winter months set in Barry started to give me lots of work whilst at the same time the advert started to pay off; all of a sudden I was very busy. Mum enjoyed answering the phone and booking the jobs. She loved playing an active role in my business venture and was very proud of my success.

Chapter Eighteen
Flying the Nest

Ronnie and I had by now become good friends with a group of lads who all lived close by. The group consisted of Mick Hanratty, John Cullen, Tommy Moore, Ralph Ridley, Ronnie and me. Most weekends we would meet up and knock around together, starting the weekend with a Friday night pub crawl that inevitably ended up at one of the night clubs in the city centre.

One cold Friday evening in February, Ronnie and I met up with the lads at The Princess. We were all sitting in our usual corner when Mick and Tommy started to tell us about the holiday camp where they had worked the season before. Mick was funny and could tell a good story, he was a natural born comedian and Tommy was happy to confirm everything he said throwing in his own small anecdote or two.

Mick and Tommy were describing a young man's paradise. They told of a world where there were no parents to answer to, a world where you were a free agent, responsible to no one else other than yourself. And this was a world full of beautiful girls. Gorgeous holiday makers and fabulous coworkers, chalet parties every night – what young man could resist.

This story telling went on over a period of several weeks, one tale after another, each one about a different girl or situation that they had found themselves in; the stories just kept on getting better and better. There was no holding back on the details and if the four of us listening had closed our eyes we could have almost smelt the perfume worn by the girl that Tommy or Mick were describing.

Apparently the work wasn't too bad either. Although the pay was pretty poor and the hours were long, there was the possibility of tips which helped boost your wages. Mick and Tommy told us that it was best to be waiters as the uniforms were the smartest: black trousers, white jackets with gold buttons down the front, and a black bow tie which magically transformed them into real lady killers.

Mick and Tommy had us convinced that the only thing we wanted to do in life was to join them working at one of the holiday camps that coming summer. We bought into the fantasy; one night we all agreed that the six of us hot blooded young men were going to Pontin's Holiday Camp in Morecambe.

When I told Mum of my plans she was obviously not very happy and pointed out the obvious; I had only just started my own business and shouldn't walk away from it. As far as Mum was concerned I was changing my mind as often as I changed my socks.

I replied by reassuring her that I was not going to walk away from my business. Aerials were more profitable in the winter, this was only a summer job, not a career change. I wanted to have some fun, an adventure or two – I was nearly eighteen and ready to spread my wings for a while.

I focused on winding down my small business for the summer and selling Blue Betty, returning her to the auctioneers where I had found her. It was a sad moment saying goodbye, but I was more than comforted by the forty pounds I raised from her sale; I hoped for her sake that the new owner would have the same patience that I'd had.

On the last Friday in April 1971 we caught the train together, six young Scousers who had given up their jobs and the security that went with them. However, once we arrived at Morecambe and boarded the Pontin's coach that was waiting for us, the party atmosphere started to kick in.

We had the camp to ourselves for the first week, all the staff arriving early for training and familiarization before the holiday makers arrived. The whole operation was run with military precision, with lists of things to do and places to report to on our first day.

Holiday Camps were a particularly British phenomenon, offering visitors a wealth of activities within a large enclosure, cocooned from the outside world by high-wire fences. Meals were eaten en masse, accommodation was basic, and free entertainment was organised. The only difference between an army camp and our holiday camp was the party atmosphere.

I shared a twin bedded chalet with Ronnie, very basic but more than enough to meet our needs and we soon got caught up in the preparations and training prior to the opening of the camp.

We thought we were ready for their arrival, but nothing could have possibly prepared us for that first Saturday opening. Four thousand holiday makers turning up in coach loads. Each bus spewing out person after person in every shape and size, each one needing to be housed and fed, entertained, looked after and fussed over, their every wish fulfilled. It was endless.

Our first Saturday night was one of the most nerve wracking I had ever experienced. We were all lined up looking spick and span in our clean and shiny uniforms, trays to the ready, positioned at our stations. The dining room doors opened and pandemonium entered, thousands of pairs of feet creating an ever increasing drumming noise as they got closer and closer, a babel of voices and children's high pitched screams drowning all coherent thought as each person looked for their allocated seat. Thousands and thousands of hungry people all wanting to be fed, and it was up to all us novices to get the job done.

Mick and Tommy had conveniently omitted to tell us about this. What else had they forgotten?

Each of us had a section to look after which consisted of a straight line of eight tables each seating four people. For every section there was a waiter's station in which we stored extra cutlery, plates, glasses etc and which we had to stand by when we were not serving. The reality was that we were constantly serving, rushing around to meet one demand after another. Within seconds of having been seated the diners were asking for more butter, more bread, more water, more everything, they had not even got to the main meal yet!

Once the food was placed in front of them a feeding frenzy would begin, almost as if one family was competing against another to see who could put the most food away in the shortest possible time.

Three course meal over they would all herd out leaving devastation behind them. What hadn't made it to their stomachs remained on the table tops, the seats or on the floor - dollops of gravy, spills of soups, crumbs galore. The dining room, once a gleaming scene of orderly readiness was now reduced to chaos.

As soon as the dining room had emptied and the doors were firmly closed a storm of activity broke out. Like an army of soldier ants we set about stripping the tables of the soiled linen and dirty crockery and cutlery, sweeping the floors and straightening the chairs, repairing the room to its former glory. The speed at which we worked would have qualified any of us for a world record as we moved about with purpose until finally it was done.

Jackets and bow ties straightened, hair flattened in place, a freshly starched tea towel draped over our arm, we lined up once again at the top of our section and waited for the onslaught to start all over again. The second seating had begun.

That first week was as nerve wracking for us as it was for our diners, they were so brave. We learned how to balance our trays stacked high with plates under metal plate warmers, how to avoid spilling hot drinks over their laps and most importantly how to remember the orders. They were on the whole very good natured, cheering loudly if anyone dropped something. By the time the third week began anyone would have thought that we had been waiters for years.

Ralph Ridley was a couple of inches taller than me, and was sturdily built. He had a nose that was a testament to the number of fights he had been involved in throughout his young life, which combined with his rugged good looks was very attractive to women. Dark short hair added to his appearance of being a hard man, not the sort of person that you would want to have an argument with. He was known for his quick temper but he also had a good sense of humour.

One Sunday morning, when a new batch of holiday makers had sat down for their first breakfast, I noticed that Ralph was rushing backwards and forwards with milk jugs all the time. As soon as I had the chance I asked him what was going on.

"It's that table there," he said pointing to a family of four. "They keep asking for milk and they are now on their third jug." I looked at him in disbelief.

"You are kidding me," I replied. "That's six pints isn't it? What are they doing?"

"I don't know what the fuck they are doing with it," he whispered to me, "but they are doing my head in!"

The next morning I saw Ralph putting three full jugs of milk on the same table. I asked him what he was doing.

"They won't catch me out this time mate," he told me. "I have got enough to do without running backwards and forwards to the kitchen for their bloody milk. And I am thinking of my tips at the end of the week." He gave me a wink, "As you know Jeff, the training says that the guest is always right."

Within a few minutes of the family having sat down I noticed Ralph going into the kitchen with an empty jug. As he walked past I could hear him cursing under his breath.

"Three jugs not enough?" I asked him quietly.

"No," he snarled as he marched straight past me in the direction of the kitchen.

The following morning Ralph had five jugs full of milk neatly arranged in the middle of the table. All the other waiters and waitress in the sections nearby knew what was going on by now, and we were taking it in turns to wind him up.

"Any bets on five jugs being enough?" Ronnie called.

"I'll have a pound that they need six," Mick shouted back.

Tommy placed his bet, "I'll have a pound on seven."

Ralph interjected at this point. "Don't be stupid, five jugs is ten pints. No way can a Mum and Dad and two little kids drink ten pints of milk! It's enough, I am telling you!" He paused for a moment, before finishing off, "And if they dare ask for more there's going to be trouble you wait and see!"

We all knew what Ralph was like. He was like a bundle of dry wood waiting for a spark to set him off. He could be dangerous.

The guests all came in and sat down and we got on serving them breakfast, whilst at the same time trying to keep an eye on Ralph to see how things were going. There must have been about twenty of us all throwing glances in his direction, the atmosphere was positively charged with excitement as we all waited to see if the fireworks were going to go off. Even some of the guests had picked up on the mood and were talking amongst themselves, also waiting to see if anything was going to happen.

As my section was next to Ralph's I was the first to notice the man was signaling for Ralph's attention. I stopped to watch. One by one the other waiters stopped what they were doing and like me stood staring at Ralph.

Ralph walked over to the table and leant forward to hear what the man had to say. Then he straightened up.

"You want more? You want more? I'll give you bloody more." His voice carried across the dining room.

Turning sharply on his heel he stormed past me, effing and blinding, heading straight towards the kitchen. I could see from his eyes that he was in no mood for a joke and that all hell was about to break out so I kept quiet.

As he approached the swinging door leading into the kitchen, he leant back, lifting his leg and kicking the door with an almighty blow. The noise was deafening as the door flew backwards on its hinges and a silence fell across our side of the dining room as several hundred pairs of eyes turned in the direction of Ralph's disappearing back. This was no waiter dropping a tray, this was a drama.

We all silently watched waiting to see what was going to happen next. Less than a minute later he emerged, red faced and angry, pushing a two wheeled metal trolley in front of him, upon which was balanced a full sized milk urn. Three feet of gleaming aluminium was being wheeled towards the family, with 100 pints of milk sloshing over the top as he navigated his way through the tables.

Coming to a standstill with a loud clang resounding around the dining room, he shouted out loudly for everyone to hear, "Sir, you asked for more? I'll give you fucking more. Here! How's that?"

Tearing off his bow tie, he continued. "I am sick of you and I am sick of this job. Here from now on, help yourself."

With one final flourish he threw his bowtie on to the family's table and turned and walked towards the dining room doors.

"I am off," he called in my direction.

A slow round of applause could be heard as he made his way to the doors, slowly building in momentum as one person after another joined in the clapping. Waiters and guests applauded Ralph loudly as he headed out of the dining room and back towards his chalet.

For all of us working in the dining room, it was a strange sight to see – we would have all loved to have responded in the way that Ralph did, however none of us had the bottle to do it.

Amazingly, Ralph wasn't sacked as the Dining Room Manager understood his frustrations and offered to transfer him to the kitchen for the rest of the week, keeping him hidden and out of the way. Ralph had made up his mind and thanked him, saying that he wasn't cut out and didn't have the patience for this type of work; he had decided to leave, to return home.

Ronnie also felt the same way, and spurred on by Ralph's sudden exit decided to depart with him leaving the four of us behind to get on with our jobs.

★ ★ ★

The 70's was the beginning of a new era. Fashions were changing, colours were vibrant, hair was getting longer and skirts were getting shorter. It was also the beginning of the sexual revolution with the birth of 'free love', and young men and women were breaking the shackles that had inhibited both their parents and generations before them.

If there was one thing that Mick and Tommy had not exaggerated about was the wealth of female talent; the girls saw themselves as being modern women, equal in terms of freedom of expression and enjoyment, and like us they were there to have fun, whether as friends or as lovers.

Men were not allowed in the female chalets and they were not allowed in ours. There were security guards who patrolled the divide between the men and women's quarters constantly on the lookout for amorous couples trying to break the rules. Dodging their watchful gaze was part of the fun, and if caught and turned back, we would only bide our time before trying again; as soon as the sun went down and the stars came out, a 'cloud of passion' hung low over the staff chalets.

We partied every night, the male staff holding parties in their chalets, the female staff in theirs. Wine and cider parties were the popular way of starting the evening, with everyone contributing towards the drink. This was a lethal combination of cheap white wine and cider, poured in equal parts into a tea urn, left to stew for a while and served at room temperature. We would turn up at the host chalet, glass in hand, and help ourselves to this vile mixture, twenty or so lads seated on every available surface, getting very drunk.

The first glass always tasted the worst but certainly improved with acquaintance; as the night wore on it became more and more pleasant to the taste buds. Effective? Highly! Especially for numbing the senses!

Chorusing loudly, different accents mixing in good natured song, we would relax, sharing stories and jokes with laughter breaking out on a regular basis, whether at the punchline or the teller's inability to string a coherent sentence together.

There was always something going on in the camp; with four thousand people passing through its gates each week, the evening entertainment was important. Swept up in the carefree atmosphere we 'holidayed' as hard as we worked, going to the pub at eleven pm for a pint or two, before going to the midnight disco.

Memories ceased after that point, with consciousness only being restored early in the morning by the loud banging on the chalet door as the Dining Room Manager shouted at us to get out of bed and report for duty immediately. Heads pounding, throats parched and not really knowing what day it was, a blast of cold water over our faces would help with recovery before we fell into our uniforms and set off at a run for the dining room, to face our happy campers who were waiting patiently at their tables.

I had been there for a couple of months when my attention was captured by a lovely waitress called Marie. I found myself making excuses to follow her into the kitchen and looking for opportunities to chat with her. She had thick honey coloured hair, and laughing eyes; she was a lot of fun, but at the same time a bit different, holding herself a little in reserve. I was smitten and falling in love.

We spent the rest of the season in each others company, and when it came to an end Marie invited me to Lancashire, suggesting that I live with her for the winter in her parent's house. It was an appealing prospect, but I wasn't completely convinced. I still had my aerials business to consider and I wanted to spend some time with my family.

I returned home but found myself missing her after a couple of weeks. Talking to her on the phone was not enough, so I decided to follow my heart, and take up her invitation moving to Burnley; her parents were lovely, and made me feel very welcome. Marie had found herself a job working in a local knitting factory, and although there were lots of jobs available in other factories, I hated the idea of being indoors. The very thought took me back to the days of being a gofer at Johnsons.

Instead I found a great job. Working as part of a sand blasting team, I spent my days high up in the air, balanced on scaffolding, blasting hundreds of years of grime and pollution off old church steeples and other ancient buildings. There was an element of danger which was exciting; restoring the buildings was rewarding; working with the other men was fun; and best of all it was outdoors.

There was also plenty of work available; I sometimes worked seven days a week soon earning enough money to buy myself a bright orange Mini. Marie and I travelled home for Christmas, pulling up in front of a snow covered house, with the back seat laden with presents. The holiday was a great success; Mum liked Marie, but was a little bit concerned that I was committing myself to something too soon. Nonetheless, we spent a very happy few days together with my family before returning to Burnley. I continued sandblasting my way into the New Year and beyond, earning enough money to trade in the Mini for a royal blue Triumph Spitfire sports car.

Marie and I spent most of the winter talking about the good times that we'd had the summer before, and were looking forward to the summer ahead. In May, we returned to Pontin's. There were many familiar faces, including Mick and Tommy, but it just wasn't the same. The excitement had gone. Shortly into the new season Tommy and Mick decided to leave, heading south to find work. With their departure I seemed to lose all desire to stay on. A feeling of restlessness came over me, not helped by the fact that my relationship with Marie was fading, and we started arguing a lot. It was time to move on, so I handed in my notice. Mick and Tommy had found work at Butlins Holiday Camp in Clacton-on-Sea and phoned me to say that there were plenty of jobs available.

Saying good bye to Marie was not easy, I felt a little bit uncomfortable and guilty as I made my farewells, but I knew that it was for the best. I was too young to settle down and there were still lots of things I wanted to see and do before I made that final commitment.

Chapter Nineteen
Postcards from Europe

It was the beginning of July 1972 and I was heading down the M6 towards Liverpool and home, when I decided to drop in to see Barry first, who was at work at the time. Apart from wanting to say hello, I wanted to show him my Triumph as he'd had one at Christmas which I'd admired a great deal.

Pulling up outside the shop front, I got out of the car and headed towards the door. Barry must have seen me arrive as he suddenly appeared at the door, a smile on his face.

"Hiya Kid," he called out. "How are things going?"

"Not too bad," I replied returning his smile.

"I can see that," he said, nodding his head, "That's a very tidy set of wheels."

"Where's yours?" I asked him, looking around.

"Over there." He pointed at a blue Land Rover parked to one side of the building. "That's mine!"

"What?" I couldn't believe my eyes, or my ears for that matter. The Triumph had been his pride and joy when I had last seen him and it was this enthusiasm for his car that had prompted me to buy mine.

"It's a long story," he said. "Come on I'll make you a brew, and you can tell me why you're here as well!"

Curiousity awakened I followed him into the building and sat down in the small back room whilst he went about making us tea.

He started to rattle on about how he and a mate had decided to work their way around Europe. He'd sold his Triumph and used the money to buy the Land Rover, and handed his notice in, then his mate had let him down and now he was committed to going but had no-one to go with!

My mind was spinning with all the information that he was firing at me. "Slow down!" I said. "What are you going to do now? Are you still going? Surely you can't go on your own!"

"Well, I have no choice," he said, "Do I? I have handed in my notice and I'm leaving work tomorrow. Plus, I am sick of Liverpool and I want to travel; I loved it last time and I want to go back. I have spent the last six months planning this trip and I am going, even if it means going on my own."

I was silent for a moment, taking it all in. "Going on your own won't be much fun!"

"Anyway, enough about me, what about you?" Barry said, changing the conversation.

I told him how I had split up with Marie and packed in my job at the camp. I was only home for a couple of days before travelling down south to meet up with Tommy and Mick.

"Down south? That's not travelling! Why don't you come with me?" Barry suggested.

For a moment I thought he was joking, as we weren't exactly close. "Are you being serious? Are you suggesting that I come with you?"

As we looked at each other I could see the idea starting to take shape.

"Yes, Kid," he said, "I am serious. Let's go together!"

"But what about my car?"

"Sell it, you'll need some spending money anyway!"

"And I haven't got a passport?"

"You can get a yearly one from the Post Office, it only takes a day. Come on Kid, stop making excuses!"

Three days later we were waving goodbye to Mum and June as we drove away from the house. Mum had found my whirlwind visit all a bit confusing, but had done her best to help getting a passport sorted for me whilst I sold my car. The last thing I heard as we headed off was Mum calling out.

"Barry, whatever you do look after Jeff; you know how accident prone he is; bring him back in one piece please!"

★ ★ ★

We talked about our plans on the trip down to Dover; as far as I could see there was no set format. Apart from arriving at Calais and heading to Paris, we were going to take each day as it came, stopping off where and when we wanted to and finding work along the way.

Barry had provided simple accommodation for us in our mobile home – the Land Rover. He'd had windows fitted down both sides, and there were curtains providing a degree of privacy. As it was a long-wheel base vehicle, there was just enough room for the two of us to stretch out full length in the back, encased in sleeping bags on top of foam mattresses which we could roll up out of the way. We even had a kitchen of sorts consisting of a double camping stove, fuelled by a small gas bottle, a saucepan and frying pan and an assortment of plates and other utensils. Jerry cans filled with petrol and fresh water were strapped on to the roof rack, and washing facilities consisted of a plastic bowl filled with cold water and a flannel. It was very basic but for two young men it worked well.

Looking back at the White Cliffs of Dover as the ferry pulled away, I was overwhelmed by the sheer anticipation of the adventures that lay ahead of us; I'd hardly explored England let alone foreign countries.

Leaving the ferry in Calais we drove out of the port heading straight for the French capital.

Although Barry and I were brothers we didn't really know each other that well as the age difference had kept us apart whilst we were growing up. Now that I was 19 and he was 25 the gap seemed to have closed; we talked endlessly, learning more and more about each other as the Land Rover ate up the miles. This was the first time in our lives that we discovered how special a relationship between brothers could be.

Whilst we were travelling through Switzerland, around Lake Lucerne, we found our first job. Pulling into a campsite on the shores of the lake, the scene that lay before us was one of the most breathtaking that we had ever come across with the blue mirrored surface of the lake reflecting the majestic mountains behind. Barry and I wanted to stop there for a while so went and made enquiries as to the cost of a pitch for a night or two. Being Switzerland it was expensive, in fact well beyond our budget. Disappointed that we could not afford to stay, we decided to take advantage of the site's free facilities searching out the shower and toilet block. Both were in need of a good clean and a lick of paint, but feeling tired and grubby ourselves we were not going to fuss, and after several days on the road, the joy of constant piping hot water was overwhelming.

Refreshed and clean shaven, we then spent the rest of the day enjoying ourselves sunbathing on the jetty, and cooling off in the fresh waters of the lake well out of sight of anyone who might have asked us to leave.

Evening drew in and it was time to go. As we reluctantly headed for the gate in the Land Rover I suddenly told Barry to pull over by the office. I went inside before emerging some ten minutes later with a piece of paper in my hand.

"Right Barry, we have to find pitch number 24."

Barry stared at me as if I was speaking in a foreign tongue. "What are you talking about?" he asked.

"Pitch 24 – it's ours for the next couple of days. I've done a deal with the man who owns this site!"

"What sort of deal?" I could see that Barry was confused.

"A cleaning sort of deal; tomorrow we start on the toilet and shower blocks and in return we can stay here for free for one or two nights."

"Well done, Kid" he was pleased, "That sounds alright to me!"

The next day we got to work and when the owner turned up in the evening he was so impressed with the transformation that had taken place, he invited us back to his house saying that we had done a great job and deserved a decent meal. After we ate, we spoke to one another in an amusing combination of broken English and German; the owner offered us a job painting the entire shower and toilet blocks, working only in the mornings. Our afternoons were free to spend relaxing and enjoying ourselves. The job lasted just over two weeks, and by the time we said our goodbyes, we'd had a wonderful time, had been well fed, and had become quite friendly with the elderly couple who owned the site. They invited us to call in any time we were passing and to stay with them for free.

Leaving Lucerne, we turned south towards Spain.

Barry had come up with a great idea – to go to Gibraltar, an English colony located on the southern tip of Spain, as he was adamant that we would find work there as we were English. But Gibraltar was a long way away and after a few days on the road we decided to stop off in Monte Carlo. The view of the harbor as we drove down through the hills was breathtaking, but it was not until we got out of the Land Rover having found somewhere to park not far from the water, that the enormity of the wealth really hit us.

Barry and I stood and stared. Neither of us had ever seen so many large yachts before, some almost as big as the small cruise liners that had occasionally moored in Liverpool. Looking at the millions of Pounds worth of boats, Barry and I were completely at a loss for words. As we walked along I noticed a young lady standing on the deck of one of these yachts, polishing the rails. She was very tall and slim, and didn't seem to be wearing very much. As we got closer I suddenly realised that she was only wearing a small bikini bottom and nothing else. She was topless!

Nudging Barry in the ribs, I drew his attention to this spectacular view. We continued our walk, eyes never leaving the vision of loveliness.

My gaze was disturbed by the arrival of another of these goddesses – also in the same state of undress. Then we realised that they were not alone – in fact there were five in total, all with long hair gently blowing in the wind, tanned legs up to their armpits, and beautiful breasts on view for all the world to see.

Like a couple of kids we started to laugh, pushing each other about, unable to believe our luck. This was something that we had never seen before, let alone dreamt would ever be possible.

We spent the next ten minutes or so, slowly walking up and down the harbor front, eyes sharply turned in the direction of the yacht. There was a man with grey hair sitting on a wooden recliner, a glass of champagne set on a small table beside him. He was reading a paper, and was not really aware of the reaction that his crew was having on two lads from Liverpool. One of his girls must have said something however, because as we walked past for about the tenth time he lowered his paper, loftily peering over the top of the page at us both, one eyebrow raised in amusement.

Spirits raised we carried on with our journey down the coast of Spain, slowly getting closer to Gibraltar.

It was a long, hot and dusty journey, and in an attempt to keep ourselves cool, we tied the Land Rover doors flush against the bonnet, holding them in place with pieces of rope wrapped around the wing mirrors.

We had never experienced such intense dry heat before, and we found travelling hard going. Sleeping at night was uncomfortable, as we had to leave the windows closed to stop mosquitoes from coming in and attacking us; they were relentless, attacking like squadrons of kamikaze pilots as soon as the sun went down. We were looking forward to Gibraltar, and what we hoped, would be a little slice of English heaven.

Finally we arrived at the border between Spain and Gibraltar. Pulling up at the Spanish side, we were told that it was closed, because of some international border dispute. Clearly in sight and less than two hundred yards away was the English border but it might have been miles away for all the success we were going to have in reaching it. The border guard told us that the only way to reach our destination was to drive further south to the nearest port, catch the boat to Tangiers and then a boat from Tangiers to Gibraltar.

Totally pissed off and weary with travel we drove to Algeciras, and were fortunate enough to arrive in time to catch the ferry across staying over night in Tangier. The following morning we caught another ferry and finally arrived in Gibraltar.

Once off the ferry, we found somewhere to park and walked around the town enjoying the very English feel of it all, with traditional pubs and fish and chip shops catering to the British troops who lived on the island. A couple of pints of English bitter and a bag of fish and chips went down a treat, and we found a cheap bed and breakfast to stay in for a few nights. Having a quick shower before setting off, we still felt optimistic about finding employment, asking people working in bars and shops for advice; we were willing to do any job to earn some money.

We soon discovered however that the only work available was with the Moroccan gangs of men who were repairing the famous Rock. Sweltering heat in the mid hundreds and a few pesetas a day was not what we were looking for. Deflated and disillusioned, with our funds running low we had to pick ourselves up and return to Spain. The whole trip had been a waste of time and money, all those miles and thousands of pesetas spent on petrol and ferries, a long way for a couple of pints of bitter and a bag of fish and chips.

After another two weeks in the Land Rover, driving around Spain continuously looking for work and still spending money on petrol, we eventually arrived in a small village not too far from Barcelona. Lloret del Mar was one of the first package holiday destinations and was popular with German, British and Scandinavian tourists.

Barry and I were beginning to hate the Land Rover for two good reasons. Firstly we were sick of spending all our time, day and night, in it, and secondly because it was a real gas guzzler, only doing about seventeen miles to the gallon. It was eating its way through our funds with an alarming speed and we were literally down to a handful of notes by the time we found somewhere to park.

This time there was no casual stroll around the village, we were job hunting with a vengeance. After going into several bars asking if there was any work available, a Spanish waiter told us of a place further up the sea front which was looking for staff. He told us to look out for the 'Sandwich Bar' as it was called, so feeling a little bit more positive we set off.

His information had been correct; there was a notice in the window saying that staff were required. Before going in, Barry told me to leave all the talking to him; he stated that he was far more experienced than me and we couldn't afford any mistakes.

The Sandwich Bar was quite small, and a welcome relief from the afternoon sun. We found the Spanish owner, Senor

Antonio, behind the bar, and Barry told him that we were looking for work. Sitting us down at a table, the owner explained in good English that he had two positions available; he needed an experienced English speaking barman to look after his tourists and a kitchen hand to do all the dishes.

Barry was in his element. "Barman!" he exclaimed, "You want a good barman?" Putting one hand on my shoulder he continued, "This young lad is one of the best, he has worked in nearly every pub in Liverpool and is a dab hand at pulling a pint!"

I just sat there completely silent, not so much because I was following Barry's instructions and leaving the talking to him, but because I was beginning to get very annoyed.

"As for a kitchen hand," Barry added, "Just show me your sink and I will make those plates gleam!"

Impressed by our credentials and Barry's enthusiasm, the owner offered us the jobs on the spot wanting to know when we could start.

"Immediately," said Barry, "There is no time like the present!"

"Tonight, six pm," we were told, "Your shift will be from six in the evening until midnight every day."

Senor Antonio told me that he would give me a red shirt and black bowtie, and asked me if I owned a pair of dark trousers.

I suddenly saw an opening, a way out of this job and was about to say that I didn't have any when Barry took over once again.

"That's not a problem," he stated, "He already has a pair!"

Barry shook hands on the deal, and we left emerging out on to the sea front. As soon as we were out of sight of the bar, I grabbed hold of his arm, pulling him to a stop.

"What the hell do you think you are doing? I have never pulled a pint in my life; I have never worked in a bar!!" My anger was obvious. "How come you didn't offer to do the bar job? Why can't I wash the dishes?"

I couldn't stop. "I am going to make a complete fool of myself. I'll get sacked before I have even started! Didn't you hear what the man said, you idiot, the man wants an experienced barman! You are such a tosser!!"

"Hey Kid, calm down." Barry interrupted my ranting. "It won't take you long to get it sussed. Within no time at all you will be pulling pints and mixing drinks like the best of them."

I still wasn't convinced and told him so.

"Well, look at it this way," he carried on, "The money is good and the prospect of tips even better. At the moment we can't afford not to work, can we?"

His words made sense. Apart from an emergency reserve (just enough money to get us home) which Barry kept hidden away, we hardly had any money left.

"And Kid?" Barry added one last remark, "Just think of all the pretty birds that you will get to meet, whilst I am up to my elbows in hot greasy water! You're the lucky one!"

I would only be lucky if I managed to pull it off, I was nervous. We went in search of a pair of dark trousers, spending more money which we really could not afford.

★ ★ ★

I spent the first night of my new job standing quietly to one side, watching the two other Spanish barman as they went through their routines, throwing ice cubes and bottles up in the air, garnishing the glasses with slices of orange or lemon. Watching them in silence I felt that I was watching some theatrical performance as they effortlessly created one masterpiece after another.

Three English tourists came up and sat at the bar. Looking around to see if either Carlos or Santos were going to serve them, I noticed with dismay that they were both busy.

"Three beers mate!" I heard one of the tourists call out. There was nothing I could do, I could not avoid the moment of truth any longer. Picking up a beer glass, endeavouring to keep my hand steady, I placed the glass under the San Miguel pump. Trying to remember how I had seen my fellow barmen do it, I slowly pulled down on the handle, waiting for the glass to fill.

There was a loud hiss, followed by a series of splatting noises, and beer came spitting into the glass. Froth flew everywhere followed closely by droplets of beer; the three men sitting in front of me were covered in flecks of San Miguel, looking totally stunned. I don't know who spoke first; whether it was one of the blokes asking what I was doing, Carlos telling me to turn the handle the other way, or me praying for the ground to open, it all remains a blur.

What I do remember however, is that Carlos threw his hand over mine, pushing the pump handle backwards and cutting off the stream of beer that was now flowing everywhere. Without any further fuss he poured three beers and gave them to the British tourists, saying that they were with the 'compliments of the manager'.

Carlos and Santos realised that I was an absolute beginner, and quietly told me that they would help me learn without Senor Antonio finding out.

Realising that the truth had been discovered by my colleagues, I felt better. The rest of the night went reasonably well, and when we finished at midnight, my two new Spanish friends invited us to a disco.

Barry and I were ready to celebrate our good fortune, and it wasn't long before we were drinking and dancing the night away. The nightclub was full of lots of young people from all over Europe having a good time, and Barry and I soon found ourselves both going in separate directions. We had agreed that should we split up, we would meet the following morning at the Land Rover, so I was not too concerned about going back to a hotel with a pretty young girl that I had met, safe in the knowledge that Barry was most probably doing the same.

My luck ended at her hotel door, so feeling the effects of too much beer, I stumbled my way back to the Land Rover, stripped off my clothes down to my underpants, crawled into my sleeping bag and was out for the count within seconds.

Barry in the meantime had been a little more fortunate, and returned to the Land Rover an hour or so later. He decided that as it was parked in a very noisy street, he would move it somewhere a little quieter and thus get a decent nights sleep. Totally oblivious as to my presence in the back, and thinking that I was wrapped up in passion, he decided he would return for me in the morning.

Leaving the brightly lit streets behind, Barry headed towards the darkness on the outskirts of town, following a narrow winding road up a steep hill. Starting to realise that he was travelling too far and couldn't turn around on the narrow road, he had no choice other than to keep on driving, hoping that there was a turning place somewhere near the top of wherever the road was taking him. Finally the road leveled out and he found himself in a tiny car park overlooking the town below. There were several other cars parked up as well, with amorous couples also enjoying the view through their steamy windows.

Cursing his bad luck, Barry decided that the only thing for him to do was to execute a three point turn, avoiding the other cars already parked there and then head back down to Lloret del Mar again.

Leaning over the steering wheel so that he could see better he inched the Land Rover forward, slowly and carefully, watching out for a car parked close by. Putting it into the reverse, struggling to get the heavy gears to engage, he drove slowly backwards craning his neck to see where he was going, but it was impossible as it was dark, he couldn't see a thing. Suddenly, he felt the Land Rover continuing to move even though he had his foot hard down on the brake. There was a loud clunk and the vehicle started to groan, as with a grinding noise Barry found himself slowly tilting backwards until he was looking directly up at the stars.

Slamming the gear stick into first, he put his foot down on the accelerator but the car did not move an inch. Totally confused Barry decided to open the door and get out. He found himself looking down into a dark space with tiny little lights blinking brightly on the valley floor some several hundred feet below.

Starting to realise the full extent of his predicament, Barry slowly lowered himself out of drivers door, reaching out grabbing on to a couple of bushes and whatever other vegetation he could find growing on the rocky hillside; he then carefully pulled himself up on to the small car park to safety. Turning around Barry now saw what he had done; the vehicle was see-sawing backwards and forwards with the heavy metal chassis groaning under the stress.

Barry stood there in horrified silence, as the full impact of his narrow escape started to sink in. Within a few minutes he was joined by other voices, as the courting couples emerged from their cars and came and stood beside him, observing that he seemed to be having 'una problema'. Even with Barry's limited Spanish, he understood exactly what they meant.

Surrounded by a group of locals, all offering advice which he did not understand (nor want), Barry stood there not sure what to do. His dazed attention was suddenly caught by the arrival of a blue flashing light as a police patrol car pulled up and two officers got out. The police officers joined the other Spaniards watching the Land Rover as it groaned with pain. Like a group of spectators watching a suicide about to leap off a tall building, they stood there in anticipation waiting for the vehicle to lose its grip on the edge of the mountain before it crashed down into the valley below ending up in a pile of twisted metal and shattered glass.

Barry sat down on a rock, his head in hands, thinking 'what have I done? Everything we own is in there!'

Suddenly a thought occured to him, as the chattering Spanish voices seem to disappear from his consciousness. His mind started to race as he tried to remember the last time that he saw me desperately back tracking. A deep rooted panic set in and he leaped to his feet, calling out for silence, one finger against his lips , waving with his free hand calling out.

"Silence please! Silence please. Ssshhhhh!"

The group of watchers fell quiet, and Barry called out "Jeff, can you hear me? Jeff are you in there?"

There was no response other than the creak of the chassis and the sound of a gentle breeze rustling through some of the bushes on the hill side.

By now the sun was beginning to rise, the sky changing colour from dark blue to a golden red. "Jeff," he called out, even louder this time a note of desperation entering his voice, whilst at the same time praying that I was still in town.

His voice must have penetrated my sleep, as I grunted out a reply, "What?"

"Jeff, wake up, it's serious! Listen to me! Speak to me Jeff, but don't move."

By now the crowd had started to talk again, and Barry turned immediately towards them telling them to be quiet. "Please shut up, my brother is in there," he tried to explain, but they didn't understand a word he said and just carried on.

Turning back in the direction of the Land Rover he called out to me again. "Jeff, please listen to what I say, I want you to slowly make your way to the front of the Land Rover and climb into the front seat. Do you understand?"

"What's going on?" By now I was really starting to wake up finding myself lying in the back of the Land Rover in a semi upright position. "What's going on?" I called out again, "What's wrong?" The effects of the deep alcoholic sleep were still making my brain slow to react as I struggled to work out what was happening.

"Jeff," I could hear Barry's voice clearly now. "Jeff, listen to me. Climb over on to the front seat, and for fucks sake don't open the back door or you'll be dead."

Turning over on to my stomach, I reached for the curtains which divided the back compartment pulling them to either side. The sight which met my eyes made me paralysed with fear, as I saw twenty or so anxious faces peering down in my direction, with Barry's being the most anxious of them all. I could feel that the Land Rover was rocking, caused by my movements, and the extreme urgency on Barry's face was enough to gain my undivided attention.

The crowd in the meantime had let out a loud gasp of horror when they saw the curtains being pulled back and my face appearing in the vehicle. Now they realised what Barry had been going on about.

"Jeff, please listen to me. I want you to carefully open the front windscreen and climb out on to the bonnet." He was pointing towards two small catches on the bottom of the windscreen, which allowed it to be pushed outwards giving me enough room to wriggle to safety.

Not realising the full extent of the danger I was in, I nevertheless carried out his instructions, moving slowly forwards into the front seat. It seemed to take an eternity, and even the smallest movement made the vehicle sway. Raising the windscreen I crawled through the gap and lay face down on the bonnet.

"Take my hand, quick Jeff, come on! Hold on tight." Leaning forward Barry grabbed hold of my outstretched hand, pulling me with all his strength as I slid forwards across the bonnet, my knees scraping against the dusty metal surface until finally I was on firmer ground.

The crowd broke into applause at my rescue, whilst Barry gathered me into a bear hug. "I thought that I had nearly lost you, that you were going down with the Land Rover," he said squeezing me tight. "What would Mum have done if I had come back without you Kid?"

Pushing me back so that he could look at me clearly, he seemed to relax a little. "Are you alright?" he asked.

"Yes," I replied, "Just a bit confused," I muttered.

I looked back at the Land Rover and couldn't believe my eyes as I saw it balanced on the edge, over half the vehicle suspended above a long drop to the valley floor below.

"Barry," I said turning back to him. "What the f…"

I didn't even get the chance to finish as he interrupted me. "Don't even go there" he said.

We stood there for a few minutes in silence, Barry's arm still around my shoulder as if he was frightened of losing me. I suddenly realised that some people were talking about us, and pulled away from my brother. "Barry, they must think that we are lovers! Just look at the way I am dressed, and you've been giving me hugs and kisses!" Looking down at my skimpy underpants Barry started to laugh.

Some six hours later, and with a lot of help from the police, a 'grande' crane came crawling up the mountain. It was the size of a small house, and as it pulled onto the car park, I understood the meaning of the word 'grande' a word that I had heard many times whilst we waited, and had begun to hate. Grande? The crane was enormous.

The Land Rover was lifted to safety, and it didn't take us too long to realise that the only damage was to the exhaust. However, Barry suffered the most as he stood counting out every peseta we had left, placing the notes one by one into the crane drivers hand; everything gone, including the money to get us back home.

Our attitude towards our Land Rover changed a lot after that terrifying incident. Although she was still a gas guzzler, her sturdy build and steel chassis had saved both our lives, and we now felt indebted to her.

We continued to work at The Sandwich Bar for the next four weeks; Barry was right as I did end up having the last laugh; I not only became a competent barman, but was also able to chat up all the best girls (before Barry) who came into the bar. We soon started to get itchy feet however and having saved enough money were trying to decide where to go next.

One night, two Germans came into the bar, regulars whom I knew quite well, so I asked them about Germany. They were very enthusiastic, and told us about the Olympic Games that were due to start soon – apparently there were lots of jobs available as well! Handing in our notice and saying good bye to everyone, we set off on the next leg of our journey.

★ ★ ★

We arrived in Munich on the morning of 1st September, and spent all that day and the next just familiarizing ourselves with the enormous Olympic Village. Soaking up the truly international feel of the games, Barry and I had a memorable time watching the swimming and boxing on our second day.

We spent the third day looking for jobs. We looked every where, and after many hours and a good few shoe miles we found a job selling ice cream. On the fourth of September we reported for work, clean shaven and hair brushed as neatly as possible; neither Barry nor I had been to a barbers for several months and both had an abundance of long curly hair! We were given striped aprons and straw boaters to wear, and struggled to keep the hats on our heads.

After a quick demonstration on the 'art' of ice-cream selling we headed off, armed with price lists, cash boxes and instructions where to set up shop, each of us pushing a beige ice-cream cart. The carts made us laugh as we unsuccessfully tried to push them in a straight line; the wheels had minds of their own.

"It's a good job that none of our mates can see us," I called out to Barry.

"Tell me about it," he shouted back, "I feel like a right clown in this get up, pushing this stupid cart along!"

The day passed quickly; it wasn't too difficult a job once you had mastered all the different words for ice-cream and at the end of it all we didn't really care how we had dressed, or what we had done, it had been good money and that was all that mattered.

The following morning as we walked through the Village on our way to work there was a strange atmosphere in the air. Groups of people stood around talking quietly amongst themselves and there were hundreds of police everywhere. The feeling of festivity and celebration had completely vanished overnight.

The man who owned the ice-cream company greeted us with a worried look on his face. "I am afraid that there is no work for you today," he said, handing us our wages from the day before. "The Games have been cancelled for today as something terrible has happened."

"Why, what's happened?" we asked him as one voice.

He told us that in the early hours of the morning, several members of the Israeli Olympic team had been taken hostage by the Black September Organisation, a group of Palestinian terrorists. There had been gunfire, and no-one knew exactly what was going on.

Advising that we keep out of harms way, he suggested that we return in a couple of days once everything had calmed down, as he would be happy to give us some more work.

Thanking him for our money, we headed back to the Land Rover trying to find out more information along the way.

"Come on Kid," Barry said, "We have got to get out of here right now. I made a promise to Mum to bring you back safe, and I mean to keep it."

The drive out of the city took several hours due to numerous road blocks and security searches, but we eventually reached the outskirts and pulled into a layby for a cup of tea and something to eat. Over the months Barry had become an expert at making spaghetti bolognaise, and it had been our staple diet throughout our travels.

Sitting at the side of the road cooking our food, we discussed what we should do next.

"What about Beverly?" Barry asked me. "Remember, our Bev who you used to go skating with? She lives somewhere in Germany. Let's give Mum a call and find out where she is."

It had been some time since we had spoken to Mum and it was good to hear that she was keeping well. She said that she had received all our postcards and had loved hearing about our adventures; we could both tell that she was much happier now that we had spoken and she knew we were alright.

Beverly lived near Wiesbaden and worked on an US Military Base. As we made our way across Germany we were glued to the BBC World Service on the radio, listening to the news reports and updates on the hostage situation that was taking place. As the story unfolded over the next twelve hours we sadly learnt that eleven hostages had been murdered, whilst six terrorists had been killed; seventeen people dead in a matter of hours. We both felt sick inside at the tragic news.

★ ★ ★

Some twenty-four hours later we were sitting with Beverly enjoying a cup of coffee. It had been a long time since we had seen each other and there was a lot of catching up to do.

Beverly lived in Army quarters and was not able to put us up for the night. However she arranged for permission for us to park our vehicle on the base, and Barry and I found ourselves sleeping in the Land Rover once again!

She also arranged for us to meet someone with regards work the following day, and so after a good nights sleep and a quick breakfast we set off in search of employment.

We were directed to a building the size of an aircraft hanger which turned out to be the biggest supermarket we had ever seen in our lives. Standing inside the entrance, both Barry and I were completely stunned as we looked around us. There were rows and rows of shelves selling almost everything under the sun, and a long row of about twenty till points.

Supermarkets like this were unheard of anywhere in the world at the time, outside of the States. This was a whole new experience, but then the Base was a completely different world. It was a slice of America transported to a foreign country, with movie theatres showing American films, bowling alleys and swimming pools, American food and American cars, and everywhere you went the sound of American accents. For the two of us, it was (I think) the greatest culture shock of all. Apart from the civilian wives and children, everyone else was in uniform and we saw every type of outfit from combat fatigues to full dress kit, with rows of medals and ribbons across the chest.

Our 'interview' was conducted by a young man sitting on top of what looked like a life saver or umpires' seat, a chair at the top of a ladder, positioned in the middle of the row of tills. Looking up at him we explained that we had come to find work.

He had a strong Southern drawl, which was a little difficult to understand, but after a few moments we were able to decipher that there was work available as 'bag boys'. In essence this meant that we packed and carried customers shopping. This all sounded very straightforward, until I asked him how much we got paid.

"You pay me ten dollars a day," was his answer.

Thinking that I had not heard him right, I asked him what he meant.

"You don't get wages here, you get tips. I don't get wages and I don't get tips because I am too busy watching out for your arses. So if you want to work here and earn loads of money, you look after me, and I will look after you."

After a quick moments silent discussion, i.e. looking at each other, Barry and I decided to give it a go, and started work immediately.

Each till had three bag boys working in rotation. Bag Boy One and Bag Boy Two packed the brown paper bags. Bag Boy Three loaded the bags onto a trolley then followed the customer out to their car walking a respectful five paces behind.

Pontiacs and Chevrolets were very popular, with long bonnets and equally as big trunks, the top of which would suddenly pop open as we approached, triggered by a press of a button. The shopper would disappear into the depths of the car whilst we loaded the shopping. Closing the boot we were told to call out "Have a Good Day, Ma'am". A gentle hum and the electric window would drop, at which point an arm would appear, the hand holding a few dollar bills for our efforts.

"Here you go boy," would be the sum total of comment from our customers, before they drove off. Hurrying back to the store, we would report to our controller, who would then tell us which till to go to. The faster you were, the more money you made. And so it would go, with each Bag Boy taking it in turn to pack the trolleys and load the cars, thus earning enough money in tips to pay our boss his cut.

It did not take Barry and me too long to realise that the best tippers were the GI's. The average shopper would have six to eight brown bags, carefully packed with all their groceries. They would give a $2 tip on average. A GI would have a half bag of groceries, predominantly six cans of beer and several packs of chewing gum.

Ridiculously, more often than not, their bag still had to be carried to the car, and we still had to walk the regulation distance behind not speaking a word, whilst they marched ahead of us at a fast pace.

"Have a nice day, Sir" we'd say, handing over their groceries.

"You too boy," would be the reply as they gave us a crisp five dollar bill. Those GI's loved the thought of us walking five paces behind them carrying a little paper bag. It was as if it was their turn to give out the orders.

It seemed to be a very long day, but eight hours later Barry and I eventually sat down enjoying a chilled beer and counting our tips. As we sorted the notes we soon realised that we had made close to $100 each, even after having paid the 'boss' ten dollars apiece. Although quite the norm in the US, earning a living from tips alone was a whole new venture for us, but we could not get over how simple it was.

We stayed there for three weeks, working almost every day, and enjoying life on the Base in our free time. Everything was subsidised, making our dollars go even further, and we took advantage of all the entertainment on offer, going to the movies and bowling almost every night. Come the end of September however, we were ready to move on.

We had learned that there was a beer festival held every year in Munich, the Oktober Fest, and so decided that we would return to the city we had left only a short while before. This time the trip passed quite quickly, and with an expertise born of practice were soon able to find ourselves somewhere to park near all the activity.

We had seen and done so much over the past few months, learning about so many different ways of life and cultures; the Oktober Fest was no different. Soaking up another new atmosphere, caught up in the midst of thousands of people from all over Europe simply celebrating the joys of beer as they drunk themselves under the table! It was an exceedingly agreeable four days sampling all the different types of beer on offer, joining in the various beer songs and taking part in the dancing that would start up from time to time as an 'oompah' band would start to play traditional German folk music. After the sadness of our earlier visit to Munich it was a brilliant way to end our travels around Europe and when Barry and I set off for England we were both full of good humour and stories to tell.

We were also both longing for our beds!

★ ★ ★

The trip back to Liverpool was in some ways the most exhausting that we did. Driven by our desire to get home and the luxury of living in a house again, (sleeping in the Land Rover for so long had both physically and mentally taken its toll on us), Barry and I hardly stopped as we crossed Europe back to Calais. On reaching Dover we decided to push on, driving through the night so that we could get back in time for breakfast. The trip passed in a blur as we struggled to keep our eyes open, staying awake by talking endlessly about how wonderful it was going to be to lie in our own beds, fully stretched out for the first time in ages and able to toss and turn without hitting someone else.

We got back home at about nine in the morning. The look on Mum's face as she opened the door was one of joy and surprise. For a second she was at a loss for words, as she surveyed the sight before her; her two sons, bleary eyed and bushy haired, looking definitely the worse for wear.

Her amazement did not last too long however, and we were soon seated at the kitchen table enjoying a fresh cup of tea whilst she cooked us a big breakfast, the aroma of bacon and sausages making our mouths water in anticipation.

Putting two full plates down on the table in front of us, Mum had the biggest smile on her face. Her sons were back in one piece; sitting down she asked us to tell her of our travels. In between mouthfuls of the best breakfast ever, we shared some of the adventures we'd had. As I finished off my last piece of toast, Mum asked what were our plans for the future.

"Right now Mum," Barry replied, "I am just thinking about my bed and nothing else."

Unusually, there was no response from Mum. Looking at her, I noticed that she had a dismayed look on her face.

"What's the matter Mum?" I asked. "You've gone as white as a sheet!"

"You should have told me that you were coming home!" was her cryptic reply. "You should have given me some kind of warning!"

"Why, what's happened? Have you rented out our room or something?" Barry was starting to look worried himself.

"No of course not," Mum tried to reassure him. "It's just that I wanted to give you boys a surprise, thinking that you would be at home for Christmas. Oh go on, go and have a look at your room and see for yourself."

Wearily we stood up, pushing our tired bodies up the stairs in the direction of our room. The door was ajar, and we could see that it was bare of furniture. Everything had been taken out, the floors were bare and the walls had been stripped back to the plaster. The only thing that was there were some rolls of wallpaper, tins of paint and a couple of paintbrushes lying on a tray.

"Mum!" I protested, "Where are we going to sleep?"

"I am sorry," she said, "I just wanted to make it all look nice for when you got back."

Seeing the degree of distress on her face, Barry and I both gave her a hug, reassuring her that it would be alright, and we would sort something out. Mum made various suggestions, including offering us June and Sheila's beds, but as we were so tired we wanted to sleep for hours undisturbed by the comings and goings of the family. We needed total peace and quiet.

For some reason, which I still cannot understand today, Barry and I opted to pitch a tent in the garden, and having crawled into our sleeping bags went to sleep listening to the sound of the rain splattering against the canopy above our heads! Our travels had come to an end in a tent in a garden in Liverpool. The last thing I heard as I drifted off to sleep was Barry muttering something to me.

Over the sound of the rain, I finally caught his words.

"What do you reckon Kid? Isn't this just bloody typical!"

Chapter Twenty
While Angels Watched

Europe had changed our lives forever. Not only had we learnt about a world outside of Liverpool, but Barry and I now shared a unique closeness, the type of bond which is not often found between two brothers with so many years between them.

Having recovered from our travels, and once again returned to our bedroom, we discussed our plans for the future, deciding to go into business together. The most logical thing was the aerials business, combining our experience and knowledge. Mum was more than happy to join our new venture, taking on her earlier role of handling the bookings and planning the jobs for us both. Apollo Aerials was born. We had some business cards printed and placed an advert in the local papers.

Barry insisted that we open a bank account for the new business, so we went in to the local branch of Barclays Bank in West Derby. I had never had a bank account before and was not prepared for all the forms that had to be completed. As I stared down at the printed pages, I felt the familiar feel of terror come over me as the words became a blur. Looking at Barry, who was busy completing his forms, I summoned up enough courage to ask him for help.

"You will have to do this for me Barry," I stated, handing him my application form.

"What do you mean?" he enquired. "It's really quite simple."

"It's not for me," I replied. "I don't understand it."

"What do you mean, don't understand it?" He was clearly puzzled by my comments.

"I can't read what's written here," I said. "I can't write or spell either."

My statement threw him off guard for a moment, before he silently took the papers from me and completed them on my behalf.

That was the first time that Barry realised that I had problems with reading and writing, and the only time we ever discussed it; it was never referred to again.

The winter months were closing in and business was good. I did most of the roof work whilst Barry looked after the customers and their televisions. Working with me taught Barry something else; he discovered my appetite for work, finding my endless energy hard to keep up with, whatever the weather. Whilst most riggers finished at four in the afternoon, I would still be going well into the early hours of the night. When it became too dark to see, I would strap a torch to my head, finally finishing at eight or nine in the evening; I felt that if there was work to be done it had to be finished, no matter what time it said on the clock.

Barry sold his Land Rover; it was sad seeing our travelling companion go after so many thousands of miles together. We replaced her with an old Morris Oxford Estate which we used for the business and a second hand Jaguar MK II for the socialising needs in our life.

We went everywhere together, during the day as we did our work, and in the evenings, dressed to kill, out on the town. It was not hard to meet girls in the various night clubs we frequented and after an evening dancing and drinking would offer them a lift home, impressing them with the elegance of our car.

Christmas Eve soon came, and having decided to go out on the town, I agreed to drive that night, enabling Barry to enjoy a drink or two. In return he would play chauffeur on

New Years Eve thus allowing me to party. It was a great night out, and we met two very pretty girls at one of our favourite night clubs. Chatting with them over a drink, we agreed to go back to our house for a final night cap or two.

It was starting to snow as we left the club, and the warmth of the car was a welcome relief after the cold of the night air. It didn't take us long to get home and after making our way into the kitchen, amongst warnings of keeping quiet so as not to wake the rest of the family who were asleep, we got down to the serious business of enjoying the rest of the night. Soon it was four in the morning and time the girls went home. We tried to call for a taxi, but the combination of snow, lateness of hour, and the fact that it was early on Christmas morning meant that we were out of luck.

Barry then suggested that I drive them home myself, my protests of having had a couple of drinks and therefore not being sober enough to drive falling on deaf ears. As far as he was concerned it was now my problem and I had to sort something out.

As I discovered, the two girls only lived about twenty minutes away in Croxteth, so putting on my new heavy sheepskin coat, we left and got into the car setting off through the falling snow.

I drove slowly. Heavy flakes were falling steadily, it was dark and the roads were very slippery. With the headlights on full, and the windscreen wipers frantically trying to provide visibility, we crept our way through the silent roads, moving through a white and sleeping world.

As I drove up Croxteth Hall Lane, I noticed that there was another car in front of me, moving equally as slowly through the now worsening snow. Blizzard conditions, and I was out in the middle of it, rather than tucked up in the warmth of my bed! Sometimes being the younger brother sucked!

Croxteth Hall Lane is not the best road for bad weather driving as it has numerous bends, some of them quite sharp.

Carefully I continued, constantly mindful of the car in front that seemed to be going in the same direction, and keeping a safe distance. Turning a rather sharp bend, I realised that the distance had dramatically closed; the car I had been following was now at a standstill and all I could do was try to avoid it.

I put on the brakes as hard and as fast as I dared but we continued to move forward, the tyres finding no grip on the snow covered surface. Slowly and silently the Jag glided forward, only coming to a stop when the two cars made contact, my bonnet right up his rear!

As the car came to a crunching halt, I quickly checked to make sure that my two passengers were both safe. Luckily no one was injured, so pulling my coat closer around my body I got out to check on the passengers in the other vehicle.

I had literally stepped on to the road and shut the car door when I saw a man rushing towards me. The snow was falling so thickly and the night was so dark that I could barely make out his features whilst his words were muffled and unclear. The tone of his voice did not sound reassuring; I sensed this was a man who was angry.

As the gap between us narrowed I realised that he had one arm raised above his head and it seemed as if he was holding something. In an instant he was upon me and I was suddenly brought to my knees as a blinding pain slashed across my head. Stunned I was unable to move, as one blow after another rained down on me, each as excruciating as the last. Something warm was trickling down my face, and looking at the snow I realised that the dark pools forming around my knees was my blood, whilst through the thick haze of pain that was enveloping me I could hear a female voice screaming out in terror.

I tried to focus on what was happening; phrases such as 'stop it', and 'killing him' penetrated my consciousness.

"Who was killing who?" I wondered. "Was it me she was talking about? Was he trying to kill me?"

By now I was bent over, doubled in pain, my face almost buried in the snow as I tried to avoid the never ending succession of blows. Raising my hands to my face I felt the flow of blood getting thicker. "My head, it must be my head," I thought cautiously inching my fingers higher searching for the source. My fingertips suddenly found what they were looking for, and I could feel long jagged edges of skin through the soaked roots of my hair.

With all the strength I could muster, I held both hands firmly in place, desperately trying to stem the flow of blood coming from the wound that I had found. Equally as carefully I straightened up, attempting to assess my surroundings and a way of escape.

I noticed that the two girls had got out of the car, and judging from the noise I could hear, were still shouting at the madman who'd attacked me. Distracted by the noise they were making he had temporarily halted his assault on my body and was shouting back at them. From what I could gather I had ruined his car, and he was making me pay!

Suddenly the two girls were kneeling beside me, each one taking an arm and helping me to my feet, shielding me from the madman with their bodies. He continued his shouting and threats as the three of us slowly tried to move towards the Jag, each step causing another shot of pain to tear through my head. I was walking agony by now, and desperately trying to fight the desire to give in to the pain, slipping into a welcome state of unconsciousness.

Suddenly I heard another male voice and opening my eyes realised that a black taxi had slowed to a halt and the driver was calling out to see if we needed help.

Literally dragging me over to the taxi, the girls asked the driver to take us to the nearest hospital, explaining that I'd been badly injured. Opening the door, they carefully manhandled me on the back seat before climbing in, seating themselves on either side of me. They had just closed the door and we were about to drive off when a face appeared at the window.

Roughly pulling the door open, my assailant climbed into the back of the taxi, sitting on one of the jump seats opposite to me and shouting that he was not going to let me out of his sight, no matter what. I was a bastard for ruining his car.

Unable to respond, I sat in a silence, focusing on keeping my hands on my head, desperately trying to stem the flow of blood that insisted on pouring down. My silence angered him further, and he started to lash out again, this time kicking my body, his heavy boots making contact with my ankles and shins and any other part of me that he could reach.

Getting bored with kicking me, he suddenly lurched towards me planting his fist in my face. Moving closer to the edge of his seat he now leant forward, as if ready to lash out at me even more. Without letting go of my head, I raised my feet in the air, trying to ward off his blows and furiously kicking back at him.

By now there was sheer pandemonium in the back. The sound of my cries of pain mixed with his roars of anger, whilst the two girls started to scream shouting at us both to stop. Suddenly the taxi pulled to a standstill, and the driver turned towards the four of us in the back ordering us to get out of his cab.

Pleading with him, the girls asked him to continue to the hospital, insisting that we weren't at fault, just this lunatic who wouldn't stop fighting. The taxi driver eventually agreed on the condition that the fighting and shouting stopped, so in an uneasy silence we continued our journey to the hospital.

What seemed like forever passed by before we finally pulled up outside the Accident & Emergency doors. It was now five in the morning on Christmas Day, just a short while since we had left the safety of the house, and in the last hour I felt as if I had been dragged to hell and back.

I felt a huge sense of relief as I struggled out of the back of the taxi, and was half carried into the hospital. Safety at last. Although warm and dry and brightly lit, it was eerily quiet with not a soul in sight. The girls propped me up on a seat, whilst one of them went to the desk to call for help.

Within a matter of seconds a nurse appeared, and taking one look at me promptly took me into a treatment room, helping me on to the bed, and taking off my coat and shoes. I was reluctant to let go of my head as I was afraid of allowing the wound to open again. It wasn't until the nurse returned with two of her colleagues in tow that I finally let go, leaving myself and my injuries to their ministrations.

A large patch of my hair was shaved off and my scalp cleaned of all the congealed blood. Silent and scared I lay there as they examined my injuries, listening to the nurses as they discussed what they had found. It appeared that I had three holes in my head, a large gash and two smaller cuts, and that stitches were required on all three. After a local anesthetic I lost all sensation as my wounds were sewn together with a total of nine stitches.

Having finished tending my injuries I was told to lie quietly for a while, and as I faded to sleep my thoughts were filled with the madman who waited for me outside.

A little while later I was woken by a nurse gently shaking my arm. Opening my eyes I saw her worried face looking down at me.

"There are two policemen outside who want to speak to you," she informed me.

Two tall policemen seemed to suddenly appear, standing on either side of me as I lay on the bed, and from where I lay they looked enormous to my befuddled brain.

"We have just come from the scene of the accident on Croxteth Hall Lane," one of the officers advised me. "There is also a man in the waiting area who has informed us that it is all your fault. You deliberately drove into the back of his vehicle, and then you assaulted him shortly afterwards. What have you got to say about all this?"

I lay there totally stunned not sure what to say. The last thing that I felt like doing at that moment was talking to anyone, never mind two official looking giants dressed in black uniforms. The anesthetic was beginning to wear off, my head was throbbing with pain, and my memories of the nights events were not very clear in any case. As I mumbled something in response to his questions, I noticed that the other policeman was writing everything down in a little black book.

"The other driver claims that you are drunk and that you were driving dangerously, veering all over the road? Is that true Sir?"

Another mumbled reply came from my mouth. I just wanted to get this over and done with and get home, and to be perfectly honest was not even sure what I was saying, if infact I was saying anything at all!

"Sir, I need you to sit up as we have to breathalise you," the first policeman continued. Helping me into a sitting position on the edge of the bed he passed me a bag and told me to blow in to it, before he took the bag from me and looked at the indicator. "You've tested positive. You're over the limit" he informed me. "We will have to take you down to the station."

I would have done anything for a little peace and quiet, just to be left alone with my injuries and pain, but this was not to be the case. The nurse reappeared and carefully helped me into my coat, the sheepskin encrusted with congealed and drying blood. It only served as a reminder of the nightmare that I had just been through.

Keeping step with my slow shuffle the police escorted me towards the hospital exit. As we got closer, the doors slid open revealing a sight I never wanted to see again.

He was standing near the doors and I got to see my assailant in daylight and therefore properly for the first time. A small stocky man aged somewhere in his forties, he was going bald and had a beard covering his face. His shoulders were so broad that his head seemed almost too small for his body, stuck somewhere in the middle of a wide stretch of muscle.

He suddenly seemed to come to life as he realised I was only a few feet away. Oblivious to the policemen standing on either side of me, he charged forwards with the same intense aggression that a Spanish bull shows when charging at a matador. Unlike a matador however quick movements were not something that I could perform, and I keeled over backwards as his body made contact with mine, my head striking against the tiled floor sending me into a world of oblivion once again.

When I finally regained consciousness, I found myself back in the same treatment room as before, a circle of familiar faces around me, as my three nurses diligently stitched away at another gash on my head.

Having tended my wounds and bound my head in swathes of white bandages, I was once again released into the care of the police. I refused to leave the safety of the room until they could reassure me that the madman was gone.

At the station I was placed in a cell. After an urine test I was charged with drink driving, having been found to be over the limit; one pint of beer when I had been out and then two in the house was all it had taken for the charge to have stuck! Taking advantage of the 'one phone call allowed' offer, I rang the house; luckily Barry promptly answered the phone next to his bed, and I asked him to come and collect me.

The look on Barry's face as I walked into the room where he was waiting for me was a sight to behold. His mouth literally dropped open as he took in the vision of his little brother wearing a blood encrusted coat, and with his head totally covered in bandages like some sort of white turban.

"I saw the car on the way here," he told me. "What the hell has happened? Are you alright?"

"Do I look alright?" I asked. "No, I don't and I am not. My head hurts and I just want to get home. Please do not ask me to talk about it right now. I just want to get to bed!"

My head finally touched my pillow at about 8.30am, and with the covers pulled up around my shoulders, and my body able to relax into the comfort of my bed, I finally went to sleep.

A terrible scream suddenly shattered the early morning quiet, and opening my eyes I saw my mother standing over me, her hand over her mouth as she looked down where I lay.

For a split second I had no idea where I was or why Mum was screaming. "What's up Mum? What's up?" I asked, trying to lift my head off the pillow. Agonising pain brought it all back.

"What's happened Jeff," she was almost in tears with worry. "What's wrong with your head? Why is it bandaged so much? What have you done to yourself?"

Christmas that year was ruined for us all; my parents went down to the police station later that day to press charges against my attacker for grievous bodily harm. They were unsuccessful. According to the police, my attacker was a taxi driver who had been quietly going about his business. The damage I had inflicted on his car, and my subsequent attack upon him meant that he would not be able to earn any money over the Christmas period. What was more, I had been found to be over the limit and was going to be charged with drink driving!

My two witnesses had disappeared at some point in the early hours of the morning once they had taken me to hospital, and although Barry and I knew their first names, we had no way of finding them. Without them I had no case to bring against the other man.

Dad was well known in the Liverpool taxi world and decided to make a few quiet enquiries of his own. He discovered that the man was not a licenced driver and had been 'pirating' that night, i.e. driving around in a private car looking for fares.

It wasn't long before Dad heard the full version of the story as told by this thug. As it transpired he had been boasting to another driver whom Dad knew about his 'heroics' on Christmas Eve. According to him he had stopped to see if a hitchhiker had needed a taxi when he was rear-ended by a young lad in a big Jag. Realising that he had been put off the road for the rest of the holiday period he decided that he was going to teach this lad a lesson, giving him a good seeing to with a starting handle he always kept under his seat.

Dad and Barry were furious when they heard this story, and wanted to do something. I just felt that it was best to leave things alone, as I was still in pain, and also afraid of any possible repercussions. I did not want to be attacked like that again!

Unbeknownst to me, a few months later, Dad had a chat with one of his friends, well known in certain circles in Liverpool as being one of the hardest men in town and good man for sorting out problems. Within a matter of days 'my problem' found himself on the receiving end of a 'good seeing to' as well!

It took a little while, but I was soon back to my normal self, always on the look out for the two girls that we had met that night as I very much wanted to thank them for having possibly saved my life on that snowy Christmas morning in 1972.

Chapter Twenty-One
Mum

Mum, Barry and I continued building our business during the early part of 1973. As it was doing so well, Barry and I were contemplating another trip to Europe during the summer months, this time planning a visit to the Greek Islands.

One day at the beginning of April, Mum sat Barry, myself and Sheila down and told us that she had bowel cancer, and told it to us straight. She was going in to hospital in the next couple of days and would be undergoing major surgery to remove the cancerous growth. Sitting there, listening to her, my mind went well and truly numb with the enormity of what she was saying. I didn't want to hear it, this was not happening to us at all!

No-one really knew how to respond, trying desperately hard to follow Mum's lead, helping her prepare her things for her visit to hospital, and trying to be as calm and as pragmatic as possible.

The morning arrived, when having kissed Mum good luck she was taken to theatre, leaving her family to spend the rest of the day waiting and hoping for the best. It is one of the most difficult things to do, waiting for a loved one to come through such an ordeal and praying that it all works out!

After what seemed like an eternity, Barry, Sheila, June and I returned with Dad to the hospital for visiting hours in the evening. We were told by the Staff Nurse on duty that Mum was doing well, however could not be disturbed as she was still coming around from her anesthetic. June's face fell, and so taking pity on her, the Staff Nurse relented, allowing us all a quick peek at Mum whilst she slept.

Pulling back the screen around Mum's bed, we were silent as we looked as this tiny frail person, so beloved by us all, lying in what seemed like an oversized bed surrounded with sorts of medical machinery. It was scary. Reassured though that she was doing well, we tiptoed out of the ward, Sheila, June and I sitting in the waiting room whilst Barry and Dad went to see the Doctor who had operated on Mum.

After some fifteen minutes or so they emerged, faces as white and as drawn as the sheets that Mum had been lying on. Realising that something was desperately wrong, we followed them in silence back out to the car. The silence was almost too much to bear, it was worse than the waiting that we had endured that day.

"What did he say?" I had to know.

Dad who was driving said nothing. Barry turned towards where I sat, and looked down at June's hand clasped in mine. After a moments silence he then looked up at me, "I'll tell you later."

As soon as we got home Sheila tucked June up in bed before hurrying to the front room where the rest of us were sitting. The atmosphere was heavy with tension as Sheila and I waited to hear what Barry and Dad had to say.

"Mum is very ill..." Dad started to speak but was unable to continue, so Barry picked up where he had left off.

"They have removed all of her bowel," he explained, "and fitted a colostomy bag. However the cancer has spread and there is nothing else that they can do." Tears streaming down his face, he lowered his head into his hands. "They have only given her three months to live."

Sheila let out a cry as if she was in pain.

I had to get out of the room, out of the house; I couldn't breathe and needed fresh air. I walked the whole way down Princess Drive as if in a trance, oblivious to the cars and people passing me by, to the chilliness of the April evening. It could have been snowing for all I cared; Mum was dying and there was nothing I could do to stop it from happening.

She was only fifty-three, too young to die. I thought that Mum was going to live for ever. And poor June, she was only eleven! Far too young to be without our Mum. In fact we all were.

Lesley came home for a few weeks to take care of Mum once she came out of hospital and having her back with us all made such a difference. Mum however, once back at home, couldn't understand what all the fuss was about. She acted as if nothing was wrong, as if there had been some terrible mistake and she had been mis-diagnosed; in her eyes the doctor had no idea what he was talking about.

It was hard for her children to know how to respond, and we found ourselves fussing around her, treating each day as if it was her last which really annoyed her.

"Just you wait and see, I am soon going to be as fit as a fiddle," was her response, telling us to pull ourselves together. She insisted that Barry, Sheila and I stopped acting as if something was wrong and told us to get on with our lives.

The impact on Dad was phenomenal. He began spending far more time at home, particularly with Mum, and as she started to regain her strength took her for days out in his car. June was too young to know what was going on and was simply happy that Mum was back where she belonged.

It was a very difficult time for us all, in particular for Mum as she was being so strong. Once Lesley returned to London,

Sheila took over helping Mum, being the oldest daughter in the house, and naturally best suited to doing so, and she too was a tower of strength.

Mum was very keen that Barry and I go off on our travels, encouraging us to go to Greece, but her words fell on deaf ears. With things as they were, Barry and I had no intention of leaving the country.

★ ★ ★

As the summer months approached the aerial business started to dry up, and there was hardly enough work for one of us, let alone a business partnership of two. We knew that our friends were working at a Butlin's Holiday Camp in Clacton-on-Sea only a few hours drive down south, which meant that we could come home at weekends.

Mum was back to her normal strength, and with her blessing we set off. We had arranged to meet up with Mick, Tommy and Danny Tallon (who was another good friend of ours) at the camp, and after the worries of the past few months, it was great to see them all again.

As we sat around enjoying a pint, they told us about their new jobs working as chefs.

"Chefs!" Barry and I nearly fell off our chairs laughing.

"Ok, cooks," Mick defended his job.

"Cooks?" I replied. "What can you lot cook?"

"Everything." Danny answered. "It easy as it's all mass produced, and what's more it is one of the best paid jobs on the camp!"

As we soon found out, they were short staffed in the kitchen, and it would be easy for us to get jobs working there as well. Barry and I were having none of it.

"You can't be serious," Barry said, "Neither of us can cook."

I had to agree with him; memories of the god-like chefs that I had come across the year before came flooding back, professionals who knew what they were doing and had no time for those who didn't.

"Seriously," Mick said, "there is nothing to worry about. You two will be fine. Let's finish off here and go to the kitchen. I will introduce you to the Head Chef; he's great, and you will really like him. He will be more than happy to have you two in his kitchen."

As we walked to the kitchen we were briefed on what to say during our interview. It all sounded ridiculous but we had no choice other than to go along with it.

Somehow we held our own during the interview finding ourselves being handed a set of keys to a chalet within a very short period of time, and being instructed to go to the laundry to collect clean uniforms. Settling down later that night, Barry and I discussed what lay ahead, and both of us had to admit we were a little bit nervous at the prospect of it all.

The alarm rang early the following morning. By six o'clock the two of us were dressed and looking every inch the professional. We had been given blue and white checked trousers and chef's whites to wear. The white's referred to the crisp cotton jacket, so heavily starched that it could stand up on its own, the edge of the round collar cutting into the skin underneath our chins. Getting our arms into the sleeves had been an event in itself, like trying to slide a hand between two pieces of cardboard glued together. To top it all off, literally, we were both wearing tall white chef's hats, as starched as the jackets, which sat stiffly on our heads.

If ever there was a situation when appearances were misleading this was it.

Our apprehension only increased as we walked across to the kitchens, passing a holidaymaker with a newspaper under his arm returning to his chalet. "Morning Chef," he called out, further emphasizing the reality of our new roles, and the significance of our uniforms.

The kitchen was huge, on the same size and scale as a football pitch, and was alive with activity. The smells of the food being prepared mixed with the heat of the cookers made the space seem almost claustrophobic, whilst a constant hum of voices, shouts and orders assailed our ears.

Steam rose up from the tops of the largest saucepans we had ever seen, so big they were more like vats. Two cooks were stirring huge amounts of porridge with large paddles, whilst another two were grilling hundreds of kippers, all laid out in a neat row, their fishy odour dominating that part of the kitchen. There was so much going on that it was almost impossible to absorb it all, and Barry and I stood at the door totally at a loss what to do next. It was time to turn tail and run all the way back to Liverpool.

Our chance was lost as a loud voice suddenly broke through the din coming from a man wearing the tallest white hat in the kitchen. It was the Head Chef. Dragging our feet slowly we inched towards him, feeling like lambs to the slaughter; we were definitely in for the chop!

Standing in front of him he gave us our orders. "Eggs for you two," he stated. "You're doing boiled," he instructed Barry, whilst I was told that I was doing fried.

"Understood?"

"Yes Chef!" Barry kept his reply short.

"Any questions before you get on with it?" Chef asked, looking at us both.

"How many eggs, Chef?" I just had to know.

Referring to a piece of paper on the top of the clip board he was holding he scanned it quickly. "Three thousand fried," he told me, "Full quota today."

Surely he was taking the piss. I was just about to say that I wasn't a chef when Danny took hold of my arm.

"I'll show him the ropes Chef," he said. I noticed that Mick had also appeared quickly going to Barry's aid.

Danny showed me where I was to be working. I stood in front of three large griddles, one meter squared in size, which had a shallow lip running around their edges. I was told they were shallow fat fryers and this was where the eggs were cooked.

The surface of the grill was covered in an inch of boiling oil, and beside the fryers were stacks upon stacks of large egg trays, each one containing at least two dozen eggs.

Balancing one tray on his left hand, Danny showed me how to crack an egg with the other, dropping the contents into the sizzling oil and throwing the shell into a bin. Quickly and methodically he worked through two trays until there were forty eight eggs cooking in neat little rows.

"Your turn now Jeff," he instructed, passing me a tray to hold.

He had been so speedy and so precise that my hands shook as I took up position. I broke the first dozen or so and burnt my finger tips countless times in the hot oil, but eventually managed to get the hang of it all. I was proud of my achievements as I lined up my eggs in neat rows and then scooped the cooked results out on to metal serving platters.

These platters, covered in eggs, were put on to large metal trolleys which the kitchen porters would then push to another part of the kitchen for plating before being served to the guests who waited hungrily in the dining room.

Three hours later, hot and tired, I served up the last egg having filled the days quota! One thousand eggs an hour – what an achievement. Barry in the meantime had boiled five hundred eggs and cooked three thousand pieces of bacon and we now felt that we could call ourselves cooks.

Our first day passed quickly as we learned how to prepare meals for the masses. The cooking side was relatively straightforward as the lads had said, but no one had warned us about the heat; it was intense in the kitchen and totally exhausting.

Barry attended his first wine and cider party that evening, and not fully appreciating the strength of the concoction had quite a few drinks whilst I was a little more cautious. The following morning, as the alarm sounded at five thirty, we both staggered out of bed and into our whites. We were on time, starting to cook as the clock turned six. I had to feel sorry for Barry as it was his turn to fry three thousand eggs, whilst I learnt the art of making thick porridge!

Holiday camps are all pretty much of a muchness, and working at Butlins in Clacton-on-Sea was virtually the same as Pontins in Morecambe. We worked hard and played hard, enjoying each others company and having a good laugh. We made new friends, and learnt new skills. Every other night we would phone Mum telling her about the funny things that had happened in the kitchen that day, whilst every weekend either Barry or I would return home, spending precious time with her.

Barry and I were dating two girls whom we had met at the camp; Barry met a lovely young lady called Linda, whilst my free time was taken up by a pretty brunette called Christine.

Whilst we were there, Barry and I arranged for Mum, Dad and June to come down for a week organizing the best chalet and pulling as many strings as possible so that it would all be perfect. Mum was as proud as Punch of the two of us in our chefs' whites, whilst June and Dad found our chefs' hats to be very amusing. We were able to cut back on the number of shifts, working in the early mornings, which meant that Barry and I could spend as much time as possible with them, enjoying the afternoons in their company and watching the cabarets and other shows in the evening. It was a wonderful family holiday.

Barry and I were also able to specially prepare their breakfasts, which were collected by their waiter and served directly to their table; this gave us both a real sense of pride as it was the first time that either of us had prepared any meals for Mum who had been feeding us both for most of our lives.

The night before they left, Mum phoned home to speak to Sheila, who had been unable to get time off work. After the phone call, Mum was very excited and couldn't wait to tell us that Sheila was engaged to be married. She had been seeing a chap from Wales, called Keith Jones, whom she had met the previous year whilst on holiday.

Keith worked as an engineer, and was a very gentle, quiet man, whom Mum really approved of and liked. They planned to get married in November and were going to live in Wales in a house that they had just bought. By the time they left at the end of the week we had had a lot of fun. Although Mum was a little sad to be leaving, she was also looking forward to getting back home and helping Sheila with the preparations for her wedding which was only a few months away.

The season eventually ended, so Barry and I returned to Liverpool, picking up where we had left off with our aerials business. It was now mid-September and with nights getting longer and the weather getting colder, business was once again busy. Mum continued to help us both with the bookings, and with all that she was doing was kept very busy. She seemed to thrive on constant activity, defying the predictions made by her Doctor earlier that year. We, all of us, almost really believed that she would go on forever.

Sheila and Keith were married on 4th November; the wedding was a lovely affair, held at the church just across from our house. Although it was only a small family affair, it was certainly one to remember. Mum in a glamorous big hat, posed with Sheila and Keith outside the church for the photos. Dad stood beside his wife, whilst June looked so pretty in the bridesmaid's dress she wore.

The year drew to a close and Christmas was upon us. Somehow we all knew that it was to be the last of its kind although nothing was ever said. Decorations went up everywhere, whilst June and I chose the largest tree that we could find which would fit into the front parlour. Laden with decorations, the old ones from Durden Street, and the new ones that had since been collected, the branches gently bowed under the weight of all its festive glory. Presents were stacked high, and the kitchen filled with goodies to eat. If there was a time to eat, drink and be merry this was truly it.

A constant stream of visitors to the house meant that there was always something nice to eat and drink, and every available surface was hidden under Christmas cards and other mementoes. As Christmas day itself dawned, we laughed about the Christmas before with Barry wrapping a white bath towel around his head, saying that it was his turn this year to look like a mummy!

Lesley and Roy with their small son David, and Sheila and Keith spent New Years Eve with us. The house was full to overflowing, and as the clock struck midnight we all joined in verse, singing the well known words of *Auld Lang Syne* standing there holding hands. Mum had so far defied the odds, she was a walking miracle and it was as if our prayers had been answered.

As the New Year started I clearly remember the image of Mum sitting in her favourite armchair in our front room, with a little boy on her lap. David had a mop of ginger hair and was the spitting image of me when I was that age. With their heads bent together, as Mum told him familiar stories, it took me back to my own childhood, not that many years before.

It was a bittersweet start to 1974.

This was the year in which I officially became a man. Mum had established a family tradition, giving each of her children a gold ring of their choice as a twenty-first birthday present, and as I sit here writing this story some thirty-four years later, it rests beside me on my desk.

Barry and I had returned to Butlin's in Clacton-on-Sea for another season, and were once again working in the kitchens.

This time however, there was no need to talk our way in as we well and truly knew the ropes, having 'graduated' from the season before.

We both had the weekend off for my birthday and spent it at home with the family. Although there was no big party, only a small family affair, Mum had, in her usual way, made it special. Driving back to Clacton I half expected to feel like a man, but in reality I felt just the same.

The antics continued at Butlin's in our pursuit of fun and laughs. Barry and Tommy had been out for several drinks one night, and were heading back to the chalet block, arms across each others shoulders, weaving from side to side and singing out loud.

Walking past the swimming hall, Barry suggested that they go for a swim, "Let's check if the doors are unlocked," he said, trying the handle to see if it would open. Tommy agreed that it was an excellent idea, saying that he really fancied the idea of a dip!

The hall was not locked, eerily quiet and dark, and the pool looked so inviting; an olympic size expanse of still water, its surface just begging to be broken. Finding the light switch near the main doors, Tommy turned them on, before he and Barry stripped naked and plunged into the water.

Splashing about, singing at the top of their voices, Barry and Tommy were thoroughly enjoying themselves when the doors suddenly burst open and several security guards came running in. The skinny dip at midnight was over!

Barry and Tommy refused to get out of the water, suggesting that if they were to be removed, the security guards would have to come and get them. It took a good two hours, and the bravado of the alcohol to wear off before they finally emerged, and having put on their clothes, they were frog marched down to the security office where they spent the remainder of the night under the disapproving watch of the camp 'police'.

As the sun came up, Barry and Tommy were made to pack up their belongings, and were escorted off the camp before the first holiday makers had even awoken. Fortunately for them both, they soon found jobs working in a hotel just up the road in Clacton itself, and we would meet up on a regular basis, at least once or twice a week. We had a good laugh about their midnight swim, although I did find myself missing Barry's company at times – we had spent almost two years together by now living and working alongside each other.

★ ★ ★

I went home at the beginning of July; the first weekend to be precise, and I remember it as clearly today as if it had only just taken place.

I got home at around lunchtime, and walking into the house found Sheila in the kitchen. She looked worried and explained that Mum wasn't feeling too well, so she had come home for a few days to help out. "She's asleep at the moment," she said. "Go up and see her in a little while, just let her rest some more for now."

I was on tenterhooks waiting for time to pass, longing to go and see Mum for myself, to make sure that she was ok. I feared the worst and wanted to spend as much time with her as I could. In the end I couldn't wait any longer, so quietly went upstairs, opening the door to her bedroom as carefully as possible, not wanting to make a noise at all.

"Who's that?" Her voice sounded so tired.

"It's me Mum," I whispered back.

"Jeff, is that really you?" I could hear the smile in her voice. "Come over here son and help me sit up."

Gently I put my arms around her, helping her lean forward so that I could rearrange the pillows, before finally laying her back against them. Mum had always been slender, never a heavyweight, but now she was literally as light as a feather which could be swept away by the gentlest of winds.

"That's better," she thanked me, before telling me to open the curtains to let a little light in the room, and asked me to make us both a brew.

I carried out her instructions, returning to her room with two cups of tea in my hands. She patted the space beside her. "Come on Jeff, sit down here and get comfortable. I need to talk to you, there is so much I have to say."

As we sat there side by side, propped up on the pillows with her hand in mine, Mum told me the strangest thing.

"You will never guess where I have been." She was speaking to me as if she was in a dream, her voice soft and gentle. I didn't answer so she continued. "I have been to heaven. God came down and took me with Him for a visit. It's so lovely there. I saw my Mother and Father, and my brothers who were killed in the War. Everything is so clear up there, you can see it all."

I was totally unsure of how to respond, thinking that perhaps it was the medication making her speak like this, so all I could do was to sit there and say yes, agreeing with her comments.

As she continued to tell me what she had seen, her voice was getting stronger, and there was a greater degree of urgency about her. "Jeff, pay attention. I am being serious; this is important."

"I am listening Mum," I replied, "I am listening to everything you're saying."

"God is coming to take me soon, and I am going to heaven. I know it, and I know that I will be so very happy there. I don't want you to worry at all, everything will be alright. I can watch over you from up there, and help you every day."

I could feel the tears stinging my eyes, and was unable to stop them from welling over and running down my cheeks. This was unbearable.

"Jeff, my dearest Son," Mum said. She had put down her cup of tea and had my hand in both of hers. "Please stop crying, I need you to be strong for me. I need you to do what I ask, do you promise?"

Hardly able to speak, I nodded my head in response, "I promise Mum I'll do what you want."

"First of all let's talk about June. You must make sure that nobody takes her away from this house."

"I will Mum," I told her, making my first promise.

"As for your Dad," she continued, "As soon I am gone, he will stop drinking. He will also look after June from now on, and be a good Father to her. For all his faults I love him and always will, and I want you to promise me that you will look after him as well."

This was not such an easy promise to make, but I did, assuring Mum that I would take care of them both.

"Now, all that remains is to talk about you." Mum smiled at me, squeezing my hand with hers. "I know that you struggle with your reading and writing, but I also know that you are very clever in so many other ways. You will be very happy and successful, and you will be famous one day. Don't ever forget that I will always be watching over you. I promise."

Words failed me, there was nothing I could say. Putting both my arms around her I held her closely against me; we lay there side by side not saying a word, for what seemed like an eternity. I never wanted to let her go; she was the most important person in my life and I wanted the moment to last for ever.

I spent most of the following day with Mum, talking about my childhood and all the things that had happened. We were able to laugh at the crises I had caused, the endless doctors and hospital visits, and the stupid things that I had done at school. It was a lovely time, each and every second so very precious.

Before I left that evening, I once again held her close in my arms; this woman whom I loved so much and who had given me so much. Putting her hands on either side of my face, she looked into my eyes, reminding me of what she had said and the promises that we had made, before finally placing a kiss on my forehead, and as I drove back to Butlins, I could still feel the touch of her lips on my skin. A part of me wanted to stay with her, yet another part of me could not bear to see her go.

There was little time for thought the following day, as we were as busy as usual cooking for the thousands of holiday makers all expecting their meals on time.

On Tuesday morning, I had literally just got in to the kitchen when I heard the Head Chef calling my name. Not giving it too much thought I made my way towards him. He had a small office in the kitchen, and was standing by the door, beckoning at me to come over.

"There's a phone call for you Jeff. Take it in here," he said, and with that he walked back into the main kitchen, shutting the door behind him.

I knew that this was the moment that I had been dreading. Putting the receiver to my ear, I said hello, before I heard Dad's voice on the other end of the phone. He was hardly able to speak as he told me that Mum had died peacefully in her sleep only a few hours before. We talked for a further minute or two, during which time he asked me if I would be alright telling Barry.

I stood in the Chef's office for a while trying to gather my thoughts. What now? Asking for some time off work, I told Chef what had happened, and having changed out of my white's, walked into Clacton-on-Sea to find Barry. On foot it took about half an hour and whilst my body went through the motions of walking, my mind was a whirl as I tried to understand what was going on. Mum had died this morning, how was I going to tell Barry? What would life be like without her? It was all a terrible dream.

When Barry opened the door and found me standing there, there was no need for words – he knew that something was horribly wrong. "It's Mum," I managed to say, "She's gone!" before I broke down and cried.

Sitting in his bedsit, side by side on his bed, we didn't speak. We took comfort from one another's presence, shedding our tears together.

The days leading up to the funeral were a blur; we must have travelled home together, but I cannot remember much else, let alone anything in particular about the funeral service itself. I do recall being back at the house afterwards, watching everyone and everything around me, as if I was not a part of it at all. The whole family was there, many aunts and uncles whom I had not seen for a long time and quite a few old friends and neighbours.

I clearly recall hearing Roy, Lesley's husband, telling one of my cousins how Mum had arranged her whole funeral. "She was a truly remarkable woman," he was saying. "As soon as she knew what was happening, she organised the whole thing: the hymns with the vicar, the flowers for the church, the arrangements with the crematorium. She even asked Mrs O'Toole next door to take care of the sandwiches and refreshments for the wake; no, she left nothing to chance."

This amazed me. Even in the last days of her life, Mum was thinking of her family, and what she could do to make her death as painless as possible for the rest of us left behind. I could see Dad in the garden talking to his brothers and sisters, whilst Barry stood quietly to one side. Thinking of my promise to Mum, I went in search of June to make sure that she was doing alright.

She was sitting on a chair in the front room, and looked like a little girl lost; totally on her own, although she was surrounded by lots of people. As I stood by the door I could hear some of my aunts talking with Lesley and Sheila, and realised that they were trying to decide what to do with June, discussing where she would live. It seemed that they felt that if she didn't go to Lesley or Sheila's she would have to move in with one of them; in their opinion Dad would never be able to care for my sister.

Walking over to where June sat, I took her hand suggesting that she come with me, so she got to her feet and followed me to the door. Just before we left the room, I turned around and asked for silence.

"Just so that there is no misunderstanding, June is staying here. That's what Mum wanted, and that's what I promised her would happen. She is not leaving this house." The two of us went for a very long walk, during which time we talked about Mum, finding warmth and comfort in our shared memories and by the time we eventually returned, nearly everyone had gone.

Mum was right though; Dad did stop drinking from that day on and looked after June very well, becoming a proper Father to her.

Barry and I came back from Clacton and lived at home. Between the three of us we shared the duties of looking after June, whilst Barry and I rekindled Apollo Aerials.

Dad took over Mum's role in his own male way, and with three men in the house June got a great deal of affection and attention. We all wanted to protect her making sure that she was as happy as possible.

At the weekends Barry would often disappear, catching the train down to London, to spend time with Linda whom he was still seeing, and had been for over a year. I too would occasionally travel to London to visit Christine, though our relationship was not as serious as Barry and Linda's.

In the summer of 1975, one year after Mum died, June and Dad had settled down into a comfortable routine, so Barry and I agreed to go off on our travels once again, but decided to take Linda and Christine with us this time. Having discussed where to go, Barry found a book on the Greek Islands, and we chose Lefkada as our destination. Rather than buying another gas guzzler, we found a pale blue Bedford Comer van, and paid the princely sum of £30 for it at auction. We christened her Old Beauty. On the surface she was ideal as she had windows down the side, and a roof rack; she even had sliding doors that could be pulled back when the summer heat became too much. She certainly looked the part, but whether she would get us there and back was another matter. It was agreed that if she broke down along the way, we would remove the number plates, abandoning her in favour of hitchhiking the rest of the way.

Chapter Twenty-Two
Boats and Bond Girls

E arly one morning in May, we picked up the girls in London, before setting off on the next leg of the journey to Dover. Linda and Christine were good friends by now, so conversation and laughter filled the van as we navigated our way through the streets of London, heading for the road to the coast.

We had only been driving for about twenty minutes when Barry commented that Old Beauty was refusing to go any faster than ten miles an hour. As Barry pulled over, and I got out, the smell of burning rubber wafted towards my face. There was smoke rising in to the air from the front passenger wheel.

Getting closer, I could feel the heat from the tyre; the brakes had seized. Crawling under the engine I managed to loosen a small bleeding nut on the brake pipe which allowed red fluid to squirt in every direction, this released the brakes. The problem was solved.

We could now continue on our way, but our joy at having fixed the problem was short-lived because within a matter of miles Old Beauty was seizing up yet again. It dawned on us that every time Barry put his foot on the brake to stop for traffic lights, the problem would re-occur. We hadn't even got out of London and Old Beauty was proving to be a Beast.

We limped in to a garage close by and asked if Old Beauty could be repaired. A mechanic agreed to have a look and slid under the front bonnet. A few minutes later he re-emerged, with a look on his face that said it all.

"It's a big job," he said, "Because the van is so old it looks as if all the brake pipes and cylinders need replacing."

Asking how much it would cost, he said he would need twenty minutes to make a couple of phone calls.

Eventually he returned, "It's going to take about a week to get all the parts in," he informed us, "And will cost in the region of £100.00."

In one blow our dreams were shattered. We couldn't afford to spend that much, and we certainly didn't want to waste a week hanging around London. Thanking him, we discussed our options.

"Drive her to the nearest scrap yard and leave her there," I suggested.

"How about we go as far as we can in the van, getting as close to Dover as possible?" Barry suggested. "If she breaks down completely we'll just abandon her like we always said we would, and then catch a bus or hitch-hike the rest of the way."

"Don't be mad," I argued, "We'll never get anywhere near Dover like this."

"We just might." He was not giving up. "If I keep my foot off the brakes as much as possible using the gears to control our speed, and avoid as many towns and built up areas as I can, we might just make it."

He was right I suppose. A few miles further on was definitely better than no miles at all. I sat next to Barry with a spanner in my hand, ready for the moment when I would have to jump out and disappear under the van. Despite careful navigation, we could not avoid every traffic light, so as soon as the van pulled to a halt, I would be lying on my back in the dirt, releasing the brakes, doing my best to avoid getting brake fluid in my eyes, before climbing back into my seat in time for the lights to change.

A queue of traffic would inevitably build up behind us, and I would often find myself carrying out my repair work to the sound of beeping horns. As we carried on travelling, Barry got better at using the gears to slow us down, and I was certainly a great deal faster with my pit-stop-mechanics, and with nothing in her way Old Beauty was happy doing fifty miles an hour.

A little later than anticipated, and incredibly enough, we pulled into the Port of Dover. It had taken some twenty mechanical maneuvers, but we had reached our destination. Once again it was decision time on the fate of Old Beauty; were we prepared to pay for her passage, or were we to abandon her there at the docks? Barry and I were not the types to accept defeat easily and even though she was literally a pain in the arse, we decided that she was coming with us whether she liked it or not.

The ferry crossing to Calais was a welcome break from our travels so far and once in France we headed off, crossing country after country as we headed for Greece.

Come nightfall we would stop wherever we could; roadside picnic areas or on the edges of fields away from the main road. Not only did we need a break, but it was important for Old Beauty as well, allowing her engine the chance to cool down. She offered comfortable shelter for two of her passengers, whilst the remaining two slept in a tent, each couple taking it in turns on alternate nights. Simple meals were prepared on a gas burner, and although all very basic, it was highly effective. Listening to Rod Stewart's *'Gasoline Alley'* blaring loudly from Beauty's cassette player we soon burnt up the miles on our way towards the Mediterranean.

After travelling for well over two weeks and driving through ten different countries, we successfully clocked up three thousand miles. I couldn't tell you how many pit-stops I carried out – well in to the hundreds by the time we finally arrived. Changing currency at all the different borders we crossed, buying fresh bread, milk and other basics in different languages were all part of the learning curve. Tempers frayed at times as we drove for hours trying to find somewhere suitable to stop for the night, or the perfect bush for the girls to hide behind whilst they went to the toilet.

We finally caught sight of our destination in the distance, the four of us standing on the deck of the small ferry with Old Beauty tied down nearby, as the boat crossed the waters to our Greek island of Lefkada. I am sure that we all felt a sense of achievement as we edged our way gently across the blue Mediterranean the excitement getting stronger and stronger as we got closer. It appeared to be a small island with its mountains pointing up towards the midday sun, and very soon we were able to see the waves lapping against the golden sandy beaches.

Finally the ferry docked, and having off loaded our old chariot in Vassiliki, we explored our island paradise in search of somewhere to set up camp. Climbing one of the mountain roads that took us high above the coastline, we spotted the perfect location, and after some clever navigation found ourselves on the beach.

There was no need for conversation as the four of us changed into our swimsuits, plunging into the fresh sea water and reveling in the coolness against our skin. Fourteen days in a van seemed to disappear as the waves lapped over our bodies. Sheer paradise.

As dusk fell we set off on foot heading towards the small harbour we had passed through on our way to the beach; it was the main habitation with the only bar on the island. There were boys playing football outside whilst their parents sat inside, watching the island's only television. Our arrival caused a stir, with the lads forgetting about their game, and the locals losing interest in the Greek drama on the small tv. After much pointing and smiling we managed to get some drinks and whilst Barry and I played football with the kids, the girls sat on the steps of the bar sipping small glasses of ouzo.

Although nobody seemed to speak English, and we certainly didn't speak Greek, there are some things that are universal. Pointing to me with a cheeky grin on his face, one of the boys called out 'Kevin Keegan'. This made Barry laugh.

"It's your hair," he teased, "not your skill with a ball!"

We were as much a novelty to the islanders as they were to us. Four young people from England who had arrived in a battered old van and were living on the beach. Our appearance must have been quite a contrast as well; our brightly coloured fashions and hair down past our shoulders worn in an Afro were a long way from the simple clothes worn by the men and the traditional black worn by the women.

Our language problems did not last forever as we found that there were two young men who had been seamen for a major shipping line and had travelled the world. They now owned a small fishing boat. Their English was quite good, thank God, and over a few days and a lot of chatting to one another we soon became friends.

Although Linda and Christine's dreams of adventure were being fulfilled, living on the beach was difficult at times, with the heat during the night almost becoming unbearable. It was certainly too hot to sleep in a tent or a van.

Mentioning this to our two Greek friends, they must have put the word about, as the villagers took pity on us and two rooms were found in nearby houses. The joy of a bed with a mattress and a shower as well only increased the perfection of our paradise island.

Barry and I were invited to go fishing with our English speaking fishermen so we went out with them on their boat on several occasions. Leaving at five in the morning, the boat chugged out of the harbor, making its way across the smooth water's surface to the blue sky beyond. We would prepare the nets as we travelled, ready to throw them over the side once we neared our destination, only to haul them in several hours later, nets misshapen with an enormous quantity of fish, differing types and sizes, thrashing about as we lowered them on to the decks. Barry and I helped as best we could, rank amateurs in comparison to the Greeks who had been fishing all their lives, and constantly mindful of keeping our fingers clear of some terrifying looking sea creature who glared menacingly in our direction.

Our morning's work was always rewarded with a fresh fish of our choice which would then be cooked for us in the evening, flavoured with local herbs and olive oil made on the island. Knowing that we had played a part in catching our evening meal only improved its flavour, as we sat under the summer stars, enjoying the warmth of the night air drinking local wines and ouzo. It really was another world.

Despite the simplicity of our way of living, our financial resources started to dwindle after six weeks which meant that it was time to return home. Before we could leave, Old Beauty needed some significant repair work on her exhaust and with the lack of a garage on the island, we paid a visit to the local blacksmith. After a day in his care, Barry and I found ourselves driving back down to the village in almost near silence. Our van no longer rattled and sputtered, she positively purred – a new exhaust pipe having been fitted to her workings. This was no ordinary exhaust pipe however, but an assortment of old pieces of metal sheet and pipes which the blacksmith had forged together, creating the perfect replacement.

Once again on the ferry, but this time heading away from the shore was a sad moment as we had all enjoyed ourselves in so many ways. Language barriers had not prevented friendships from forming, and there was a considerable turn out of people waving good-bye from the harbour, as the ferry bore us away.

Returning back to England was once again exhausting, with never ending mechanical repairs *enroute* to keep Old Beauty going. Finally the city streets of London welcomed us. Scraping together what little money we had left, we managed to book into a hotel, we went out for dinner to celebrate the last night of our trip, laughing out loud as we reminded one another of the adventures we had shared together. Barry and I then dropped the girls off early the next day before completing the final leg of our journey up North, arriving home in the late afternoon.

Dad and June were at home when we finally arrived, and their smiling faces were a welcome sight to two bone weary travellers. June loved the presents we had bought her, a collection of small souvenirs bought at various stages of our trip, and Dad laughed at some of the crazier stories we told. All that was missing was Mum; it was strange coming home after some time away not to find her there to greet us.

As for Old Beauty she managed to produce a final Ace from up her sleeve. Despite the numerous breakdowns and the constant bleeding of brakes, she had carried us safely clocking up nearly ten thousand miles. And then having brought us back to Liverpool she excelled herself putting on such a good show at auction that she sold for £40.00 – ten pounds more than we had originally paid.

Old Beauty lived up to her name in the end, and as I look through the photos some thirty years later, I am even more amazed at what a remarkable companion she turned out to be. As for Barry, he must hold the world record for driving the longest distance - Greece and back – hardly using the brakes!

★ ★ ★

Not long after we got back, Barry rented a flat in Wavertree, close to Sefton Park where we had played as kids.

Although Christine and I had drifted apart, Barry and Linda were still close, and she left London coming to live with Barry. Within a few weeks of Barry moving in to his new flat, another came vacant next door, and so deciding that the idea of having my own space appealed, I signed the lease and moved in.

We continued with our aerial business, which thanks to the good reputation we had previously earned, was flourishing. Linda answered the phone and took the bookings and Barry and I found ourselves with plenty of work to fill our time and bank account.

In the Spring of the following year, Barry and Linda announced that they were having a baby so Barry now started saving for the new arrival taking his responsibilities very seriously. I however, was still only 23, a young bachelor full of enthusiasm for life and not ready to settle down!

Looking for adventure I bought myself a lime green MGB convertible. I was quite content with my purchase until one day I saw a similar car towing a boat. The combination of sports car and speed boat really appealed to me, and thinking that there would be no shortage of pretty young women to take out for the day, I convinced myself that this was what I needed. It did not take me long to find a 20 foot Fletcher Speed Boat, brilliant white in colour, with a nippy 40hp Johnson engine on the back, and kitted with all the extras, water skis and wetsuits, the lot! I was ready for action. All I needed was my own Bond girl!

She soon materialized, in the shape of a glamorous blonde called Karen. We met one night in town, and got on well, so it was not long before she was being invited for a day out. I picked her up early one Sunday morning and she slid into the passenger seat of my car, admiring the gleaming white lines of my brand new speed boat. Little did she know it was my boats first day out, and although I seemed calm on the surface, I was extremely anxious that the launch went well!

I had therefore arranged for Sheila and Keith to meet up with us in Colwyn Bay, Keith to provide assistance and manly moral support and Sheila to provide a picnic and female company for my new friend.

As Karen and I drove on to the beach, I spotted my sister and Keith, and parked my car next to them. The weather was not at its best – overcast and quite breezy, whilst the waves breaking against the shore were fairly choppy. Determined not to let it spoil my latest challenge, Keith and I speedily changed into our wetsuits, as I issued instructions. Keith was to help me pull the boat on its trailer down to the water, and once the boat was afloat the girls were to come down and join us. There was no time to be lost.

There was a row of about twenty boats at the waters edge, still on their trailers waiting to be launched, with their owners standing nearby watching the waves crashing towards the shore. Undeterred by the lack of enthusiasm shown by my fellow boat owners, we made our way past them down into the water. As the water flowed around the hull of the boat, lifting her off the trailer, I told Keith to take the trailer back, returning with the girls, whilst I held on to the boat.

Waist deep in water, keeping the bow of the boat facing towards the open sea was proving to be difficult. As the waves swirled around us both, they were dragging me further and further away from the shore, trying to snatch the boat from my control, dragging us out into the deep. Suddenly my feet lost contact with solid ground and I found myself holding on tightly to the edge of the boat, kicking against the pull of the tide, as I tried not to lose control. It did not take long for the sea to get what she wanted, and within a matter of seconds both the boat and I were turned sideways, the waves crashing into my back, over my head and filling up the boat. I could barely hang on as the waves played their games, becoming more and more aggressive in their attack as I tried to fight back, determined not to give in.

By now my boat was filling rapidly with water, and I no longer had the strength left to hold on. A decision had to be made, it was me or the boat, so I let go and swam, exhausted, back to the shore before staggering, breathless up on to dry land.

A large crowd awaited me as I made my way out the sea and I was conscious of their stares. Wondering what they were looking at, I cast a glance over my shoulder back towards the waves and saw that my new pride and joy had disappeared from sight; she had sunk to the bottom!

Fatigue and frustration got the better of me as I collapsed on to the ground. What a great seafarer I had proven to be- Captain Jeff who had managed to sink his boat on her maiden voyage. And to add insult to injury I had done it for the benefit of a watching audience, a gathering of superior sailors, who had loved every minute of the drama unfolding before their eyes, revelling in their knowledge and experience, and indulging in numerous snide comments interlaced with countless 'I told you so!' to one another.

Getting to my feet, I walked past them, aware of their smirks and their smiles, and heard their comments as they discussed the stupidity of launching in a turning tide. It was all too much, and I stopped in my tracks, directing my annoyance at no one in particular but at the crowd in general.

"Why don't you all piss off and leave me alone, you *helpful* bastards!" I felt as if I could have died out there and they would have put it down to a good morning's entertainment!

After I had dried myself off, I finally plucked up the courage to look at Karen, the woman I most wanted to impress. What did she now think of me? My action hero image was now rather soggy and damp.

Sheila broke the atmosphere insisting that we have our picnic. Conversation was a little bit difficult to start off with as no one knew quite what to say, but the obvious absence of my new boat could not be avoided and my lost battle against the sea quickly became the topic of conversation. I soon heard what it had been like from a spectators point of view, and found comfort in their shared opinion that the professional boaters could have easily come to my assistance.

Keith summed up his opinion of the whole adventure beautifully. "I thought it was a bit strange that there were no other boats in the water."

Looking at my brother-in-law sitting on the sand, I appreciated the irony. "You could have shared your observations with me before I tried to set sail!"

"Much good it would have done me," he replied. "Your Captain's hat was pulled so far down over your eyes, it covered your ears as well!"

It took a good three hours for the tide to recede, leaving a marooned speed boat sitting on the sand, full of water and seaweed. Not one to be put off by the recent traumas Keith and I spent the next two hours bailing her out and then taking the engine to pieces so as to dry it all off.

Whilst we were occupied with our repairs, the other boat owners had successfully launched their own craft and were taking great pains in putting on an extravaganza for our benefit, skiing past where we sat, hands raised in salute in my direction.

By the time I managed to get the engine started, the beach had virtually emptied and I had the water to myself – there was no audience to witness my remarkable comeback! The girls sat in the back of the boat whilst Keith drove, towing me behind on the end of the rope trying to ski. It was slow going at first, and I spent a great deal of the time face down in the water, but after a while managed to get the hang of it all. By the time we had all had a go, and finally returned to the car the night was drawing in, and it was time to leave.

It seems that boats and Bond Girls are not what they are made out to be, and my relationship with both were equally as short-lived; the three of us parted company around the same time.

* * *

In September that year, Linda gave birth to a lovely son whom they called Danny. Barry was very proud and took fatherhood extremely seriously. Whilst I was more than happy for the two of them, I was even happier that Danny was going to carry on the Pearce family name, and I knew that Mum would have been so proud.

Christmas came and went, and despite my social life being filled with activity, I began to feel restless and bored with the same routine week after week. I needed to get away and my itchy feet were begging for adventure!

My usual travelling partner, Barry was no longer available. To my surprise, Mick, Tommy and Danny were not interested in going abroad either, so I decided to go on my own.

Looking for inspiration as to where I should go, I found myself standing outside a travel agents contemplating the bright sunny holiday pictures before emerging less than an hour later clutching tickets to Spain. I was booked on a two week package holiday to Benidorm flying out in the first week in April. I believed that in arriving so early into the season I would have little or no problems finding a job with my bartending skills.

Several weeks before I was due to depart I bumped into my old friend Kenny Walker whom I had not seen since I left school; it was great catching up with him. Once he realised that I had travelled and worked abroad, he asked me to do him a favour. He wanted me to have a word with his sister Elaine, whom I remembered as a child. Apparently she and her best friend wanted to work in Europe, and he wasn't too keen on the idea, so I agreed to meet the girls.

Two nights before I left, I met up with Elaine and her friend Gina. I told them of all my different adventures and explained that it was far more difficult for young girls travelling and working abroad. They were not deterred and asked me to give them a ring if I thought that there was work available.

Being my usual optimistic self, I paid the rent for the next six months on my flat, and covered my car with a dust sheet; forty-eight hours later I was taking off for Spain.

Chapter Twenty-Three
Solo in Spain

This was a journey of firsts. It was my first package holiday not to mention travelling by 'plane, and the first time I had travelled alone. Not being particularly comfortable in my own company, I was happy to be herded along, until I found myself in the hotel.

As soon as I could, I unpacked my suitcase in my tiny single room before setting off to familiarize myself with the town of Benidorm.

Benidorm was bigger than Lloret del Mar, but similar in many ways. The coastline seemed to stretch for miles, and as I looked out to sea I was reminded of all the times that Barry and I swam together some four years earlier.

Being on my own just didn't feel right. I felt that everyone was staring at me; old Billy-no-mates all alone. I found myself quickening my pace as if I was on my way to meet someone. How stupid was that?

Returning to the Hotel Raymar, I showered and dressed for dinner, before making my way to the large restaurant for my meal. A table for one is a lonely place to sit, and the noise from all around seems even louder than normal than when you are sitting with somebody else. Eating my dinner as quickly as possible, I literally fled the hotel, in search of a bar where I could find some company and conversation, no matter what the topic.

I visited a number of bars and only managed to find the local bartenders to talk to. As I drank my San Miguel I asked if there was any work available for experienced barmen, however I was told the same wherever I went. I was too early in the season; extra staff were only taken on at the end of May when the season picked up. My well made plans of being first in line for a job were a little premature.

The night wore on as I drowned my nose and disappointment in numerous glasses of beer, trying to forget that I was all alone and without any hope of work.

It was well past midnight when I found myself sitting in the middle of a large bar, one of the last customers nursing a drink whilst the barman cleaned his glasses and tidied away. Looking around to see who was left, I realised that apart from a Scandinavian looking man with long, almost white blond hair who was at the other end of the bar, I was the only other person there.

Feeling a little bit tipsier than normal, I ordered a drink and suggested the barman have one himself as well as pouring one for my distant drinking companion. As I looked over, the stranger raised his San Miguel in acknowledgement of the drink which I had bought, and a short while later the barman gave me a drink and indicated that it was from the other man. Similarly I raised my glass in thanks.

By now however, the beer was beginning to lose its appeal, so getting unsteadily to my feet I decided to see if I could find my way back to my hotel. Walking past the stranger on the way out I stopped to thank him, holding my hand out as if to shake his. I was not in the mood for an exchange of conversation, particularly in some foreign language, so wanted to keep it brief.

"Thanks for the beer," he said, a strong Yorkshire accent catching me off guard. "Where are you from?"

"Liverpool," I replied, my words somewhat slurred with fatigue and Spanish beer.

Nodding his head towards the barstool next to him, he ordered two more beers and we soon found ourselves talking about the North of England and the places we knew. As it turned out he had been born in Burnley, and was now working for a company building villas in Benidorm. The bar finally closed and I found my way back to the hotel, before falling into a deep sleep.

What seemed like only minutes later, a loud banging and shouting outside my door dragged me from the depths of oblivion. A man was shouting in broken English, telling me that it was a wake up call. My head pounding from the lack of sleep and excess of beer, I wondered what was going on. Was I dreaming or had that stranger last night really given me a job.

Trying to work it out made my head hurt even more; I could not remember a thing from the previous night. I took a cold shower to see if that would help my memory, half of me thought that I was to be collected at seven thirty whilst the other half did not even know what day it was.

I stood outside the hotel entrance in the early morning sunshine, still not sure what I was doing. Dressed in a small pair of white tennis shorts and vest to match, with white sports socks and pumps, I must have looked as if I had just stepped off a tennis court.

As I sobered up, it was easy to convince myself that it had all been a dream. On the point of giving up and returning to the comfort of my bed, I heard a horn beeping behind me. Turning in the direction of the noise I saw a battered old truck parked down by the road. The driver's window lowered, and a familiar head of white blonde hair appeared.

"Hey Scouser, get in!" he called out.

The flat bed of the old truck was filled with a gang of about six men. Getting closer, a hand extended down towards me, accompanied by a loud cockney accent.

"Come on Scouser," I was told, "Grab a tight hold of my hand." Taking his advice I found myself sitting amongst several other men, squatting on the dirty surface whilst the men around me started to introduce themselves. As thoughts of "what was I doing? and where was I going?' filled my head, I soon found out who my travelling companions were.

There was Cockney Steve and Alan, Geordie John and Freddy, and Scottish Mick as well as Dave the Driver and Boss, whom I had only met a few hours before. All the lads had nicknamed him Rubio, the Spanish word for blond.

I felt a right plonker with my lily white skin and matching 'tennis' outfit. Who in their right minds would dress like that to go to work on a building site? They all looked the part with their brown muscles and tattooed arms for all the world to see; god alone knows what they thought of me!

After forty minutes of being thrown around in the back of the truck and getting to know the motley crew, we arrived at a building site somewhere up in the mountains. There was only one villa completed whilst several others were half completed, and I could see the local bricklayers hard at work. As my eyes scanned the scene in front of me, trying to take it all in, I heard Rubio calling out.

"Right come on Scouser, follow me!" As I walked behind him to a large mixer, he asked me if I had ever mixed concrete before.

This was not the time nor place for blagging. I had managed to get through a few hairy moments in my life, but this time I was on my own so I told him the truth.

"Not to worry," he reassured me, "It's easy. I'll show you how."

Having learnt how to make the concrete, I then had to pour the mix into a wheelbarrow and then push it some fifty yards to a trench, where the barrow had to be lifted and the concrete poured out. This was almost the hardest part of it all, and tipping the barrow required nearly all of my strength.

I made and tipped concrete all morning, the hot sun burning down on me. I could feel myself getting burnt, and knew that if I wasn't careful I would end up getting sunstroke so I tied my vest over my head and neck. Thankfully we stopped for lunch at 12 o'clock, taking shelter in the shade of the half finished villas and a three hour siesta was a welcome break. I was starving, and had not brought any food of my own, so Cockney Steve came to the rescue offering me one of his sandwiches. I then spent the rest of the siesta asleep.

Rubio decided that I had done enough concreting so handed me a pickaxe and told me to work with a couple of the other lads digging a trench. This was also hard going, as we had to break through large amounts of rock that the mountain was made of.

My first day was definitely an endurance test to see what I was made of, and if my aching muscles weren't proof enough the blisters on my hands certainly let me know how hard I had worked. It was way after seven by the time I was dropped outside the hotel. My body ached all over as I climbed out of the truck and I was starving. Rubio gave me 700 pesetas, pushing a bundle of notes into my hand. "Well done Scouser," he said, "You did well today! Same again tomorrow?"

Before I could say yes, one of the lads on the back of the truck asked me if I was coming out for a drink. "We always meet up at the Robin Hood Pub at around ten," he said. I said I would be there.

As I entered the hotel I had one thing on my mind. Food. I was so hungry I could have eaten a horse, and afraid that the restaurant would soon be closing decided to get my dinner as soon as possible. There was a long buffet set up that evening, so I joined the queue at one end, tray in my hands, and made my way along piling it high with bread rolls and ham to make sandwiches for the following day, as well as lots of fresh hot food to enjoy there and then.

I walked through the busy restaurant to my table, and sat down oblivious to nearly everything around me as I got stuck in. After a few mouthfuls and feeling a little less focused, I noticed that the restaurant was almost silent, there was no chatter of voices or clatter of tableware. Pausing in putting a forkful of food in my mouth, I looked around and realised that every eye was on me.

Suddenly it struck me that the hand holding my fork was a thick grey white, and so were my arms and my top. In fact, apart from two circles around my eyes, the whole of my body, from the top of my head right down to my shoes, was covered in thick grey cement dust. I was a living statue! Too tired to care, I threw a smile in the general direction of my fellow diners, and continued eating. Within a minute or two the noise in the restaurant had returned to normal, the evening's entertainment over and done with. Thinking back, my mind boggles at what they must have thought.

Having eaten, showered and changed I met up with the lads in the Robin Hood. The Pub was run by an English couple and all the English workers gathered there most nights, the focal point of a small community, welcoming to strangers like me.

I continued to work on the building during the remaining two weeks of my package holiday. Considering the heat of the sun and the fact that it was hard physical work, the money was actually quite poor, but it wasn't about the money; it was about doing something different with my life. I decided to stay in Benidorm, carrying on where I was before getting a better job as a barman later on in the season.

I broke the news of my plans to the Thomas Cook Rep on the last day of the holiday, telling her that I had sold my ticket to another English guy who wanted to get back home; after numerous phone calls the other guy was eventually given permission to take my place.

On the day of their departure, I sat on my suitcase watching my fellow passengers getting on to the coach before they left for the airport. Just before the coach pulled away, an older man opened his window and called out to me.

"Hey, you!" He shouted, "Not being funny or anything, but please tell us what you have been doing for the past two weeks? We are all dying to know!"

"Working on a building site," I shouted back. "Building villa's in the mountains!"

"You're bleeding mad!" he called back as the coach headed away. "There's plenty of work back in England!"

He had to be right – I was mad – there was definitely a screw loose somewhere!

Cockney Steve came to collect me, and we went in search of a place to share together. It took us all day, but by the end of it we had found an ideal reasonably priced two bedroom apartment which we agreed to rent until the end of the season. Steve and I became great mates whilst continuing to work together.

* * *

I rang home and spoke to Barry, Dad and June and told them my plans. They also thought I was a little bit mad, but wished me good luck nonetheless. I also called Elaine to tell her that there were hardly any jobs, especially at this time of year. It didn't matter however, as she told me that she and Gina had already booked a two week holiday in Benidorm and were coming out at the end of April.

Being a bachelor in Benidorm was good fun. I found myself getting on well with the thirty or so other English people that lived there, and spent most night going out clubbing and meeting lots of different girls from all over Europe who were enjoying some holiday fun.

April soon came to an end, and with it and Elaine and Gina's arrival. I had agreed to meet up with them on their first night, so Steve and I took them on a tour of Benidorm, showing them where all the best bars and clubs were, introducing them to the English and Spanish people we knew. Both girls were very pretty, and I found myself protecting them from all the young handsome Spanish lads.

I hadn't planned on playing the big brother role, but nor did I want them to get hurt by some hot-blooded Spaniard only interested in a one-night-stand.

Towards the end of their two week holiday, it soon became apparent that they did not want to go back, preferring to stay and find work. They planned on living off their savings, but finding an apartment which they could afford was proving to be impossible, so Steve and I decided that we would share a room at our place, offering the other to the girls. It made good sense splitting the rent four ways, so the girls agreed and promptly moved in.

My interest in Gina started to grow. There was something special about her which set her apart from the rest of the girls in Benidorm. If anything she was the exact opposite of everyone else; whilst they wore the shortest skirts possible, hers were down to her knees; whilst their necklines plunged to their navels, her collars were done to the top; she had a 'Mary Poppins' way about her. I found myself thinking about her more and more. There was just something very special about Gina.

Playing the role of chaperone was driving me mad. I was now well and truly in love with Gina myself, so it was not surprising when it all came to a head one evening.

We were out at one of our favourite bars, when I realised that Gina was being chatted up by a Spanish guy. It started to irritate me 'something wicked' particularly as I desperately wanted her to know how I felt about her. She had never given me any indication as to how she felt, but it seemed that I would have to make my move and, by the looks of things, would have to make it fast.

Taking a deep breath I made my way over and gently took her to one side. My heart was almost in my mouth I was so nervous. Without time to think it through, to practice what I wanted to say, I just blurted it all out.

"As from tonight I am not chaperoning you and Elaine any more," I stated. "You can see whoever you want!"

She just stood in front of me, a confused look on her lovely face. This was going well, I thought, this really is not the way to tell a girl how you feel, but I have to tell her.'

I continued, "I want you to know that I fancy you myself!" As I stood there waiting for a laugh of rejection, all I could think was that was one of the worst chat up lines ever! What an idiot! A complete tosser!

Gina gave me the most amazing smile I had ever seen in my life. "I fancy you too." Her words were so quietly spoken that I could hardly hear her; I just stood there, speechless for once in my life.

As we left at the end of the night, I took Gina's hand in mine and as we walked along I felt an overwhelming desire to kiss her, but still feeling a bit awkward I wasn't sure when the right moment would come. As we walked a bit further I couldn't wait any longer. I stopped and pulled her close to me. And I kissed her.

As from that night the rest was history.

★ ★ ★

Day after day the girls continued their efforts to find work, but they were not having any success. However, the season was getting busier, and more and more bars were starting to open, ready for the influx of tourists during the summer months. One evening Steve and I called into one of our favourite bars for a cold beer after work, and I got chatting to a couple of English guys I knew called Dave and Jerry. They sold necklaces which were known as 'love beads' on the beach during the day, and by all accounts made a good living out of it. They asked me if I knew anyone who would be interested in buying their remaining beads as they were going back to England the following day. Not one to miss out on a good deal, I asked them to show me what they were selling.

Dave kept them in the boot of his car, and I was amazed at how many strands of brightly coloured beads he had. I asked how much he wanted for them, and he told me to make him an offer. This was a little more difficult, as it was hard to tell how many he had. So I asked.

"Maybe six to eight hundred strands of beads," I was told, "It's anybody's guess."

Returning to the bar, I decided to give it some thought as I was not sure what I would do with them all. Jerry, however, was keen to close the deal. "Go on Jeff," he insisted, "make us an offer." Quickly trying to calculate the potential profit on this bizarre offer I came up with a figure.

"Eight thousand pesetas."

"Make it ten and you have a deal," Jerry hustled.

"Meet you half way," I replied, concerned with his desire to get rid of them so quickly, "Nine thousand pesetas!"

"Deal" was their immediate and joint response, and so once we had all finished our beers, they dropped me and Steve off back at our apartment, before emptying the car boot of numerous plastic bags bursting at the seams with hundreds of strands of beads. I handed over the money, equivalent to around £40, and having wished me good luck, Dave and Jerry left to return to England.

Steve and I struggled carrying all the bags in. Placing them on the dining table I called out to the girls to come and have a look at my new purchases, wanting to share my excitement with them. Instead of sharing my enthusiasm they merely stood staring at the piles of beads covering the table top, completely quiet.

The silence was too much. "This is how you two are going to make loads of pesetas from now on!" I enthused.

"What do you mean?" Gina was clearly puzzled.

"You and Elaine can sell these on the beach for 100 pesetas each," I explained.

"Nice idea," Elaine said, "But we can't sell them!"

Before I could ask why, Gina finished explaining. "We're too shy to go up to strangers!"

I was disappointed with their lack of interest in my great find. "Don't be daft," I told them. "It's easy. Look tomorrow is my day off; I'll show you just how easy it really is."

The next morning as we made our way to the beach, I stressed to the girls how important it was not to get caught by the police. It was against the law to work in Spain without a permit; if caught I could either end up in jail or be deported. They had to keep a good lookout for the police as they slowly walked along the promenade. It was agreed that if they spotted a policeman on patrol, they would signal me by waving their arms up and down, enabling me to make my getaway.

I had prepared for the burning hot sand and only wore a pair of jelly shoes and swimming trunks, with a plastic bag tucked in at the waist band to keep the money safe. My arms were draped with over one hundred beads, and ready for business I headed out on to the crowded beach.

Spotting a group of young women sunning themselves together, I walked over, greeting them with a cheeky hello asking them if they were enjoying their holiday. Showing them the love beads draped over my arms, I soon made a sale with nearly everyone buying a strand or two either for themselves or as presents for people back home.

Sales went from strength to strength, as did my confidence. Business was good and the money was coming in fast. Keeping an eye on my lookouts on the promenade, I made my way from one group of sunbathers to another, covering most of the beach in about two hours.

Taking a quick glance over towards my lookouts I realised that both Gina and Elaine were waving their arms frantically up and down. Quickly stuffing the remaining strands into the plastic bag that held the money I legged it into the safety of the sea, and swam out a safe distance from the shore. I did not want to end up in jail so this seemed a much safer option to me.

Just about able to stand, with only my head above water, I looked back towards the promenade, and could just about make out the two girls; they seemed to be signaling at me to come over. I couldn't see any police so headed back to the shore, my progress now slowed down by a plastic bag full of water.

It was a long way to where the girls were standing, and by the time I reached them my legs felt like jelly.

"What's wrong? What has happened?" I breathlessly managed to get out.

"We thought you would like a drink with it being so hot?" Gina replied.

"We were trying to get your attention," Elaine explained, "That's all."

Still finding it hard to breathe, I was choking on all the salt water I had swallowed; snot was running down my nose and I was feeling sick.

"What did you say?" Not wanting to believe their stupid comments. "No police at all? I have just nearly drowned myself out there!"

We went and had a well deserved drink, a new problem now faced us. My plastic bag, still full of water, contained our first days takings, five thousand pesetas, and the notes were swimming around like fish in a tank. After paying for our drinks with a handful of dripping pesetas, we headed back to the apartment, we then spent the rest of the day hanging the money out on the washing line to dry.

I eventually managed to sell all my beads, working the beaches at weekends, and sharing the profits with my two partners in crime. The three of us enjoyed every minute of it.

At the beginning of June Gina and Elaine found a job working for an English couple who owned a café/bar. They took it in turns, one of them waitressing during the day, whilst the other babysat their four year old son, Steven, in the evening.

Meanwhile the lads and I were making good progress building the villas until one day when the ground suddenly gave way beneath me, sending me flying into a small ravine several feet below. As I fell my right shin caught on a jagged edge that stuck out of the rock face , tearing through the skin and leaving a long gash up my leg. The pain was horrendous.

Big Alan drove me back to the apartment. Both the girls were at home, and having taken one look at my leg insisted that I get medical treatment. We were directed to a convent where the nuns ran a small hospital of sorts. It was more like an old peoples home than anything else, but we were told that they could help.

As I lay down on a bed a nun set to work dry shaving my leg with a cut-throat razor. The pain was so excruciating I nearly hit the ceiling so Big Al (all 6'4" of him) had to lie across my chest to pin me down whilst another two nuns held on to my ankles. The air soon became blue with my swearing and shouting as they stitched my up, and I was thankful for the human restraints on my body otherwise I would have leapt up and disappeared for good.

Ordeal over and wounds dressed, Gina made me laugh in the car on the way back describing my performance worthy of a woman giving birth to a very large baby. I had apparently been very loud!

Hobbling around the apartment for well over a week was driving me insane so I talked a friend of mine into selling me his Honda 50cc moped for £40, a small two seater which made my life a lot easier.

It wasn't long before I was out looking for work; my accident had put me off working on the building site. I had heard about a new discotheque 'Tramps' which was due to be opening shortly, run by an English man called Billy Lorrins. I eventually managed to track him down. I explained how I had worked in a bar in Spain some years before. He told me that the Spanish owner only employed local barmen, and that he had already employed four other English lads as glass collectors; there were no jobs to be had.

Not to be defeated I asked him if there was anything else available other than bar work, assuring him that I could turn my hand to anything.

He stared at me for a moment. "Can you paint?"

"Yes," I nodded, "No problem."

He took me outside the club and pointed to a small bright red Citroen 2CV, more commonly known as 'The Duck'. It appeared to be in good condition.

"Are you saying that car needs painting?" I asked

"Yes," he told me. "I need it turning into a propaganda car to promote the club. Come with me I'll show you what I mean."

Going back into the building, I followed him down the stairs to the disco, where the walls were covered with photos of Charlie Chaplin. Pointing to the pictures, he explained that he wanted to recreate the same look on the car.

"Do you think you can do it?" he asked.

"Well," I replied, choosing my words carefully, "I am not Picasso, but I'll certainly give it a go."

The following day I bought some black paint and brushes and managed to find some large pieces of cardboard. I cut out a large silhouette of a bowler hat and walking stick and placed them on the bonnet and doors, drawing around them to give me the perfect outline to paint in. On the back of the car I painted clear black letters saying "Follow me – I am going to Tramps, Benidorm's Number One Discotheque!"

It took me two days to complete the car. Billy was more than pleased with my artwork, and liking the bowler hat so much he asked me to paint them on the ceiling in the club which made a big improvement.

Tramps was now ready for its opening in a few days, and my work was finished. Calling me into his office to pay me, he said, "You have done a great job and I like your enthusiasm for the club. With that in mind I think that I have come up with the perfect job for you. I want you to work the door dressed as Charlie Chaplin!" he announced. "Do you think you can pull it off?"

I laughed, "Of course I can!"

Having discussed the job for a little while, Billy handed me a bowler hat and a thin cane and told me to be ready to start at 7pm on opening night. I couldn't wait to get back home to share the good news with my flatmates. They all thought that it was hilarious especially watching me mimicking Charlie's famous walk, heels together, toes pointing out as I shuffled along, swinging my cane and casually tipping my hat. I spent hours upon hours practicing until I had mastered the routine.

On the big night I wore shoes, trousers and waistcoat which were all black whilst my collarless shirt was white; Gina pencilled a black moustache on my face which with my bowler hat on my head and cane swinging as I walked completed the image.

Once outside Tramps I spent the evening walking Chaplin style up and down the pavement, talking to customers and making them laugh as they entered, calling out to passers-by inviting them in, all the time catching peoples attention with my impersonation of the famous man. As a marketing ploy it worked, the club was soon full. The success continued night after night.

Tramps was a popular place, and with hardly any problems or breakouts of trouble. This was mainly due to Billy's many years experience in running clubs; he had cleverly employed five guys from different parts of the UK to work in the club – the four glass collectors represented Scotland, Newcastle, Manchester and London, whilst I was his Scouser. The idea was if a group of lads were getting too rowdy and there was the chance of a fight starting up, having found out which part of the UK they came from, we would send over one of the lads from the same place to sort it out offering them all a small beer 'on the house' to calm the situation down. It nearly always worked.

I soon found that the best way to discourage groups of drunken lads from wanting to come in was by telling them that Tramps was a gay club, and that the club across the road was much better, with lots of young girls out for a good time! (Not too ironically there were fights nearly every night at that particular club across the road!!)

I had found myself the perfect job and what's more, I was good at it. Tramps soon became the second most popular night spot in Benidorm, the first (The Istanbul), being the sister club owned by the same Spanish family.

Elaine started to get homesick and decided to return home at the end of July, so Steve Gina and I stayed on in the apartment together. Gina chose to work evenings only, babysitting little Steve, which meant that we had the days free together. We explored the whole of Benidorm and the surrounding villages on the little moped, having, literally, the time of our lives.

In August, Ronny, Danny and John, my good mates from back home came out to visit me for their holidays. At the same time, Gina's friend Wendy arrived so our small apartment was full of bodies sleeping everywhere. John found the bath very comfortable, whilst the rest slept on blow up lilo's on the floor.

Towards the end of their two weeks stay the lads were in Tramps one night having a good time downstairs whilst I was working the door. I planned on joining them later once Gina arrived. Then Danny suddenly appeared.

"You had better get downstairs now. There's going to be trouble," he told me. "One of the Spanish lads has just grabbed Ronny's bird's arse; he won't go away."

"You're joking," I said as I headed down the stairs.

I wondered which Spanish lad it could be; I knew most of them pretty well by now. Tramps was quite full, with about 300 people in that night, but I could see Ronny and the others by the bar.

I knew that Ronny could look after himself so was a little surprised when he told me that he didn't want to cause any trouble for me or for the club. "But you had better have a word with him," he said, pointing to a Spanish guy standing a small distance away.

Peering through the darkened smoky atmosphere I could see whom he was talking about and was surprised. It was a man called Cossi whom all the staff knew; he worked in one of the kitchens at a nearby hotel and had never been any bother before. He had been coming in every night for almost two months, and we all knew that he was a slightly retarded; he was a loner and did not seem to have many friends at all; I got on well with him and always let him in for free.

Smiling at Cossi, I gently put my arm around his shoulder and suggested that we go somewhere else. He wouldn't move, instead he spat straight into my eyes. I stood there, my face covered in spit; if it had been anyone else I would have punched their lights out on the spot.

However, it was Cossi, so I grabbed him in a headlock moving him towards the stairs and out of the club. I planned to send him on his way with a warning, and advice not to come back for a few days.

As we got half way up the stairs he began to resist my grip. His strength came from nowhere as he started to go berserk. I felt like a cowboy holding on to a young steer by the horns as he was tossing me all over the stairs. I couldn't let go of him as I didn't want him returning to the club, so I held on as best I could determined to get him outside.

Then all of a sudden I felt a sharp pain. It was coming from my chest. Looking down I could see a red stain spreading across my shirt – Cossi had sunk his teeth into me and was not going to let go.

Now I was really frightened of loosening my grip incase he ripped a chunk out of my body. Pleading with him to let go, my eyesglued to where his mouth was attached to my body, I heard the familiar voices of the glass collectors standing behind me.

Instructing them to back off, they stood behind me helplessly, unaware of how serious the situation really was! Cossi had to release his grip sooner or later – he had to breathe! As soon as I felt his teeth slackening I loosened my grip. Within a split second he threw himself backwards with all his strength sending me and everyone else hurtling down the stairs; a mass of bodies landing on top of each other at the bottom.

Cossi was the first to his feet, running into the club and somehow managing to get over the bar. Within seconds he was hurling bottles of spirits randomly into the dancing crowds. The two barmen had fled, locking themselves into a small back room. In the short time it took us to get to our feet and into the club, pandemonium had broken out.

The DJ, safe in his sound-proof booth was oblivious to what was going on so the music continued to play; he controlled the lights. We needed the lights on fast, so I shouted to one of the lads to sort it.

The rest of us leapt over the bar, and quickly overpowered Cossi, pinning him to the floor. He was going nowhere, at least not until the police arrived.

The full extent of the damage only became clear once the lights went on.

It was hard to accept that one man could have inflicted so much trauma and pain in such a short time. There were half a dozen or so young men and women with blood pouring from bad injuries, caused by bottles hitting them with full force in the face and on the head. I could not believe that only minutes before everyone had been having such a good time.

The ambulance and police arrived not long after. The police were aggressively arresting anyone they could get their hands on – innocent holiday makers that had nothing to do with what had happened. I tried to intervene, to explain what had happened and to tell them that they were arresting the wrong ones but they just threatened me with their truncheons and threw me into the back of a jeep.

After much confusion at the police station, I found myself locked up in a prison cell. A couple of hours later two policemen entered and started to interrogate me. Their English was poor, but I could make out that they were accusing me of having caused the trouble and had picked on a Spanish man with mental disabilities.

They were getting very angry and started to beat me with their truncheons, hitting my ribs and my legs. I tried to show them where Cossi had bitten me, but they were not interested in what I was saying – they just continued to lash out at me, verbally and physically.

I curled up in a small ball on the floor, and covered my face and my head with my arms. I could now feel their boots kicking my back as they set about me. The fear seemed to make the pain go away, and the only sound that I could hear was their shouts of 'English Pig'. I seemed to be rolled up in that small ball forever, and even after they had left, I was reluctant to move, so frightened for my life and the thought of this bad dream never ending.

Some hours later my cell door opened and a well-dressed man appeared. He spoke to me in English and told me that he had been hired by the owner of the nightclub to represent me in Court. In very precise words, he came straight to the point.

"Listen very carefully to me Senor," he said. "You are in a lot of trouble and could go to prison if you do not listen to what I say and do what I tell you to do. Do you understand?"

I mumbled a yes in reply to his question.

"You do not tell the Judge that you work at the Club if he asks you. You say that you are here on holiday, and it was your girlfriend who the man was annoying. Leave all the talking to me and do not say any thing. Do you understand?"

Again I said I did.

He then left; an hour later, I was escorted by two policemen to the Court Room which was in the same building. Standing in the dock, numb with pain, tired from lack of sleep, scared by what was happening, and terrified at the thought of what might happen, I waited for the Judge to arrive.

As I looked around me I notice that Cossi stood directly opposite me on the other side of the small court room. We all stood as the Judge entered, and then as the procedures began, all conducted in Spanish, I sat there lost in visions of spending the rest of my life in a Spanish prison cell.

Time flew by; the Judge gave his verdict talking to my lawyer, who solemnly nodded his head in agreement. My lawyer never once looked at me, and I had no idea what was going on, but then it was all over. My lawyer walked over to me and told me that I was a very lucky man, but I had twenty-four hours in which to leave the country. As we walked out of the Court, I asked him what was going to happen to Cossi, what sentence had he received. His answer was simple.

Nothing; apart from being told to keep away from Tramps – he had been allowed to walk away free!

Gina and a group of my friends were waiting for me outside the building, with anxious looks on their faces; when I told them what had happened they too could not believe it. Gina was happy to see me, but more concerned by my blood covered shirt and the teeth marks on my chest. Once again I found myself being sewn together by my 'friendly' Spanish nun, who was concentrating on her needlework skills; she still did not understand what my cries of "Pain, pain, pain" meant. Even today the memories like the scars have not faded.

Gina and I quickly packed up, saying goodbye to all the lovely friends we had made over the five months we had spent in Spain. Although disappointed at the way in which our time in Benidorm had come to an abrupt end, we were, however, both relieved that I wasn't serving a prison sentence! Despite it all the summer of 1977 was one of the best summers ever.

Chapter Twenty-Four
Neck on the Block

Our unannounced arrival home was a shock to everyone. Gina's parents were pleased to see her, though I am not so sure what they thought of my having been chased out of Benidorm by a Judge.

I stayed with Dad and June for a week before returning to my flat and worked with Barry on the aerials yet again.

Soon winter had once again set in, and life returned to normal. Gina worked as a barmaid four nights a week, leaving her Saturdays free to help her Father selling shoes on his market stall. I sold my sports car to raise enough money to buy another van and Barry and I were soon very busy. With two vans on the road we could cover Liverpool more easily.

One Saturday, a few weeks before Christmas I was on my way to put an aerial up close to Park Road Markets where Gina was working. I decided to call in and surprise her. She was hard to find at first as a big crowd had gathered in front of the stall, but as soon as she spotted me she called out.

"Jeff! Great to see you! Come and help me, I am on my own as Dad has gone for more stock!"

Standing next to Gina I soon found myself serving a customer.

"Brown size nine and size four in pink," one lady called out, referring to the slippers, the best selling Christmas present. The slippers were stacked high and Gina and her father, Bob, were selling them cheap. I carried on serving until Bob returned and then set off to get on with my afternoon's work.

I picked Gina up at around 7.30 that evening and we went to the Brook House for a quiet drink and spent the evening talking about the markets. I couldn't believe how much I had enjoyed myself helping Gina for just a short while. Memories came flooding back from when I was a young boy working with Mum down on the Market and selling stockings out of a suitcase with Dad. By the end of the night I had managed to talk Gina and myself into going into business together on the markets. Convinced that it was fate and meant to be, considering we both had originated from Liverpool market trading families and that destiny had brought us together three thousand miles away in Spain. We spent a day visiting as many markets as we could looking at all the competition, and what people were selling. The possibilities were endless, but we wanted to sell something completely different to all the other stalls.

It was a tough decision but in the end we decided to go into business selling teenage girls fashion clothing. I gave up the aerial business and by the time Christmas was over we had announced to every one our intentions registering J&R Fashions as our trading name – the R standing for Regina. Bob gave us an old market stall plus a canvas sheet that he didn't need and I already had a van.

Now all we needed was something special to sell. Not having a clue where to find it or where to go, we were almost stopped at the first hurdle. However, June had recently purchased a checked shirt that we both really liked, and the label in side said Kumar Brothers.

Calling Directory Enquiries, I was given an address in Manchester and so on Thursday the 5th January, 1978, a twenty year old Gina and I, a slightly mature twenty-four year old, set off to Kumar Brothers clutching hold of our joint life savings - £300!

The address led us to a huge old office block in the heart of Manchester City Centre. We made our way down a dark and dingy stairwell in to the depths of a large cellar where we were met by an elderly Indian lady, whom we later discovered was Mrs Kumar, the mother (and boss by all accounts) of the two brothers who owned the wholesale fashion company.

Introducing ourselves as market traders from Liverpool we were allowed to wander up and down the line of hundreds of cardboard boxes laid out on the floor, bursting with clothes of every description and colour. Walking slowly down the lines inspecting every item of clothing in almost every box was exciting at first, but after well over two hours we started to realise that the majority of styles on offer were not what we were looking for. We did however manage to find thirty-six checked shirts and twenty-four pairs of denim drain pipe jeans that were just starting to come into fashion in the UK. Gina also liked the look of a cowl necked jumper; we chose a dozen in different colours.

Handing over all our savings to Mrs Kumar was worrying to say the least. She informed us that Friday night at around 7 was the best time to come along as the big deliveries arrived from London full of the latest styles. With no money left we took on board what she had said and made our way back to Gina's house. As we drove along we convinced one another that we had made the right purchases. The next day was spent around at Gina's parent's house getting everything ready.

Robert and Brenda Jones were a fantastic couple. Bob as he liked to be called was a very talented man and could put his hand to most things. After leaving school he served an apprenticeship as a carpenter before joining the Army. He then drove large oil tankers as well as selling a variety of different items on Park Road Market every Saturday.

Brenda stayed at home caring for her family. Susan, the eldest daughter had recently been married to John and they now lived in the Old Swan area. Gina was their middle child and Robert, aged seventeen, was the youngest. They lived in a comfortable semi-detached house in Chilwall, one of the better areas of Liverpool. Bob and Brenda were the type of parents who would do anything to help their children.

It was still dark and very cold at five in the morning when I arrived at Gina's for our first Saturday's trading. The Hall light was on and the front door slightly ajar. Gina was in the kitchen pouring hot soup into a flask. She was wearing several layers of warm clothing, protection against the cold January air.

We left, making our way to Great Homer Street Market, ironically the same place that I had started out with Mum. Organised chaos greeted us; at least fifty vans, if not more, were trying to find somewhere to park in the darkness of early dawn, their headlights blinding me as they bumped on and off the sidewalk, a law amongst themselves. They were obviously experienced and knew what they were doing. We parked a short way away from all the commotion.

As I got out of the van I could not help but feel a sense of urgency hit me at the speed in which they were emptying their vans and the tremendous noise made by the metal bars hitting the concrete ground was deafening at times. I told Gina to stay in the van whilst I went looking for a space to set up. Five minutes later I returned advising her to come quickly as I had found the perfect spot. We soon emptied the stall from out of the van, both of us working equally as speedily as everyone else and soon had piled everything up in the space I had chosen. Putting a stall up for the first time is very similar to erecting a tent for the first time when you go on holiday. Nothing ever seems to fit together.

After an hour of wrestling with the stall we eventually completed the task and stood back for a moment to admire our new business venture. I put my arm around Gina's shoulder and squeezed her towards me.

"This is it love," I told her, "The start of something big."

Our special moment was quickly cut short by the arrival of a man the same size as a block of flats. He told us to move our 'fucking' stall or he would do it for us. He was angry.

"What do you mean?" I asked. "We were here first."

"Don't be stupid," he replied. "This is my pitch and has been for years. You can't just set up wherever you like." He stopped for breath. "You have to go to the office and see the inspector if you want a pitch. You'd better hurry up and take this down as I haven't got time to stand here chatting to you all day. So move it or I will crush it with my bare hands."

I am sure that he could (not doubting his ability to carry out his threat) I had to accept defeat and told him to keep his hair on as anyone could make a mistake.

Gina and I spent the next half hour taking it all down again and putting it back in the van. By the time I got to the office there was a queue of at least twenty people waiting outside. I asked a man at the back what the procedure was for this market, as if I knew the score. He gave me the run down; apparently the inspector would appear at nine o'clock, and we follow him around the market. If any of the 200 regular traders have not turned up he allocated their pitch to the first in the queue and keeps on going until the market is full. Anyone left without a pitch has to go home and try again the following week.

By 9.30 all the available spaces had been filled and the inspector announced that he was sorry, but there were no more left before turning away and heading back to the warmth of his office. The remaining small crowd dispersed as Gina and I just stood there looking at each other in disbelief. Our dreams of a business together was becoming a nightmare. Not prepared to give up that easily, I returned to the Inspectors office.

He was sitting behind a desk with a large mug of tea in one hand and a juicy bacon and egg butty in the other and was just about to get stuck in.

"I am sorry to bother you," I interrupted him before he could take his first bite, "But there is no way I can go home. My life's savings are stuck in the back of a van our there and I need to sell today. Surely you must have some spaces available?"

He had obviously been in the job a long time and had seen a lot of Oscar winning performances before as he didn't flinch. He just took a bite and chewed. Speaking with his mouthful, he replied, "I told you no and that means no. Now shut the door on your way out!"

I couldn't bring myself to tell him that he had egg yolk dripping down his chin and it was just about to land on his official Corporation tie, thinking that it would be best if he found out for himself. So I quietly left, closing the door behind me. However I was not totally convinced by what he had said, so I searched up and down the place myself, and found the smallest of spaces around the back of the market where all the second hand clothes were sold.

The Inspector was rubbing his tie with a damp cloth when I returned. He wasn't too pleased when I told him about my great find, though he seemed to change his mined when I said that there would be a fiver in it for him.

Gina and I made the best out of a bad situation making our first sale at eleven o'clock; after that there was a steady flow of customers and by the end of the day we were please with the way things had turned out.

As I drove home, Gina sat next to me counting the takings. Her smile was getting bigger and bigger the more she counted. "Jeff, how much do you think we took?" she asked me. "Go on, have a guess!"

"About £70 pounds," was my estimate.

"No double that," she couldn't contain her excitement.

"One hundred and forty pounds? You have got to be joking!" I couldn't believe my ears.

"That's right," she said, "One hundred and forty pounds!"

"One hundred and forty pounds on our first day," I was almost singing with happiness, "and from such a bad position! Yippee, we are going to be rich."

The following Saturday, in a better position this time, we took three hundred and fifty pounds, selling out on a lot of the styles we had chosen. We were now up and running, but still had a long way to go.

We followed Mrs Kumar's instructions and arrived at her warehouse on Friday at 7pm in the hope of finding some decent stock to sell. The place was full of Indian traders standing around and talking in their own language, at least 30 or 40 of them, also waiting for the deliveries to arrive from London. We were the only two white faces there.

At 7.30pm a trapdoor was opened on the pavement outside and men were unloading boxes off a huge wagon and sliding them down a chute into the depths of the cellar. As they landed with an almighty bang on the floor, Mrs Kumar stood on guard with two of her men who opening the boxes and pulling out one style or another for everyone to see. Mrs Kumar would be calling out the quantity and the price.

Within a split second, one of the other men put his hand up and said something in a language which I did not understand. The box was then put to one side exclusively for that bidder. These were definitely big buyers and they knew what they were doing, whilst we were still small fish with only a little bit of money.

This went on for hours until there were no more boxes left. We got home at midnight, not a single sausage to our name, so I had to put my thinking cap on. The following Friday, I arrived half an hour early with a big bunch of flowers which I handed to Mrs Kumar. She was taken by surprise by my gesture, whilst the other traders stood around looking as if I knew something they didn't. Very quietly I murmured in her ear, "Please Mrs Kumar, please give some small traders a chance to survive as well."

The simple token of a bunch of flowers clearly worked as Mrs Kumar always offered us first refusal and we went from strength to strength from then on.

The next obstacle we had to overcome was trying to establish ourselves as permanent stall holders on as many markets as possible in and around Liverpool. This proved to be difficult as firstly you had to get there very early and sign on the casual list, and then eventually after some months and sometimes even years you would be offered a permanent pitch.

Gina and I were lucky as we started in January in all the bad weather, so a lot of stall holders stayed away and in just five months we became established on four different daily markets.

Business was good but it was still hard to find the right stock to sell; we spent days at a time walking around the Manchester fashion district and knocking on the doors of the larger fashion labels bit it was not working. Once they heard the words 'market traders' they would literally shut the door in our faces saying that they didn't want their brand being sold on a market stall.

Feeling rejected and frustrated we decided to try and make our own styles. I placed an advert in the local paper for a pattern cutter and machinist who worked from home; the response was very good. Finding a fabric merchant to supply us was a task in itself, but eventually we did. I spent hours upon hours driving all over Liverpool dropping off bundles of fabrics at machinists houses and going back four days later to pick up and pay for the finished products. It was a lot of hard work but the only way we could get what we wanted.

The first style which we put into production was a checked, pleated mini skirt. In the first week we sold almost sixty pieces on our four market stalls – Garston, Speke, Park Road and Paddy's, and we went on to sell around seven hundred in total. Making our own styles proved to be good business, shifting large quantities week after week. Gina and I worked well together building up the business, in no time we had a lot of regular customers. Mum had taught me how to survive on the markets and I had not forgotten what I had learnt. I clearly remember one particular Tuesday when we managed to get on to Garston Market. As we started to set up, Gina noticed that the stall opposite was selling the exact same coats as we were, the only difference being that theirs were five pounds cheaper than ours, which was a lot of money in those days.

Gina asked if she should take the coats off and put them back into the van or should we reduce ours in price to the same amount. I told her that we should leave them as they were.

The stall opposite was run by Isaac, an old Jewish man who had been trading from the same spot for donkey's years. He was more than established and was literally an institution as all the women bought their coats off Isaac. We were amateurs in comparison, he was the master and the better trader by far, everything I wanted to become.

As the day came to a close, we were packing up to go home, I heard Isaac calling me over. Thinking he was going to have a go at me for selling the same coats I hesitantly walked towards him.

"Hey kid!" he called out. "I don't know what you have got, but whatever it is you should bottle it and sell it!"

I looked at him, confused. "I am sorry, I don't understand, what do you mean?"

"I have watched you sell at least four of those coats for five pounds more than I am selling them for – I haven't even sold one!" he explained. "In all my years on the markets I would never have believed it possible if I hadn't seen it with my own eyes. What an extraordinary gift you must have."

I smiled and thanked him for his compliment and returned to help Gina pack up, whilst at the same time thinking to myself that it was a good thing that he had not heard me telling my customers that my coats were perfects and not rejects that are sometimes found on other market stalls. Only then did I appreciate how valuable all those years spent with Mum on the markets had really been.

June, my little sister now worked with me on Saturdays at Paddy's Market just like I had done with Mum – she would have been so proud of us working together.

Six months had passed since we had started and business was very good. We had built up a good stock level and bought a larger van. Gina and I worked non-stop and were ready for a holiday. Choosing Benidorm as our destination we thought it would be nice to see all our old friends. And if that was not a good enough reason, it seemed as if half of Liverpool was living and working out there by now.

Barry, Linda and their son Danny were there, plus Mick, Tommy and Danny. Even John Cullen had moved over. I had more friends in Spain than I did at home – what an amazing turn around it was that year!

We took June and her friend Mary with us as they had never been out of Liverpool before, let alone travelled on a 'plane, and the idea of a holiday was therefore an exciting prospect for all of us.

I filled an extra suitcase with fifty Hawaiian mens shirts that I had bought from Mrs Kumar and sold them all in the first two days in bars around the town, whilst the profit I made gave us our spending money.

Gina and I took a walk down memory lane visiting all our favourite haunts; Rubio drove us to see the finished building site which looked very impressive with the villas completed. I felt a little bit proud at having made a small contribution to their construction. Showing June and Mary Tramps disco was even more memorable for me, and they even had a new Charlie Chaplin working the door.

Barry, Linda and Danny were all doing well – Barry was working for a baker delivering pies to all the bars and cafes whist Linda and Danny enjoyed the Spanish sun.

All my old mates from Huyton were working in a new bar called the Talk of the Town. It was obvious that they were having the time of their lives and the most bizarre thing of all was that they were sharing an apartment with Cockney Steve, whom Gina and I had lived with the year before!

A small part of me wished that I could be there with them all having a good time, but the greater part of me wanted to be with Gina.

On our last night I took Gina out alone to a beautiful restaurant that overlooked the coast line. We had the most romantic candlelit dinner and held hands, talking about the past year we had spent together. I was madly in love with Gina and knew from that moment on that I wanted to spend the rest of my life with her.

As the evening was coming to an end, we walked back along the beach arm in arm. A familiar clear sky with bright stars glittered above our heads and a full moon seemed to shine down just on the two of us. It was completely silent except for the sound of the Mediterranean Sea gently washing up on the sand. The whole experience was magical.

I stopped and turned Gina towards me. Holding both her hands I got down on one knee in the sand, and asked her to marry me.

Gina gave me the most radiant smile and softly said 'yes'. Getting to my feet I held her close in my arms and we kissed for what seemed like the longest time ever – a totally spontaneous proposal, and it could not have been more perfect even if I had planned it!

Again Benidorm was the place of a perfect holiday, and once again we left with happy memories to last a life time.

On returning to England, we couldn't wait to break the news that we were getting married, and both Gina's family and mine were more than happy for us both. A date was set for the following year, May 19th 1979.

Not long after we got back from holiday Gina passed her driving test which enabled us to put another van on the road. She now went off with Sue, her friend, to trade on four markets a week, whilst I managed to do five, with Alan, another friend of mine. The remaining two days were spent trying to find stock from all over Manchester.

If I had learned anything in my short time in the fashion business it was that the buying was the most important part. Finding the right product to sell was the key to success. Liverpool teenage girls were some of the most fashionable in the country and it was our job to come up with the styles that they wanted to buy.

I had no other alternatives than to go to the big city of London in search of new companies. Leaving home at 4.30 in the morning I set off on my 500 mile round trip in the van to London dressed in a smart suit, shirt and tie. With two thousand pounds in my pockets in cash, I headed straight for the West End, where allegedly the large fashion houses were located which sold to the trade. I certainly looked like the young successful business type if nothing else as I walked up and down all the different streets. Looking in the windows at the fantastic displays excited me, even though I was more nervous than usual. Having finally built up enough courage to go in side and have a look at one, I opened the door and was greeted by a polite good morning.

"How may I help you?" I found myself being greeted by a well dressed middle aged woman.

Still feeling nervous, and a little intimidated by her posh voice, I kept up the pretence of the successful business man. "I am looking to buy some stock for my company," I replied.

"Well, you have certainly come to the right place," was her response. "Follow me, I'll show you our latest styles." I followed her into a larger show room where there were thousands upon thousands of the most fabulous garments hanging on rails. My wildest dreams could never have imagined such a place like this.

"Is this the sort of thing that you are looking for?" she asked, gesturing towards the racks of clothes.

Speechless, I could only nod, silently saying yes to everything, style after style which she showed me. Everyone equally as good as the first. I wanted to buy them all, and it all was going extremely well.

"Where is your shop?" she asked me.

"Liverpool," I replied.

"Whereabouts?" she pressed on for more answers.

I started to feel very uncomfortable with her line of interrogation, and knew that she probably wouldn't like the truthful answers if it came out. Still avoiding a direct answer, I carried on talking, whilst a 'hole' started to appear at my feet.

"All over really." Clearing my throat, I kept on digging.

"How many shops do you have?" she was really interested, whilst I was up to my knees by now in the ever increasing pit I was making.

"Several," I replied. Looking at her face, and knowing that she would continue asking me questions, I carried on. "They are not quite shops though," I paused for a moment, "More like very nice stalls."

"Stalls!" her softly spoken voice turned to a shriek of horror as I was quickly ushered to the door. As I stepped out into the street I heard her final comments.

"I am sorry, but we couldn't possibly supply the likes of stall holders. Good day!"

Turning around to protest, I was faced with the door being slammed firmly shut in my face.

After bravely trying to convince a couple of other larger fashion companies to supply me and receiving the same response, I gave up and made my way home, desperately disappointed and feeling rejected. I couldn't stop wondering what was wrong with market stalls considering that was how retail first started thousands of years ago; people forget that Marks & Spencer started out as a small market stall.

Gina and I were really proud of what we had achieved in such a short time and we enjoyed the market way of life. We felt a sense of being part of a small community. The majority of traders are some of the most genuine, kindest and hard working people that you could ever wish to meet; a very special 'breed' in their own right. It is not an easy life, setting up shop in the early hours of the morning in all weather conditions, serving for ten hours at a time, taking your stall down at the end of the day, only to repeat the whole process all over again the following day requires a great deal of dedication. But the reality is that markets are a focal point of a community, somewhere to buy their day to day necessities, and more importantly somewhere to meet other people, to chat and say hello to friends both old and new.

Gina and I worked hard that winter. The weather was nearly always horrible, and I got so fed up getting blown to bits in the wind and rain, that I bought a large box trailer and converted it into a small mobile shop. The back and one side could be opened up to create awnings and steps leading into the trailer allowed our customers to come in out of the cold. It even had a changing room in one corner which gave people privacy when they wanted to try things on. Our trailer was the first of its kind and admired by all. It soon was nicknamed the 'Harrods' of the markets, most probably because I had plush red carpets laid down on the floor.

Chapter Twenty-Five
Three Wise Men

Another Christmas came and went and our wedding day was drawing closer. We still hadn't found a place to live, not having a lot of time left over – we were working all the hours God gave.

One night Gina went to visit a friend of hers who had just got married and moved in to her own house. The next day Gina told me how gorgeous it was, and that there was one for sale a few doors down so we made arrangements to visit it the following Sunday.

As we drove through Whiston (at that stage a small rural village) on the outskirts of Liverpool, I couldn't get over how quiet it was. Gina gave me instructions to Foxshaw Close, a quite cul-de-sac surrounded by fields, and pointed Number 23 out to me.

As soon as we saw it, we fell in love with it. Number 23 had a small front garden and a larger one at the back, its own drive leading to the garage; it was a three bedroom semi-detached house. After a thorough guided tour of the inside, and two hours of hard negotiations, I shook hands with the owner agreeing a purchase price of £16,000. It was hard to believe that soon it would be ours, and in our desire to move in as quickly as possible, we agreed to the one condition made with the sale; Bert and Doris were to be allowed to live with us even after Gina and I had moved in.

Putting a small deposit down, we managed to get a mortgage for the rest and bought our first house. We moved in to our new home, and Bert and Doris remained in residence in the garage for a further three months. They were normally no trouble at all, except in the evenings, when we had to persuade them to go back to the garage. At times it was very hard, as they were both fairly old and stubborn, and required a lot of persuasion, but we would eventually win out, coaxing them into their temporary home with a carrot or two. Aside from that however, they were good guests, two pet donkeys who had belonged to the previous owners and had lived with them for many years, and we were actually quite sad to see them go when it was time for them to move on to newer pastures.

Bob, Gina and I gave the house a complete overhaul, spending every evening decorating the rooms from top to bottom before moving our furniture in, and we managed to complete the task two days before the wedding.

On Saturday, 19th May 1979, the weather was at its best with not a cloud in the sky; a perfect day for getting married.

Looking at my reflection in the mirror, attired in a new light grey suit worn over a white shirt and smart tie, I was proud of myself and particularly of getting married to Gina in a few hours time. I did, however, feel an emptiness, as if something was missing, which of course it was. Mum. She should have been there to share in my happiness; if only she could have met Gina she would have adored and loved her as much as I did. Taking comfort from looking up at the blue sky, I remembered her words and how she said she would be looking down on me, and I knew she was.

My thoughts were interrupted by Barry who was going to be my best man, calling up the stairs to me, telling me that the hire car had arrived. A short while later as we pulled up outside the church, I noticed a group of women standing by the entrance. Not recognizing any of the faces at first, I thought that they must be 'left-over's' from the previous wedding, but as Barry and I got closer they started to call out.

"Good luck, Jeff!" and "All the very best!" I couldn't believe my eyes as I realised that this gathering of well wishers were actually some of our regular customers from the markets. They had travelled quite some distance to see the bride and to wish us both luck, and their presence made me feel even more special.

The small church was full. I saw a lot of familiar faces from my side, whilst Gina seemed to have an even larger gathering of friends and family, many of whom I had yet to meet. As I sat in silence, nervously waiting in the front pew, Barry broke the silence.

"Are you sure you want to go through with this?" he asked, "Or should we just quietly leave, go and buy an old banger of a van and spend the next six months driving around Europe?" His comment broke the tension, and we both burst out laughing, making the vicar peer over the top of his glasses as if telling us to be quiet.

As our laughter faded away, the organ came to life, filling the church with music as we all stood to our feet.

As I stood in front of the altar, the temptation to look over my shoulder was too great to resist. Turning slightly, I watched as Gina walked slowly up the aisle towards me, a vision of loveliness in her wedding gown. I felt a lump forming in my throat as I glimpsed a sight of her face through her long veil; her beauty was hard to miss. Close behind Gina were her three bridesmaids, her sister Susan and best friend Wendy, and my little sister June.

The rest of the day seemed to pass in a blur, one of the most important days, but definitely the fastest.

Wedding celebrations over, Gina and I returned to our new home in the early hours of the morning, excited at the thought of spending our first night together as man and wife in our very own home. Getting out the car, we closed the doors as quietly as possible not wanting to bring any attention to ourselves by disturbing the neighbours. Opening the gate to the footpath, the nighttime silence was disturbed by a horrendously loud clashing and clanking of tin cans. We had been sabotaged by our neighbours!

Looking up to see if we had woken anyone, we noticed a large banner stretched across the width of the house. In large, clear letters, we could read the message from our neighbours 'Welcome to Foxshaw Close Jeff and Gina'. Not only did our new neighbours have a great sense of humour, but they had made us feel very welcome indeed.

We couldn't afford a honeymoon or the time off work for that matter, but living in our new home as man and wife was special in itself. Like all young couples committed to sharing a future together, we had dreams of one day having children of our own, and enjoying the happiness that a family could bring.

I had always had a burning ambition to better myself, and now it was even stronger with the prospect of a family of my own to provide for. Being a loving husband and a caring father was something that was important to me as I had no intention of letting Gina experience the same things that my mother had. Nor did I want my children to grow up with an absent father; I was determined to ensure that my family was protected by a loving and happy environment.

The small market business Gina and I had started just two years before was doing very well and we had achieved so much in such a short time; but we could do better. I didn't want Gina to have to get up at four o'clock on a freezing cold morning to go to work on the markets for the rest of her life. I wanted to expand my business, and at the same time make Gina's life easier. The best way to achieve this, therefore was to open a shop, so the next six months were spent looking for the perfect premises in our spare time.

Every month, Gina and I would spend a day in the city centre, visiting the larger stores, studying the designs they had on offer, and more importantly looking at the prices they were charging. Although we were market traders we still had to do our homework so we could stay ahead of the competition.

One day, whilst we were on our city centre visit, we noticed a fairly small shop on Church Street pretty close to some of the larger high street stores. Not only was it empty, but there was a large board on the building front which said that it was for lease or for sale, and gave the contact details of the agents.

Fired by determination to fulfill my ambitions I soon made enquiries about the lease, and discovered that it was available for £15,000. With 22 years left to run on the lease, and a rental premium of £9,500 per annum it seemed like a good opportunity. We talked about it over the next few days, and in the end Gina and I decided to see if we could acquire the shop.

Although I needed to raise enough money, I also found that my enthusiasm was dampened by my lack of education and poor literacy skills. I needed the help from some 'educated' men and the only three I could think of were my bank manager, my accountant and my solicitor. They were the only ones with whom I could discuss the possibility of becoming the proprietor of a shop.

I set up the appointments for the following day, one after the other, and with some trepidation set off. By the end of the day, and earfuls of advice from my chosen advisors, I felt like jumping into the Mersey in order to drown my sorrows. Any dreams I may have had had been destroyed in a matter of hours by the three wise men.

Gina and I had been invited to dinner at her parent's house that evening, and as we sat around the table, Gina, Bob and Brenda were all eager to hear my news. They all wanted to know how I had got on with my important meetings.

I spent the next hour or so explaining how disappointed I had been with the advice which I had received. My bank manager had lectured me on the perils of the High Street and said that although I was a good market trader this alone would not be enough for me to take on the big boys of the High Street. On that basis he was refusing to lend me any money.

My accountant, Alan Gorst, had been more sympathetic, and had felt that my market business was thriving, but did not believe that we had enough retail experience to take on a shop. In his opinion we were being too ambitious and had advised me to continue with the market business, to enjoy the success we were having and to forget about a shop.

My final appointment that day had been with Alan Espley, my solicitor, who had helped us buy our first house. Alan had explained, in great detail, the numerous pitfalls regarding a lease, and how once you had signed a 23 year lease, it was your responsibility. In essence, if my idea for a boutique failed, I would still have to find a way of paying the rent, and just like the others, he told me to stick to what we knew best – market trading!

When I had finished telling them about my day, Bob wanted to know how I felt – what my thoughts were, now that I had received the professional advice. I told him that I felt that they were wrong, and in my heart, I believed that I could do it.

"We can compete with the big boys," I told him. "Every day our stalls are busier than all the rest – Gina and I have a gift!"

With that, Bob stood up and went over to the mantelpiece. He picked up a large envelope which was propped up behind the clock and place it in the middle of the table.

"This envelope contains the deeds to my house."

Gina and I sat in silence looking at him.

"I have just finished paying off my mortgage after twenty-five years and I have all the faith in the world in you two; that you and Gina can make it work."

Bob passed me the envelope and told me to take it to my bank manager the following day, using it as security against a loan from the bank.

Words failed me, and I looked at Gina, wondering if she was going to say anything, but like me she was silent.

"Enough of the misery," Brenda broke the silence. "Let's have a cup of tea to celebrate."

I took Bob and Brenda up on their exceptionally generous offer, and as a result Gina and I were soon the proud owners of our first shop premises on Church Street, Liverpool.

On the day I went in to pick up the keys, my solicitor mentioned something to me that took the wind out of my sails. He told me that Harold Bagenski, the owner of the premises before me, had said that I would only last 12 months. Apparently I didn't have a clue what I was doing and if he couldn't make it work despite many years experience in the menswear fashion business, then there was no way that I was going to succeed specialising in fashion for teenage girls!

I felt doomed before I even got going. Putting the miserable thoughts to the back of my mind, Bob, Gina and I got stuck in doing the shop up.

The shop was named after a song by Dave Edmunds called 'Girls Talk'. Once we had purchased the new stock and recruited four staff to work alongside Gina we were ready.

On Saturday, 26th April 1980, we opened the doors of our first shop to the public. I had set up my stall very early that morning at Paddy's Market in readiness for the days trading; Bob and June, in addition to our Saturday staff were going to run the stall whilst Gina and I focused on 'Girls Talk'.

By 12 o'clock I was getting worried as we'd hardly done any business. The place was empty. I found this hard to accept as we were offering the same stock at the same price in the shop as we had on our stall in the market.

As I paced up and down, all I could think to myself was that I had set my sights too high. Holy shit, my father-in-laws house deeds, all the advice I had ignored – there was a lot riding on the shops success.

Gina knew I was worried by the shops first day's trading, so that night as we settled down at home she decided to cheer me up with some good news. It was news which I had been waiting for, for some time. Gina was expecting our first child – something we had planned ever since we got married. Now our dreams had come true, and the new member of our family was expected to join us in November. Everything was happening so fast.

★ ★ ★

We soon got into a routine; I worked the four best market days and then helped Gina on the two other days at 'Girls Talk'; Gina remained at the shop every day. The markets continued to be very busy but the shop was almost too quiet for comfort and I believed that it was because no-one knew we were there.

Except for Mr B, (I am going to refer to this gentleman as Mr B for obvious reasons!).

We had only been open for a week when he paid me a visit, coming in to the shop and informing one of our staff that he wanted to speak to the new owner.

I was down in the basement organising some stock when I was called to the shop floor. Walking towards the strange looking man standing by the shop entrance, I was thinking that it was all a bit odd. He was well groomed and tall, and wore a long black overcoat and black leather gloves, which on a warm sunny day made him stand out.

"Hello, can I help?" I asked.

"If you are the owner, you can." He spoke in a raspy voice.

"I am the owner," I replied, trying to be helpful, but at the same time wondering what a funeral director wanted from me.

"Good, then I will call every Friday, at the same time, four o'clock. You got that?" He looked at me sternly, almost daring me to say no.

I just looked at him blankly; he had to be some kind of nutter.

"When I call I want you to have an envelope with £200 cash inside. Do you understand?"

I was no clearer now than when he had arrived. "Why would I do that?" I asked, confusion written plainly across my face.

"Don't be fucking funny with me kid, or you will regret it. You are on my patch and that's the way it works."

I could see that he was getting angry. "What happens if I don't?" I didn't want to ask, but I needed to know.

"I'll torch it!"

"What do you mean torch it?" I was still lost.

"Burn the fucking place down!"

"Why would you want to do that?" I asked. He had to be mad, and I needed to be polite not to upset him any more.

"Because that's what happens if you don't fucking pay you idiot. See you next week." And with that final comment he turned and left.

I was totally gobsmacked and did not know which way to turn. That night, on the way home, I stopped at my gym on the north side of the city to do my regular workout. One of my mates was lying on the bench pressing weights whilst I was lifting them on and off for him. I was telling him about my strange visitor at the shop and the demands that he had made. I hadn't even finished speaking before the owner of the gym appeared at my side and asked me to come in to his office. He must have overheard me, because as I followed him in he told me to close the door – he had something he needed to discuss.

Johnny was in his sixties; built like an ox he was one of the fittest and strongest men I had ever met. I had been going to his gym for two years and got on well with him; we had sparred and worked out together and he seemed to like me. After I had finished telling him what had happened, he told me that he knew Mr B and said that he would be at my shop at four o'clock on the Friday.

I told Johnny that I didn't want any trouble and felt sure that I could sort things out myself. Looking at me from across his desk, he quietly assured me that there would be no trouble whatsoever, and that I would definitely not be able to sort things out on my own.

The following Friday Johnny arrived at the shop at about 3.30 as promised. I made him a cup of tea and we sat chatting in the staff room. At four o'clock on the dot the intercom sounded, it was one of the staff.

"Jeff, Mr B is here to see you," she announced.

Getting to his feet, Johnny told me to stay close and to leave all the talking to him. Walking two paces behind him, we headed on to the shop floor. Mr B was standing by the door, dressed in the same black clothes as before, but looking even more menacing this time.

"Hello Johnny." Mr B seemed to know my companion.

"Hello Tony." Johnny returned his greeting.

These were obviously men of few words.

"Tony, I am going to ask you to do me a favour." Johnny got straight to the point.

"What's that Johnny?" Mr B asked in his husky voice.

"Tony, this lad is family." Johnny nodded his head in my direction. "I want you to leave him alone."

"Can't do that Johnny, you know that. He's on my patch; you know how it works; I look after the south side and your family look after the north." All of a sudden Mr B didn't look quite so powerful.

Johnny continued speaking, his quiet voice making it difficult for Mr B to argue. "I am asking you to do me a favour on this one occasion. Just leave this lad out."

Mr B said nothing for a moment, just looking straight at Johnny in the eyes, one giant to another. Finally he spoke.

"You owe me one Johnny." With that he and Johnny shook hands, and then embraced before he turned and left.

I was mesmerized by what I had just seen and heard. It had been like a scene from 'The Godfather', only this time set in my small shop in Liverpool.

For the next six months or so, every Friday afternoon at 3.30 Johnny would drop into the shop for a cup of tea; apparently he was always just passing by. I knew however, that he wanted to make sure that Mr B never bothered me again although Johnny and I never discussed it at all.

In the ten years I remained on Church Street I never saw Mr B ever again, and often wondered why Johnny had gone out of his way to help. At the end of the day it was probably because he was a genuinely nice guy.

Chapter Twenty-Six
Mannequins and Nappies

I didn't have any money to spend on advertising, so I had to come up with something fast. One day, I was walking through Church Street, not too far from our shop when I noticed a crowd of people gathered together. They were watching something going on in the pedestrianised part of the road, so being the the inquisitive type, I decided to go and see what was happening.

The crowd were watching two teenage black girls dancing like robots to music coming from a ghetto blaster on the pavement next to them. Robotic dancing had just come out and their amazing routine lasted for about three minutes. Once the music had finished, the girls started to pass a hat around, causing the crowd to quickly disperse. Only a few people bothered to throw in a couple of coins.

I had found their performance mesmerizing, and immediately went over to congratulate them and have a chat. They seemed like nice girls so I invited them to join me for a cup of coffee back at the shop. A few minutes later, sitting in the warmth of the staff room, I found out that they both wanted to become professional dancers one day; their street performances were a way of earning college fees, but didn't actually pay very well at all.

I had a brainstorm moment. "How about working for me? I'll pay you £20 each a day; what do you think?"

"Yes!" They both replied at the same time. "Yes, please!"

Shaking their hands on the deal, I told them to report back to the shop at nine o'clock the following Saturday morning.

I now had a week to turn my idea into reality. I immediately had 2000 flyers printed announcing the arrival of Liverpool's newest boutique; 'Girls Talk' was now open for business selling all the latest styles. The flyer gave an example of our amazing prices and included a small map showing our location on Church Street.

I then purchased two bright white boiler suits from the local hardware store, and two baseball caps to match. I then had the shop's name embossed in brilliant red letters on the front of the caps and the backs of the boiler suits.

The girls turned up the following Saturday, and once in their outfits looked really spectacular. They completed the look with black stockings over their faces and black gloves on their hands, making them appear even more like anonymous robots.

The girls were soon into their performance and a crowd quickly gathered, keeping Gina and me busy handing out flyers. As we gave out the leaflets we pointed towards the shop, encouraging the passers by to go and have a look. Within an hour 'Girls Talk' was packed with eager shoppers, all happily spending their money; this lasted for the rest of the day.

Towards the end of the afternoon, my two 'robots' returned to the shop accompanied by two bizzies.

"Excuse me Sir," one of the policemen addressed his comments to me. "Are you responsible for these two young women?"

"Yes, I am," I replied, "Why? What's wrong?"

"I am afraid that we cannot allow them to continue their dancing," he explained. "It's against the law."

"Against the law?" I was puzzled. "They are not busking or doing anything wrong – just entertaining the shoppers as they pass by." This seemed to be a stupid situation, and one that was beginning to annoy me a little.

"If we let it continue," the policeman replied, "Soon everyone will be doing the same thing, and the area will become congested. I am sorry sir, no more dancing and that's final."

The girls had been listening to the policeman's words and watched them go with disappointed looks on their faces. The day had been going so well for all of us and now it was ruined. However, by the time that they had changed out of their costumes I had come up with a solution to our problem.

"Don't worry girls," I told them. "Next Saturday you can perform in our windows!"

The following Saturday I removed a mannequin from each window and Gina dressed the girls in two of our latest styles instead of their boiler suits. Once they had put the black stockings over the faces and the gloves on their hands they looked just like the real mannequins in the window.

They were brilliant; standing completely motionless in the window until somebody walked passed or stopped to have a look, whereupon they would make a small movement, frightening the life out of whomever was looking. It was hilarious watching the people's reactions and listening to their screams of surprise. Within a very short time a crowd of curious onlookers had gathered, with people crossing over from the other side of the street to come and see what was going on.

Our living mannequins were attracting a lot of attention, and soon the tills were ringing non-stop as people started coming in to the shop to spend their money. My idea had worked – I had got customers through the door.

Everything was going much better than I had anticipated until the bizzies once again decided to turn up uninvited. Walking towards the policeman standing at the front of the shop, I recognized him from the week before.

"Sir, am I right in thinking you are the proprietor of this shop?"

"Yes," I responded, "I am. What have I done this time?"

"Well, Sir, I am not sure," he replied. "But whatever it is you have to stop."

"Stop what?" I was confused. "What do you want me to stop?"

"I don't know what you're doing sir," he said, "But all I do know is that you are causing an obstruction on the pavement outside."

The penny dropped. I now knew what he was talking about, but had to smile at his blindness. Even this sharp eyed bobby had missed the obvious – my window was the stage for two living dolls!

"You cannot be serious!" I protested. "Last week you told me that I couldn't promote my business outside, and now you are telling me that I can't promote it from inside? How do you expect me to do it then?" I was definitely annoyed by this narrow minded approach.

"I don't know, Sir," was his answer. "But I cannot allow you to cause an obstruction on the sidewalk."

I muttered a few angry words under my breath as he left. This was too much – I was trying to make my business busy, but the bizzies wouldn't let me!

As the weeks passed by, 'Girls Talk' was becoming a little better established though the pressure was still there to do a lot better. If I really was going to compete with the 'Big Boys' I had to start thinking like them.

Now that we had shop premises, many more doors were opened to us. This enabled me to drive to London once a week and successfully acquire the latest styles from the larger fashion houses. The only drawback with this was that they were expensive, and I hated selling them at a similar price to my competitors; my aim was to be a lot cheaper than the rest so every time I went to London I spent many hours searching for small factories.

The fashion industry, like many others, has it's own language, for example it refers to itself as the rag trade, whilst small factories run by immigrants (both legal and illegal) are referred to as sweat shops. Sweat shops were popular with the rag trade as labour costs were low, and most importantly they operated at great speed.

If a sweat shop was given a winning style on a Monday, it could be manufactured, delivered to the high street and on sale in the department stores by Saturday; the speed in which they produced finished garments was amazing.

My job was to find 'cabbage', but not the cabbage we eat. It is an expression which dates back many centuries, and refers to the left over fabric or cloth. Most of the big fashion houses would design a garment, source and pay for the cloth, and then give the design and cloth to a known manufacturer on a (CMT) cut-make-trim basis. This meant that the factory owner would only get paid a minimal amount for making the garments; however, if he was clever the cloth would be cut very carefully, allowing for no wastages. Thus the expression, cutting your cloth according to your means also came into being.

Once the order had been completed, any left-over fabric now traditionally belonged to the factory owner. Factory owners could often achieve between 10-15% which on the basis of a 1000 blouse order, could mean that the fabric left over could be converted into somewhere in the region of 100-150 over-makes. Because the cloth was free, the over-makes or cabbage could be sold at a very low price. I was therefore able to sell up to the minute garments for a much lower price than the competition, which soon became one of the fundamental reasons why 'Girls Talk' was able to survive.

* * *

Gina was blooming; eight months pregnant she was in full sail, and with only a month to go needed lots of encouraging to take time off, resting and staying at home. But being obstinate she wouldn't listen and insisted on continuing to work.

One Saturday morning, whilst I was at the market, Gina was working in the shop with five of our staff. She was serving someone at the till when two females in their mid-twenties interrupted her conversation. Throwing a carrier bag down on the counter, one of them, a blonde, demanded her money back.

Gina picked up the bag, and handed it back saying, "Do you mind? I am serving some one at the moment, but I will be with you in a minute."

Once she had finished at the till, she turned to the young women who had been waiting. "How may I help?"

Pointing to the bag, the blonde woman stated, "I bought this last week and it has already fallen to bits. I want my money back now!"

Opening the bag, Gina was hit by a strong smell of alcohol, and on closer inspection she found a stained blouse with its collar hanging off. "How did it get in this condition?" she asked.

"That's none of your business," she was told. "It's faulty so just give me my money back."

Gina put the blouse back into the bag and handed it back to the customer. "This is my business and I am sorry but I am not prepared to refund your money, particularly as it looks as if someone has tried to rip the collar off."

The young woman was not going to give up. "I am going to take this to the Citizens Advice Bureau and see what they have to say."

"Please do," said Gina as the two of them stormed out of the shop.

Half an hour later the phone rang, and Gina answered. A voice spoke.

"This is the Citizens Advice Bureau here. We have just had a woman come in with a blouse that she bought from you; we think that you should give her the money back." And before Gina could say anything the line went dead.

Her immediate thoughts were that it had been a strange telephone call and mentioned it to one of the staff who told her that the Citizens Advice Bureau was not open on a Saturday. Deciding to check to be sure, Gina called the Bureau only to get a recorded message saying that the Bureau was closed on a Saturday, giving the opening hours during the week. Just as she had hung up the phone she noticed the two trouble makers walking back through the door.

As she threw the bag down on the counter again, the blonde arrogantly informed Gina that she should have had a call from the Citizens Advice Bureau by now. "They told us that they have spoken to you," she whined, "And that you have to give me my money back."

Looking at the two women in front of her, Gina replied. "I don't know which of your friends I spoke to but it certainly wasn't the Citizens Advice Bureau as they are closed all day Saturday."

The women started cursing at Gina quite loudly, angry at having been caught out. Gina came out from behind the counter and towards the door as if encouraging them to leaving the shop. Taking one look at Gina, standing there is a well filled maternity dress, the blonde leaned towards her hissing, "I'll put you and that fucking baby through that window you bitch!" whilst her companion moved closer and spat in Gina's face.

Seeing what was happening, two of the staff who had been standing nearby ran over to assist Gina, and after much arguing, eventually managed to steer the two women out of the shop.

When I arrived at the shop at five o'clock that afternoon Gina was in a terrible state. The staff told me what had happened and where they thought that the women had gone to. Taking one of the staff with me to identify the troublemakers, I headed to a pub around the corner.

It wasn't hard to spot them as they were sitting at a large table with lots of other men and women making a lot of noise. The pub was poorly lit and full of smoke, and the loud atmosphere clearly told me that everyone there was well into a Saturday afternoon drinking session.

I was so furious at what had happened I didn't stop to think and stormed straight over. Putting my hands firmly down on the table I leaned in close to the pair.

"If you two bitches come anywhere near my wife or my shop ever again, I'll put you through every fucking window in this place." My voice was so loud that the whole pub must have heard what I said, as the place fell quiet.

"Do you understand?" I finished off. "Have you got that?"

My outburst had caught them off guard; thank God no one said a word or did anything in retaliation!

In the early hours of the following morning, Gina woke me to tell me that her waters had broken and she was going in to labour. I carefully drove her to the Oxford Street Hospital when she remained in labour for a further thirteen hours before finally delivering our daughter.

I was present when she was born. She was four weeks premature and only weighed five pounds and spent the first week of her life in an incubator in intensive care. Being such a young couple we found the whole thing terrifying; we had come so close to losing our baby girl and all because of the distress caused by those vile women.

The day after Gina gave birth I was running around telling everyone that I was a Dad, as well as trying to organise the markets and the shop. I was like a headless chicken. Arriving at the hospital just as they were opening the doors to the Maternity Ward for visiting times in the evening, I noticed that all the other proud fathers were carrying bunches of flowers.

"Oh shit!" I was carrying the company account books and wage slips!

My wife and daughter were eventually allowed home; we named our precious little girl Katie May, giving her the same middle name as my Mum, Elsie May. In the early months of Katie's life Gina took her in to work so that she could breast feed her. There was no alternative at the time as we really could not afford any more staff.

Once Katie arrived our luck seemed to change for the better over the next twelve months. Our business went from strength to strength, for the first time we began to enjoy the financial rewards of all our hard work. By the end of the year we had saved enough money to pay back Gina's parents and move to a bigger house. It wasn't so much the house, but we needed more space to accommodate the large market trailer and vans as well as Gina's car so we were looking for something a bit bigger with a little more land.

We came across a Victorian house for sale set in half an acre of land ideal for all the vehicles. It was a mansion in comparison to Foxshaw Close with six bedrooms and two bathrooms. Although structurally sound it needed a lot of updating as it had been built in the late 1800's originally for Lord Latham who had owned most of the land in Huyton in the last century; his coat of arms still remained above the front door.

It seemed that Gina and I were the only ones mad enough to buy it and in March 1981 we moved in.

We found it rather spooky at first with its dark cellars and large staircase leading up to an even larger landing. There were eight tall doors facing you when you go to the top of the stairs, and with its high ceilings and big windows it seemed like a very large house for two young people and a tiny little baby. Even with Carla and Ranger, our two German Shepherds, we still rattled around.

One day there were two unexpected callers at the house. Opening the door, I found two policemen standing on our front step. One of them looked me up and down before speaking.

"Morning young man, is your Dad at home?"

"No he isn't," I replied, "How can I help?"

There was a moment's silence. "We need to speak to Mr Pearce."

"Yes, that's me," I informed them.

"I don't think you understand young man. We need to speak to Mr Pearce, the owner of the house."

"That's me." I said it with pride.

They weren't the only one's who found it hard to believe that such a young family could own such a grand house.

It took Gina and I a year to put our stamp on the big house but then it really did feel like our home; in the middle of all this Gina announced some further good news – she was expecting our second child who was due to arrive the following year. The pressure was now even greater than before to make a success of the shop.

Chapter Twenty-Seven
By The Seat of My Leather Pants

It was the early part of December 1982 and I was on my regular once a week journey from Liverpool to London, my part time driver and old mate George was at the wheel. I was looking for good quality stock for the Girls Talk sale that always started the day after Boxing Day. We needed to become more established and I was looking for something different that would make us stand out from the rest of the competition.

By five o'clock that day, I must have visited between 20 to 30 factories all over London and I had managed to fill three quarters of the van with pretty good deals. By now we would normally be heading back for Liverpool, but something was bothering me; there was still something missing and I felt we could do better.

Then it hit me. I gave George instructions to drive us across London to Brick Lane near Spitalfields Market in the East End where I used to buy leather trousers.

Brick Lane was not for the fainthearted; a maze of dingy streets and poorly lit, narrow alleyways leading off the main thoroughfare. It was somewhat reminiscent of a Kasbah, with doors on all sides of the narrow streets, leading to small factories, which would take up several floors of the small houses that crowded the pavements. There would be a faint smell of foreign spices, and a distant murmur of foreign voices, and you always felt as if there were eyes watching. These factory/houses were in poor condition, and dirty. Each of the floors would be packed with sewing machines and work benches, and no doubt during 'factory hours' countless illegal immigrants pedaling away at the machines producing garments for the more fortunate population.

The dark alleyways outside were always full of shifty, slightly menacing looking characters, of Asian origin, predominantly Indians and Pakistanis. They would be wearing their native dress, a long shapeless tunic, invariably dull in colour over baggy shapeless trousers. Their heads would be adorned with a small white crocheted hat, and their faces would often sport a beard of varying length and shape. Dark eyes, and dark skin, with teeth and gums stained red from years of chewing on small herbal beads – beetlenut I believe.

By the time we arrived, evening was setting and I was soon standing in front of Rashid, the owner of the leather factory.

He had not changed too much, and apparently neither had I as there was a clear look of recognition on his face.

"Mr Jeff, greetings" he said, gesturing towards his office. "Please come, sit and have a tea". All business negotiations began with this traditional gesture of hospitality, however this time I took the precaution of politely asking for a can of coke, the recollection of the dirty cups from an earlier visit being somewhat off-putting. The hospitality completed, it would then be time to get down to business.

I mentioned that my van was full of stock outside, with only George looking after it – so he sent two of his men to keep an eye out in case anyone tried to steal something. Finishing our drinks he opened negotiations.

"Mr Jeff," (they would always prefix your first name with the title of 'Mr'), "Tell me what you are looking for…"

"Girls leather pants," I replied, "At a very cheap price. I want to buy them for my sale and then be able to sell them at half the price - half of what I paid you last time." (For regular stock I normally paid £35 per pair and then sold them for £70. On this occasion I now wanted to pay no more than £17 per pair which would enable me to sell them at £35 in the sale.)

"Impossible," he whined. "I would go out of business, it would ruin me. Mr Jeff, the raw leather costs me that much! Are you mad?"

We continued in this vein for the next twenty minutes, bartering for the best deal, but making no real progress, so I decided to pull out my ace card.

Putting my hand into the inside pocket of my overcoat, I pulled out one thousand pounds of used £20 notes, bundled together with an elastic band, which I then threw on the table for him to admire.

"Rashid," I said pointing to the money, "It is getting late, and I want to finish our business. I am quite serious about the leather pants, so if you want any of that money, show me some stock now." This was my 'party piece' and had never failed to work in the past. I knew for a fact that there was no way on this planet he was going to allow me to walk away with all those lovely pound notes, to take them back to Liverpool

Rashid bent towards the money, quickly grabbing it off the table, raising his tunic and stuffing it into a sort of money belt that he wore around his waist, "come he said, come with me Mr Jeff."

I could not stop smiling as I followed him up the stairs. The cash on the table trick never failed.

After climbing three flights of narrow stairs, Rashid led me into a small dark room at the top of the building. In the corner of the room, was a pile of leather pants in all colours and sizes, literally just thrown one on top of the other.

Pointing towards them, Rashid said, "You can have these for £20 a pair, good quality leather, nothing wrong with them."

I started to pick them up, examining them carefully for serious faults, such as rips and holes. Years in this game had given me an 'experienced eye' and I was not easily fooled, but this time around the only problem that I could find was that all the side zips were broken. After checking each and every pair, and counting them in the process, I realised that there were seventy-two pairs in all, a real treasure!

Throughout my inspection, Rashid has stood quietly to one side, his beady-eyes never once leaving me

"You must be joking," I said, "£20 a pair when they are all faulty? They cannot be worth more than a fiver in this condition!" (I found that by starting at the lowest price was often the best way to plant a seed of doubt on the sellers mind, and would help me get a price that I wanted to pay.) "The colours are horrible," I continued, "and the sizes...." I paused for effect, "they are all big sizes!"

"There is nothing wrong with them," countered Rashid, a note of anxiety in his voice.

"No, nothing good here," I said.

"They look good to me." Once again Rashid sounded hesitant. "£15 a pair then," he offered.

Turning away so that he could not see the smile on my face, I almost felt sorry for him. Although noted for their trading skills, Rashid and his kind suffered from one great disadvantage – they had not been trained from an early age by my Mother.

Gathering my composure and putting on a poker face I looked him straight in the eye. "No, I am not interested, and to be honest I can't think of anyone else who'd be daft enough to buy 72 pairs of faulty trousers!" Putting my hand out towards him, I continued, "I am sorry, but if you could hand me my money back, I am going to head off now. I have a long drive ahead of me."

Rashid dropped his head to one side as if in deep thought. "Make me an offer," he said.

"Ten pounds a pair," I replied, "that is my last and final offer. Ten pounds, take it or leave it." Poor Rashid; his face looked as if he had just received some tragic news. I started to make my way downstairs as if I was no longer interested, when I was stopped by a shout.

"Ok Mr Jeff, alright, it's a deal." He stood at the top of the stairs, a defeated man. "You had better come and help me load your van."

Within twenty minutes the van was loaded, he had given me my £280 change, and George and I were setting off for Liverpool. As the van turned the corner I started to laugh.

"What is so funny?" George asked.

"You should have seen it, George," I replied, "the whole deal. It was poetry in motion. Oh my Mum would have been so proud of me. Twenty pound a pair was a good deal, but no I kept on haggling with him for over an hour, and in the end got them for just a tenner each."

We finally got home in the early hours of the morning. Gina, who was now six months pregnant, had not been able to sleep and had got out of bed as soon as she heard the van pulling up. Opening the door, I was greeted by a rather tired, and slightly annoyed wife.

"Where have you been?" she demanded, "Do you realise how late it is? I have been worried sick thinking that something might have happened to the pair of you!"

"Put the kettle on," I said, giving her a hug. "I will tell you all about it over a brew." As I sat there, sipping a hot cup of tea, I told Gina all about the day's adventures.

"I have had an idea," I said. On the way back in the van, I had been thinking of ideas that would make us stand out from all the other shops in town.

"Rather than sell these leather pants at £35 a pair, making a £25 profit, I want to sell them for £1 a pair." I paused, waiting for the explosion that I knew was coming.

"You can not be serious," Gina replied, looking at me as if I had lost my mind. "Nobody sells leather pants for £1 a pair. Think of how much money we could make if we sold them for £35 each. That is still a fantastic bargain, half the normal price, and we would make about two and a half thousand pounds! You just really can't be serious."

"Just think of all the publicity," I countered, "Selling leather pants for £1 a pair would make us the talk of the town. We would never be forgotten."

I could see that it was going to take a while to bring Gina around to my way of thinking, so leaving it at that, we both headed off for bed.

I managed to find a local man to replace all the broken zips, who charged us one pound per pair; I could not help smiling at the irony of it all – he was charging the same price as I planned to sell them for!

It took a few days, but I eventually managed to talk Gina around to my way of thinking, agreeing that the loss of £720 was more than worth the potential publicity. It was a gamble; we knew we were taking a risk. In the hopes of minimising the risk, I placed an advert in the *Liverpool Echo*, appearing on December 24th, wishing all the Girls Talk customers Seasons Greetings for Christmas and the New Year, and thanking them for all their support over the past year. I also used the advert as a means of inviting them to our sale, starting on the 27th of December, and mentioned that in addition to all the fabulous half price bargains that would be on offer, we were also going to be selling leather pants, reduced from £70 to £1.00. If anything was going to grab their attention, it was going to be that!

On Christmas Eve, we started preparing the shop; reducing all the old stock by 50% and introducing the new stock brought in for the sale. We had eight staff working for us by now, all lovely young girls, and naturally enough, they each wanted a pair of the leather pants. I explained to them however, that I would rather wait and see what happened on the first day of the sale; they agreed that this was fair.

By about 3.30 in the afternoon, with everything ready for the sale, I told the girls to go home and wished them all a Happy Christmas. Once they had left I locked the door, and went about my usual routine of checking the store, before shutting the shop down for the next two days.

Overcoat on, alarm set, I had locked the front doors and was just about to pull down the steel security shutters when I noticed a young woman sitting on the ground with a blanket around her shoulders. She seemed somewhat out of place, as the homeless/ street dwellers of today were unknown back then, and so I politely asked if she was alright. I hated locking up on Christmas Eve. The City Centre was notorious for groups of tipsy workers, who having finished early, had been to the pub, and were well on their way to becoming totally drunk. Locking up any day of the week was bad enough, I liked to do it as quickly as possible, before heading for the safety of my car, and as I was on my own I was even more aware of how vulnerable I was to potential trouble.

However the girl just grinned at me. "I'll be alright if you have got a black pair of size ten, leather pants for just one pound!"

I looked at her, still not sure what was going on. "Yes, we will have leather pants for a pound in the sale, and I am sure that there is at least one pair of size ten's!"

Her response was to the point. "That's good," pulling the blanket further up around her shoulders and huddling down into the warmth.

This was frustrating. I wanted to get to my car, to get home, and yet I was standing here having a conversation with some strange young girl who was sitting outside my shop with a blanket wrapped around her shoulders in the middle of winter. I needed to get to the bottom of this.

"How did you find out about the pants?" I asked, wondering if the *Liverpool Echo* had made a mistake, and put the wrong date in the advert.

"*The Echo*," she replied.

"Well, when did *The Echo* say the sale was starting?"

"The day after Boxing Day," she answered.

I couldn't help myself, this was totally weird. "Well then why are you here, sitting outside the shop, with a couple of days to go before the sale starts?"

"I want to make sure that I get a pair of leather pants for just one pound" she said.

By now it was dark, cold and starting to snow. It was also Christmas Eve, a time when normally, people would be at home with their families, getting ready to enjoy Christmas. "You cannot be serious," I was getting irritated. She was just not listening. Injecting a more forceful tone in my voice, I told her, "I have got seventy two pairs of leather pants. Go home now and then come back at 5am on the morning of the sale. That's all you need to do!"

She didn't move, and it seemed as if my words of advice had fallen on deaf ears.

"You must be mad." I couldn't think of anything else to say, other than goodbye and headed off to the car park. As I drove back down the road ten minutes later, I passed by the shop front, and saw this solitary figure sitting there. She looked so sad, alone on a cold dark night, with wet snow all around her. In the car, I couldn't stop thinking about her, comparing the situation with my own; Gina and Katie were waiting for me.

It was so wonderful coming home any day of the year, but over Christmas it was even more magical and started the moment I opened the door. Gina welcomed me with Katie in her arms, and gave me a hug and a kiss. Katie was just over two years old, a great age for climbing all over me and calling out my name.

Putting Katie on my back for a piggy back ride, Gina and I headed for the kitchen whilst I told her about the day, the events of closing time with the girl setting up camp outside our shop. I don't think that Gina really believed me, as she laughed and looked out the window, observing that the snow was starting to stick.

"I am sure that she will have gone home by now," she said, "Come on dinner's ready. Let's go and enjoy ourselves – and Jeff? Will you stop talking about work."

We had a lovely dinner, settling down in front of the fire and watching tv afterwards.

When nine o'clock came, I found myself still thinking about the girl outside the shop. Was she still there? Was she alright? Had she fallen prey to some drunkard, or been harassed and taunted by a group of lads out on the piss? It was bothering me.

Once Katie was tucked up in bed, I told Gina that I was going to the shop.

"I feel like Ebenezer Scrooge," I said. "Here we are, all nice and cosy, and she could still be out there in the freezing cold. If she is, I am going to tell her that I promise her a pair of leather pants on the day of the sale, and then send her back home. That's the only way that I am going to be able to enjoy Christmas with my family, if I get her off my mind by knowing she is ok." I gave Gina a kiss, and set off, promising that I would not be much longer than an hour.

The weather outside was bitter and had now turned to sleet, the snow no longer sticking. As I turned the corner and got closer to the shop I could see boxes lined up on the ground outside. Pulling up, alongside the pavement, I could not believe my eyes. There were now 12 people gathered there, sitting inside cardboard boxes trying to keep warm. As I stepped out of the car, the girl who had been there earlier shouted out, "That's him! That's the owner of the shop, the man I was telling you about."

I suddenly found myself being bombarded with questions; did I have a size 14 in brown? Had I a size 12 in black? Were they really one pound? The noise and the commotion were starting to worry me, as the last thing that I needed was the police to turn up thinking that there was trouble.

Holding my hands up, I raised my voice so that I could be heard. "Calm down everyone. I have got 72 pairs of pants in all different colours and sizes. You don't have to stay here - come back on the day of the sale. It is not starting for 3 days!"

There was a chorus of 'that's ok's and 'we're going to stay as long as you have got our size'.

I despaired. "Don't be daft. You are going to freeze to death." I noticed that some had blankets whilst others had sleeping bags. There were girls with their boyfriends, even a father with his daughter. It was crazy.

"For the last time," I pleaded "Please, please go home." But no, they were determined to stay put!

I was getting cold and decided to get back into the car. Looking at them all huddled together in now wet boxes I couldn't help but feel sorry for them, whilst at the same time thinking that they had to be mad to stay out all night in the freezing cold.

With these thoughts in my mind, I started the car, and headed back out of town. On my way, I spotted a fish and chip shop on the corner of Brownlow Hill which was still open. I parked in front, went in and ordered 12 portions of fish and chips and 12 cans of coke.

As he was packing the box, the man asked me if I was going to a fish and chip party.

"You don't want to know, "I answered, taking the box, "it is a long story." I thanked him and got in the car, and turning around, headed back to the shop. When I arrived, I went down the row of people, giving each one a packet of fish and chips and a can of coke. With every portion I handed out, I asked that person to go home, confirming that I had 72 pairs of leather pants, telling them that there was no need for this madness. However each and everyone said the same thing, they were staying. Finally, admitting defeat, I wished them all a Merry Christmas before getting back into the car and leaving. It was midnight by the time I got home.

Gina was as shocked as I when I told her what I had found. We talked about it for a while, before going into the Katie's room to leave her presents at the bottom of her bed. Then we went to bed ourselves.

After breakfast, at about 9am, I wondered about the people outside the shop. The weather had changed overnight for the better and the sun was now shining. Thinking to myself that they must surely have gone home by now, being Christmas Day, I decided to call Gina's brother Robert, who lived quite close to the shop.

I dialed his number, and asked him if he could do me a quick favour. "Could you drive past our shop and see if there is anyone outside?" He was puzzled and asked me what I meant.

"Look, I know it seems daft on Christmas morning, but I would really appreciate your doing this. It is a long story, but I promise I will tell you about it later."

A short while later Robbie rang me back. "What on earth is going on?" he asked. "There must be around 80-100 people queued up out there!"

I was astounded. "Are you sure? There can't be that many!" I said.

"Well I didn't get out of my car and start counting each individual one," he replied, "I just estimated that's all, but it certainly seemed close to 100!"

Saying that I would call later, I thanked him and hung up. I was starting to panic. This was all starting to get out of control. I only had 72 pairs of pants, there were still two days and two nights to go, how many other people would start to queue up, how was I going to cope? What the hell was I going to do?

When I told Gina that Robbie had counted about 80-100 people outside our shop, she was silent for a moment or two. "You idiot," she finally said, "You smart-arse! What are we going to do now?" Although she wasn't shouting at me, I could see that she was beginning to feel as worried as I was, however her attention was soon caught by the other more pressing tasks associated with Christmas Day.

I started to think positively about ways of cashing in on what seemed now to be something remarkable. It was no small achievement getting people to give up their Christmas holidays, to camp outside a shop for three nights and three days just to buy a pair of leather pants for one pound. I still found it all a little hard to believe, it was incredible.

My mind was racing with ideas; I needed to do something. I could not just sit back and wait for a few hundred people to queue up outside our shop on the morning of the sale without taking advantage of it. One publicity stunt had led to this bizarre situation, and here was the perfect opportunity for another. It had to be really good, really different.

As I sat there, sipping on yet another brew, it came to me. I needed to speak to Paul Feathers, a young guy I knew, who was an up and coming hotelier. Paul owned several small hotels and an outdoor catering company which worked in and around the Liverpool area. I had met him on numerous occasions and got on very well with him. He seemed to be my sort of guy, up for anything.

After numerous calls, I eventually tracked him down at one of his hotels.

"Paul," I started, "I am putting together a PR opportunity that might interest you. Tomorrow morning, Boxing Day, I reckon there will be between 100-150 people queued up outside my Girls Talk shop in town; they are waiting for the doors to open at 9am the following day. Do you fancy joining me with one of your mobile catering units, you know the ones with *Feathers Catering* written all over them, to serve hot drinks around 12 lunchtime?"

"I plan on contacting Radio Merseyside, Radio City, *The Liverpool Echo*, *The Daily Post*, Granada Television, and any others I can think of." I continued, "I reckon it will make a fantastic news story." Letting my imagination run away with me I added, "Can you just see the headlines? 'Shop owner Jeff Pearce and Paul Feathers, of Feathers Hotel and Outdoor Catering Company, took time out of their Christmas holidays to serve the public with hot drinks in the freezing cold. When asked why they had done this, we said that we felt that as the people of Liverpool had slept out in the freezing cold it was the least we could do to make sure that they had some warmth at Christmas'. Oh Paul, they will love it. What do you think?"

I could hear the smile in Paul's voice as he answered. "Jeff you are a genius. I can't come myself as I am tied up completely with the hotels at this time of year, but I will send two of my staff and we can do tea and coffee and loads of bacon butties. How is that?"

I told him that it sounded fantastic. After wishing me good luck, and each other seasons greetings I hung up, and then spent the best part of the rest of Christmas day speaking to the various news desks which I had mentioned to Paul, tipping them off for 12 o'clock the following day.

Boxing Day morning came, and after Gina and I dropped Katie off with Gina's Mum, we headed to the shop. We pulled up across the road, a short distance away and sat there in silence. By now there were easily 150 people, maybe more all sitting down in a long line with their backs leaning against neighbouring shops fronts. They were chatting to each other, all seemingly enjoying this bizarre outing, as if it was a day out at the sea-side or some great camping adventure. There seemed to be no aggression, no problems, and no need for the police. In the cold sunshine, we could see that they were all wrapped up in their blankets sitting on the cardboard boxes. It really was quite something to see and Gina and I just sat there, staring out of the car window, at a loss for words.

Soon afterwards, the Paul Feathers Catering van pulled up and two members of staff started to unloaded the heated catering trolleys from the van. These trolleys were similar to the service trolleys you find on aircraft. Gina and I went over and introduced ourselves, to Paul's staff, before getting down to the important task of serving the people sitting on the pavement. We started with those directly outside the shop, as they had been there the longest. Gina was doing the teas and coffees laughing with all the different customers. Everyone seemed to be in good spirits and kept asking about the leather pants.

In the meantime, I was being interviewed by all the journalists from a variety of news desks whom I had spoken to the day before. They were all there and we ended up on air live with BBC Radio Merseyside. Radio City had us on their news updates every hour on the hour, whilst the newspapers were interviewing people in the queue and taking lots of photographs. There was so much going on, that it must have been at least three o'clock by time we got finished.

On our way home and feeling worn out, Gina started to voice her concerns, asking me how we were going to handle the first day of the sale, with all those people, and more importantly, how were we going to ensure that those people who had been queuing longest were not done out of the chance of getting their leather pants.

I had been thinking about this and had come up with an idea. We were going to control the people, as the leather pants sold, each person would fill out a piece of paper:

I explained that she and I were going to prepare these pieces of paper at home that night, and then as the leather pants were sold, each piece of paper was to be pinned to the wall behind the till, for everyone to see.

As the only man who worked in the shop, I had also been giving some thought to 'security'. Gina had organised extra sales staff so I knew that the floor was well covered; I wasn't too concerned about thieves and shop lifters either, it was more about crowd control, the thought of hundreds of stampeding female teenagers being a daunting one for the even the biggest and bravest of men, I needed men for the doors.

Therefore when we got back to the house, I got on the phone almost as soon as we walked in, phoning around to all and everyone I knew who might be up for the job. My luck was in, as I managed to get hold of John, my brother-in-law, and then Paul, Phil and Albie, three mates of mine. All four of them were tall and well muscled. Having explained what I wanted them to do, we agreed that in order for them to look the part they would need long black overcoats, white shirts and black dickie bows. They were being paid good money for the following days work, and as I found out later, all four of them spent the evening tracking down the appropriate clothing, a process involving a certain amount of begging and borrowing (!) in order to be ready for the 8am start the following morning.

> *I have purchased one pair of leather pants for just one pound.*
>
> *Name:* ....
>
> *Date:* ....
>
> *Address:* ....
>
> *Signature:* ....

Gina and I were too tense that night to sleep much, and it was almost a relief when the day of the sale dawned. Getting up early, we were ready to go by the time Bob and Brenda arrived to look after Katie. We left shortly after 7am, both of us apprehensive about what would be waiting for us when we got to the store.

On our way in to town, we came to a halt at the traffic lights at the bottom of Brownlow Hill, near the Adelphi Hotel. Looking at the Army & Navy Stores across from us, I commented to Gina that there were lots of people queuing up, and it was almost a relief to see that we were not the only shop with a long line of people forming outside. The traffic lights changed and as I drove off down towards Renshaw Street, I found myself almost following this long human chain, around the corner, and the whole way down the road until it came to an abrupt halt. Outside our shop. The Army & Navy Stores queue wasn't theirs at all, it was ours, and what I had seen from my vantage point at the traffic lights was actually the tail end of it all!

I hadn't counted the number of people as I drove past, but there were definitely more than a few hundred lined up. The sheer quantity of people was a terrifying thought. We weren't one of these large department stores which could handle such a large volume. We were small, modest, humble..... even our doors suddenly seemed too small to cope. My mind was racing as I passed the shop on the way to the Car Park. I could see my four 'security guards' positioned outside, all looking very professional and well turned out, but not nearly sufficient in quantity to cope with the thousands of people looking for a bargain at Girls Talk.

To say that I was sh****ng myself was an understatement. I am not a person given over to swearing often, but the 'f' word was going through my mind as I parked up. I needed a frigging army, not four brave lads and a handful of sales assistants. All I could see at that point was riots, people getting hurt, ambulances pulling up, the shop getting damaged, it was almost too much. I parked the car, and looked at Gina. Her face showed the same degree of disbelief mixed with concern as mine. All we could do was sit there and look at each other in horrified silence. I knew that she was thinking exactly the same thoughts as I, what were we going to do? I think we both felt like turning the car around and heading home; I know that I certainly was extremely unwilling to get out of the car, let alone open the shop. The thought of being stampeded in a crush of bargain hunters was keeping me glued firmly to my seat. However, I had started this, and I had to finish it.

Gina looked petrified, close to tears. Taking a deep breath I looked at her, "Come on love, let's go face the music, this is not going to go away. I will think of something on the way over, I promise you. It will be alright."

As we walked along Renshaw Street I held Gina's hand tightly, trying to give her a sense of strength and togetherness. In reality, I was the one quaking inside, and I was feeling guilty as well. I alone was responsible for creating this mess, and it was up to me to sort it out. As we turned the corner on to Church Street, we could now see the shop. Keeping my eyes pinned on the shop entrance, I focused on John, Paul, Phil and Albie almost as if they were rocks in a stormy sea. My head and shoulders were tense, staring straight ahead, unable, unwilling to look to the right, towards the long queue of people just in case somebody recognised me and called out my name.

We both quickened our pace. John, Paul, Phil and Albie were like the Four Musketeers, standing bravely solid against a large force of the King's troops, the only difference being the troops in this case predominantly wore skirts and carried handbags as opposed to swords and knee high leather boots. They greeted us both with a cheery "Alright Boss?" and as my mouth was dry I was only able to mutter a strangled "Morning" in response. I fixed a smile to my face, as if nothing was wrong, and removing the keys with a truly shaking hand started to open up the security shutters.

An unusual noise caught my attention. Turning my head to the left, in the direction of where the noise was coming from, I saw to my utter amazement and surprise, about forty people standing outside Chelsea Girl, clapping and throwing comments in our direction. Chelsea Girl was the biggest fashion store in Liverpool at that time, and was very successful. It was like the grand lady when compared to the younger Girls Talk.

The people gathered outside were the sales staff, and they were clapping at us, cheering us in our success and wishing us luck. The ovation, the applause was for us.

The manageress, who I admired very much, called over to me, "Well done Jeff. Good luck with the Sale!" The sense of pride that I felt at that moment was overwhelming. Only a few minutes earlier I had been overcome with panic and concern over this 'monster' that I had created, and then I find myself being congratulated and applauded by one of the biggest fashion names in the country. It was a moment of contradiction, and one that I wish I could have enjoyed for longer, but the moment passed and I got back to the task of opening up.

Once the shop was opened, I asked Paul and John to come inside. I instructed them to keep the door locked and to only let staff in, until we were ready. They were under no circumstances to leave the door unattended. Phil and Albie, in the meantime, were to walk up and down the queue telling everybody to keep in line, to keep order if possible. Whatever happened, they were not to let the customers rush the front of the shop.

The truth of it stared me in the face. Despite our best endeavours, my four musketeers were not enough - I really needed an army of men. The only army that I could think of, who would be readily available was the police, and so at about 8.20am I rang Cheapside Police Station which was the main police station in Liverpool.

The phone was quickly answered, and I introduced myself to the officer on the other end. I explained that I needed to speak to whoever was in charge that day as a matter of some urgency. The response I received was far from satisfactory, as the policeman who I was talking to seemed to be almost disinterested in my predicament. I could hear it from the tone of his voice, and the way in which he responded with questions of his own.

"What did you say your problem is Sir?" he asked, even though I thought I had already made myself clear.

Slowly, as if talking to a child, I explained, "I have a shop with a sale starting today. In that sale I have 72 pairs of leather pants which I am selling for one pound each. My problem is that there is somewhere in the region of well over 1000 customers queued all the way up the road, past the Army & Navy Store."

"One thousand people?" he asked. "Do you know, Sir, what 1000 people look like?"

"Well if I didn't before," I retorted, "I do now. They're queued up outside my shop!" Time was ticking and he was starting to annoy me. Raising my voice slightly, (perhaps he was deaf as well as slow), I continued. "Some of these people will be really pissed off, as they have been camping outside, in the freezing cold for the past three days and nights, and if this gets out of hand, and they lose their hard earned place at the front of the queue, there will be trouble."

It must have worked, as I heard the phone being dropped on the desk. When he came back on the line, the tone in his voice had changed considerably. He was finally taking things seriously. He asked me for my name again and telephone number and instructed me to wait by the phone as someone would call me back as a matter of priority.

Within ten minutes the phone rang. Snatching the receiver up, I answered. A voice on the other end introduced himself as the Sergeant in Charge and asked me to tell him what was going on. Repeating my story for the third time, I stressed my concern that something could go terribly wrong, it could all get out of hand, and how people could get hurt.

His response was like music to my ears. He told me that they would be there as soon as possible, and within no time at all a police van arrived and stopped outside the shop. The Sergeant got out of the van, a tall man with a truncheon under his arm, who looked very impressive in his immaculately pressed uniform, highly polished shoes, three stripes on his arm and the silver pips gleaming on his shoulders.

Coming inside the shop, he told me that he had brought five men with him and they would spread out along the queue in an effort to keep everything under control. He also told me that he was sending for reinforcements as the five he had brought with him were not nearly enough.

The sheer number of people lined up was causing problems for the other stores along the way. The weight of bodies leaning against plate glass shop fronts was causing the windows to bow inwards and there was fear of glass breaking and people getting hurt and shops displays being damaged. Furthermore, the shop entrances were being blocked, making it impossible for staff let alone customers to go about their business. It was agreed that the police would also address this problem, clearing a space where necessary.

Nine o'clock came, the police reinforcements had arrived, and a degree of control had been established. We were ready to start trading. On my suggestion, we were going to start by letting customers in one at a time. I don't think that this idea really appealed too much to the Police Sergeant; however he agreed to give it a try.

The doors opened, and that very first girl, from all those many nights ago, came in. I couldn't help but like her, and served her as quickly as possible, whilst she tried on three pairs of pants before finding the right pair. As she paid for her pants, I gave her a lovely jumper worth about £25 as way of a thank you for her perseverance.

We continued in this manner, one shopper at a time, for the next hour. At the end of the hour I could see that this method was not going to work as we had only served 7 people and the queue was still endless.

Taking me to one side, the Police Sergeant muttered in my ear. "Excuse me Sir for being blunt, but are you taking the piss? At this rate we will be here until midnight, and my men and I have better things to do than hang around here all day. You had better get a move on."

I returned to the floor, trying to speed things along as quickly as possible, until all the leather pants had been sold, and the sales notes completed and pinned up on the wall behind the till. It was now 11am. Walking over to the Sergeant, I shook his hand, and thanked him for all his help. I told him what a relief it had been to us all having them there; they had given us a sense of security.

"Without wanting to presume too much," I added, "Would it be possible to leave two police officers with me for an extra half hour, whilst I walk up and down the queue telling everyone that all the leather pants have been sold!!!"

I felt sure that once everyone knew that all the pants had gone, the crowds would disperse and all would return to normal.

He agreed. Shaking my hand he observed that the last time he had seen such a gathering of teenagers had been when the Beatles were at the height of their popularity. I felt a huge degree of pride; being (indirectly) compared to the Beatles was quite something.

Just before walking out the door he laughed, and said "You would have made a good copper!"

Funnily enough, some customers did leave the queue once they heard there were no more leather pants left, but most stayed the whole day, we took more money in sales that day than we had ever done before. The shop buzzed with activity, the staff, although tired said that they had loved it, and even my four musketeers seemed to have enjoyed themselves.

By days end, Gina and I were exhausted. We walked back to the car, holding each others hand, the adrenalin and elation putting a spring in our step, which might not have been the case if things had gone wrong.

The next day, Tuesday, 28th December 1982, after picking up a copy of the *Liverpool Echo*, I couldn't believe my eyes. We were front page headlines. Gina and I stared at the oversize print from one side of the page to the other which proclaimed:

'THE BIG SALES SPREE'

with two large photographs of our shop dominating the front cover. It then went on to add:

'*...shoppers packed Liverpool City Centre today..... fashion was the biggest attraction with long queues outside Girls Talk boutique on Church Street. At the head of the queue, and now the proud owner of a leather pair of trousers for just one pound was 18 year old Amanda Oprey....... Police battled to control the teenagers,....... whilst one police officer said it was similar to Beatle Mania.*'

The exposure from being on the front page made me want to do it again so I put the pieces in place to ensure that our headline success would continue for years to come.

Wednesday, 28th December 1983, the *Liverpool Echo* front page headlines shouted:

'QUEUE CRAZY. SALES FEVER'.

Again there was a large photograph along the top of the page showing the queue outside our shop and a small photograph of Christine Shaw, the first shopper in the queue that year. These first customers were becoming celebrities in their own right.

December 27th 1984, and the Girls Talk Sale made its third appearance on the front page of the *Liverpool Echo*. This time I shared the front page with a photograph of Princess Diana of Wales holding Prince Harry for his first public appearance - his christening. My headlines read:

'SALE MADNESS!'

Inside the newspaper, on page three, the *Echo* continued its coverage of the Girls Talk phenomenon. There were two large photographs of our customers sleeping in cardboard boxes in a long line. Girls Talk boutique had now become a household name on Merseyside.

A spokesman from the *Liverpool Echo* once told me that in the 130 years that the paper had been in print, there were only three people in its entire history that had achieved front page headlines on three consecutive occasions; these were Jack the Ripper in the late 1800's, for his heinous crimes, Prince Charles, next in line to the throne, and Jeff Pearce a young Scouser possessed of a vivid imagination and a degree of sheer audacity. An idea that was born one night in a van coming back from London led to great things, and three newspaper headlines, the originals of which I still have in my possession today.

Chapter Twenty-Eight
From Little Jumps to Hurdles

The decision to sell leather pants for just £1 had changed our lives completely. The front headlines turned Girls Talk into Liverpool's Number One fashion boutique, with queues at the till's a regular sight and customers snapping up the latest styles.

Even better was that the phone never stopped ringing with garment manufacturers wanting to supply us for a change. I received a telegram from the previous owner of the shop congratulating me on the phenomenal success which we had achieved, which I thought was brave of him considering his earlier comments about me not lasting more than twelve months. I also found myself having to refuse invitations to lunch from my Bank Manager on more than one occasion as I was far too busy.

Life was good and became even better with the birth of another special little girl on the 25th of March 1983. Faye Louise weighed in at nine pounds ten ounces, nearly twice the size of her older sister. Gina and I were so proud of our two precious daughters, and so thankful for being blessed with two healthy little girls.

Shopping for fashionable clothing for Katie and Faye was proving to be difficult and Gina and I were amazed that there wasn't a boutique specialising in fashionable clothing for children. So when a shop became available four doors away we jumped at the chance and opened Kids Talk Boutique, the only one of its kind in the city centre which specialized in trendy clothes for trendy kids. It took off like a rocket, and in less than a year the Kids Talk Boutique became equally as popular as Girls Talk.

The day soon came when I had to make a very important decision – whether or not to give the markets up. It was both tough and sad leaving the markets behind as Gina and I would not have been able to have achieved what we did without them. I made sure that all our regular customers knew where to find us, as they had become friends over the years, and saying good bye to all my fellow traders was just as hard.

Having experienced the success of Girls Talk and Kids Talk I felt I had the urge to expand, and I started looking further afield, away from our shops in the city centre. Having visited Chester, a very popular city with shoppers only an hour's drive away, I decided to concentrate my search for premises there. After weeks of trying to find the right size shop in the right position without any luck, I was left with no alternative other than to approach another retailer who had the perfect site right in the middle of East Gate Street, the main shopping street in the town centre.

This was the street where all the large multiples had their stores, just where I wanted to be. The negotiations went on for several hours at the end of which I made him a substantial offer which he would have been mad to refuse. It was another large gamble on my part, but I believed, as always, that I was capable of making it work.

It was a very hot summer in 1985 when Gina and I opened the doors on our newest venture. The premises were big enough to accommodate both Girls Talk and Kids Talk under the same roof, and were able to provide a new shopping experience for young mums with small children. Our quarter of a million pound investment soon became the Number One fashion spot in Chester, and in no time was as successful as our other boutiques in Liverpool.

I had to pinch myself to make sure that I wasn't dreaming about this phenomenal success. We now had four shops that were doing exceptionally well; my only problem was finding the winning styles week after week.

'Top of the Pops' was one of my favourite ways of coming up with best sellers. What ever the pop stars were wearing the public wanted the following week.

One Thursday night as I was watching the show, (searching for inspiration for the shops) when Wham started to perform their Top Ten Hit, 'Wake Me Up Before You Go Go!'. Most importantly however was that George Michael was wearing a large white baggy t-shirt with 'Go-Go' printed on the front.

The following morning when I arrived in my office above my favourite Girls Talk shop I was immediately on the phone to our suppliers looking for XXL plain white t-shirts. I was in luck as one of the suppliers had them for £1 each so I ordered one thousand over the phone. As he was based in London I asked him to do me a favour – to take them to Euston Station and put the boxes on the next train for Liverpool and then ring me to let me know what time they were due to arrive.

It was now 10 o'clock and I had to find a local screen printer who could print the t-shirts. I rang all the people I knew but kept drawing blanks. In desperation I rang Liverpool University's Art Department, I chatted to a very helpful lady, and asked if she knew of any students that had left and were capable of screen printing; she said that I was to leave it with her and she would try her best to find someone.

Not convinced that I would find anyone able to print my t-shirts this late on a Friday afternoon, I headed to the station to pick them up. A short while later, when I returned to the shop I found two dodgy looking characters waiting to see me. Dressed like tramps they looked out of place and I was curious as to what they wanted with me.

"Can I help you?" I asked.

"You're looking for someone to print something," one of the youths mumbled.

This was not quite what I'd had in mind, but I continued.

"Who told you?"

"The bird from the Uni." The other one spoke.

"Right, ok." Taking a t-shirt from the box I showed it to them. "Can you print 'Go Go' in big black letters on the front of this?" I asked.

"No probs."

I stood there wondering what the hell he meant.

"No probs." The other one spoke.

"What does that mean?" I was finding it difficult to communicate.

"We can do it!"

Right! I was now beginning to get the hang of their business negotiations.

Eventually it was agreed that they would charge me one pound per print and they could start immediately. The only thing was they had no money for ink and no transport, so I gave them fifty pounds for materials and an extra ten pounds for a taxi, and after loading a taxi with my boxes of t-shirts I waved them good bye.

My staff told me I was mad, saying that I would never see the students, my money or my thousand t-shirts ever again, but I simply said "Oh ye of little faith."

The following morning I arrived early at the shop and found the two young men standing outside with the boxes on the ground beside them. Both of them had their arms full of t-shirts hot off the press. They had worked through the night and had managed to complete 500 t-shirts which looked fantastic.

As soon as I put the t-shirts on the mannequins in the front window they sold like hotcakes, literally flying out the door; by the end of the day we had sold out – less than forty-eight hours after seeing them on 'Top of the Pops'.

That year we sold 250,000 t-shirts in every possible print that you could think of. 'Frankie Says Relax' was our best seller in our four shops, particularly in the smaller sizes for kids.

My two dodgy looking friends printed every single t-shirt and went on to be very successful printers in their own right. However my biggest thanks still have to go to George Michael, for helping me revolutionise the printed t-shirt business. I am sure that my two printing friends would like to do the same thing as well!

Gina and I became very wealthy, and along with the money came all the trappings that accompanied it. Gina now drove a black Mercedes sports car, whilst my choice was a Jaguar. One evening, arriving home in the dark after work, I was going through the large metal gates at the bottom of the driveway when a man suddenly jumped out from behind the hedge, his face appearing at my window.

He frightened the life out of me, and I did not actually start to breathe normally until I realised that it was an old friend from years ago, John Cullen. Lowering the window I was about to say hello, when he started to speak very quickly.

"Jeff, I don't know what you are doing, but they are on to you." He was speaking very quickly and quietly. "They are tapping your phones and following you!"

Whilst he paused for breath, I managed to ask him, "Who are?"

"The bizzies. They are asking informers to grass on you!"

Suddenly he was gone, disappearing into the darkness without another word, leaving me not only stunned, but very confused by what he had said. John knew, and associated with, a lot of real villains in the city, but he was a pretty straight guy himself.

I went in to the house and told Gina what had happened, but her response was to tell me not to be daft, John had most probably been drunk.

"Gina, I am telling you he wasn't drunk. In fact, he was as sober as a Judge! Something must be going on!" I was thinking out loud.

Gina wasn't interested. I was going back over everything that John had said to me in those few minutes.

Having my phone tapped and being followed stood out clearly in my mind, so I walked over to the phone and picked up the receiver, listening intently, but I could hear nothing unusual. I then called Gina's parents and as Bob answered the phone I heard a strange sort of beep-beep, click-click before I heard Bob's voice saying hello.

"Sorry Bob," I said, "It's Jeff here, but I think that I have dialed your number by mistake."

Putting the receiver down I told Gina what had just happened, attempting to convince her that our phone was being tapped, but she wasn't having any of it and just kept telling me not to be silly.

"Who do you think you are? James Bond?" was her logic, "Who could possibly be interested in what you do?"

I was still feeling suspicious when I went to bed, knowing that John would not have said what he did without a good reason.

The following morning, I kept checking my rear-view mirror as I drove to work to see if I was being followed. I was slowly becoming paranoid, imagining that someone in the stream of traffic behind was tailing me.

Once in the office, the day-to-day routine pushed it to the back of my mind until Gina called me at around noon. Once again I heard the same beep-beep, click-click noise.

"Did you hear that?" I asked Gina.

"Yes," she replied, "It did make a funny noise."I told her that I would talk to her later and hung up, before leaving for the Kids Talk shop where I called my solicitor and told him what had been happening.

"Stay there Jeff," he said, "I'll call you back shortly."

A short while later he rang back and told me that he would pick me up. Ten minutes later I got into his car and he drove me to the Cheapside Police Station where he had made an appointment for us to see an Inspector from CID.

Seated in a small room, Alan told the Inspector that his client had reason to believe that he was being followed and that his telephones were being tapped. The Inspector had a file in front of him on the table, and as he opened it, he confirmed that my suspicions were correct.

I nearly fell off my chair with shock.

Flicking through the file, the Inspector continued to talk. "Six weeks ago we had a tip off that Mr Pearce could possibly be laundering drug money through his shops. We therefore had no alternative but to carry out a thorough investigation into these allegations, and had to inform Customs & Excise and Inland Revenue as to this matter."

"We followed Mr Pearce to London in the early hours of the morning on numerous occasions, and yes we have been tapping his phones. These were serious allegations, but I am pleased to inform you that we are more than happy with Mr Pearce's business activities and can see nothing suspicious going on. We are therefore now closing the file."

As he apologised for any inconvenience that might have been caused he explained that tip-off's were a very important part of police business and a good way of catching criminals, so they could not be ignored.

When I thought about it later, I figured that the only reason why it happened was the speed in which Gina and I had expanded our business, and the wealth we had accumulated in such a short time; someone must have been very jealous, or we must have rattled somebody's cage somewhere along the way.

There was a hilarious end to the story though. Whilst the investigations were being carried out, I was ironically involved in the *Liverpool Echo's* annual fashion show. Girls Talk and Kids Talk had two scenes on the catwalk, modeling our latest collections. The show ran for four evenings, with about five hundred guests coming to watch each event. I thought that it would be a good idea to give each customer a one pound voucher to spend in any of our shops.

I had instructed our printer who looked after all our stationery printing, to print me green one pound notes, identical in size to the legal one, but instead of saying The Bank of England he was to replace it with The Bank of Girls Talk. The other big difference was that my notes were printed on ordinary paper, and only on one side!

The shows were proving to be busier that expected, so I had called my printer innocently asking him to print me an extra thousand one pound notes as quickly as possible and unaware that my phone was being tapped. Although he agreed to do it, they never turned up, and it wasn't until a couple of weeks later when I called in to pay him and to find out why he hadn't delivered that I discovered the truth.

"Don't talk to me about printing money!" he exclaimed. "Not long after I spoke to you on the phone the police burst in and arrested me, keeping me in a cell overnight until they had searched my shop and house! They thought I was forging real bank notes!"

I didn't have the heart to tell him that it was all my fault!

What has always amazed me, however, is how wealth can sometimes make you feel uncomfortable. As a child I had dreamt of one day owning a Rolls Royce; when Gina and I started on the market I one day mentioned in passing that when I was thirty I would own such a car. She hadn't forgotten.

A couple of weeks before my 30th birthday, Gina insisted that I buy one. I didn't take much persuading and almost immediately traded in my Jag for a magnificent dark blue Rolls Royce Silver Shadow with a light beige leather interior.

One afternoon Gina told me that she was just going to nip to the butchers to get half a pound of mince for the spaghetti she was making that night, so I volunteered to take her there; finding any excuse to drive my new toy. As I waited outside whilst Gina went in to the shop, I noticed the butcher admiring the graceful lines of my elegant car. When Gina returned she told me that my luck was in!

"We're having fillet steak tonight," she exclaimed, "There was no way that I was going to ask for half a pound of mince after having got out of a car like this!"

It was the best looking car I had ever seen but after a while I began to feel uncomfortable driving it. When I stopped at traffic lights I felt like a horse with blinkers on unable to look at people sitting in their cars either the left or the right of me in case they thought I was looking down on them. Instead I would sit behind the wheel staring straight ahead, feeling very self-conscious.

On the first Saturday I took Katie out for drive in the country; she would have been just three years old at the time. On our return we stopped at some lights; I clearly had my blinkers on unaware of anything that was going on outside of the car.

"Daddy," Katie caught my attention, "Daddy, one of your friends is waving at you!"

Katie was sitting to the left of me in the passenger seat, and looking out of her window I could see two men in the car next to us. The driver was waving the 'V' sign at us, whilst his passenger was leaning forward waving his fist in what is commonly known as the 'wanker wave'. Their message was clear; they thought I was a wanker for driving such a nice car.

That was the final nail in the coffin as far as the car was concerned. It had to go. I took it back to the showroom as soon as I could, and fortunately they still had my Jag. Exchanging the Rolls for my old car, and losing £2,000 in the process I drove away a happier man. I had only had the Rolls for five days, but at least I could say that my dreams had come true, if only for a moment or two!

Gina's dreams also came true one Christmas morning. It had soon become a family tradition for Katie and Faye to drag their sacks full of presents in to our bedroom, opening them in front of us whilst sitting on our bed. Once the girls had finished I would pass Gina a present, one at a time, from me.

The first box she opened contained a pair of jodhpurs and a riding hat, whilst the second box had a pair of black riding boots and a crop. After a little bit of encouragement I managed to get Gina to try them on for me; she was a bit puzzled.

"Are you getting kinky in your old age?" she asked.

"Not yet!" I assured her.

Standing in the bedroom, dressed in her full riding kit, she certainly looked the part, the only thing missing being a horse. The curtains were still drawn so I suggested that she open them, so that we could see what the weather was like.

Suddenly there was an almighty scream. "Jeff there is a silver grey horse in the garden, tied to a tree!"

Coming over to stand beside her, I whispered in her ear. "Happy Christmas Gina. Her name is Foxy lady and she's all yours!" I could hardly get the words out for the tears running down my face.

Gina had often told me that when she was a little girl she had often dreamt of owning a horse, and that it had to be silver grey as no other colour would do.

Suddenly she was off, out of the bedroom, down the stairs and running out in to the garden. Katie and Faye stood and watched as she ran out to the horse; they were both amazed that Father Christmas had brought their mummy a horse and had left it outside because it wouldn't fit down the chimney!

By the time I had got the girls dressed in their wellies and coats, and had gone outside Gina had disappeared. We found her trotting up and down St Mary's Road, riding like a true professional with her new clothes and hat on; Foxy Lady and Gina were getting along fine. I had rented a stable at a riding school close by in Netherley. A good friend of ours Lisa Haynes had gone there early on Christmas morning and ridden Foxy Lady to the house and tied her to the tree as instructed, underneath the bedroom window.

Foxy Lady was to change our lives.

By the middle of 1986 J&R Fashions had expanded to seven properties with four retail shops, two distribution warehouses and a head office, stretching from Warrington to Chester. Adding the weekly trips to Manchester and London I was spending too much time driving all over the place, so one day I got a map and marked out X's showing where all our properties were located. I then dropped my pen in the middle of the X's and it landed on a place called Whitegate in the County of Cheshire.

Showing Gina what I had done I told her that we should be living in Whitegate.

The following day Gina drove out that way with a friend to have a look around and see if there was anything for sale. Over dinner that evening she showed me some property brochures that she had picked up of three houses in the Whitegate area. The first two did nothing for me, but the last one was perfect. On the front page was a coloured photo of a magnificent house set by a lake with ducks swimming on the surface. The print under the picture told me that it was Abbots Walk, a fine country house in a secluded and private setting.

"I like this one," I said to Gina.

"I knew you would," she smiled. "It's my favourite too."

We viewed the property and a few days later and bought it on the spot.

Chapter Twenty-Nine
The Outback of Nowhere

We were all sad to leave our mansion in Huyton; although it was old and somewhat eerie, the four of us loved it. If we could have picked it up and transported it to Cheshire we would have!

We had sold it to two doctors who were going to convert it in to a thirty bedroom residential care home for the elderly – a good idea as to how big it was.

We set off in convoy on a fresh November morning in 1986. I led the way with Katie who was now six years old and so excited with the whole adventure of moving house. Ranger, our pet dog was sitting in the back with his long tongue hanging out, hoping that he wasn't going to the vets. Gina was close behind with three year old Faye sitting next to her (not quite understanding what was going on), and our other dog, Carla. Bob and Breda were towing a horse trailer with Foxy Lady, her head peering over the top of the door – she too seemed to be excited by all the attention she was receiving. And then, last but not least, bringing up the rear was the huge removal van full of our possessions.

As we drove into the hamlet village of Whitegate, the first sight that greeted us was the magnificent steeple of the 16th Century Church. Taking a sharp left opposite the church, we made our way down a narrow lane with one hundred year old oak trees on either side, their branches forming a thick canopy overhead almost blocking out the daylight. This tunnel of trees led all the way to Abbots Walk, our new home.

Luckily there was a large drive leading into the property as we just managed to get the whole convoy in. Once we had parked, Gina gathered Katie and Faye in her arms and went off to show them our new pet ducks, whilst I went to chat to our removals men.

The next minute I heard a woman's voice shouting loudly. Turning in the direction of the noise, I saw Mrs Woods, the lady whom we had bought the house from, having a go at Gina and the girls. I quickly went over to see what was wrong, only to discover that she was demanding that we left the property immediately as it did not belong to us yet.

"Go on," she screeched, "Get the hell out of here now!"

We had no other alternative than to leave as she becoming hysterical and totally unwilling to listen to reason.

Our convoy was once again on the move. This time however we ended up in the car park of the Blue Cap Pub, a large country pub some two miles down the road; it was the only place that I could find that was big enough to accommodate our convoy. I rang my solicitor and told him about the unpleasant reception we had received. He told me to stay put as he was going to ring their solicitor to find out what was going on. Calling me back in a few minutes he informed me that the property would not become legally ours until twelve o'clock noon and from then on we were in our rights to tell her to 'get-the-hell out of there'!

What a ridiculous situation to be in! Six adults, two children, two dogs and a horse, not to mention four vehicles all waiting on a pub car park because some mad woman wouldn't let us wait outside the house for an hour.

We arrived back at five minutes past twelve only to find that there wasn't a soul to be seen. The front door had been left ajar and that was it. When Gina and I had moved out of our old house, we had left a bouquet of flowers and a card wishing the new owners success in their new venture. Still they do say that 'there is nothing stranger than folk' and that old expression certainly rang true.

We could now enjoy the rest of the day familiarising ourselves with Abbots Walk. It was a sprawling 18th Century house which had formerly been the hunting lodge on the Delamere Estate. The house was surrounded by six acres of farmland and woods; there were stables for Foxy Lady as well as Katie and Faye's ponies which were due to arrive on their next birthdays. As far as I was concerned, I quite fancied the idea of being 'Lord of the Manor'. Feeding and naming the ducks kept Katie and Faye busy, whilst Gina and I tried to count the number of carp we could see swimming around in the lake which was massive.

We found our new rural surroundings gave us quite a lot to take in; my only regret was that my beloved Mum was not there to enjoy it with us.

By late afternoon most of the unpacking was completed; Bob, Brenda, Gina and I were sitting around the kitchen table enjoying a well deserved cup of tea whilst Katie and Faye were sitting on the floor playing together.

I heard the sound of a car pulling up and went to see who it was. I was curious as to whom it could be, as we didn't know anybody. Looking out of the window I noticed a man of the cloth getting out of the car.

"Gina, quick, go and grab Katie and Faye. It looks like the vicar is here to welcome us to his parish!"

We both picked up the girls and opened the front door, cheerful smiles on our faces. "Hello Vicar," we chorused.

"Are Mr and Mrs Wood still here?" he was almost stern in his response.

"No, I am sorry you've missed them." I replied. "They have already left."

"Oh dear, I called to say goodbye." He was obviously disappointed.

Gina and I stood there still smiling, waiting for him to say hello and to welcome us to his parish. I was on the point of asking him in for a cup of tea when he turned his back on us and walked away without so much as another word or even a mutter, before getting in to his car and driving off.

Gina and I were speechless, standing in our doorway in total disbelief. He hadn't even said hello! There were only thirty human beings living in the village and we accounted for four of them. Another strange happening on our first day.

Little did we know that there would be a third strange occurrence. It arrived on a clear Sunday morning; the sky was a lovely blue although there was a frost on the ground. Certainly too good a day for staying indoors so after breakfast I suggested to Gina that we take the girls and dogs for a long walk.

She thought it was a great idea, suggesting that we go through the woods which were conveniently placed just past our boundary fence. Wrapping Katie and Faye and ourselves up well to protect us from the cold with hats, gloves and scarves, and whatever else we could find, we set off. Carla and Ranger weren't bothered as they had thick coats and spent most of the time running around which also helped them keep warm.

Setting off at around ten o'clock we made our way over the field and then climbed the fence and headed into the woods. We felt like explorers as we walked through the trees and across the adjacent land. We picked up pocketfuls of conkers so that I could show the girls how to play with them whilst the dogs looked more like wolves as they sloped through the undergrowth, picking up the different scents of the wild foxes and rabbits that lived there.

We must have covered six miles or more by the time we got back to the house and were all ready for a hot drink. We were sitting around the kitchen table when the phone rang.

I picked up the receiver, "Hello?"

A well spoken lady asked if I was the new owner of Abbots Walk. Taken aback by her posh voice it took me a second or two to reply.

"Why, yes I am. How can I help?"

"Oh excellent. My name is Nancy Wright and I own the farm just next to you. We're all members of the same Neighbourhood Watch Group here in Whitegate," she explained, "and if anything untoward or suspicious happens we immediately ring around to inform our neighbours to take care and keep a look out."

She was efficient as well as posh!

"Are you still there?" My silence must have made her pause.

"Yes, I am," I answered, impressed by what she was telling me.

"Okay, right. I am ringing to tell you that there are lots of gypsies in the area and that I was concerned by what I saw."

She went on to explain that she had seen some gypsies that morning, describing them in great detail.

Looking out of the kitchen window, I could just make out her farm buildings in the distance.

"Oh yes, I can see your place now," I told her.

"Well, keep alert and let me know immediately if you do see something," I was instructed. "Here's my telephone number." She read out the number which I wrote down on a pad by the phone.

"Thank you very much Mrs Wright. I assure you nothing will get past me," I said before putting down the receiver.

Brimming over with enthusiasm I couldn't wait to tell Gina the news.

"We're going to love living here! Can you see that farm over there in the distance?" I asked her pointing through the window, "Well it belongs to a lady called Nancy Wright. I have just been talking to her on the phone and she was telling me that we are members of the Neighbourhood Watch Committee."

"Oh," Gina looked impressed. "What does that mean?"

"Well, if we or any of our neighbours see anything suspicious like thieves or dodgy looking people hanging around we ring up each other and warn them."

I couldn't take my eyes away from the window as I continued to look across the many acres of farm land, searching for a sight of gypsies. This was a serious matter and so I went upstairs to look through the bedroom window which gave me a much better bird's eye view of whole area from above. Disappointingly, there was nothing to see.

As I headed back downstairs and into the kitchen my mind was occupied by the description that Mrs Wright had given me of the travellers she had seen; she had mentioned a gang with children and wild dogs. Stepping over Carla and Ranger who were lying sprawled full length on the kitchen floor tired from their long run, it suddenly dawned on me.

"That cheeky cow was describing us!" I called out to Gina.

"What are you talking about? What do you mean?" Gina was clearly confused by my outburst.

"We're the bloody gypsies she was talking about!"

"Give over Jeff," Gina replied. "Don't be silly."

"I am not – look at the evidence." I was taking this very personally. "She said she saw a group of men and women with children and dogs on her land this morning. That was us – we were walking close to her land today, and what's more we were dressed more like townies than people who lived in the country; I mean I was wearing a black leather coat and a black wool hat!"

Gina started to laugh at my reaction.

"I don't know what you're laughing about," I told her, "Your choice of clothing wasn't much better!" Within a few seconds we were all laughing at the silliness of it all, including the girls who loved the idea of being called gypsies.

A few days later, however, we went out and bought ourselves four Barbour Jackets and four pairs of green wellingtons so that we could blend in better with the countryside and not be mistaken for gypsies again.

It took many years for our neighbours to accept us city slickers, and in the beginning it was very hard; it was like being stranded in the middle of the outback of nowhere. If Katie and Faye had not settled in so well into their new school, Gina and I would have most probably returned to somewhere closer to Liverpool.

We persevered and eventually settled in and made a couple of new friends. We bought Katie and Faye ponies for their birthdays as promised and I ended up with a mad Arab cross called Diego who spent most of his time throwing me to the ground! On the odd occasion when I did manage to stay on, we would all go out riding together as a family; even I began to feel like a Lord of the Manor!

Bob and Brenda used to love coming to stay at weekends and so did my Father and June; the house was always full with family and friends, most of whom were from Liverpool. I kept my promise to my dear Mum and made sure that Dad and June did not want for anything.

It was strange however, I could never bring myself to call him Dad, always referring to him as 'Boss', the nickname that had been used for years and which he liked; he and June were my close family, as Lesley, Barry and Sheila had all moved away. I came to love him over the years and we became good friends, and even though he never said it, I knew that he was very proud of me and all I had achieved.

Chapter Thirty
Sport of Kings

I n May 1987 on a glorious Saturday afternoon I was driving along the A49 simply enjoying myself. I was only a mile away from our house when I noticed a sign at the side of the road saying *POLO 3pm TODAY*.

Glancing at my watch, I saw it was only ten past three, so I pulled off the road into a large field. Looking to the right I could see lots of horse boxes lined up with dozens of horses tethered alongside them.

Straight ahead of me cars were parked next to each other in a long line, people standing around watching the game. I quietly parked the car hoping not to bring attention to myself as I had no idea whether or not I was allowed to be there. Getting out, I leant against the bonnet, and quickly became absorbed in the game.

I had never seen anything like this before. I had never, until then even heard of polo as a game; it is not the sort of thing that a boy growing up in Liverpool would have heard about.

The horses thundered past, their hooves pounding the turf and sending vibrations through the ground. The riders in different coloured shirts and white trousers tucked into brown leather boots, shouting out instructions to one another, all the time chasing a small white ball up and down a field hitting at it with long mallets.

There and then I just knew that I wanted to play this game.

My head was filled with questions - How do I learn to play? Who do I ask?

A short while later a bell sounded and the players started to ride off the field, heading towards their wagons to change their horses. I was close enough to see that the horses' flanks were heaving as they struggled for breath, their sides lathered in sweat, whilst the riders looked equally as hot!

Within minutes most of the players had returned to the field, except for one rider, who remained seated on his fresh horse at the edge of the field. He appeared to be doing nothing. Thinking that this might be a good moment to find answers to my questions I walked over to him. Screening my eyes from the sun with my hand, I looked up in his direction.

"Excuse me," I asked, in my best spoken English, trying to eradicate as much of my Scouse accent as possible, "How do I learn to play polo?" I stood there, smiling and waiting for him to reply.

"Fuck off," was the response, the tone loud and clipped. "Can't you see I am bloody playing? Just fuck off."

I stood there gob-smacked, feeling as if my jaw had hit the ground, as kicking his horse quite hard in the ribs, he turned and galloped back on to the polo field. Shock was soon replaced by embarrassment, and I prayed that nobody had heard his reply.

My face glowing, I went back to the car before spending the next 30 minutes or so watching the game. There was a man on a microphone providing a running commentary on the game in progress which was interesting to listen to. I was still determined to get involved in this game as it appealed to me on several levels. First of all it was played on horses and I was just starting to learn to ride; secondly it was a team game, which I preferred; and thirdly you played with a ball. What appealed most however was the adrenalin rush, such was the air of excitement and danger, that you could almost smell the adrenalin in both the horses and riders as they charged past in full play.

Who do I ask for information? I was determined to find an answer to my question. Once the game had ended the two teams shook hands with each other before riding back to their horse boxes. The man at the microphone looked more approachable so I decided to go and have a word with him. I introduced myself and asked him how I could learn to play polo. Introducing himself as Mike Taylor, he kindly indicated in the direction of a dark green horse box.

"Doodle Long," he advised, "You need to speak to him. That is his box over there; he gives polo lessons."

Thanking him, I went off in the direction of Mr Long's horse box. As I got closer, I could see that there was a man kneeling down with a bucket of water and a sponge in his hand washing his pony's legs.

Once again using my best English accent, I enquired if he was Doodle Long.

"Yes," he muttered, as if talking to the water bucket.

"My name is Jeff Pearce," I continued, "And I would like to learn to play polo."

"For God's sake fuck off," he said, "Can't you see I am busy?"

I just turned and left. I couldn't believe my ears. As I walked back to my car I was astounded. I had only spoken to three people, and two of them had said almost the same thing – they had told me to fuck off. In the world that I grew up in, that was fighting talk and I felt like knocking their lights out. I couldn't stop thinking what a strange group of people they were.

I had no sooner arrived home than I was telling Gina about this wonderfully exciting game of polo that I had discovered. I was speaking so quickly, that she had to tell me to slow down! The excitement was getting the better of me as I laid out my plans for the following day.

"It is on again tomorrow afternoon, at three o'clock. We will bring Katie and Faye and take a picnic. You can see for yourself then. It will be great!" I was so positive. "Oh Gina, you are going to love it. You can learn to play as well!"

Gina naturally didn't quite share my enthusiasm, as she was thinking about the encounters I had had, and the response I had received from two of the three members. However, I told her not to worry as there were lots of other people there.

On Sunday afternoon we packed the boot with a picnic basket full of goodies and we set off. Finding somewhere to set our picnic out, we settled down and the first game soon got underway. I found it as exciting as I had the day before but kept glancing in Gina's direction to see how she was reacting. She seemed to be equally engrossed, and it soon became apparent that she was as captivated as I had been.

Whilst we had been sitting there, Katie and Faye had found some other children to play with, and they were running around having a good time. A little while later Katie came over to where we were sitting bringing one of her little friends with her.

"Daddy, Daddy, this is Sarah. She is in my class at school! She is my friend. Her Daddy plays polo, and he is over there!"

She had no idea what she had done! I now had an opening.

Gina and I went over to introduce ourselves as Katie's parents, and soon started chatting about schools and children, but I soon turned the conversation to polo.

Sarah's parent, Geoff and Jenny Marshall were very nice people, and I found out that Geoff had only just started playing the game himself. All of a sudden Geoff got up and announced that he was going on to play. Gina and I remained with Jenny, standing on the line watching the game, and chatting about the game in play. When the game was finished, they invited us in to the Club House for a drink and introduced us to a couple of other members. It was a brilliant end to a great afternoon.

Over the following week Gina and I discussed taking up polo as a sport, and we both decided to become involved. She was great; not only was she the perfect mother to our children, as well as being the best business partner anyone could ever want to have, she was my soul mate, and was willing to have a go at every sport became involved in; she had tried windsurfing and alpine skiing, and now she was giving polo a go as well.

The next weekend we went back to the Polo Ground, and I found myself talking to a Chinese man called Steven Leung who had been a member for the past two seasons. In his stilted English, he gave me an insight into the strange people that played there.

As I discovered, the first man who had told me to 'f★★k' off was Michael Camm. Steve explained that when Michael was playing, he became so involved with the game he will not speak to anyone, never mind a stranger. Doodle Long, on the other hand, was very much old school and a bit pompous, however he was a very good player. He was the official club coach, but lost all signs of patience and encouragement when it came to teaching.

Steve was a character, and summed up his place in the club to perfection, laying on a thick accent to highlight his point.

"Me Chinee man. They don't likee me velly much. You long haired Liverpool man. They not likee you either."

A good friendship was formed, and we spent a great deal of time in the years to come together.

Gina and I wanted to get into the game as quickly as possible. In hindsight our enthusiasm led us to be somewhat naïve, and we bought two ponies from fellow members. The ponies were sold to us as schoolmasters; a schoolmaster is an experienced horse which had been playing the game for many years and knows the rules better than the rider, i.e. a great asset for any beginner. We paid £3,000 for each pony.

Within a week both ponies had gone lame, and continued to do so week after week. As if this wasn't enough they hated getting in to the horse box, bought for £2,500.

Gina and I felt that we had been like lambs to the slaughter in every way.

As it soon transpired, the horse box soon proved to be 'lame' as well, breaking down on regular occasions. How we ever made the two mile journey from our house to the polo ground I will never know. If we did manage to make it we were always put in the last two chukkas at the end of the day with the junior boys and girls aged between 12 and 16.

Polo is a complex and dangerous game with rules that are hard enough to understand, without having to include the skill of horsemanship required.

By the end of the season I was frustrated. Having forked out £8,500 and gone through a lot of hassle and bother over the past couple of months, I was no closer to learning the game, let alone being able to hit the ball. This was definitely not what I had hoped for.

I had overheard the experienced players talking in the Clubhouse about Argentina, and how it was the best place to learn to play polo. You could also buy young polo ponies at good prices.

I had even had the chance of meeting one of these Argentineans, Alejandro Mihanovich (known as Alex) when he had been on a promotional visit to the UK. He was well known to several members of the Club and stayed with them whenever he was over here. On this particular visit, he had given me a business card, with details of the Polo school that he and his colleague Manuel Llinas ran in Argentina. I had not thought much of it at the time, and had filed the card away.

I was talking to Stephen Leung one day, telling him that I wasn't making any progress and unless I did something drastic nothing much would change. I told him that I needed to go to a polo school where I could learn to play properly, and that I was thinking of going to Argentina. Steve thought it was a great idea, and asked if he could join me. It was agreed there and then that the two of us would go.

With Gina's encouragement and assistance, the wheels were set in motion. The first thing I did was to ring the number on the card and spoke to Manuel. His English wasn't that good and I certainly couldn't speak Spanish. With the aid of a fax machine the dates were agreed, flights booked and Steve and I set off on our big adventure.

I would like to point out, that when I embarked on my trip to Argentina, I had no idea where it was, let alone that we had recently been at war with them over a remote group of islands.

When booking our flights, we must have chosen the long way around. We changed planes four times, we spent several hours sitting in transit lounges waiting for our connecting flights, and it took us over thirty-six hours to get there. We arrived at Buenos Aires International Airport at ten pm local time. It was dark outside, and as we made it through customs we were on the look out for somebody holding up a card with our name on.

There was nobody there to meet us. The airport emptied and still no one turned up, so after an hour or so Steve and I agreed that I was to call Manuel. It was a bad line, making Manuel's English even harder to understand. We shouted to each other a bit, and eventually I managed to catch the words 'Jose', 'outside' and 'waiting' interspersed between the crackles and other interference which made up the greater part of the conversation. I assumed that he meant that there was someone called Jose waiting for us outside.

Leaving the airport building, I started to look for a man called Jose. There were several taxi drivers lounging around smoking, one or two guys sitting in cars, and others just hanging about.

It was like looking for a needle in a haystack, and a stupid thing to have to do - walk up and down, asking for a Jose who knew Manuel? For all I knew Jose was the most popular mans name in Argentina and they could all be called Jose.

I had no success, and after about fifteen minutes went back to where Stephen was sitting on the cases, supposedly looking after them. He was in fact half asleep (though I don't know why as he had slept most of the way over from England). I was pretty annoyed by now, and did not appreciate being made to feel like an unwelcome stranger in a foreign country. This was not what I had hoped for, and I was beginning to think about checking into a hotel for the night.

For some unknown reason, my attention was caught by an old dirty grey truck parked some way in the distance.

"I don't believe it" I muttered out loud, to no one in particular. "What's the betting that's frigging Jose?" Tired, frustrated, annoyed I ran down to the truck.

There was a man sitting behind the wheel, his chin resting on his chest and a straw cowboy hat pulled down over the top half of his face. He was snoring loudly, and to someone as tired as me, this was like a red rag to a bull. I pulled a coin out of my pocket and rapped loudly on the car window, almost shouting at him to wake up.

I woke him up. Or should I say he woke with a start. Leaping out of his seat, bumping his head on the car roof, he stumbled out of the door, almost landing at my feet.

"Jose?" I demanded loudly.

Nodding his head frantically, he replied, "*Si senor, si senor*".

"Manuel Llinas?" I asked.

"*Si Senor, si senor.*"

This was informative. No matter what I said he would just say "si senor, si senor". At this stage I was so fed up I just pointed to Stephen a huddled mass of human being and suitcases in the distance. This could be Stephen's problem now.

Without waiting for me, Jose had jumped in the truck and reversed it at high speed back towards the airport terminal. By the time I caught up, I found our suitcases tied down in the back, covered with a large piece of tarpaulin.

My legs could hardly carry me as I made my way back to the truck. If anything kept me going it was the thought of Stephen and Jose communicating with each other, one in heavily accented Chinese English and the other with no English at all and a vocabulary limited to *si senor!*

They must have achieved something however, because we were ready to leave by the time I got back, and I did not even pay any real attention when Stephen held the door open for me and suggested I sit in the middle.

Cunning oriental! I found myself sitting on the hardest bench, more like a wooden plank than a seat, wedged between a large Argentinean 'bandit' on one side, and my snoring Chinese travel companion on the other. The gear stick was strategically placed between my legs, which made changing gears an embarrassing operation for both Jose and me. The handbrake was also limiting my leg room, and in the end I found myself sitting with my legs almost cramped up against my body, heels precariously gripping the edge of the seat.

Stephen was obviously exhausted, and having made himself comfortable went straight back to sleep. If I had been any less tired or preoccupied this would have driven me mad, but I had something new and 'exciting' to keep me awake!

The road out of the city was smoothe and pleasant, and the first hour passed without event. Storm clouds were gathering and it was beginning to rain, with the rain drops getting larger and the thunder being accompanied with streaks of lightning across the sky.

Suddenly tarmac turned to dirt track, as we headed inland. The road became bumpy, mounds of hardened dirt, interspersed with small rocks, dotted between large potholes. The rain was lashing down, the headlights gave off a faint beam, and the windscreen wiper was just not up to the job.

We had been travelling for about two hours now, and we hadn't seen any other vehicles. I did feel a moment or two of concern, wondering if everyone was saner than us, staying in the shelter of their homes. However Jose seemed to know this road well, clinging to the edges of the track, and avoiding the danger zones as if he knew where each and everyone was.

I won't say I relaxed, but I felt that he knew what he was doing. Suddenly the truck swerved, heading into the darkness. Alarmed I looked over at Jose to see what he was doing! Like my Chinese friend, Jose was asleep, lulled like a baby by the swaying and rocking of the truck.

I thumped him, and shouted his name. Grunting, he opened his eyes, straightened the truck and we continued on.

The rest of the journey continued as a white knuckle ride. Stephen, oblivious to it all, lolled against me, his weight bearing down on my shoulder, his snores rumbling in my ear. Jose lit cigarette after cigarette, filling the cab with a foul smelling smoke, his head occasionally falling forward. Each time this happened, I would thump him again. I was vigilant, sitting beside him, my eyes never leaving his face; this was serious, this was my life he had in his hands and I was not going to let it end in the middle of nowhere, squashed between an overweight Chinese man and a chain smoking Argentinean gaucho and a gear stick stuck between my legs.

Waking up the next morning I was disoriented. I found myself in a single bed, in a simply furnished room, on my own. Staggering across the tiled floor, feeling a degree of panic, I pulled back the curtains on the window, nearly blinding myself in the process.

Strong sunlight filled the room, and I could see fields and trees all around me. Looking away, I realised that I was still in the clothes that I had been wearing since I had left England.

Seeing a door across from the window, I opened and found myself in a larger room, furnished with a table and some chairs. Steve was sitting at the table, obviously enjoying some breakfast, as if he had been there all along.

On his greeting of "good morning" another door opened and a man came through bearing a fresh pot of coffee.

He introduced himself to me as Roberto, and told me that he was here to look after us both, for the duration of our visit. I soon found out this meant that he looked after nearly every aspect of our stay, from cleaning our rooms, to cooking our breakfast, tacking-up our horses and even cleaning our boots.

During breakfast Manuel arrived and after introductions, sat down to tell us about the forthcoming schedule of events.

During our two week visit, he told us, we would start each morning with the ride over to the main house, which was known as the estancia. This ride would take about thirty minutes at a leisurely pace.

After arriving we'd spend the first two hours of the day learning how to stick and ball, which involved standing on chairs following Manuel's instructions on how best to hit the ball. There would then be a midday break for lunch, at the main house, before heading back out to the polo field by one o'clock to learn the correct way of riding a polo pony. This would involve taking a horse from a standing start into a full canter within second; stopping and turning the horse on a sixpence; and most importantly 'riding off' an opponent.

This is one of the most important aspects of polo. If an opponent has the ball and is heading towards your goal, there are only two options available. Either you 'ride him off' which means you come up alongside him and lean your horse into his horse steering him away from the ball, (which became quite physical)or alternatively you 'stick him' which meant using your stick to stop his stick from hitting the ball.

This part of the day over, there was time then for a dip in the outdoor pool before the big game of polo at four o'clock. By five thirty we would be finished.

If I had any misgivings about coming to Argentina, they soon disappeared as Manuel outlined the itinerary. I couldn't wait to get started. For the first time I would be playing polo as it should be played.

After a quick shower and changing into my polo gear, we were mounted and heading over to Manuel's estancia. We were pleasantly surprised that first morning to find that we were not the only pupils at the polo school. Our fellow students were from different parts of the world, and once introductions were made we got down to the serious part of the day.

We soon found that we had a lot in common, sharing jokes and stories of our mistakes over lunch, enjoying a refreshing dip in the pool mid afternoon, and entering into the competitive spirit of the game before days end.

Returning in the evening for dinner, Jose would pick us up in the truck. There would be at least ten of us gathered around a large table, formally set with gleaming silver wear and crisp white linen. There were beautiful heavy crystal glass filled with local wines, and the food served was all from the land.

The meal completed, the table would be cleared, but the evening was not over. Using the table covered with a piece of green cloth as a polo field, Manuel would continue to talk us through the rules of polo, moving small models of horses about to show us what he meant.

After four days I had really settled in and found it easy to mix with the other guests. I could sense however that Steve was not as happy and certainly was not enjoying himself as much as I. Therefore it was not too surprising when he suddenly announced that he was leaving, on the pretext of going to Hong Kong to visit his family.

I remained in the guest room on my own and continued to practice very hard every day. I made two good friends whilst I was there, a young guy from New Zealand called Mark and a young woman from America called Pamela. Before we left and went our separate ways, we exchanged phone numbers and addresses and arranged to visit each other one day soon.

A few days before I left Manuel and Alex took me shopping for polo equipment. I had no idea as I set out with them that it would be quite so interesting or enjoyable.

Our first stop was a boot-maker, who made nothing other than polo boots. I had a pair especially made for me and ordered a pair for Gina, both with our initials engraved on the side.

The prices were so reasonable compared to England, with an average saving of at least one third, whilst the quality was excellent. Loving a good deal, I couldn't help but take advantage of it all. I bought two sets of six polo sticks, with my initials embossed on one set and Gina's on the other as well as two small sticks for Katie and Faye. I also had a special leather carrying case made for them whilst I was there.

I snapped up four complete saddle 'sets', matching bridles, Argentinean head collars; you name it I bought it. Essentially I bought anything to do with polo, and completely forgot that I was going to have to get them all home!

On the last day Manuel took me in his own car to the airport. It was such a contrast to my earlier journey of a few weeks before. This time it was nice and comfortable. We spoke of my buying young horses and discussed prices and transportation. He said if I came back he would take me all over Argentina looking for good ponies and would help me organise their transportation back to England. I really appreciated his offer, as I knew that if anyone was going to help me buy the right ponies it would be Alex and Manuel, both because of their contacts but also because they were good judges of horseflesh.

I thanked him very much for my stay and told him that I had really enjoyed myself and had learnt an awful lot about polo in such a short time at his school. Shaking his hand, my last words were a promise to return. I would be back.

Arriving at the check in desk, with my huge mountain of luggage, I was beginning to dread the journey ahead. The thought of all those changes, and masterminding all my suitcases through to the right destination was pretty daunting. However, I was in luck and was told that my assortments of goods were all checked through to London Heathrow. After that it was up to me to get them all safely to Manchester!

The journey home to London was relatively uneventful and I spent a great deal of it reflecting on the fabulous time I had had. I was looking forward to sharing it all with Gina and the girls, and to giving them some of the gifts I had bought, knowing that Gina would chuckle at the savings I had made!

I arrived at London Heathrow, and made my way to the baggage hall to collect my luggage. Grabbing a trolley, I positioned myself by the carousel and was soon surrounded by my baggage, an assortment of shapes and sizes. There were about fifteen pieces in total, and I had great fun stacking them all on to the trolley, trying to get them to balance and stay on.

Time was ticking by, and I was conscious of the fact that I only had one hour to get to another terminal for my shuttle to Manchester. As everyone who has pushed a luggage trolley will know, they have a mind of their own, and this trolley was no exception. Heavily laden, I was trying to head towards the Green Channel, whilst my trolley wanted to go to the Red.

Strength and sheer determination won the day in this case, and I managed to get myself down the Nothing to Declare route without any further mishap. Walking past those Customs officers is an uncomfortable feeling at the best of times. But I knew that I was being slightly naughty, I was definitely pushing my luck, and as the saying goes, and 'as luck would have it' I was stopped.

I had neared the end of the corridor, when a voice called me back. I was about the only passenger there, and was in no doubt he was talking to me. Reluctantly turning around, I headed back to the table where he was standing.

It was not my appearance that would have caught his attention. I was dressed smartly, especially for my meeting with Gina and I wanted to look my best. I was wearing a pair of chinos, a white shirt with blue and red striped tie and last but not least a very smart navy blazer with brass buttons on the cuffs and front and an embroidered badge on my breast pocket. The badge had no particular significance, having been put there mainly for decorative purposes.

The Customs Officer started to open my luggage, revealing saddles, and bridles. The smell of new leather, and the contents of the bags, plus the fact that I was returning from South America were grounds enough for suspicion.

"Well," he asked, intrigued by the contents, "Where have you been Sir?

"Argentina," I replied, trying to look as calm as possible. Someone had once told me that nervous people blink a lot, so I most probably stood there looking like a glazed idiot, trying hard not to blink too much. It would have been a dead give away.

"What were you doing there, Sir?" he asked.

"Playing polo," I answered.

He stopped what he was doing and started looking at me a bit more closely.

"Hmmmm, playing polo." He paused for a moment before adding, "With Prince Charles I suppose?"

"No, not this time," I said, desperately trying to gain a little respectability.

Throughout our entire conversation, he had been staring at the embroidered badge on the chest pocket of my blazer, so his next question threw me a little.

"Playing for England were you?"

The penny dropped, and wanting to take advantage of the direction he was taking in his questions, I crossed my fingers and replied with a simple yes. He must have been thinking that I was a player from the English Polo Team.

"Did we win?" he asked.

"Of course," I muttered, trying to play the whole thing down.

"What score?"

That threw me, oh shit I thought. What do I say now?

"Six goals to three," I informed him.

Turning to a fellow Customs Officer on a nearby desk, he called out, "Hey Billy, we beat those Argies again."

I just wanted to get away and wished that I could mutter a "beam me up Scotty" and find myself being transported magically to another realm. Glancing down at my watch I must have let out a quiet groan of despair.

"What is the matter Sir?" he asked.

"I have missed my shuttle," I replied, my disappointment clearly written all over my face, "it was the last to Manchester tonight."

He looked at me for a split second, and then suddenly turned away, picking up the phone and talking to someone on the other end.

I believed I was in for it, he was going to arrest me and I had visions of spending a night in a cell. Why oh why hadn't I been a little more honest and gone through the Red Channel? "You Stupid Scouser" I thought to myself, "you stupid git."

I must have been standing there paralysed for a few minutes, because the next thing I was aware of was a small buggy pulling up alongside us. I glanced over at it, this was all rather strange – people did not get taken to jail in buggies!

Moving out from behind the desk, the customs officer started to load my luggage on to the buggy.

"Come on," he insisted, "Give us a hand. I have made some calls, and they are going to hold the plane for you. This guy will take you there."

I sat next to the driver, before turning to the Customs Officer.

Shaking my hand he apologised, "I am sorry for the delay Sir," adding "Anyone who plays for our country is alright by me. Good luck Sir."

I thanked him for all his help, whilst at the same time feeling a little remorseful. I had been so lucky, when in reality I had not been overly honest, and had got away with it.

It was a long way to the plane even on the buggy. I sat there with my heart in my mouth, silently urging the driver to go faster. I would never have made it on foot, even if I had not been stopped, and it was only when I sat back in my seat, fastening my seat belt did I finally let out a sigh of relief.

Smiling to myself, I realised that playing polo does having it advantages!

Gina and the girls were waiting for me in Manchester when I arrived. Coming out into the arrivals terminal, and seeing their faces after what felt like an eternitywas the most wonderful feeling in the world; I was overwhelmed with my love for them all.

★   ★   ★

Over the next few days my enthusiasm and excitement for polo and everything I had experienced in Argentina seemed to rub off on Gina. I tried to impress on her how beautiful the horses were, how well they were trained and how they responded to the lightest of signals. I so wanted her to come out with me again, and that way we could choose our horses together, as well as benefitting from the lessons at Manuel's school.

So it was decided. We would return as soon as possible, and having approached Gina's parents, arrangements were made for the girls to stay with them. This in itself was a big decision, as Gina and I had never left the girls for such a long period of time ever before.

Within four weeks of my return to the UK, Gina and I were setting off to Argentina. Having learnt from my earlier trip, I took charge of the travel arrangements. The flights were more direct this time, cutting a good few hours of the travel time. More importantly, however, was that during my conversations with Manuel I had insisted that I did not want to be met at the airport by Jose. There was no way that Gina was going to go through the 'fun and games' that I had endured on my first trip out.

So Manuel was there to meet us at the airport, and we returned to his estancia, chatting like old friends and enjoying the trip. This time we stayed as his guests in the main house, and this time Gina and I were the only two guests at the school. This was fabulous as it meant that we had more intense one-to-one lessons in the morning, and then played polo in the afternoon.

This was a truly fabulous experience; being in the position where we were able to travel to Argentina to pursue a sport which we were both beginning to love was the sort of thing that we had worked hard for. Polo is known to be the sport of kings and I felt like a king during those two weeks. It was lovely to see Gina having proper lessons and benefitting from them; it was fantastic having her riding along by my side every day; and best of all I could share it with her.

Manuel and Alex kept their word and drove us all over the place looking for ponies. They helped in the selection, advising us on the blood lines and training, until we managed to finally choose six youngsters that we both agreed to buy, paying £1,000 each. The cost of flying them back to England worked out at an extra £3,000 per pony.

As soon as I arrived back home I found my time taken up with building six new stables, and overseeing the creation of a polo ground. Bringing in large earth movers and diggers, I set to work on one of the bigger fields near the house, firstly draining, then leveling and finally grassing, until I had my own bespoke polo field. This would enable both Gina and me to continue to practice everything that we had learned, readying ourselves and our ponies for the coming season without having to leave our home.

We couldn't help but smile at our new acquisitions when they arrived six weeks later. A similar four or five year old, bought in the UK would have cost at least £8,000 so even with the cost of transport included they were still a bargain!

Six more girls for me to contend with! Calandria, Rubia, Tordia, Primavera, Nutria and Coco, came off the wagon, stiff from the journey, and after a short while settled into their new home. We loved our beautiful new animals, and enjoyed riding and getting to know them. Without a doubt these youngsters would now get us into the game.

Once we started riding them, it did not take long for us to realise that the key to successful game is horse power. Polo is all about getting in to the action and just as importantly getting out of harms way. Therefore, with a pony contributing towards as much of 80% of the game, the better the pony, the better the player.

That winter I bought a brand new horse box and had it specially converted to accommodate our new ponies. As usual I was thinking business, knowing that it would be a great advantage if I could share the cost of the coming polo season with someone. But I would need a sponsor.

After giving it careful thought, I decided to approach Jaguar. It seemed like an obvious choice, as I had bought four of their cars over the years. Calling Richard Greenwood, the Sales Director at Jaguar House, I made an appointment to meet him in their Liverpool Office. Jaguar House owned a few Jaguar and Mercedes dealerships in and around the North West.

The meeting went well. I presented him with a proposal outlining my ideas for sponsorship. The first item to carry the logo would be the horse box which would be repainted in Jaguar Racing Green, with their logo emblazoned across the sides of the wagon.

Our polo ponies were to wear saddles cloths, horse rugs, leg and tail bandages in racing green, and where possible would have the name Jaguar embroidered on them. As for the players they would look professional in their traditional white trousers and brown boots with racing green polo shirts, again showing the Jaguar logo across the front.

In addition to the team livery, Jaguar would sponsor a silver cup, played for each year. They would provide the hospitality in a marquee, laying on a champagne luncheon for their VIP guests whilst displaying the latest cars around the polo ground.

Richard was enthusiastic about my proposal, and after going through the figures with him, told me that it would be only a matter of a few days before I got an answer as he needed to discuss it with the other directors.

He called me and gave me the good news. I was now the official captain of the Jaguar House Polo Team and it was up to me to bring it all together. That was quite an undertaking in itself as all the fabric used in both the horse wear and the outfits for the players had to be specially dyed to get the colour perfect. I wanted to present a professional image, and to do things right was an expensive undertaking. Phoning Richard regularly, to keep him informed of the costs and what was going on, he never once blinked an eyelid, continuing to give me his support.

When everything was finished I invited Richard and a couple of his directors to come over and have look. It was an impressive turnout - the horse box looked absolutely fantastic with the green and gold artwork on the sides; the six ponies in their racing green livery looked equally as professional. My two grooms also wore the Jaguar house polo shirts continuing the corporate team theme.

Jaguar were more than pleased with what I had achieved, and were very much looking forward to the polo season getting underway in the next couple of weeks.

By now I had accumulated ten horses. In addition to the six polo ponies, there were also those belonging to Katie and Faye, so we now had to employ two full time grooms, Louise and Toria. This made a huge difference not only with the mucking out, etc, but also because polo ponies have to be exercised every day. Getting ready for a polo match also takes a fair amount of time grooming, and preparing them, so extra pairs of hands were always welcome.

On a sunny Saturday afternoon in May 1988, almost a year to the day when I had first turned into the Polo Ground as a spectator, Gina and I arrived in a beautiful horse box with some serious polo ponies on board. We'd made a major financial investment (I recall it was somewhere in excess of £70,000) and although a bit nervous were looking forward to a good season. We'd certainly come a long way in the past twelve months and both felt very committed.

Arriving at the polo ground, the new horse box with the logo on the sides made a few heads turn, however it was nothing compared to the commotion caused as our six ponies trotted down the ramp. A crowd gathered on the terrace of the club house, watching avidly and I could overhear some of the comments, carried towards us on the afternoon breeze.

"Who the hell is that?" asked one individual.

"Bloody man. It must be that Jeff Pearce fellow," commented another.

"The long haired Scouser," said a third. "Last year he had two knackered ponies and he couldn't even play!"

"Where did he get those ponies from?" asked another.

"I hear he went to Argentina," said the first, "and flew those horses back with him!"

"He has even built his own polo ground at home!"

There were other mutters but we didn't care, we were here to play polo. We weren't surprised however, as sponsorship was unheard of in those days; and as for the horsebox it did stand out amongst the plainer and older wagons parked nearby.

That first afternoon, the Club Manager, Michael Taylor put me in a decent match. During the first three chukkas I played reasonably well, the lessons I had learnt in Argentina proving to have been worth the time and money. On the third chukka our team was awarded a penalty which was to be taken from the sixty yard centre spot; the norm being that the better player always takes the penalties, and in this case it was Doodle Long who was a three goal player.

Polo rules state that there are five different types of penalty hits. For each of these penalty hits the players have to be in certain positions; i.e. a different penalty, a different position.

I did not know where to position myself for this particular shot so I decided the best thing to do was to ask Doodle. Riding over to him I said,

"Where would you like me to be positioned for this penalty?"

With that he shouted at the top of his voice, "Off the fucking ground! I hate it when people like you don't know the fucking rules."

Again I could not believe what I was hearing; I had asked a simple question and had been given a load of verbal abuse! I rode over to where one of our other players was standing, reining up alongside him, and although the game continued, I couldn't stop thinking about Doodle's comments; I was furious – he had pushed me that little bit too far, enough was enough.

The goal was scored, the bell rang and it was the end of the third chukka. Everybody rode back to their wagons to change their horses. As soon as I arrived at my box I jumped off my horse handed the reins to Louise and ran, raging, towards Doodle's dark green horsebox which was at least 100 yards away.

As I was running I threw down my polo stick and took off my helmet and gloves casting them to one side. It was difficult running in boots and knee pads and by the time I got there I could hardly breathe. Red faced, puffing and panting I looked up to see Doodle standing at the top of the ramp of his wagon. I felt dwarfed in comparison but there was no turning back.

In a blind rage, fuelled by temper, I ran up the ramp like a charging bull my head hitting him straight in the groin. I was David, he was Goliath. The sheer force from my assault pushed him backwards and the two of us were carried towards the rear of the wagon, ending up on the floor, fists flying, covered in horse shit and hay.

As I managed to get a couple of punches in, I told him in no uncertain terms that I'd had enough of his rudeness. He needed to learn some manners and I was going to teach him a lesson. We scrapped like a couple of raging terriers, not letting go off each other as we rolled around on the floor, oblivious to everything around us. Someone must have called for help as two male grooms soon arrived on the scene and pulled us apart still snarling at each other and punching the air with our fists.

Mike Taylor had been attracted by all the noise and commotion and came over demanding, "What the hell is going on?"

"It's between him and me," I said, still staring at Doodle.

"It's not," said Mike, "We will not tolerate this kind of behavior. Come with me."

He took me into the Club House, telling me to sit down and wait. A few minutes later he returned with Sebastian de Ferranti, the Club President, and official Steward for the Hurlingham Polo Association, the governing body. They don't come much bigger in the polo world - Mr de Ferranti was definitely top brass, and he was highly respected by everyone.

I had seen Mr de Ferranti on earlier occasions and was really looking forward to being formally introduced to him, so meeting him under such embarrassing circumstances was not a good start to my polo career.

The clubhouse quickly emptied as we sat down at a long table. I sat on one side whilst Mr de Ferranti and Mike Taylor positioned themselves directly opposite, two judges facing the guilty party. Mr de Ferranti spoke first.

"This type of behaviour is not acceptable," his quietly modulated tones making the words seem even more serious. "We don't tolerate this sort of behavior in Polo."

"This is a gentleman's club, and gentlemen do not resort to street fighting to resolve issues. There are established procedures for resolving issues and we adhere to those procedures. The penalty for fighting is instant dismissal from the club, a revocation of your membership."

Looking at them from across the table, I replied.

"Gentlemen, I appreciate your rules, I accept them, and I am willing to abide by them. However, before I go I think that it is only fair that you know what drove me to behave this way."

I then went on to tell them about how I had originally approached Doodle Long the year before to ask him for polo lessons and how he had told me to fuck off.

"The second time that I spoke to him just a short while ago, I asked him a perfectly normal question. He was about to take a penalty, and I asked him where he wanted me to be positioned. This time he decided to shout at me, in front of everyone, telling me to fuck off the ground!" I explained. "I felt he was unbelievably rude and he had embarrassed me for no good reason. I am sorry, I had to teach him some manners as he shouldn't speak to people that way."

The two gentlemen listening to me were visibly shocked by what I told them, finding it hard to believe that one of their 'gentleman' members would behave that way. They asked me to wait outside the Club House whilst Doodle Long was sent for.

I couldn't believe what had happened. I stood outside, thoughts rushing through my head. "What had I done? Six new horses? A new wagon? All that money spent on the stables and polo ground? My sponsors and all the money that they had spent – what were they going to think?" Although I felt pretty lousy, a sense of self dignity and value stopped me from feeling too bad - just because I was from humble beginnings did not mean that I was a lesser person and should be spoken to like that.

After ten minutes Mike called me back. Mr de Ferranti was standing up by now, and gesturing towards me, said that Doodle had something to say.

"I am sorry," he said, "Will you accept my apology?"

I couldn't ignore his outstretched hand and returned the handshake, acknowledging his apology.

Mike, standing between the two of us clapped us both on the back, "Come on you two, that's the end of it. No more swearing and certainly no more fighting."

Doodle and I shook hands again and we all smiled.

I looked over at Mr de Ferranti, trying to work out if a verdict was written on his face; would I have to go, or would I be allowed to stay? He too put his hand on my shoulder, took me to one side and apologised for the welcome I had received, assuring me that I would hear no more of the matter.

It took a while for Doodle and I to become friends although we played lots of polo together. I found him very helpful over the rules after that day. Mike Taylor and I always got on – he was impressed by my enthusiasm for the game and for the Club. A couple of years later Mike arranged to go the

Guards Polo Club at Windsor, for a special four week course on becoming a Grade One Umpire.

He invited me to go with him and I immediately agreed, enjoying every minute of it, both passing our exams with flying colours. He also invited me to play polo with Prince Charles.

Unfortunately, Prince Charles fell off his horse and injured his arm badly just four weeks before we were due to play. The match was naturally cancelled but I ended up umpiring the game that took its place that day at Hembury Hall, the highlight being the presentation of prizes by Princess Margaret one of which she gave to me.

Sebastian and I got on very well and also played polo together. We often played at his fabulous home Hembury Hall, and after a game, Gina, Katie and Faye were invited to swim in his indoor pool. He enjoyed our company and we certainly enjoyed his.

The rest of that season was a great success; Gina and I enjoyed playing polo and my sponsors were more than happy with their financial commitment agreeing to finance the Jaguar polo team the following year. We had made lots of good friends, Geoff Marshall sometimes played for my team, and I on lots of occasions played for his Causeway Racing Team. Jenny, Geoff's wife also started to play and Gina enjoyed the female company. Polo took us all over the UK, playing in different clubs, and meeting all sorts of different people.

The following year half way through the season I got a phone call out of the blue. It was Pamela, the young woman I had met on my first visit to Argentina. She was in London and thought that it would be nice to come and visit. I gave her instructions on which train to catch and agreed to pick her up from our local station at five pm on the Friday night.

Having collected her, I brought her back to the house, and introduced her to my family. Pamela got on well with Gina and the girls, giving both Katie and Faye a bath before putting them to bed. Over dinner, Gina kindly offered Pamela the use of her ponies for the matches over the weekend and Pamela happily accepted.

It was getting late, about 9pm and I realised that I needed to inform Mike of the changes as he always arranged the chukkas and the team for the weekend's play. I rang him at his office at home and mentioned that Gina was not going to be playing as we had a guest staying with us who would be taking her place.

Mike said that wasn't a problem and asked me her name.

"Pamela," I told him.

"Pamela who?" he asked. "What is her second name?"

Not having ever thought of asking her, I told him to hang on whilst I checked. Putting my hand over the receiver I called out, "Pamela, what's your second name?"

"Sue Martin," she replied.

"Sue Martin," I told Mike.

"Thanks Jeff," he said, "I'll see you tomorrow," before hanging up.

The three of us were all in the kitchen tidying up after our dinner. Pamela offered to wash the dishes while Gina dried them and put them away. I was tidying up and talking about Argentina when the phone rang. It was Mike again.

"Jeff, did you say Pamela Sue Martin?"

"Yes, that's right Mike," I answered.

"The Hollywood movie star?" he asked.

I looked over at Pamela. She was standing at the sink washing the dishes. Barefoot, in faded jeans and an old t-shirt there was nothing about her that resembled a Hollywood star.

Shaking my head I said, "No Mike, I don't think so."

"She must be," he said, "I have looked her up in the Hurlingham Book. There's only one Pamela Sue Martin that plays polo and she's a movie star. Just ask her what does for a living!"

This was all becoming a bit of a saga. "Pamela, what do you do for a living, love?" I called out.

"I am in the movie business," she answered, her voice unmistakable with its West Coast American twang.

I nearly dropped the phone. "Shit, Mike you are right. She is in the movie business."

Mike was almost silenced, bring the conversation to an abrupt halt with a cursory, and "See you tomorrow."

I sat down at the kitchen table and Gina and I looked at each other baffled.

"What do you mean you're in the movie business? What do you do?"

Pamela went on to say that when she was young she had starred in the first Titanic film and told us about the other parts she played after that. However as she explained, she was probably best recognized for her role as Fallon in Dynasty, an America soap starring Joan Collins, which was at that time a phenomenal success in the UK. On this trip over however, she was promoting a new film in which she played a starring role.

It took a while for all of this to sink in, and we sat around talking and asking questions, listening to her stories before finally going to bed.

As soon as we were in the privacy of our bedroom, Gina went quietly mad at me hissing "You have invited a Hollywood movie star here without knowing it. What did you think she did for a living?

"I don't know" I said.

"Why didn't you ask?" Gina demanded.

"I didn't care what she did for a living!" I replied, "We just talked polo all the time."

Gina quietly reminded me of what had happened that evening. "You let her bathe the girls, and put them to bed. You even let her wash the dishes! How embarrassing is that?!"

Gina was now totally convinced that I was a complete idiot and told me so in no uncertain terms. Finally, we went to sleep agreeing on one thing, that it really didn't matter what she did – Pamela was a nice person and that was that.

After breakfast, Gina showed Pamela the ponies that she would be playing on. Pamela continued to assist around the place, insisting on helping the grooms prepare the ponies for the forthcoming polo that afternoon.

Michael, in the meantime, had rung me early in the morning suggesting that we should throw a party that night for all the other Club members and their wives. As he pointed out it wasn't every day that we had a Hollywood movie star playing polo here in Cheshire.

I put the idea to Gina, asking her whether she thought it would be a good idea. She agreed and immediately rang a friend of ours in Manchester who owned an Indian restaurant. After some discussion, Gina arranged to collect a selection of traditional dishes later in the afternoon, thus giving our guests an Indian banquet to feast upon.

Leaving Gina to make the preparations, Pamela and I set off with Louise and Toria following in the wagon with the horses.

When we arrived at the polo ground we were mobbed by photographers. Mike, like me, knew how to take advantage of a publicity opportunity to promote the Club and had been in touch with the local media.

Pamela took it in her stride. Getting out of the car she told waiting reporters that she would allow them a short interview and a few photographs on the understanding that we would be left alone for the rest of the weekend. The press, knowing they had no option, agreed, and the interviews were over and done with in a few minutes.

Pamela joined the Jaguar House team that weekend alongside Mike, Steve Lung and myself. She played well, and we were all proud when we won. After the game we ended the afternoon with a few drinks in the Club House enjoying the banter and laughs about the afternoons play.

As for the Saturday night party it turned out to be hilarious. Pamela had travelled light only bringing with her jeans and t-shirts. At 8pm everyone started to arrive. As they parked their cars and got out became apparent that the wives had made a special effort with party dresses, hair do's and their best jewellery in honour of meeting our movie star.

Power dressing was at its most extreme in the late eighties with large shoulder pads sewn into the sleeves of just about everything. It was all about big, and on this occasion there was no exception. As some of the guests approached our front door, a 'traffic jam' started to build up. In their glamorous outfits, with their wide shoulders, the ladies could only enter one at a time and even then at a slight angle. It was like watching a parade of beautiful crabs make their way, sideways into our house.

Once again Pamela rose to the occasion. Wearing her jeans and t-shirt she immediately put them at ease, offering her apologies for not having dressed up on such a special evening. She explained that she had travelled light, with only enough room for her polo gear, and had brought nothing other than what she was wearing.

The party was a great success and everybody had a night to remember.

Over the following week, the local papers were published and there were many pictures of Pamela and me wearing Jaguar House polo shirts. The headlines read 'Hollywood Movie Star Comes to Cheshire to Play Polo', followed by a write up of the game. Mike was obviously pleased with the media coverage and good press that week, giving Cheshire Polo Club some well deserved PR.

My sponsors were over the moon with the mentions of Jaguar House and the link to the 'Hollywood Movie Star', so I framed one of the photographs and gave it to them as a present. They put it up in prime position in one of their showrooms for everyone to see.

The following year Jaguar flew Pamela over from America so that she could play with their team again; she stayed with us again – in what she termed 'her English home' with her 'adopted English family'.

Chapter Thirty-One
Tickled Pink

There I was at the young age of thirty-five, a millionaire living the dream with everything I could possibly wish for. I had a gorgeous wife and two lovely, perfectly healthy daughters, a large house in the country, stables for our horses and garages full of new cars.

I also had a successful business that was doing unbelievably well.

Our Girls Talk and Kids Talk boutiques had become so popular that we had queues at the doors every Saturday. Lots of young customers would often ask us to sell them carrier bags with the Girls Talk logo on the front to carry their books in on their way to school and back.

One day, I heard a mother arguing with her young daughter. When I asked what the matter was, the mother replied

"She wants me to buy something just so she can have your carrier bag to show off to all her friends."

I told them there was no need to argue and gave the daughter half a dozen bags for free. The power of the Girls Talk and Kids Talk name had become phenomenal. Teenagers were saying "If it's not from Girls Talk and Kids Talk it's not fashionable." I encouraged my staff to give away carrier bags as often as possible for free; this was the cheapest way to promote our shops.

Karen Foster had joined me in 1985 when we opened our Chester Girls Talk and Kids Talk branch. She started as a part time sales assistant and after many promotions eventually became the Area Manageress, looking after all our shops. Karen knew how Gina and I worked and how attention to detail was very important. Karen was absolutely fantastic at her job and took a lot of the pressure off Gina and me. My baby sister June, who by now had grown up to be a lovely young lady was the manageress of my first and best shop in Church Street, so I knew everything was in good hands.

I was in a more than perfect situation to be in, certainly for someone so young. However, I just could not sit back and enjoy what Gina and I had built up over the past ten years; it was not in my nature to sit still, I was a work-a-holic and loved every minute of it. I was only happy when I was running at one hundred miles per hour; maybe it had something to do with my childhood, or my mother continually telling me to better myself every day, or just maybe it had something to do with Mrs Jones, my old form teacher, and her scathing comment when I had left school.

I was still driven, wanting to achieve more; I had untold energy spurring me on; I was constantly hungry for success. Money never motivated me but being the best at what I did mattered more.

Ironically I still could not read or write and it haunted me nearly every day of my life. I lived with the shame and embarrassment and tried to hide it from the world like some hideous scar. I couldn't even read to my two little girls at bed time, for fear of them finding out that their Daddy couldn't read properly.

Gina was very happy and contented with our life.

I, however, was beginning to realize that retail was not giving me as much of a buzz as it used to.

One night, when Katie and Faye had gone to bed, Gina and I sat and talked for hours about the different business ventures that we could possibly go into. A couple of weeks later, having discussed it some more, we eventually narrowed it down to two; the first option was property development. It seemed to be an attractive proposition considering how over the past ten years we had already bought and sold nine properties, selling three of them for a very good profit. We were in a financial position to buy old, run down buildings and restore them sympathetically before selling them on at a profit. The timing was perfect as there were a great many potential properties near where we lived and the property boom had just started.

The second option was to launch a new clothing brand in to the fashion industry, this time selling our own brand to other retailers. This was even more of an obvious choice as we were constantly receiving enquiries from other smaller retailers who wanted us to supply them. They had heard and seen how successful our boutiques were in selling our own designs and wanted to enjoy some of our success.

With these two choices in front of us, we had to make a decision.

After many long conversations over a four week period, we both agreed to stay in the fashion business, agreeing that it was a case of 'better the devil we knew than the one we didn't'.

We were going to set up a new fashion company, designing all our own styles under our own brand name, primarily specialising in teenage girls clothing which we knew so well. It was very exciting.

The first step was to choose a name that sounded special for the brand, one with global potential, and one which would appeal to the female population. We chose an old English expression 'Tickled Pink' meaning delighted or happy, which we decided would make a great brand name.

I applied to register the name as a brand for clothing and within a few weeks it was accepted. Then we had to find suitable premises to trade from. London would have been the ideal choice but it was too far away; I did not want to be away from my family for long periods of time. Basing ourselves in Manchester made better sense as it was only one hour from home, with our shops in Liverpool and Chester also being the same distance away; it was also the busiest city outside of London for fashion. There were also lots of companies supplying the trade in this area.

Not long after starting our search I found the perfect two and a half thousand square foot show room in Stephenson Square, near Piccadilly, surrounded on all sides by all the other fashion houses. Ironically, it was also just around the corner from my old friend Mrs Kumar.

Wasting no time, we opened on Sunday 2nd October 1988, just in time for the busy Christmas trade. I took a full colour page in the Drapers Record, a fashion weekly trade magazine, inviting everyone in the fashion business to a Tickled Pink grand opening; we served Pink Champagne and pink cakes and it looked so professional. Well over one hundred inquisitive customers turned up, even my nervous competitors (who all anticipated that I would be a threat).

We had spent a lot of money on the look of the show room, with ultra modern pink neon lights arranged round the inside of the windows and very trendy mannequins, wearing up-to-the- minute styles. To begin with we sold other company's designs and even a little bit of 'cabbage'(!) as we needed six months to organize our own designs. My plan was to get the show room up and running before introducing our own label.

Starting off as wholesalers, essentially a cash and carry, meant that shop owners from all over the North of England could call in once a week to buy their stock, paying for it there and then.

I employed new staff. There was Lillian, my sixty year old secretary/book keeper, who was obviously Gina's choice! No dolly birds for me! Then there was Paul, a twenty–one year old who was my warehouse boy; Paul was as strong as an ox and ideal for loading and unloading deliveries. We found a young graduate fashion designer, straight out of university, twenty–two year old Kirsty and finally, Tina Brown, whom I head hunted to run Tickled Pink show room.

Tina used to work for 'Joe Bloggs', the most exciting menswear fashion company at the time. Shammy, the owner was not happy about the move as Tina was so switched on and knew everything there was to know about selling and distribution in the fashion industry. We had known each other for years in the business and when I told her I was going to launch Tickled Pink as a teenage girls' brand and that I would love her to join my team, she jumped at the chance. Tina was the spitting image of Janet Jackson and was especially good at communicating with all the customers.

By now I had learnt the power of the media and advertising through my retail businesses, so from the very beginning I set up an advertising campaign to market our Tickled Pink brand, starting with a front cover on the Draper's Record (dated 12th November 1988). The picture was a coloured photograph of a top model wearing Tickled Pink's newest look. To go on the front page cost a fortune but it was worth it because it generated a buzz; everyone in the fashion business was talking about Tickled Pink wanting to know "Who are they?" and "Where did they come from?"

Kirsty, Gina and I set about putting a Spring/Summer collection together for the 1989 Season. We wanted to be different from our competitors and to stand out so we decided that our very first Tickled Pink designs were going to be made in fluorescent colors – neon pink, yellow and green. Bright!

It was a very brave decision as a couple of years before it had been tried by other companies but it had failed miserably. We felt however, that if the bright colours were trimmed in black they would then become more fashionable.

The relatively small collection consisted of ten different styles; tops and t-shirts all bearing the Tickled Pink logo embossed in black on the back. We had five different styles of 'bottoms' which included black lycra cycling shorts. To complete the collection we added a washed-out denim range all with three-coloured neon cotton embroidery on each style.

The samples were so fabulous that we decided to put ourselves under even more pressure by producing all the styles for younger girls aged between two and twelve; it had proven to be so successful in the past that it was worth taking the risk.

Once all the final designs were made, I set off all over Europe looking for factories to produce them, and ended up in Greece as they specialized in manufacturing light-weight cottons and lycra. Having spent time visiting and inspecting a number of possibilities, I felt that it would be best not to put all our eggs in one basket so chose three; one to manufacture the cotton garments, one for the lycra, and a third to produce the washed-out denim story.

Ten days later, having worked at least twelve hours a day with the respective factories on the collections, I placed orders for sixty thousand garments, the value of which came close to three hundred thousand pounds!

There are many saner people who would have said I was totally crazy to have taken such a big risk in the first place, and in our first season, and I think that I would have had to agree. However, if I had learned anything in life it was there are 'ditherers' and there are 'doers' and there are those with 'lots of balls'!

I was aware that I stood to fall at the first fence, losing a lot of money, and possibly ruining the Tickled Pink Brand overnight, but I knew that we also stood to make a huge amount of money as well if we had 'got it right'.

Being successful in the fashion business means spending all your time gambling on your beliefs. It is all a numbers game and not for the fainthearted, as long as you win more than you lose you are doing alright. I never had the need to gamble on anything else in life as I did it for a living.

On the plane returning home, I was thinking that I would certainly be buying the styles for our shops, when a thought suddenly dawned on me – both Girls Talk and Kids Talk might end up having to shift the whole bloody lot anyway!

As soon as I got back to the UK I had to immediately open three irrevocable letters of credit from my bank, guaranteeing the Greek factories money. Without this they would not start producing our designs and the clock was ticking away especially if we wanted a February delivery. There was no going back; I had once again put my neck on the proverbial block, and yet again we just had to keep our fingers and toes crossed.

All the stock was due to arrive at the end of February just as the spring/summer season was about to start. I booked a stand at the Birmingham N.E.C. fashion trade show to help minimize some of the risk and produced a small glossy brochure featuring all our collections.

Tickled Pink soon became a 'family' fashion business with Katie and Faye modeling the clothes for the kids range, and Tina's nieces Jade and Javeen modeling the teenager's range for the brochure.

All our merchandise arrived from Greece on time. Both the quality and packaging were of a high standard, whilst our show room looked fantastic with all the new neon styles in position. Despite all this I still had a sick feeling that the collection would not be as successful as we had prayed for.

No sooner had our stock arrived than Gina, Tina and I immediately were in Birmingham showing our new collection. The big trade fair takes place twice a year, in February and September, when all the top fashion houses show their new collections for the season ahead. The show runs for three days, and is the biggest gathering in the industry, with hundreds upon hundred of stands displaying every kind of product.

We set up our stand the day before the show opened. I'd had a large, electric fluorescent sign made with the word 'Tickled' in blue and the word 'Pink' in pink. It hung in the middle of our stand with mannequins on either side dressed in our new designs.

Exhausted but proud at how brilliant it looked, we finally finished setting up and returned to the hotel nearby. Both Gina and I were excited at the thought of the following day; we had attended enough exhibitions in the past as buyers but this time we were there as exhibitors!

The next morning before the show started, Gina and I were feeling more nervous than ever before. Would the buyers like our styles and the bright neon colours? Even more worrying though was the uncertainty of the buyers actually placing any orders with us for immediate delivery?

Nearly all the other companies at the show were ahead of the game showing styles for an autumn delivery, some six months ahead, whilst we were showing for that season.

Nine o'clock sharp when the main doors opened thousands of buyers rushed in and within what seemed like minutes we had a large gathering around our stand asking questions regarding Tickled Pink. They wanted to know how long we had been established, and how competitive were our prices.

Despite this, they seemed to love our styles. We spent the next eight hours doing nothing but taking orders. We were literally mobbed, and it was impossible to leave the stand. The show was supposed to close at six pm, but we still had people on the stand. At six thirty one of the security guards had to show us out through a back door, along with our last two customers, as they wanted to close the show for the night. It was literally mad, absolutely, wonderfully mad!

Gina and I were in a state of shock. All the buyers wanted our concept immediately in their shops. At the end of the show three days later we had sold over 25,000 pieces and opened 67 new accounts all over the U.K. We had sold over a third of our initial 60,000 pieces in an unbelievably busy three days.

We were also inundated with enquiries for fashion agents wanting to carry our samples and represent Tickled Pink in their regions. They had seen that our stand was one of the busiest at the show and wanted to be involved, so I took their names and phone numbers and told them I would get in touch.

Back in Manchester we found out that the show room had also been very busy with the cash and carry customers and that the Girls Talk and Kids Talk shops had sold out of certain styles in just a couple of days. Some of the most popular styles had to be repeated from Greece to keep up with demands; an extra 20,000 pieces in all and by the end of August we had sold every last piece.

Gina and I found it hard to believe how quickly everything sold out. The Tickled Pink brand was up and running, with the decision to do the children's sizes proving to have been a good one and we went from strength to strength over the next few years becoming the fastest growing brand of our time.

In order to keep up with demand, we ended up having to borrow a large amounts of money from the bank; the more accounts we opened, the more stock we had to carry. We now dealt with factories all over the world, and I found myself travelling to Hong Kong, Thailand, and China at least once a month.

We no longer needed the cash and carry business, all our work being forward order, and with the volume and size of our clients soon outgrew the Manchester showroom. We rented larger premises in Runcorn, a brand new forty thousand square foot warehouse, and based all our operations from there.

We were supplying over 600 independent shops throughout the U.K. and parts of Europe, and had customers which included most of the High Street big names such as, House of Fraser, John Lewis, Selfridges, Fenwicks, Beatties, Dickens & Jones and Harrods. We even supplied Lane Crawford's, referred to as the 'Harrods of Hong Kong'. It had only taken us two years to win the top accounts in Europe.

I now employed thirty-eight staff in total, with seventeen sales representatives out on the road showing our latest collections. Karen Foster, my Area Manager from the shops was promoted, working alongside me controlling the volume of stock coming in and going out.

The Tickled Pink children's range had now expanded into boys wear, making clothes for two-ten year olds. As young boys would not want to be seen in the girly Tickled Pink name we kept the 'TP' initials and decided to register Tom Pepper as the brand for the boys clothing; it had a more boyish feel to it.

We also had to protect the prestigious Tickled Pink and Tom Pepper brands, selling them only to the exclusive, top-end department stores and up market boutiques. I therefore insisted that the larger, price conscious department stores such as C&A were only allowed to stock different styles under our Girls Talk and Kids Talk labels, which had also become brand names for two further collections.

I will never forget the first time I visited C&A in London, a journey which had started some days earlier sitting in my office late one Friday afternoon in Runcorn with my Sales Director, Peter Wallace.

Peter's job was to open new accounts with large multiples, and I wanted to know why we were not doing any business with C&A. In answer to my question, Peter explained that we were a relatively young company and the likes of C&A preferred to do business with more establish brands, which is why we were having no success.

"That's absolutely ridiculous." I would not accept his reason. "The children's products which I have designed exclusively for the multiples are perfect for them."

Peter told me that he had already sent the children's wear buyer one of our new brochures and had also rung the buying department on occasions, but he'd had no success in getting an appointment.

"Jeff, I am telling you they are not interested in doing business with small companies like ours." He was adamant.

"Nonsense!" I replied. "Get the buyer on the phone now so that I can speak to him." I was confident that I would get a meeting arranged.

"You have got to be joking," Peter said. "It's five to four on a Friday afternoon! All the buyers leave at four on a Friday for the weekend; you'll never get hold of him." Peter was adamant that my call would be a waste of time.

"Just give me his name and the number," I told Peter. "I'll ring him myself."

Peter did as I asked, and I sat there listening to the phone ring. It rang out, so I dialled the number again. This time however it was answered.

"John Smith speaking."

"Mr Smith, good afternoon, it's Jeff Pearce, the Managing Director of Tickled Pink." I went straight in for the kill. "I'm calling to see if you have had a chance to look at the new brochure which we have sent down to you."

"Yes," and then there was silence.

"Good, then I would like to make an appointment to come and show you samples from our fantastic children's collection." This was not the time for idle niceties.

"I am just about to leave the office," he advised me.

"Not a problem, I won't keep you," I assured him. "Can we quickly pencil in a date in our diaries for next week then?"

"I have to catch a train in ten minutes," he replied.

I could almost feel his desperation to get out of the office coming down the phone.

"Mr Smith, all I need from you is a date and a time, and then I won't keep you any longer."

"Right then," he gave in. "Nine o'clock sharp, Monday morning." And then the phone went dead.

Peter had been listening to my side of the conversation, and found it hard to believe that I now had a foot in the door; I had managed to arrange an appointment with C&A.

Peter and I agreed that he would collect me in the early hours of Monday morning if we were going to achieve the nine am deadline at their Head Office on Oxford Street in London's West end.

We arrived in London, and eventually managed to find somewhere to park. By the time we had pushed a rail full of samples the mile or so through the busy streets to the C&A building it was ten minutes to nine when we signed the visitor's book. Peter and I ended up with time on our hands to recover from our mad rush to get to the offices, as Mr Smith left us waiting in the Reception Area for three hours before eventually calling us in to his office.

As Peter and I manoeuvred our sample rail into the small room, I noticed that there were two men, both in their mid-thirties sitting at a desk. After shaking hands and introducing ourselves, Peter and I sat down opposite them both.

"Thank you for agreeing to see us Mr Smith." I decided to get the meeting going, at the same time becoming aware of the small clock which was placed on the desk, and which was ticking away loudly.

Ignoring the clock, and concentrating on the two men in front of me, I proceeded to tell them a little bit about Tickled

Pink and how I felt that our product was right for their company.

Mr Smith decided to interrupt. Rudely.

"You have got ten minutes left Mr Pearce," glancing down at the clock. "You had best show us your samples quickly."

I couldn't believe what he had said, nor his degree of rudeness.

"I am sorry what did you say? Would you mind repeating yourself?"

"At C&A we only allow fifteen minutes for a manufacturer to show their samples," he replied.

I was simply furious. In a loud and clear voice I made my position clear.

"I cannot believe what you are saying. Fifteen minutes of your time! I have travelled two hundred and fifty miles to get her, leaving at three in the morning so as to be on time for nine o'clock and then waiting three hours until you could be bothered to see me! If fifteen minutes is the best you can do, I do not feel that I should bother showing you our designs, as I don't believe you deserve to see them!"

As I finished speaking there was a moment's silence, and then a voice broke the silence. Whilst I had been telling Mr Smith what I thought about his approach to meetings, another man had quietly entered the room and was standing directly behind me.

"Turn the clock off Mr Smith, and allow Mr Pearce the time to show us his samples."

Peter sat there frozen, not moving and not saying a word, so I carried on, taking the garments off the rail to show each one.

It was quite obvious that both Mr Smith and his colleague liked our designs very much, but thought that they were too expensive.

"We sell this type of garment for £4.99" Mr Smith said, holding up a cardigan to fit a six year old girl. "You're recommending we sell it for £16.99?"

It was now my turn to convince him.

"Mr Smith, I have two daughters of my own. One is aged ten and the other is seven. On numerous occasions my wife and I have tried to shop at C&A to buy fashionable clothes for our girls but with no success."

"The reason for this," I continued, "Is because of the drab colours and boring styles that you have on offer." I was being honest. "My wife and I are not alone; there are many other customers out there who feel the same way and who are prepared to pay more for a product with more design input."

He still wasn't convinced.

The man standing behind me took this moment to speak, introducing himself to me as Mr Roberts, the Head of the Buying Department, before turning to Mr Smith.

"Place a sample order with Mr Pearce for our fourteen best stores," he instructed.

"That way we can see if you're right Mr Pearce," he said, turning in my direction. "However, please don't call us we'll call you."

As Peter and I walked out of the building, clutching a £35,000 order, I was over the moon. This was my big chance to prove myself to C&A, the largest retailers in the world at that time.

A week after the samples had been delivered to the fourteen stores, Mr Roberts rang me inviting me back to London. He told me that within two days of my styles going out on to the sales floor, they had sold out. This time when I left the meeting it was with an order worth a quarter of a million pounds for the Kids Talk Brand. My designs were now going to be sold in every one of C&A's two hundred stores.

The following season I received a further, larger order for my children's collection, but then the orders abruptly stopped. I had clearly proven to the C&A buyers that a garment with greater design input sold for a higher price and I soon found out that they started to do it themselves.

From then on I kept a very close, interested eye on their children's wear department; at the beginning of a new season I would always pop in and have a look at what they were designing and was pleased to note that the styles were back to normal, still pretty dull and not selling.

Perhaps C&A should have listened to my Mother's wise advice about biting the hand that feeds you.

Chapter Thirty-Two
Two Wrongs Don't Make A Right

I was riding on the crest of a wave by the time we entered 1991. Tickled Pink was heading for its best year ever with two million pounds worth of forward orders on its books. All four brands were performing well on the High Street. Tickled Pink, Tom Pepper, Girls Talk and Kids Talk. I was feeling quite proud of what we had achieved in just two and a half years.

Then something drastic happened; I well and truly found myself in the wrong place at the wrong time.

The recession of the early nineties started to hit the High Street. Consumers suddenly stopped spending. Fashion, often regarded as a luxury, was one of the first to be hit, and boy was it hit hard. The speed in which the knock-on effect happened was frightening.

Our big department store buyers were having their budgets cut in half, forcing them to immediately reduce their orders by half as well. Whilst the 600 small independent shops which we were supplying were also cancelling orders left, right and centre.

It was a nightmare. By now I was working on orders six months in advance, i.e. for the coming season, and was heavily committed to factories all over the world. They in turn had large quantities of garments in production and there was no way of stopping them.

Whilst I was putting out fires on one side, the bank decided to throw a spanner into the works on the other; they were demanding that I reduce my overdraft limit, which was £570,000. Typical! Just when I desperately needed the overdraft they wanted to take it away. It was like being given an umbrella when the sun shining, and then having it snatched off you at the first sign of rain.

As the recession worsened, many of the small independent shops that we were supplying were seriously struggling to stay in business; the reality was they were losing with almost one a week closing down.

The bank kept increasing the pressure, and I was left with no other alternative than to put my shops on the market. The timing could not have been worse as property prices were starting to fall and were in fact reaching the lowest they had been for many years.

My only saving grace was that all the shops were in prime locations.

First to go was the Chester shop, then Kids Talk in Liverpool and finally Girls Talk on Church Street. That hurt the most as it had always been my favourite, and having been our first had been a part of our lives for so long. Both Gina and I felt as if we were losing an old friend.

In total we managed to raise £200,000 which enabled us to reduce our overdraft limit, leaving us with £370,000 to trade with.

The loss of our retail business was hard to take, but I was even more convinced that supplying retailers was the way forward. Optimistic about the future with the brands we had created and the accounts we had opened, all we had to do was to ride the storm through, and the next six months certainly proved to be tough. Keeping on going, constantly tightening our belts, we hoped that the recession would soon come to an end.

By the middle of 1992 we were still doing reasonably well, and were on target to make a profit, albeit only a small one. However, it was still a profit and I was quite pleased; we had managed to survive when so many of our competitors had gone out of business along the way.

Then once again, disaster struck. Black Wednesday. Like a hurricane flattening everything in its path, Black Wednesday was a day of untold devastation and ruin.

On the 16th of September 1992 the European ERM fell apart, with catastrophic effect on the pound. In a bid to prop up the ailing sterling, announcements were made that interests rates were going to go up to 15%. Banks were in a blind panic, pulling the plugs on any small business they could get their hands on and mine was not to escape.

A few days after the 16th I received an extraordinary phone call from my Bank Manager. He did not sound his usual polite self.

"I want you in my office at ten o'clock tomorrow morning," he demanded.

Completely thrown by his abrupt and rude manner, I told him to fuck off and then hung up. I just sat there, stunned. How could he have been so rude, talking to me as if I was the lowest of the low, a less than junior clerk in a large bank?

The following day I received a letter from him apologising for his manner the day before. He asked me to be 'kind enough' to call his secretary to make an appointment to see him as soon as possible.

Accordingly, I spoke to his secretary and arranged to meet him at 2 o'clock the following afternoon. Before I hung up she told me to bring the company cheque books which I found a little bit odd, and made me feel uneasy.

I arrived on time and was escorted to his office. He was behind his desk as usual except this time he had a very serious look on his face. As I came in he stood up and shook my hand, apologising once again for his unprofessional phone manner.

Sitting back down in his chair he indicated that I should sit in the chair opposite him, and then got straight to the point.

"Have you brought your cheque books with you?" he asked.

"Yes," I replied, opening my briefcase and placing them on the desk in front of him.

He didn't speak or even look at them, as he slid them across the desk surface and into a drawer. He then locked the drawer, putting the key in his pocket.

"As from today," he informed me, "We are no longer prepared to finance your business."

"You can't be serious! You have enough security to cover my loan." I was shocked.

"Not any more," he replied. "Property prices have halved since we last agreed your facility. I am sorry Jeff. It's not me; my instructions are from Head office."

He was passing the buck.

"Aubrey, please, you can't do this to me." Reaching into my briefcase I pulled out my paying-in book. "Look. On Monday I paid in £30,000." I was desperately trying to reason with him, thinking that he would see sense.

"We have half a million pounds still owing to us," I continued. Before I could carry on, he interrupted me.

"Yes, and we believe you won't realise more than a third of it in this current economic climate."

"I won't receive a penny of it if you won't let me keep trading. What about the stock we own in the warehouse? It must be worth about £150,000 and I only owe you just over £370,000! Aubrey, we can work this out together. Please don't do this to me, please!"

I was begging him as if begging for my life.

"I'm sorry it's out of my hands." He wasn't interested.

"Well then, what do you suggest that I do with no cheque book? I have staff wages to pay!"

"I suggest you go into voluntary liquidation," was his reply.

"Why on earth would I want to do that?" I demanded. "After sixteen years of breaking my back to build up a business from nothing, why on earth would I do that?" I was beginning to shout with frustration.

He stood up and walked to the door and opened it. Looking at me he said, "There is no more that I can say or do in this matter. Good day."

At that point I felt both physically and mentally battered. I don't remember walking out of there, but I can remember being violently sick in the car park as the reality of it all hit me. After the vomiting came tears. How on earth was I going to tell Gina? And what about my loyal staff who had been with me for so many years? How was I to tell them that we were finished.

My mind was in a turmoil, trying to come up with answers. Sitting in the car I was searching for a way out of this mess; I had been in tight spots before and had overcome them. But this time it was no good, this was far, far worse.

The more I thought, the more I realised that there was no way out. I felt like I was stuck on the back of some horrendous monster that was racing away from me, there was no way of stopping it, no way of controlling which way it went, and no getting off. As I drove back to the office, I rang Jaguar House (from where I had bought my cars) and spoke to Richard Greenwood, asking him how much my Jag was worth.

"Sixteen thousand pounds is the best price I can do," he told me.

I asked him to help me out, to bring sixteen thousand pounds in cash to my office the following morning. He may have thought it was a bit strange, but agreed anyway.

That night I sat down with Gina and explained everything. As we talked into the early hours, I told her that I felt as if I had failed her, had let her down badly. She tried to comfort me by saying that it wasn't my fault, but it didn't make me feel any better.

The next day I gave all our staff five hundred pounds each from the sale proceeds of my car and told them to go home as Tickled Pink was now finished. There were lots of tears shed that day, including mine and Gina's as our staff had been so special. The atmosphere at Tickled Pink had been fantastic, everyone loved working there and we had been a dynamic team. For it to have ended in such a cold hearted way left us all feeling devastated.

All the staff eventually left, except for Karen Foster. Over the many years that we had worked together, not only had she become a very good friend but was also an essential asset to the company. Karen insisted on staying on to help Gina and me and we couldn't have got through it without her.

With just the three of us left we set about trying to raise as much money as we could for the £150,000 stock which had been paid for and was now sitting in boxes in the warehouse.

More importantly however, was the need to recuperate as much of the half million pounds still owing to us, and we needed to get it back as quickly as possible.

As the Bank held a charge over our house as security against the £370,000 overdraft facility, I felt that time was against me and was afraid that it would not be long before they forced us to sell our house, the only property we had left.

After three weeks of doing everything we possibly could we only realised about forty thousand pounds for most of our remaining stock, the huge loss in value being due to the fact that it was now a buyers market, and the major fashion clearance companies were offering as little as possible for it all. Considering what they acquired, they paid peanuts!

Collecting the money still owed to us was equally as difficult. I spent day after day driving Gina's car all over the country, personally calling in on all our customers and demanding payment on the spot. Getting blood out of a stone would have been easier, as the recession had hit them all hard as well, and they were struggling to survive themselves.

One look at their shops told me all I needed to know; I had little or no chance of walking away with the money I was due, whether it was two or ten thousand pounds. By the time I had finished debt collecting I had managed to claw back one hundred thousand pounds and had to kiss the rest of it good-bye.

We paid the £140,000 we had raised into the bank but were still short by £230,000.

As if to add insult to injury, the bank were now charging me £1,000 a week interest on my overdraft facility, making themselves an additional £52,000 a year! I begged them on numerous occasions to freeze the interest on the outstanding loan on the grounds that I no longer had a business and had already paid them some £300,000 in interest and bank charges alone over the past four years, but they refused to listen or to help.

Instead they demanded that I now sell my house to pay off the balance of the money still owing.

A few years earlier, our house had been worth half a million pounds, but with the fall in property prices I would be lucky if I raised enough to clear my outstanding debt to the bank.

The For Sale board went up outside Abbots Walk, and it was now time for me to put my beloved Tickled Pink into voluntary liquidation.

I contacted Ernst & Young in Liverpool to arrange an appointment. I was advised by the gentleman I spoke to that it would cost me four thousand pounds and it had to be paid in cash on the day of the meeting.

More money to pay out! With more problems than pennies, I had to borrow the cash from my old friend and former driver, George Haynes.

As we walked into the Ernst & Young offices on the day of our appointment, something was annoying me. I wasn't happy at all with the payment terms that I had been told about, so before going into the office for our meeting, I quickly removed a thousand pounds worth of notes from my briefcase, rolled it into a small bundle and then shoved it into my coat pocket. Gina wanted to know what I was doing, but I just gave her a wink and opened the office door for her.

Our liquidators greeting was very direct.

"Good morning Mr Pearce. Have you brought the four thousand pounds as requested to start this whole process?"

"I am sorry, but I have only been able to raise three grand," I explained, placing three bundles, each containing one thousand pounds, down on his desk in front of him.

"Ok, that fine." Picking up the money our liquidator locked the money in a drawer in his desk and then turned to us both, offering us a seat. "Let's get on with it shall we?" he said.

Once I had answered half a dozen or so of his questions he got to his feet.

"Mr and Mrs Pearce, I suggest that the two of you go and have a long lunch somewhere nice and come back in about three hours time by which stage I will have gone through all your accounts and will have a much better idea how to proceed."

As Gina and I walked out of the building we were greeted by a blast of cold air. It was a crisp autumn's day so we decided to head down to the Pier Head which ran alongside the Liver Building to get some fresh air. The last thing on our minds at that point was a long lunch, in fact neither Gina nor I had actually eaten a decent meal since the whole ordeal had begun some four weeks earlier.

We both felt sick to the stomach, literally nauseated by what had been happening to our lives; everything had been turned upside down and we felt a huge sense of loss, as if a loved one had died. For fifteen years we had helped our business grow bit by bit, nurturing it from a small market stall worth a couple of hundred quid to a company turning over millions.

I held Gina's hand as we strolled along the seafront towards Otterspool. We killed time in silence, an unnatural feeling of quiet between us tinged with a degree of uneasiness as to what was coming next.

As we neared the Ernst & Young building on our way back, I pulled the thousand pounds out of my pocket, trying to lighten the moment.

Showing it to Gina I said, "I haven't lost my touch yet, even with all this agro going on around me."

The humour was good for us both.

Back in the liquidator's office the meeting continued.

"Mr and Mrs Pearce," his tone was official, "There is something terribly unusual about your Accounts."

Gina and I looked at him in disbelief. What? Another disaster?

"In what way?" I asked, but at the same time not really wanting to hear his reply.

"You don't owe anyone any money. There is a small amount of VAT and PAYE still owing, but that is hardly worth talking about." He paused for a moment looking at us both.

"In fact there is only the bank to settle with, and they hold the deeds to your house as collateral, so you now stand to lose your home."

He sat back in his chair, removed his glasses from the end of his nose and continued in a quieter tone.

"Most companies which I come in contact with in liquidation situations like this, would have paid off their personal guarantees, i.e. their bank loans rather than paying their creditors. But your accounts show me that you have paid the factories which you dealt with well in excess of the outstanding balance that you owe to the bank, and you have done this recently. There are not many who would do this."

He fell waited for my reply. I remained silent for a moment before I spoke, choosing my words carefully.

"Two wrongs don't make a right," I explained. "Just because the bank have shafted me doesn't mean that I have to shaft somebody else."

He looked at me with surprise, and then smiled at my summary of the whole affair.

"Right. I cannot see any need to hold a Creditors Meeting and will therefore tie up all the loose ends before writing to you in due course."

As he walked Gina and me to the door, he thanked us both for having chosen Ernst & Young to handle our affairs and shook us both by the hand. As we left, I couldn't help but think that must have been the easiest three grand that he had ever earned.

Chapter Thirty-Three
Silent Prayer

Gina and I shared the car home together, but little else. We were both lost in our thoughts, most probably similar in nature, and conversation seemed unimportant.

I had made eighteen successful business decisions in my life but the nineteenth collapsed like a house of cards and cost me everything.

I felt a strange sense of relief in a way now that it was over, but I was deeply scarred inside by what had happened and the way I had been betrayed by the bank. What the bank had done had been immoral and cruel. In fact, comparing the bank to some of the more colourful characters I had met in my life, I could honestly say that there was indeed greater honour amongst thieves.

But the greatest sense of betrayal was my own. I had placed my family in a privileged world where they could have anything that they wanted, and now I had taken it all away. I could never forgive myself for losing Gina's home, and now I would have to remove Katie and Faye from the private school which they loved so much.

My ambition had brought us to this point and my ambition had lost it all. My need to succeed and the desire to prove my worth had put my family in a situation which was unforgivable.

At forty years old I was more than a failure, I was lost with nowhere to go; a man alone.

I silently said the first of many prayers to my Mother, asking for help.

Epilogue
2002 – Cap and Gown

Ten years on and the champagne was flowing; it was the night of the 14th of November 2002. We were sitting at a table placed near the back of the Dinosaur Room of the Natural History Museum in London.

I had been invited to attend the Drapers Annual Awards, referred to as 'The Oscars' of the fashion industry. My store, Jeff's of Bold Street, had been shortlisted as a finalist for the Independent Womenswear Retailer of the Year category, one of the hardest category's of all as there were literally thousands of very good women's wear retailers from across the UK and the Irish Republic to choose from. My relatively small business in Liverpool was up against some very tough opposition.

Gina, Katie and Faye were there to support me along with some close friends of ours. We were seated at large tables, laden with silverware and sparkling crystal, ornate floral arrangements filling the air with their heavy scent. Course after course of elaborate dishes were set down in front of us, but I found myself totally unable to eat.

I was so tense that my stomach was refusing to take part; more nervous than I had anticipated, my mind constantly wandered back to my childhood and the beginning of my career.

In contrast I was now sitting here in the same room alongside all the top names in the fashion business; household names like Phil Green, the billionaire who controlled most of the big names on the High Street such as Top Shop and BHs, and George Davies (the mastermind behind Next, and George at ASDA) as well as Stuart Rose the new Managing Director of Marks & Spencer to mention just a few. They were all there that night.

As soon as the meal finished the awards ceremony began, hosted by Trinny and Susannah, television fashion celebrities in their own right.

The awards were presented from a large stage at the far end of the room, and covered seventeen different categories – all the different aspects of the fashion business. The Independent Womenswear Retailer Category was a prestigious award, given towards the end of the evening, and sitting and waiting for the award to be announced was painful.

Finally it was 'our' turn and as they called out the nominees I held Gina's hand tight. Everyone's attention was fixed on the stage except for mine; I just couldn't look, and stared at the table instead.

As the envelope was opened a silence fell, not a sound could be heard.

"And the winner is..." there was a long pause, "Jeff's of Bold Street."

I leapt to my feet with excitement lifting Gina with me, embracing her so tightly she could hardly breathe. Beckoning to Katie and Faye, the four of us walked towards the stage, applause ringing out around us. It seemed like such a long way to walk as we snaked our way through the forest of tables.

When we reached the stage, a two foot tall, maroon velvet statue shaped like a mannequin, was placed in my hands and we all received a congratulatory kisses both cheeks from Trinny and Susannah. As we stood in a row next to each other with the press taking photos I realised that this was the moment that I had been dreaming of, for most of my life. To receive recognition from my peers for being the best Women's Wear Retailer in the whole of the United Kingdom and Ireland was something special, particularly in the presence of my family.

As we got back to our table, my friends were more than pleased for me, continuing the celebrations with more champagne. An announcement was made that there were a further two Gold Awards still to come, the first being Fashion Retail Personality of the Year. Six of the very top names were shortlisted, and Philip Green was announced as the winner. As he collected his gold statuette, he thanked his 48,000 staff for helping him to win such a prestigious award.

Finally Eric Musgrave, the Editor-in-chief of the Draper's announced the most prestigious award of the evening. It was the highlight of the whole event – the Gold Award for the Independent Retailer of the Year. The nominations had been selected from all the winners of the Independent Retailer Categories, and were regarded as being the best of the best. As the Award was being explained, Gina noticed that I was staring fixedly at the gold statuette standing alone on the stage.

"Stop it Jeff," she interrupted my thoughts. I was lost in a world of my own.

"Stop what?" I asked her, dragging my gaze away from the stage.

"Stop thinking that you are going to win that award. You won't; there's no chance, we're too small. We have come here to win this," she said, placing my statuette in front of me.

"I am excited," I told her. "Can't you see that I am happy? We are taking this home with us!" I picked it up as if to admire it one more time, before she looked away.

Gina was right, but she also knew me well enough to know what I was thinking.

I wanted that gold award more than anyone else in the room. My desire was greater and came from the heart. My thoughts were interrupted by the announcement coming from the stage.

"And the winner is.... Jeff's of Bold Street!"

In disbelief I nearly dropped to the floor. The expressions on everyone's face made me realise that it was true. I had won the highest accolade the fashion industry had to offer.

As they stood applauding me, the girls told me to go up on my own. It didn't feel right however, this momentous occasion had to be shared with the ones that I loved, so I insisted that they come along too.

Making our way to the stage for the second time was proving even more difficult as we were now receiving a standing ovation. The continuous patting on my back of fellow guests, and shaking of hands made me feel like a film star on the way to collect an Oscar.

If this was a dream it was the best one that I had ever had. Can you wish for something so much that it becomes true? Or was it a genuine acknowledgement of my hard work and determination? Being applauded by the most recognised people in the fashion industry meant more to me that night than any financial reward that I had received in my business career.

Just before I stepped down from the stage, I walked over to the microphone and raised the gold award high above my head.

"I owe this to two remarkable women," my voice rang out around the room, sounding frighteningly loud. "My Mother for teaching me how to survive in the rag trade, and my Wife for putting up with me for so long in this crazy business that I love so much."

I could not have said another word as I was overcome with such strong emotions.

All the winners were called back on to the stage for a final photograph together. As I stepped up, Phil Green put his hand out to shake mine.

"Well done," he congratulated me. "You must have a remarkable business. How many staff do you have?"

"Fifteen," I replied. With all the noise going on he must have misheard me as he repeated, "Fifteen thousand? That must take some looking after!"

"No, no, I think you misheard me. I said fifteen; one five!"

He looked at me in astonishment, I smiled and thanked him for his kindness, before turning to stand next to my girls in readiness for the photograph.

In the taxi back to the hotel Katie and Faye summed up the evening beautifully.

"Dad, it was the same as you receiving your cap and gown. You were recognised by the fashion business for your outstanding contribution. We are so very proud of you!"

The perfect end to a perfect night.

The next day Katie and Faye stayed on in London whilst Gina and I took the train back to Liverpool. We couldn't wait to show our staff the two awards and tell them about how the night had unfolded.

We got chatting to a lady who was sitting opposite us on the train. It wasn't long before we were explaining where we had been and what we had been doing. She equally found it fascinating and as we departed at Lime Street Station her parting words to me were that I should write a book. A week later I received a letter from the stranger on the train inviting Gina and me to join her for lunch at the House of Commons. As it turned out she was Private Secretary to Gordon Brown, the then Chancellor of the Exchequer. Unfortunately we were too busy with the run up to Christmas and were unable to take her up on her kind offer.

Leaving Lime Street Station we walked around to the store. As we approached I took the two large awards out of our bag and held one in each hand before walking in to the store.

"Guess what!" I shouted out, "We didn't win one award! We won two!!!"

All the staff dropped what they were doing and came running over. As I stood there engulfed in their embraces I found myself getting very emotional and started crying. It had been ten long years, more or less to the day, since I had started making my come back. The journey had seemed long and hard at times, with sheer grit and determination keeping me going. Years of emotions which had built up inside found their release, like rain water breaking the flood barriers, leaving me feeling complete for the very first time in my life.

The following week an article appeared in the press. One of the lines stated that *"Jeff Pearce is a paragon of independent retailing"*. I didn't understand the word paragon, so looked it up in the dictionary and was very pleased to find it meant an unflawed diamond weighing at least 100 carats.

Those ten years had been another journey, and will easily fill another book, but for now, I have reached the end of this story.

PS. It's going to be interesting to see how I get on in the brutal publishing world!